The UK Guide To Online Investing

Michael Scott

THE McGRAW-HILL COMPANIES

London · Burr Ridge IL · New York · St Louis · San Francisco · Auckland
Bogotá · Caracas · Lisbon · Madrid · Mexico · Milan
Montreal · New Delhi · Panama · Paris · San Juan · São Paulo
Singapore · Sydney · Tokyo · Toronto

The UK Guide to Online Investing

by Michael Scott

McGraw-Hill Publishing Company

Shoppenhangers Road
Maidenhead
Berkshire
England SL6 2QL
Telephone +44 (0) 1628 502500
Facsimile +44 (0) 1628 770224
Website http://www.mcgraw-hill.co.uk

Find the online version of this book on the World Wide Web at:
http://www.investment-gateway.com

Publisher: Alfred Waller

Commissioning Editor: Elizabeth Robinson

Cover design by Simon Levy

Notice of Rights

Notice of Liability

ISBN: 0-07-709672-X

Printed in the United Kingdom

For my Sins

Special thanks to:

Aidan Pickering, *at Fox 11 News for providing his luxurious apartment in Los Angeles, complete with free internet access and a spanking new computer!*

Craig Becker, *at Imagitech Inc for technical assistance, a great Thanks Giving party and introducing me to the modern wonders of 'QuarkXPress'.*

HC, *for giving me something other than finance and the internet to think about.*

Contents

Introduction

For many people, there could not be a more daunting prospect than combining investment and computers with the internet. Typing personal or business letters on the home computer is one thing. Connecting to the internet and using the computer to look up useful investment information, is something that many people assume is for the more technically minded.

This book is designed to be as 'jargon' free and simple as possible, so you don't need to be a sophisticated investor, or a computer genius to use it. Each Chapter contains numerous pictures which show you what you will actually see when you visit a particular internet site. Furthermore, there is a detailed Glossary at the back of the book to explain some of the more commonly used terms which you may not be familiar with.

Once you know where to look, you'll be amazed at how quick and easy it is to look up relevant information on the internet. Almost everyone will find something in this book to interest them. You can buy and sell shares over the internet, as well as check out the best rates of interest for your cash.

It has often been said that 'Time is Money' and in the case of the internet, this is certainly true. With over 1500 investment orientated sites on the internet, it would take over 4 years to explore them all if you spent an hour every day. The purpose of this book is to save you both time and money by revealing exactly where to find the best FREE financial information on the internet. The CD Rom which accompanies this book, gives you FREE internet access and shows you how the information in this book can be of use to you.

The internet is becoming ever more popular and growing at an explosive rate. Internet sites are constantly being updated and the quality and quantity of free financial information is improving all the time. To keep you up to date with these changes, there is an internet site which accompanies this book at: *http://www.investment-gateway.com.*

Getting Started

Once you have 'logged on' to the internet, you will see a place at the top of your screen in which to type internet addresses. This is known at the 'location bar', and will generally be labelled with either 'Address' or 'Netsite' depending whether you are using the 'Explorer' or 'Netscape' browser. The Figure below is an example of what the 'Internet Explorer' 'location bar' looks like.

Fig A *At the top of your screen, there is a place to type in internet addresses.*

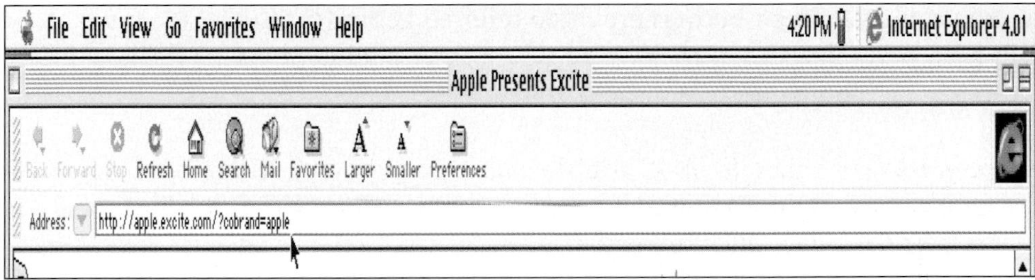

The 'location bar' will generally contain the internet address of the internet page which is displayed on your screen. Internet addresses usually start with 'http://www......' . Using your mouse, you need to click in the 'location bar' and delete any text that may be there. To do this, use the 'delete' or 'backspace' button which is usually located in the top right hand corner of your keypad.

Fig B *Delete existing text and enter the address of the internet site you want to visit.*

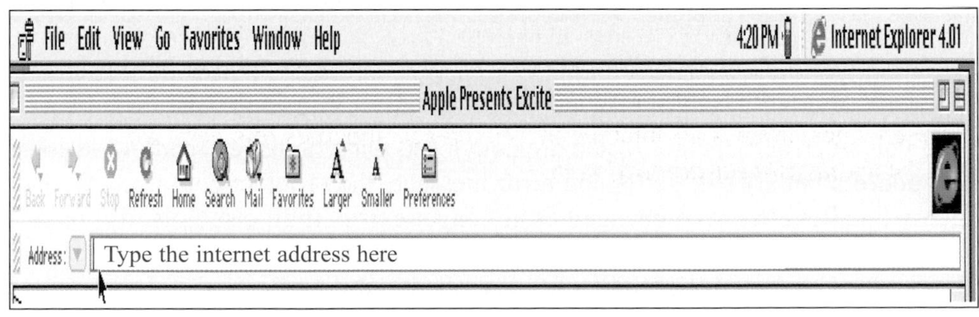

Getting Started *(con't)*

Once you have deleted any text in the 'location bar', you can type in the address of the site you wish to explore. For example, to access the page relating to shares at the web site which accompanies this book, type: http://www.investment-gateway.com After a short moment, the screen shown in Fig C should appear on your screen. The headings in the left hand column of the screen correspond to Chapters in this book. The headings in the centre of the page correspond to the internet sites described in each Chapter. When you roll your mouse over one of the buttons alongside these headings, the name and logo of a company appears. This is the internet site you will be taken to if you click on your mouse. These buttons are often referred to as 'Hot Links'.

Fig C *The 'Shares' page of the internet site which accompanies this book.*

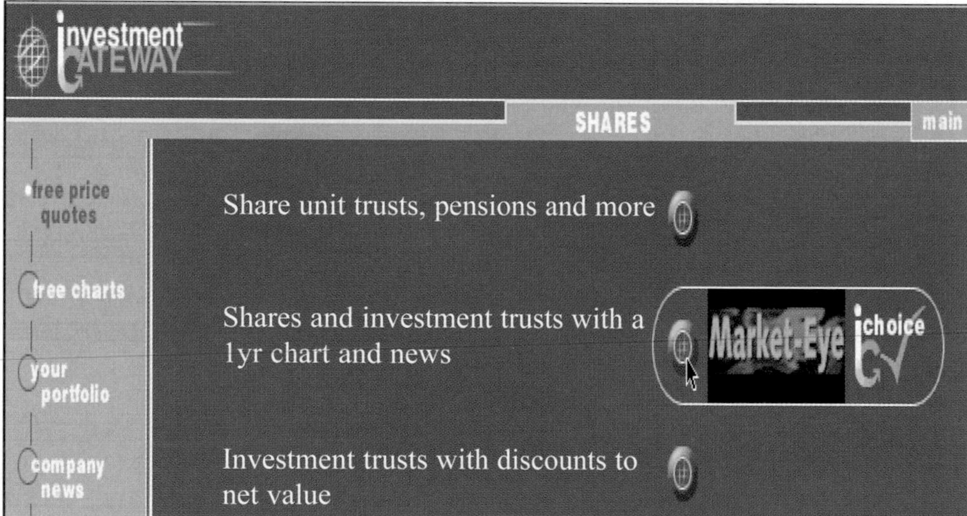

It is important to make sure you type an internet address exactly how it is written. If you accidentally miss out a full stop or a back slash, the computer will give you an error message. If you are convinced that you have typed in the correct address but are still getting an error message, the problem could be that the internet address has been changed or no longer exists. If all else fails, try looking for the site you are attempting to access in Appendix B which lists the 'Home Pages' of all the internet sites described in this book.

Saving internet addresses

Some internet addresses are quite long and complicated. To save time, you can 'Bookmark' a page. In future, when you want to access that internet site, you don't need to type in the address again. Simply click on the 'bookmark' icon and scroll down until you see the page your want. You should find the 'bookmarking' facility at the top of your screen. If your are using 'Internet Explorer', the bookmarking facility comes under 'Favorites'. If your are using 'Netscape', the bookmarking icon is a small green book. The example below, shows you how to save the address of the page in Figure C using the 'Internet Explorer' browser. First click on 'Favorites' and the screen in Figure D should appear.

Fig D *You can save time by saving long internet addresses in your 'Favorites'.*

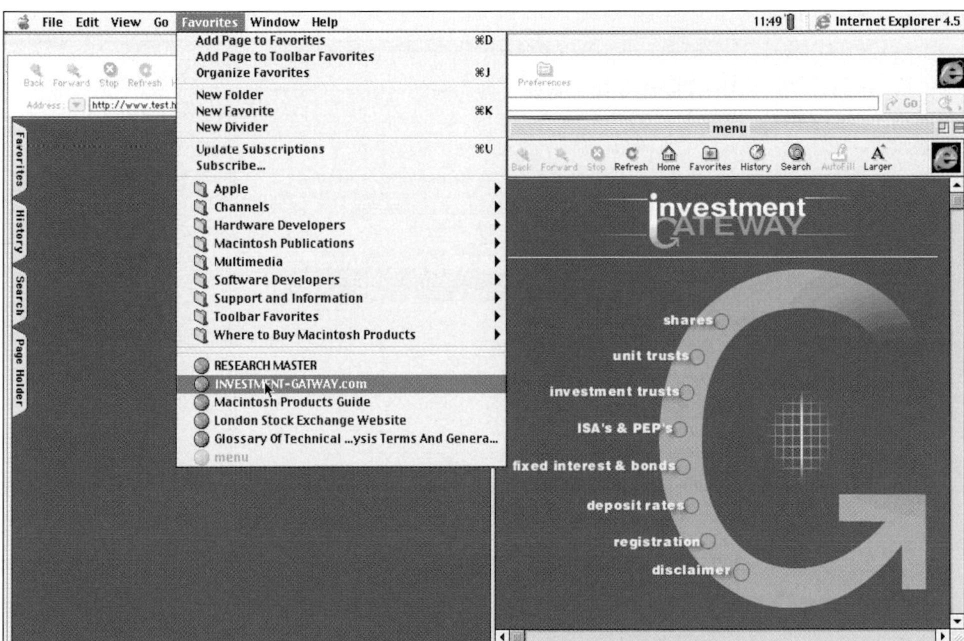

Click on 'Add Page to Favorites', and the internet address is automatically saved on your computer. Each internet page has a title. In this example, the title of the page saved was 'INVESTMENT GATEWAY'. In future when you want to access this internet site, simply click on the name of the page in your 'Favorites' list.

Accessing an internet site

One way to access any of the internet sites described in this book, is to type the correct internet address in the 'location bar' at the top of your computer screen. To enter an internet address manually, first clear any text in the location bar as shown in Figure A and Figure B. Type in the correct internet address in the location bar and press the 'Return' or 'Enter' button on your computer. The internet address of each site described in this book is given in *blue italics* at the top of each page, under the name of the internet site.

Fig E *Copy of a page in this book showing the location of the internet address.*

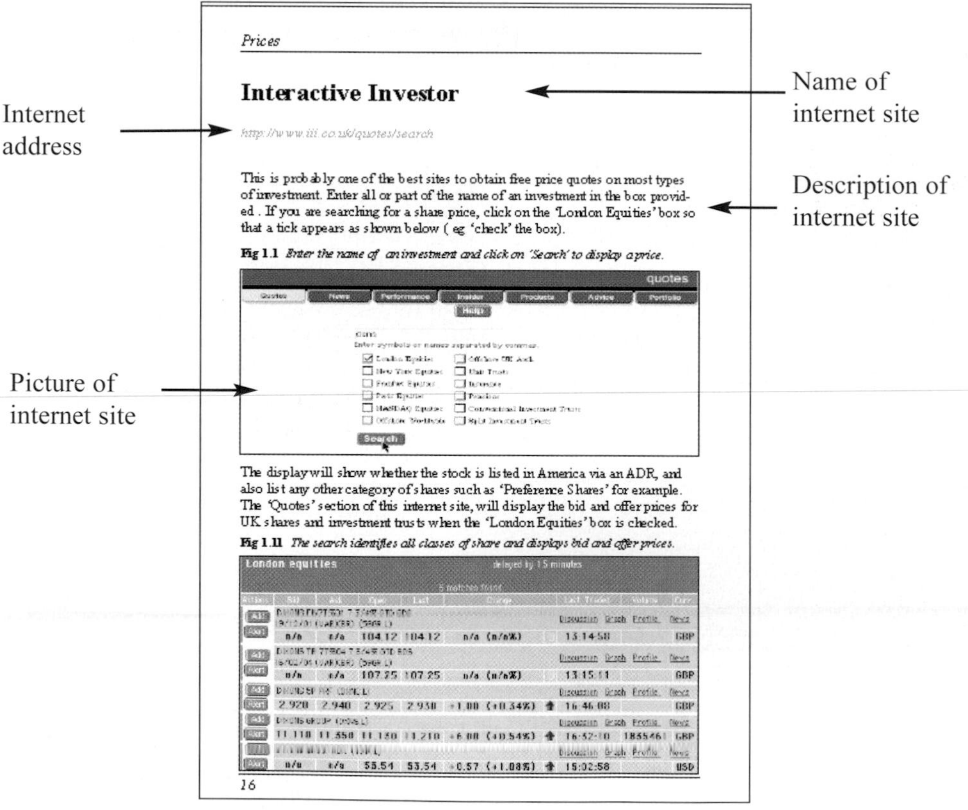

Prices

Interactive Investor

http://www.iii.co.uk/quotes/search

This is probably one of the best sites to obtain free price quotes on most types of investment. Enter all or part of the name of an investment in the box provided. If you are searching for a share price, click on the 'London Equities' box so that a tick appears as shown below (eg 'check' the box).

Fig 1.1 *Enter the name of an investment and click on 'Search' to display a price.*

The display will show whether the stock is listed in America via an ADR, and also list any other category of shares such as 'Preference Shares' for example. The 'Quotes' section of this internet site, will display the bid and offer prices for UK shares and investment trusts when the 'London Equities' box is checked.

Fig 1.11 *The search identifies all classes of share and displays bid and offer prices.*

16

Using 'Hot Links' to access internet sites

All the internet sites described in this book have been conveniently grouped together and linked to one internet site at http://www.investment-gateway.com Each web page at this internet site almost exactly corresponds to the first page of a Chapter in this book. At the internet site, the 'Hot Links' you see listed at the beginning of each Chapter become live, and enable you to access the sites described in that Chapter directly. Rather than type in the exact internet address each time, simply click on the appropriate 'Hot Link' and the computer will take you to that internet site automatically.

Fig F *Copy of the first page of Chapter 1 showing the list of 'Hot Links'.*

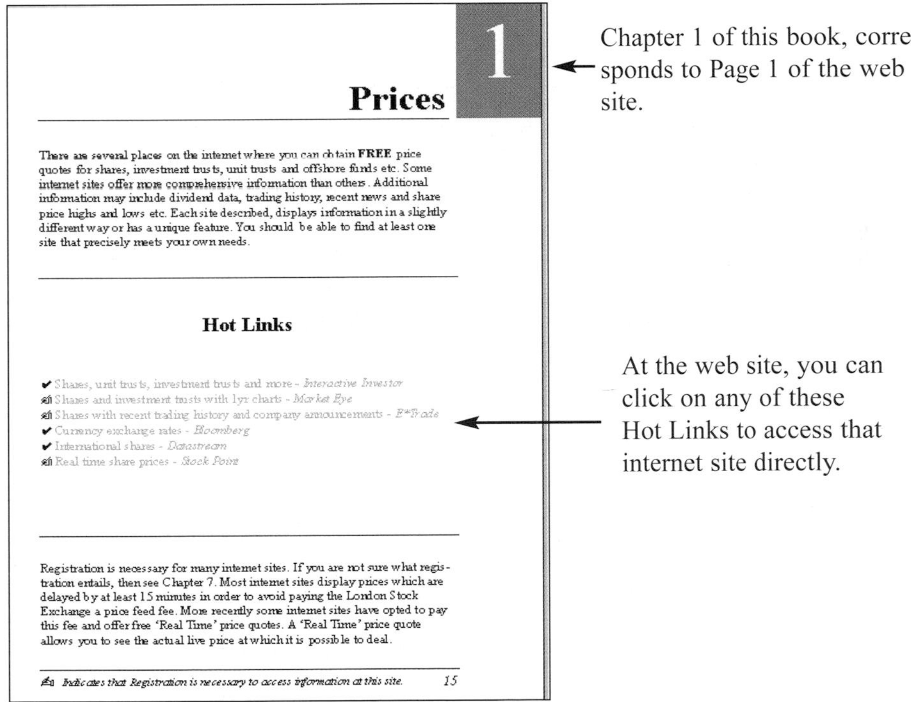

1

Prices

There are several places on the internet where you can obtain **FREE** price quotes for shares, investment trusts, unit trusts and offshore funds etc. Some internet sites offer more comprehensive information than others. Additional information may include dividend data, trading history, recent news and share price highs and lows etc. Each site described, displays information in a slightly different way or has a unique feature. You should be able to find at least one site that precisely meets your own needs.

Hot Links

- ✔ Shares, unit trusts, investment trusts and more - *Interactive Investor*
- ✍ Shares and investment trusts with 1yr charts - *Market Eye*
- ✍ Shares with recent trading history and company announcements - *E*Trade*
- ✔ Currency exchange rates - *Bloomberg*
- ✔ International shares - *Datastream*
- ✍ Real time share prices - *Stock Point*

Registration is necessary for many internet sites. If you are not sure what registration entails, then see Chapter 7. Most internet sites display prices which are delayed by at least 15 minutes in order to avoid paying the London Stock Exchange a price feed fee. More recently some internet sites have opted to pay this fee and offer free 'Real Time' price quotes. A 'Real Time' price quote allows you to see the actual live price at which it is possible to deal.

✍ *Indicates that Registration is necessary to access information at this site.* 15

Chapter 1 of this book, corresponds to Page 1 of the web site.
At the web site, you can click on any of these Hot Links to access that internet site directly.

This book enables you see what information is available at various financial web sites without having to be logged onto the internet. Once you have decided which internet sites have the information you require, you can click on the appropriate 'Hot Link' to access that site.

Last but not least.......

Some of the internet sites described in this book require you to register before you can access any of the free data. Registering is usually quick and easy and is fully covered in Chapter 7. The first page of each Chapter will tell you which internet sites you need to register for. Under the heading of 'Hot Links' there is a list of the internet sites described in that Chapter. If the site has a tick (✔) next to it, you don't need to register.

Fig G *The first page of a Chapter shows which sites require registration.*

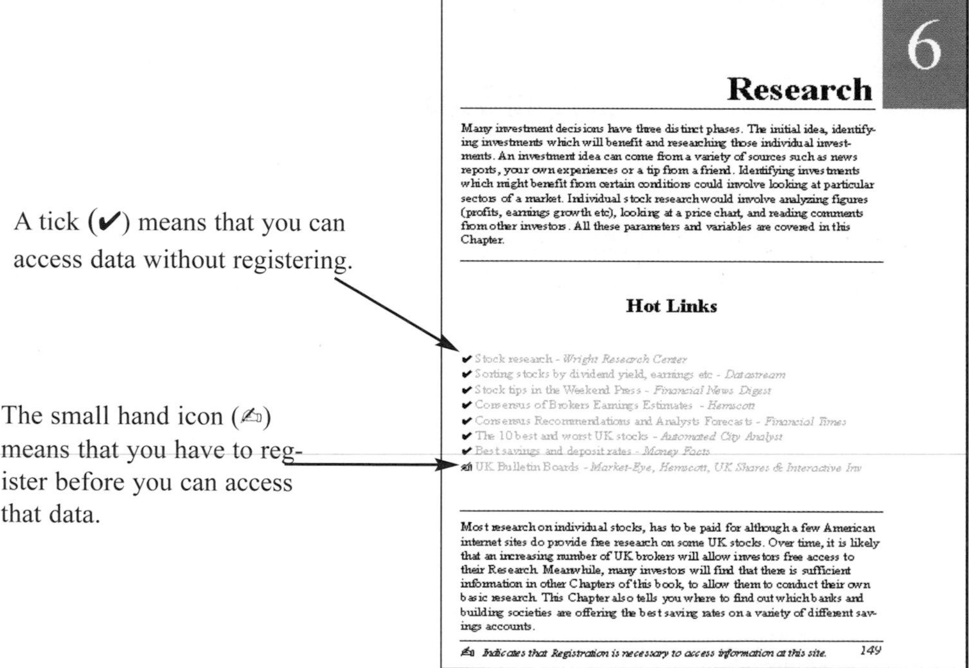
A tick (✔) means that you can access data without registering.
The small hand icon (✍) means that you have to register before you can access that data.

6

Research

Many investment decisions have three distinct phases. The initial idea, identifying investments which will benefit and researching those individual investments. An investment idea can come from a variety of sources such as news reports, your own experiences or a tip from a friend. Identifying investments which might benefit from certain conditions could involve looking at particular sectors of a market. Individual stock research would involve analyzing figures (profits, earnings growth etc), looking at a price chart, and reading comments from other investors. All these parameters and variables are covered in this Chapter.

Hot Links

✔ Stock research - *Wright Research Center*
✔ Sorting stocks by dividend yield, earnings etc - *Datastream*
✔ Stock tips in the Weekend Press - *Financial News Digest*
✔ Consensus of Brokers Earnings Estimates - *Hemscott*
✔ Consensus Recommendations and Analysts Forecasts - *Financial Times*
✔ The 10 best and worst UK stocks - *Automated City Analyst*
✔ Best savings and deposit rates - *Money Facts*
✍ UK Bulletin Boards - *Market-Eye, Hemscott, UK Shares & Interactive Inv*

Most research on individual stocks, has to be paid for although a few American internet sites do provide free research on some UK stocks. Over time, it is likely that an increasing number of UK brokers will allow investors free access to their Research. Meanwhile, many investors will find that there is sufficient information in other Chapters of this book, to allow them to conduct their own basic research. This Chapter also tells you where to find out which banks and building societies are offering the best saving rates on a variety of different savings accounts.

✍ *Indicates that Registration is necessary to access information at this site.* 149

Some of the internet addresses given in this book may change over time. Appendix B at the back of the book lists the Home Page addresses for all the internet sites described in this book. If you cannot access an internet page with the address given in this book, try typing in the address of the Home Page for that site and accessing the page that way.

1

Prices

There are several places on the internet where you can obtain **FREE** price quotes for shares, investment trusts, unit trusts and offshore funds etc. Some internet sites offer more comprehensive information than others. Additional information may include dividend data, trading history, recent news and share price highs and lows etc. Each site described, displays information in a slightly different way or has a unique feature. You should be able to find at least one site that precisely meets your own needs.

Hot Links

✔ Shares, unit trusts, investment trusts and more - *Interactive Investor*
✍ Shares and investment trusts with 1 year charts - *Market Eye*
✍ Shares with recent trading history and company announcements - *E*Trade*
✔ Currency exchange rates - *Bloomberg*
✔ International shares - *Datastream*
✍ Real time share prices - *Stock Point*

Registration is necessary for many internet sites. If you are not sure what registration entails, then see Chapter 7. Most internet sites display prices which are delayed by at least 15 minutes in order to avoid paying the London Stock Exchange a price feed fee. More recently some internet sites have opted to pay this fee and offer free 'Real Time' price quotes. A 'Real Time' price quote allows you to see the actual live price at which it is possible to deal.

✍ *Indicates that Registration is necessary to access information at this site.*

Interactive Investor

http://www.iii.co.uk/quotes/search

This is probably one of the best sites to obtain free price quotes on most types of investment. Enter all or part of the name of an investment in the box provided. If you are searching for a share price, click on the 'London Equities' box so that a tick appears as shown below (eg 'check' the box).

Fig 1.1 *Enter the name of an investment and click on 'Search' to display a price.*

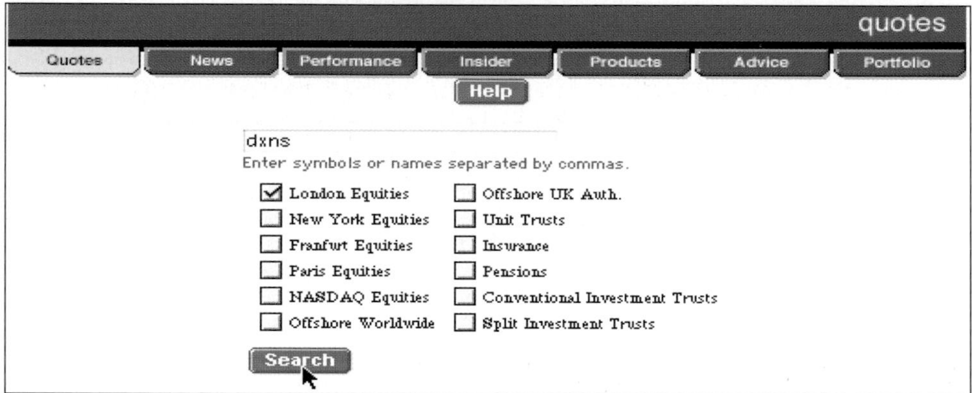

The display will show whether the stock is listed in America via an ADR, and also list any other category of shares such as 'Preference Shares' for example. The 'Quotes' section of this internet site, will display the bid and offer prices for UK shares and investment trusts when the 'London Equities' box is checked.

Fig 1.11 *The search identifies all classes of share and displays bid and offer prices.*

London equities — delayed by 15 minutes

5 matches found.

Actions	Bid	Ask	Open	Last	Change	Last Traded	Volume	Curr.
Add / Alert	DIXONS FIN7T%01 7 3/4% GTD BDS 19/12/01 (VAR)(BR) (58GR.L)					Discussion Graph	Profile	News
	n/a	n/a	104.12	104.12	n/a (n/a%)	13:14:58		GBP
Add / Alert	DIXONS TR 7T%04 7 3/4% GTD BDS 16/02/04 (VAR)(BR) (59GR.L)					Discussion Graph	Profile	News
	n/a	n/a	107.25	107.25	n/a (n/a%)	13:15:11		GBP
Add / Alert	DIXONS 5P PRF (DXNC.L)					Discussion Graph	Profile	News
	2.920	2.940	2.925	2.930	+1.00 (+0.34%) ↑	16:46:08		GBP
Add / Alert	DIXONS GROUP (DXNS.L)					Discussion Graph	Profile	News
	11.110	11.350	11.130	11.210	+6.00 (+0.54%) ↑	16:32:10	1835461	GBP
Add / Alert	DIXONS GROUP ADR (79IR.L)					Discussion Graph	Profile	News
	n/a	n/a	53.54	53.54	+0.57 (+1.08%) ↑	15:02:58		USD

Interactive Investor *(con't)*

http://www.iii.co.uk/quotes/search

If you want to display bid and offer prices for investment trusts, then you need to check the 'London Equities' box and enter the name or 'Ticker Symbol' as shown below. If you check the 'Investment Trusts' box, a different screen is displayed as shown in Figure 1.16.

Fig 1.12 *To display bid and offer prices for investment trusts, check 'London Equities'.*

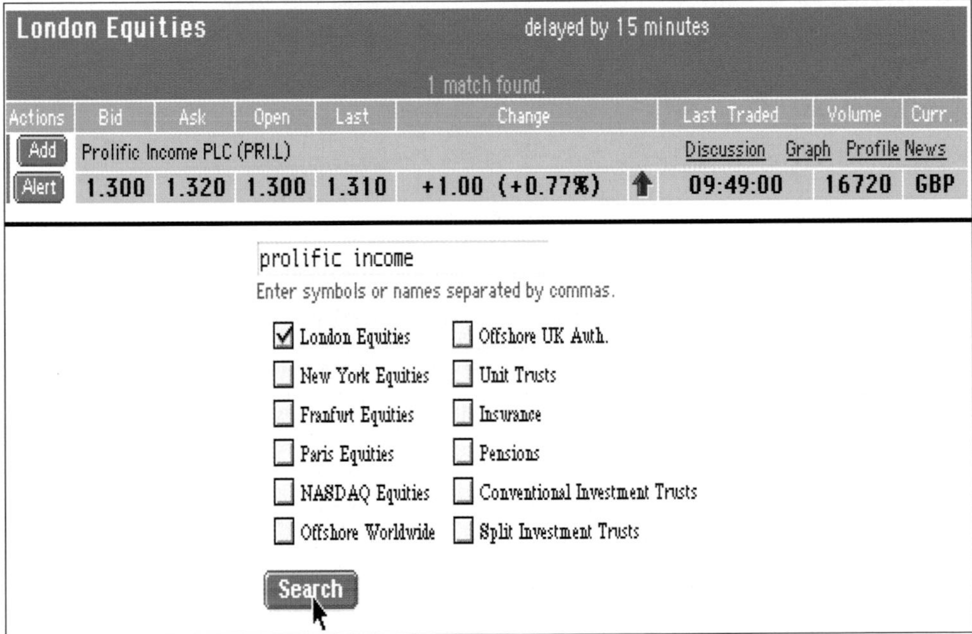

On the right hand side of the screen in Figure 1.12, there are several icons on which you can click to display other information relating to that investment. The 'Discussion' icon is a relatively new addition, and displays comments and questions relating to that stock made by other private investors. The graphing function generated by clicking on the 'Graph' icon, is excellent and fully described in Chapter 2. The only potentially useful information you get by clicking on the 'Profile' icon is details of when the last Report & Accounts came out and when the next ones are due. Clicking on the 'News' icon gives access to a comprehensive list of news stories relating to that investment. Unfortunately, you have to pay to view these news items. However, the same story can frequently be accessed for free from other news sources highlighted in Chapter 4 of this book.

Interactive Investor *(con't)*

http://www.iii.co.uk/quotes/search

A good feature of this site, is the ability to be notified by e-mail when investments rise or fall by a certain percentage. To set this up, you need to click on the 'Alert' icon on the left hand side of the screen in Figure 1.12. There are three parameters you need to specify. In the example below, an 'Alert' has been set up for Dixons Group. The parameters have been set so that an e-mail is sent when the 'Bid' price of Dixons is 'greater than' '1200p'. The 'Field' box can be set to either the 'Bid', 'Mid' or 'Offer' price. The 'Event' box can be set to either 'greater than', 'equal to' or 'less than'. The 'Value' is the price in pence at which you want the 'Alert' to be activated.

Fig 1.13 *Set an 'Alert' to be notified by e-mail when a stock reaches a certain level.*

Set an Alert

Display portfolio, Edit portfolio, View/Reset Alerts
Help

London equities — delayed by 15 minutes

Bid	Ask	Open	Last	Curr.
DIXONS GROUP (DXNS.L)				
11.110	11.350	11.130	11.210	GBP

Contact:	scottitonline@hotmail.com
Fund Name:	DIXONS GROUP
Field:	Bid
Event:	greater than
Value:	1200

☐ Please continue to inform me after this event has occurred.

Set Alert

After you have set the desired parameters, click on 'Set Alert'.When you initially register for this internet site, you are asked to specify an e-mail address. This is the address to which the e-mail Alert is sent. In this example, you would automatically receive an e-mail telling you that the bid price of Dixons Group had moved above 1200p. You can use this facility to set selling prices for stocks you own, or buying prices for stocks you are interested in.

Interactive Investor *(con't)*

http://www.iii.co.uk/quotes/search

To access unit trust prices, enter all or part of the name of a unit trust, check the 'Unit Trust' box and click on 'Search'. If you enter part of a name like 'jupiter income' for example, then all the unit trusts with 'jupiter' and 'income' in the title will be displayed as shown in Figure 1.15.

Fig 1.14 *Check the 'Unit Trusts' box and enter all or part of a name such as 'Jupiter'.*

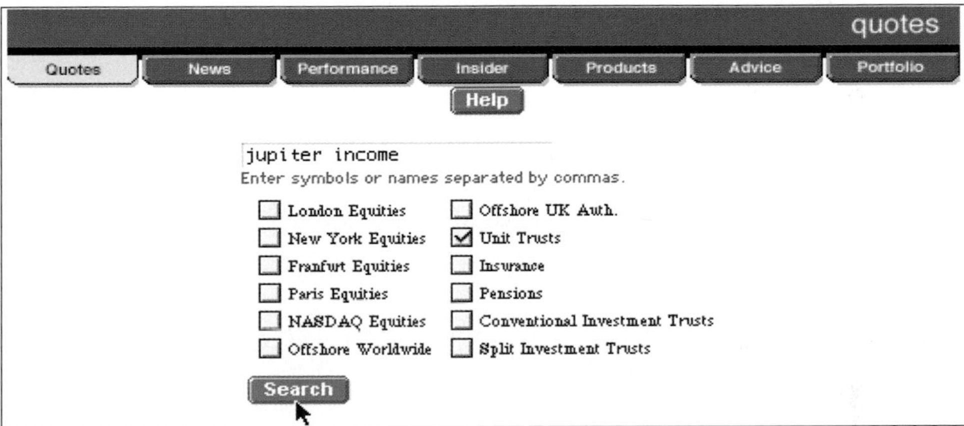

Bid and offer prices are displayed for unit trusts together with the gross dividend yield, the daily price change and whether the fund is ex-dividend. Clicking on the 'Graph' or 'Performance' icon will lead you to the very comprehensive charting facilities available for unit trusts. These are described in Chapter 2.

Fig 1.15 *Bid and offer prices are displayed for unit trusts together with dividend yield.*

Unit Trusts

3 matches found.

Actions	Bid	Offer	Yield	Daily Change	xd	Curr.	Price Date
Add	Jupiter Growth & Income Fd						Graph Performance
Alert	0.5828	0.6216	1.69	+0.06 (+0.10%) ↑	n/a	GBP	08/10/1999
Add	Jupiter High Income						Graph Performance
Alert	0.744	0.7935	3.52	-0.24 (-0.32%) ↓	D	GBP	08/10/1999
Add	Jupiter Income						Graph Performance
Alert	3.5504	3.7769	2.84	-0.22 (-0.06%) ↓	n/a	GBP	08/10/1999

Interactive Investor *(con't)*

http://www.iii.co.uk/quotes/search

If you check the 'Conventional Investment Trusts' box and search for an investment trust by name, the data shown in the figure below is displayed. This is different to the information displayed when you search for an investment trust and check the 'London Equities' box (see Figure 1.12). The screen now displays the gross dividend 'Yield', 'Last xd Date', 'Current Net Asset Value' and 'Current Discount'. Only the previous day's mid price is displayed as opposed to the current bid and offer prices in Figure 1.12.

Fig 1.16 *Initially only the previous day's mid price is shown for investment trusts.*

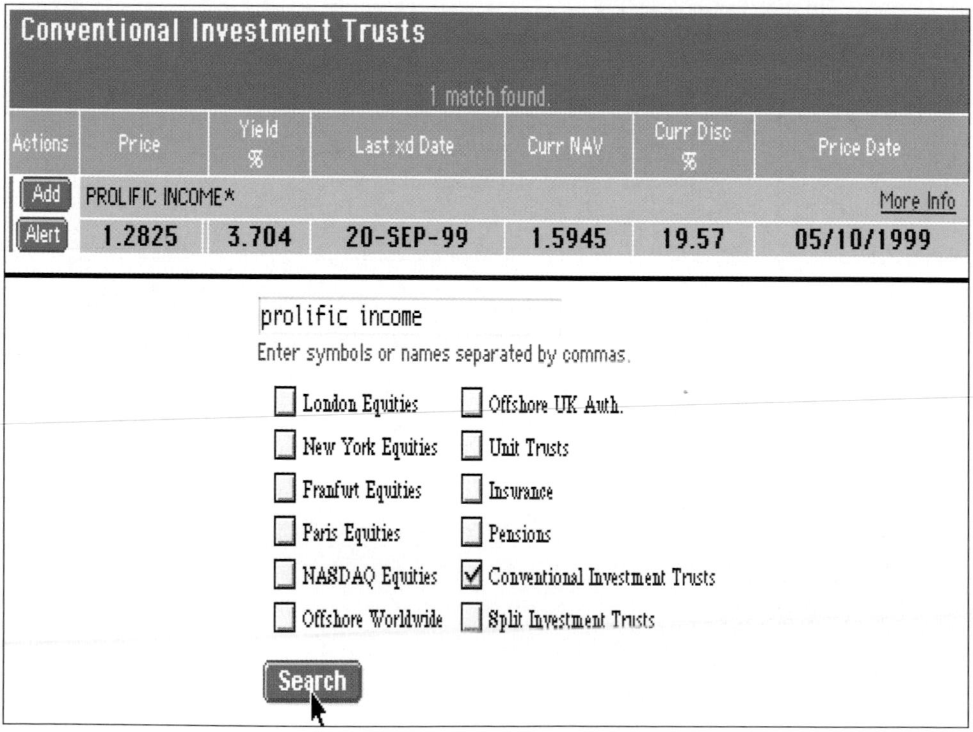

Conventional Investment Trusts

1 match found.

Actions	Price	Yield %	Last xd Date	Curr NAV	Curr Disc %	Price Date
Add	PROLIFIC INCOME*					More Info
Alert	1.2825	3.704	20-SEP-99	1.5945	19.57	05/10/1999

prolific income

Enter symbols or names separated by commas.

- London Equities
- New York Equities
- Franfurt Equities
- Paris Equities
- NASDAQ Equities
- Offshore Worldwide
- Offshore UK Auth.
- Unit Trusts
- Insurance
- Pensions
- Conventional Investment Trusts
- Split Investment Trusts

Search

When you click on the 'More Info' icon in the top right hand corner of the screen shown above, a whole host of useful information relating to that investment trust is displayed.

Interactive Investor *(con't)*

http://www.iii.co.uk/quotes/search

The top of the screen displays the investment manager of the investment trust, the sector in which it appears and a Micropal star rating. You can see that in the example below, Prolific Income, is managed by 'Aberdeen Fund Managers', appears in the 'UK Income Growth' sector and has a one star rating. The bid and offer price of the investment trust is displayed together with the 'Opening Price', the 'Last' price, the percentage 'Change' and the time of the last trade.

Fig 1.17 *Clicking on 'More Info' displays useful data for that investment trust.*

Conventional Trusts 6/ 10/ 99

Today | Conventional Trusts | Split Trusts | Warrants | Sectors | Management Groups | Knowledge Bank |

Prolific Income PLC

Manager: Aberdeen Fund Managers Sector: UK Income Growth

Current Market Information 09:44:24

	Bid	Ask	Open	Last	Change	Last Traded
Add / Alert	1.290	1.290	1.290	1.290	0.00 (0.0%)	9:40:00

Micropal Performance Graph

Price Performance

Price: 150, 145, 140, 135, 130, 125, 120, 115, 110, 105, 100

Sep 98, Nov 98, Jan 99, Mar 99, May 99, Jul 99, Sep 99, Nov 99

Asset Allocation

Region

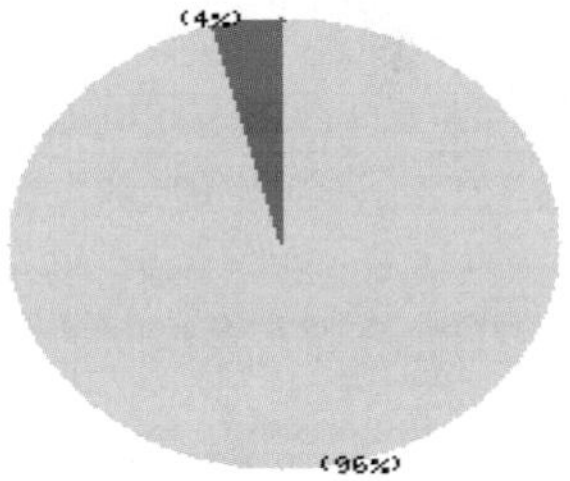

(4%) (96%)

Distribution %	
United Kingdom	96
North America	4

Quotation basis : Mid-Mid, Net income reinvested

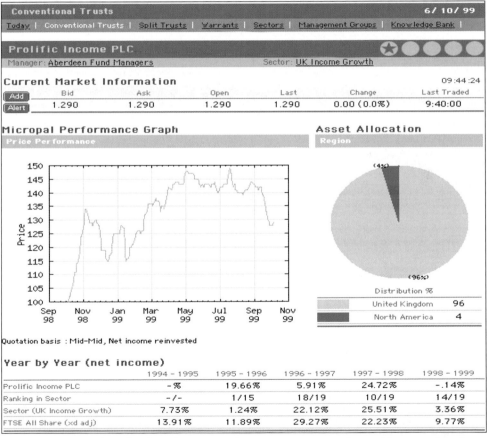

Year by Year (net income)

	1994 - 1995	1995 - 1996	1996 - 1997	1997 - 1998	1998 - 1999
Prolific Income PLC	-%	19.66%	5.91%	24.72%	-.14%
Ranking in Sector	-/-	1/15	18/19	10/19	14/19
Sector (UK Income Growth)	7.73%	1.24%	22.12%	25.51%	3.36%
FTSE All Share (xd adj)	13.91%	11.89%	29.27%	22.23%	9.77%

A 1 year price chart is also shown on the same page together with a useful pie chart showing asset allocation. The performance figures shown at the bottom of the page give a good indication of how consistent performance has been against both the relevant sector, and the FT-SE All Share Index.

Interactive Investor *(con't)*

http://www.iii.co.uk/quotes/search

If you click on 'UK Income Sector' in the top middle of the screen in Figure 1.17, a list of investment trusts in the same sector is displayed. The screen automatically displays up to 30 funds on the same screen, but you can change this to either 10, 20, 30, 50 or 100. Click on any of the funds shown to display a 1 year performance chart and asset allocation pie chart as shown in Figure 1.17.

Fig 1.18 *Click on the Sector to display the list of trusts in the same sector.*

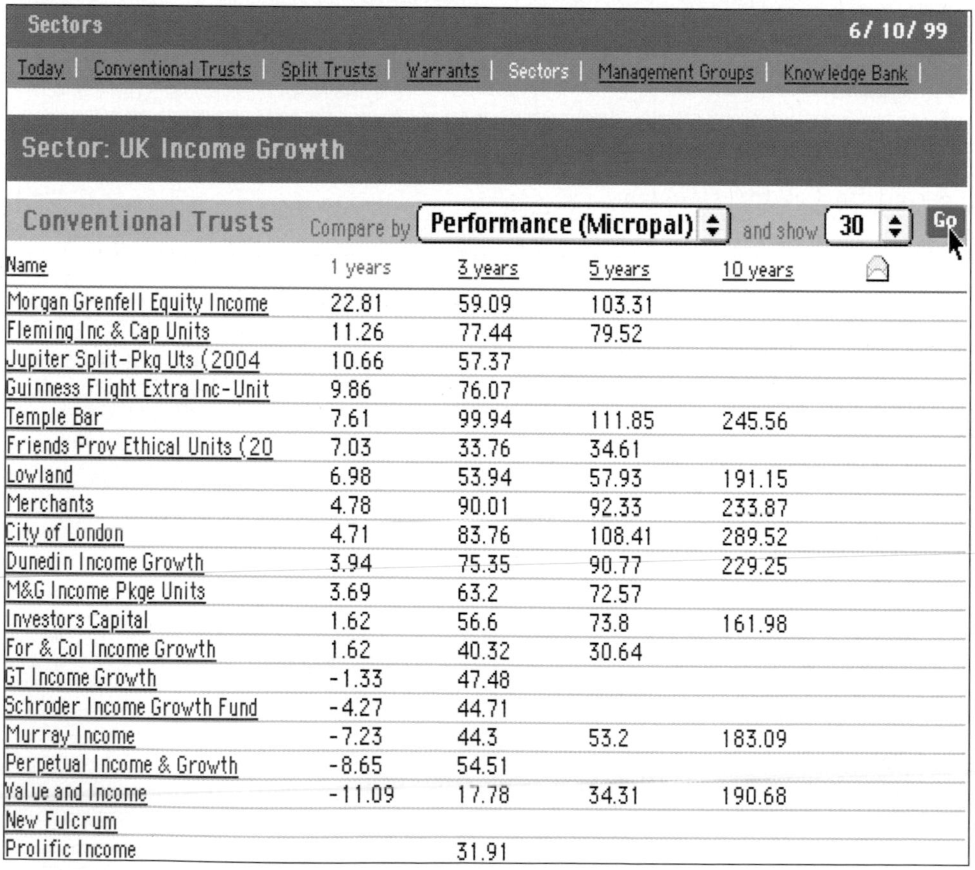

Sectors 6/ 10/ 99

Today | Conventional Trusts | Split Trusts | Warrants | Sectors | Management Groups | Knowledge Bank |

Sector: UK Income Growth

Conventional Trusts Compare by Performance (Micropal) and show 30 Go

Name	1 years	3 years	5 years	10 years
Morgan Grenfell Equity Income	22.81	59.09	103.31	
Fleming Inc & Cap Units	11.26	77.44	79.52	
Jupiter Split-Pkg Uts (2004	10.66	57.37		
Guinness Flight Extra Inc-Unit	9.86	76.07		
Temple Bar	7.61	99.94	111.85	245.56
Friends Prov Ethical Units (20	7.03	33.76	34.61	
Lowland	6.98	53.94	57.93	191.15
Merchants	4.78	90.01	92.33	233.87
City of London	4.71	83.76	108.41	289.52
Dunedin Income Growth	3.94	75.35	90.77	229.25
M&G Income Pkge Units	3.69	63.2	72.57	
Investors Capital	1.62	56.6	73.8	161.98
For & Col Income Growth	1.62	40.32	30.64	
GT Income Growth	-1.33	47.48		
Schroder Income Growth Fund	-4.27	44.71		
Murray Income	-7.23	44.3	53.2	183.09
Perpetual Income & Growth	-8.65	54.51		
Value and Income	-11.09	17.78	34.31	190.68
New Fulcrum				
Prolific Income		31.91		

Initially, the funds are displayed in order of 1 year performance. To list the funds in order of either 3, 5 or 10 year performance, click on the appropriate heading. There are 7 other criteria on which funds can be compared. At the time of writing, these different comparisons were only available for funds in the same Management Group.

Interactive Investor *(con't)*

http://www.iii.co.uk/quotes/search

If you click on 'Aberdeen Fund Managers' in the top left hand corner of the screen in Figure 1.17, the address and phone number of the management group appears. Below that, a complete list of 'Conventional' and 'Split Level' investment trusts managed by that group is displayed. The screen automatically displays up to 30 funds on the same screen, but you can change this to either 10, 20, 30, 50 or 100 as shown below.

Fig 1.19 *Click on the management group to display the list of trusts managed by them.*

Management Group: Aberdeen Fund Managers

Contact Information

Address	One Bow Churchyard Cheapside London EC4M 9HH
Tel	0171-463-6000
Fax	0171-463-6001

Conv. Trusts — Compare by Performance (Micropal) and show 10 / 20 / ✓ 30 / 50 / 100 Go

Name	1 years	3 years	5 years	10 years
Aberdeen Asian Smaller Cos	82.16	-11.84		
Aberdeen New Dawn	72.52	-20.29	-24.52	51.78
Radiotrust	43.37	92.73	127.78	84.06
Aberdeen New Thai	32.91	-64.46	-57.72	
Aberdeen High Income	6.71	157.65	87.41	
Aberdeen Emerging Economies	6.45	-27.22	-36.13	
Smaller Companies	2.85	24.87	27.77	
Taverners	-7.8	7.87		
Aberdeen Convertible Income	-12	35.29	13.43	
Aberdeen Latin American	-20.65	-18.89		
Prolific Income		31.91		
Enhanced Zero Trust				
Aberdeen Development Cap-Ord				
Aberdeen Development Cap-Zero				

Split Trusts — Compare by Performance (Micropal) and show 30 Go

Name	1 years	3 years	5 years	10 years
Danae-Inc (2002)	27.85	82.77	62.18	180.21
Jove - Inc (2004)	20.15	97.98	99.28	177.3
Jove Zero div Pref	11.76			
Aberdeen Preferred Income	5.55			
Danae-Cap (2002)	-1.69	141.67	117.5	97.73
Jove - Cap (2004)	-4.6	313.24	331.6	166.05

Initially the funds managed by a particular group are displayed and compared in order of 1 year 'Performance' with figures supplied by Micropal. There are 7 other criteria on which funds are compared, and these are illustrated on the following pages.

Interactive Investor *(con't)*

http://www.iii.co.uk/quotes/search

Fig 1.1.10 *Performance figures by Reuters include net asset value (NAV) performance.*

Conv. Trusts — Compare by: Performance (Reuters) — and show: 30 — Go

Name	3 mth price	1 yr price	3 yr price	5 yr price	3 mth NAV	1 yr NAV	3 yr NAV	5 yr NAV
Taverners	120	100.5	114		118	141	142	
Aberdeen Asian Smaller Cos	118	75.5	87		108	191	95	
Radiotrust	114	170.5	172	208	103	150	189	294
Aberdeen New Dawn	114	162.75	75	70	109	203	81	74
Aberdeen Emerging Economies	112	59.75	73	58	104	163	80	70
Aberdeen New Thai	109	56	36	38	98	162	30	27
Aberdeen Convertible Income	106	109.5	130	95	106	98	117	113
Smaller Companies	101	163.5	124	114	103	132	133	155
Aberdeen High Income	101	127.75	213	131	103	113	171	131
Enhanced Zero Trust	101	102.125			103			
Prolific Income	100	142.25	115		100	130	144	
Aberdeen Latin American	95	50.5	71		97	151	76	
Aberdeen Development Cap-Ord								
Aberdeen Development Cap-Zero								

Fig 1.1.11 *The funds of Aberdeen Fund Managers sorted by discount to net asset value.*

Conv. Trusts — Compare by: Discount — and show: 30 — Go

Name	Current	1yr av	1 yr high	1 yr low	Relative 3mth	Relative 1yr
Aberdeen Latin American	24	-1.99	45.08	15.04	2.3	25.99
Taverners	23.88		29.01	19.35		24.74
Smaller Companies	22.91	1.02	30.62	16.14	1.37	21.89
Radiotrust	22.08	-3.74	33.44	17.23	-1.63	25.82
Aberdeen Asian Smaller Cos	20.76	-6.29	49.6	14.57	-1.39	27.05
Aberdeen Emerging Economies	18.77	-5.5	41.41	11.61	-2.11	24.27
Prolific Income	15.97		24.13	6.46		15.4
Aberdeen New Dawn	15.45	-3.01	34.33	11.22		18.46
Aberdeen Convertible Income	4.17	5.41	9.17	-12.99	1.62	-1.24
Enhanced Zero Trust	1.14	1.27	3.37	-4.71		
Aberdeen High Income	-3.55	2.15	5.11	-15.64		-5.7
Aberdeen New Thai	-6.81	-8.03	13.06	-11.9	-10.41	1.22
Aberdeen Development Cap-Ord						
Aberdeen Development Cap-Zero						

Sometimes comparing the discount to net asset value of funds managed by the same Management Group can be revealing. The investment trusts of more popular Management Groups will often trade on narrower than average discounts. It is generally a bad sign if all or most the trusts of a particular group trade on above average discounts.

Interactive Investor *(con't)*

http://www.iii.co.uk/quotes/search

Fig 1.1.12 *Year by Year performance with net income reinvested.*

Conv. Trusts — Compare by: Year by Year Net — and show: 30 — Go

Name	98 - 99	97 - 98	96 - 97	95 - 96	94 - 95
Aberdeen Asian Smaller Cos	82.16	-50.33	-2.56		
Aberdeen New Dawn	72.52	-51.77	-4.2	-3.11	-2.26
Radiotrust	43.37	28.38	4.71	24.4	-5
Aberdeen New Thai	32.91	-52.21	-44.05	8	10.16
Aberdeen High Income	6.71	69.93	42.09	-19.98	-9.1
Aberdeen Emerging Economies	6.45	-37.28	9.01	4.76	-16.23
Smaller Companies	2.85	25.2	-3.03	3.94	-1.55
Taverners	-7.8	18.08			
Aberdeen Convertible Income	-12	40.41	9.49	-4.58	-12.13
Aberdeen Latin American	-20.65	-27.75	41.48	7.01	
Prolific Income		24.72	5.91	19.66	
Enhanced Zero Trust					
Aberdeen Development Cap-Ord					
Aberdeen Development Cap-Zero					

Fig 1.1.13 *Year by Year performance with gross income reinvested.*

Conv. Trusts — Compare by: Year by Year Gross — and show: 30 — Go

Name	98 - 99	97 - 98	96 - 97	95 - 96	94 - 95
Aberdeen Asian Smaller Cos	82.29	-50.19	-2.22		
Aberdeen New Dawn	72.7	-51.48	-4.08	-2.98	-2.17
Radiotrust	43.61	29	5.23	24.58	-5
Aberdeen New Thai	32.91	-51.68	-43.75	8.31	10.5
Aberdeen High Income	7.61	72.86	45.29	-18.15	-7.08
Aberdeen Emerging Economies	6.45	-37.28	9.14	4.89	-16.08
Smaller Companies	3.22	25.2	-3.03	3.94	-1.55
Taverners	-7.8	18.15			
Aberdeen Convertible Income	-11.24	41.6	11.05	-3.02	-10.92
Aberdeen Latin American	-20.65	-27.75	41.48	7.39	
Prolific Income		25.7	6.82	20.68	
Enhanced Zero Trust					
Aberdeen Development Cap-Ord					
Aberdeen Development Cap-Zero					

Interactive Investor *(con't)*

http://www.iii.co.uk/quotes/search

Fig 1.1.14 *The 'Market Information' selection displays a useful summary.*

Conv. Trusts — Compare by: Market Information — and show: 30 — Go

Name	Market Cap (£m)	Price	1 yr high	1 yr low	Yield (%)	Yield Mark	Current NAV
Aberdeen High Income	117.415	113	129.75	94.997	6.71	Q	123.37
Prolific Income	74.555	127	148.75	98.5	3.24	I	169.29
Enhanced Zero Trust	61.275		103	99.25	0	A	103.3
Smaller Companies	44.257	128	173.5	113.5	1.17		212.09
Aberdeen New Dawn	41.757	239	178.5	63.5	1.01	A	192.5
Aberdeen Convertible Income	39.778	99	118.75	94.5	7.62	Q	114.26
Aberdeen Emerging Economies	29.877	194	66.25	26.25	0	A	73.56
Aberdeen Asian Smaller Cos	26.425	232	78.5	26	.14	A	95.28
Taverners	15.927	128	100.5	61	.27	A	132.03
Radiotrust	14.663	152	172	102.5	1.87	A	218.8
Aberdeen New Thai	10.371	168	62	34.5	0	A	52.43
Aberdeen Latin American	10.1	138	62.25	27.25	0	A	66.45
Aberdeen Development Cap-Ord					0		
Aberdeen Development Cap-Zero					0		

Fig 1.1.15 '*Asset Allocation' displays the countries in which a trust has invested money.*

Conv. Trusts — Compare by: Asset Allocation — and show: 30 — Go

Name	UK	NA	JA	OP	EU	GE	FR	NE	SW	HK	SI	MA	TH	TA	LA	AS	AF	ME	US	CA	ON	AU	Other
Enhanced Zero Trust	103																						
Radiotrust	98																						
Taverners	98																						
Aberdeen Convertible Income	97																						
Prolific Income	97																						
Smaller Companies	95																						1
Aberdeen High Income	92			1																			
Aberdeen Emerging Economies					14										25	43	9	7					
Aberdeen New Dawn										18	10	10	6	5									49

The 'Market Information' selection displays the 'Market Capitalization' of each investment trust in a particular Management Group. Sometimes this information can give an over all impression of a particular group. It is generally a bad sign if a group has a relatively large number of small trusts trading on above average discounts. Sometimes this is an indication that the management group's efforts have been directed more towards raising new money via new issues, than looking after the interests of existing shareholders.

Interactive Investor *(con't)*

http://www.iii.co.uk/quotes/search

The gearing of an investment trust can be displayed as shown below. Investment trusts have the ability to borrow money or 'gear' themselves up unlike most unit trusts. Borrowing money will tend to improve performance in a rising market, but can be disastrous in a falling market. The past performance of a highly geared investment trust will often look spectacular after a period when the stock market has done particularly well - this is often not the best time to buy.

Fig 1.1.16 *'Gearing and XD' displays the trusts in order of Potential Gearing.*

Conv. Trusts — Compare by: Gearing and XD — and show: 30 — Go

Name	Actual Gearing	Potential Gearing	Last XD Date	Next XD Date(months)
Enhanced Zero Trust	171	166		6
Aberdeen Convertible Income	159	164	21-JUN-99	
Smaller Companies	154	166	16-AUG-99	6
Aberdeen High Income	128	141	26-JUL-99	1
Aberdeen New Dawn	113	115	05-JUL-99	9
Taverners	112	115	16-AUG-99	11
Aberdeen Latin American	99	100	01-SEP-98	
Aberdeen Emerging Economies	98	100	21-DEC-98	4
Aberdeen New Thai	97	100	01-JUN-99	8
Radiotrust		100	01-JUN-99	8
Prolific Income		100	06-APR-99	
Aberdeen Development Cap-Ord				
Aberdeen Development Cap-Zero				
Aberdeen Asian Smaller Cos		105	09-NOV-98	2

In most cases, you can change the way in which the funds are sorted. If you were looking to generate an income from your investments, you could sort the funds in order of 'Next XD Date' to see at a glance which funds are due to pay dividends next as shown below.

Fig 1.1.17 *Aberdeens' investment trusts sorted in order of the 'Next XD Date'.*

Conv. Trusts — Compare by: Gearing and XD — and show: 30 — Go

Name	Actual Gearing	Potential Gearing	Last XD Date	Next XD Date(months)
Taverners	112	115	16-AUG-99	11
Aberdeen New Dawn	113	115	05-JUL-99	9
Radiotrust		100	01-JUN-99	8
Aberdeen New Thai	97	100	01-JUN-99	8
Smaller Companies	154	166	16-AUG-99	6
Enhanced Zero Trust	171	166		6
Aberdeen Emerging Economies	98	100	21-DEC-98	4
Aberdeen Asian Smaller Cos		105	09-NOV-98	2
Aberdeen High Income	128	141	26-JUL-99	1
Aberdeen Convertible Income	159	164	21-JUN-99	
Prolific Income		100	06-APR-99	
Aberdeen Development Cap-Ord				
Aberdeen Latin American	99	100	01-SEP-98	
Aberdeen Development Cap-Zero				

Market-Eye

http://www.market-eye.co.uk/scripts/search/InvStockSearch.asp?

This is a very well designed site which provides investors with a whole host of useful share information on one page. Stock prices can be accessed in one of three ways. If you click on any of the letters of the alphabet, a list of stocks beginning with that letter will be displayed. Simply scroll down the list to the stock you are looking for and click on it. Alternatively, you can enter all or part of the name of a stock in the box alongside 'Name' in Figure 1.2 and click on 'Search'.

Fig 1.2 *The quickest way to access price data is to enter the correct stock symbol.*

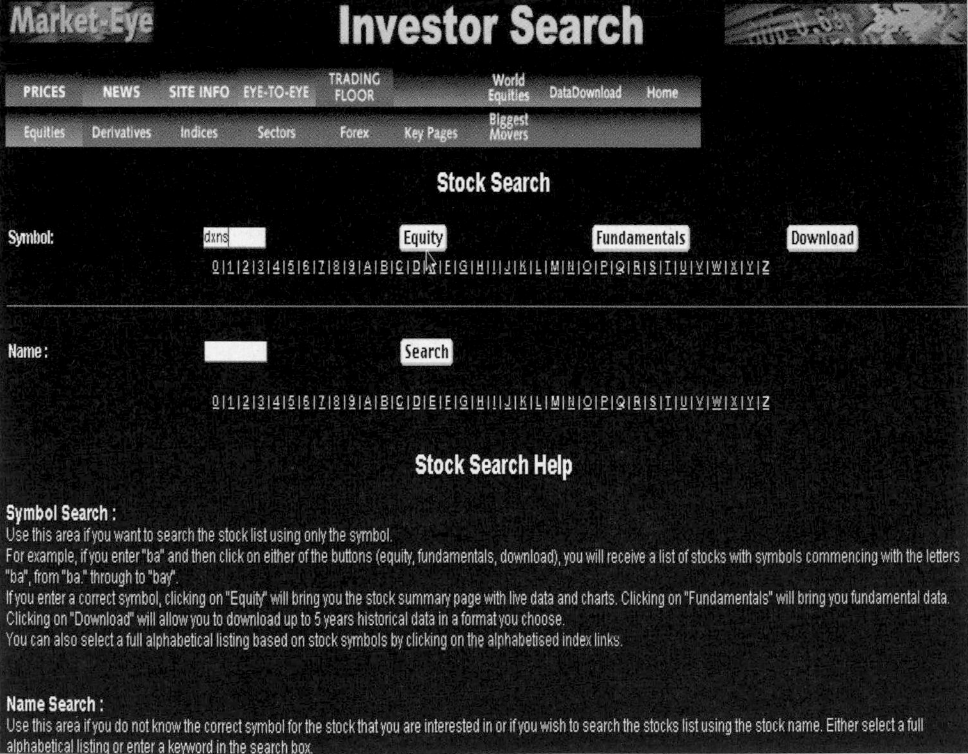

The quickest way to access information on an investment is generally to enter the correct symbol for that stock. It is worth making a written note of stock symbols which you know you will be re-using. For example, to access share price data for Dixons, enter 'dxns' in the box shown in Figure 1.2 and click on 'Equity'. The screen in Figure 1.21 should appear.

Market-Eye *(con't)*

http://www.market-eye.co.uk/scripts/search/InvStockSearch.asp?

For shares and investment trusts, the Buying, Selling and Current price (middle market) are displayed. Other price information on the same screen includes Change in price, Opening price, and the High and Low price for that day. The Trade price and the Traded Volume of the last deal are also displayed together with the Total Volume of shares traded that day. In addition to this comprehensive share price data, the Price/Earnings ratio (P/E), Dividend Yield and Earnings Per Share (EPS) are also shown. In the example of Dixons shown below, the shares have just gone ex-dividend as denoted by the 'xd' alongside the name.

Fig 1.21 *Useful trading information, is displayed alongside the bid/offer quote.*

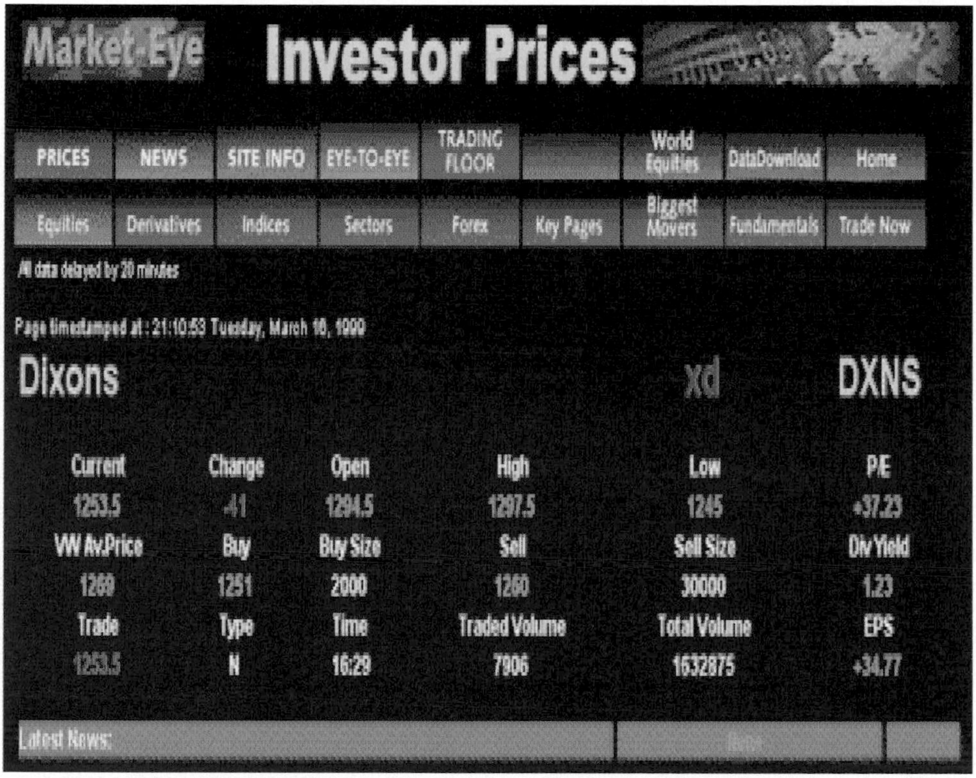

Market-Eye Investor Prices

PRICES | NEWS | SITE INFO | EYE-TO-EYE | TRADING FLOOR | World Equities | DataDownload | Home

Equities | Derivatives | Indices | Sectors | Forex | Key Pages | Biggest Movers | Fundamentals | Trade Now

All data delayed by 20 minutes

Page timestamped at : 21:10:53 Tuesday, March [illegible]

Dixons xd DXNS

Current	Change	Open	High	Low	P/E
1253.5	-41	1294.5	1297.5	1245	+37.23
VW AvPrice	**Buy**	**Buy Size**	**Sell**	**Sell Size**	**Div Yield**
1269	1251	2000	1260	30000	1.23
Trade	**Type**	**Time**	**Traded Volume**	**Total Volume**	**EPS**
1253.5	N	16:29	7906	1632875	+34.77

Latest News:

The latest up to date news headline is displayed below the price quote and the full news story can be accessed free. A large one year price graph and volume bar chart is automatically displayed at the bottom of the screen (not shown).

Market-Eye *(con't)*

http://www.market-eye.co.uk/scripts/search/InvStockSearch.asp?

The Market-Eye site has recently been upgraded and now includes additional share price information. To access this information, enter the name of a share or its symbol and click on 'Fundamentals'. The example below shows the information which is displayed for Dixons Group PLC. Under the heading of 'Fundamentals', both this years and last years High and Low prices are displayed. Also shown, are the Number of Shares in Issue, the Market Capitalization, and the Nominal Value of the shares. Under the 'Historical' heading the Price Earning Ratio (P/E), Total Net Dividend, Dividend Cover and the gross Dividend Yield are displayed. The historic Earnings Per Share (EPS) are also shown in both standard accounting formats.

Fig 1.22 *Clicking on 'Fundamentals' displays a whole host of useful data for Dixons.*

Dixons DXNS

FUNDAMENTALS

Close	1121	Shares/Issue(m)	430.925	MktCap(m)	4830.669
1999 High	1564	1998 High	845.5	NomVal(£)	0.1
1999 Low	797.5	1998 Low	472.5	Segment	SET1

HISTORICAL

PE Ratio	+32.24	Total Div(Net)	12.7	FRS3 EPS	+35.4
Div.Yield	1.13	Div. Cover	+2.92	Norm EPS	+34.77

LAST DIVIDEND ANNOUNCEMENT

Last Div.	Interim	Ann.Date	13 Jan 1999	Ex.Div	01 Mar 1999
		Amount(Net)	3.5	Payment	06 Apr 1999

LATEST COMPANY ACCOUNTS (£m) - 02 May 1998

Turnover	PreTax Profit	Fixed Assets	Cash	Curr.Liabilities	ST Debt	LT Debt
2773.8	+218.7	340.2	+38.1	607.9	37.4	199

The dividend information displayed on this page is both comprehensive and accurate. The dates on which both interim and final dividends are announced and paid are given, together with the net amounts. Last but not least there are useful extracts from the last set of Report and Accounts. These include Turnover, Pre Tax Profit, Fixed Assets, Cash, Current Liabilities, Short Term (ST) Debt and Long Term (LT) Debt.

Market-Eye *(con't)*

http://www.market-eye.co.uk/scripts/datadownload.dll?HandleEquityLink?symbol=dxns

A good feature of this site, is the ability to download the last 5 years prices for some investments. This is achieved by clicking on the 'DataDownload' icon in the top right hand corner of the screen shown below. First select an investment whose price history you wish to download. In the example of Dixons, the screen below should appear.

Fig 1.23 *Click on the 'Data Download' icon to access share prices on a particular day.*

To download the share price history on to your computer, you need to click on the 'DXNS.CSV' icon as shown above. A 'Download Manager' box similar to the one shown below should appear on your computer screen. It may take a moment or two for the data to download depending on the processing speed of your computer.

Fig.1.24 *The 'Download Manager' function on your computer should be displayed.*

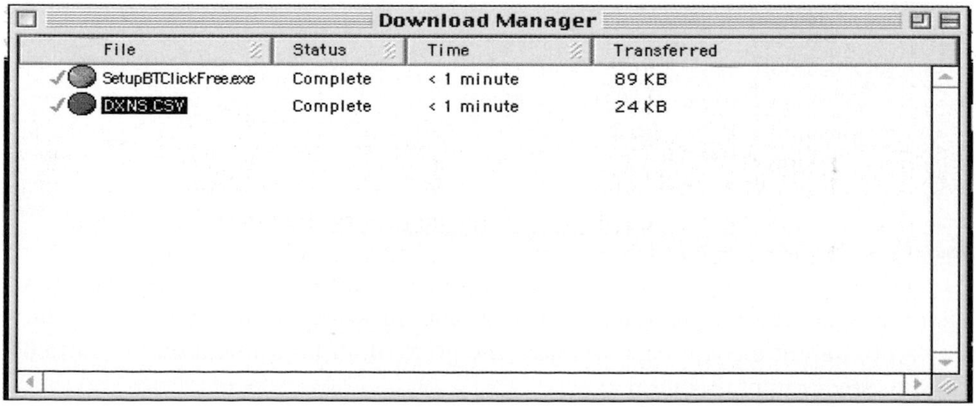

Market-Eye *(con't)*

http://www.market-eye.co.uk/scripts/datadownload.dll?HandleEquityLink?symbol=dxns

Once the data download is complete, you should be able to display a list of share prices going back five years. In the example of Dixons, the 'Download Manager' saves the share price history in a file called DXNS.CSV. The location of this file depends on how your computer is set up. In most cases, the file will be saved on your 'Desktop'. The 'Desktop' is the opening screen on your computer when you initially turn it on. To display the prices for Dixons, you need to locate the file and double click on it's name.

Fig 1.25 *Double click on the file name DXNS.CSV to display a list of historic prices.*

DXNS.CSV

	A	B	C	D	E	F	G
1	27/5/1994,186.5						
2	30/5/1994,186.5						
3	31/5/1994,189.0						
4	1/6/1994,188.0						
5	2/6/1994,188.0						
6	3/6/1994,185.0						
7	6/6/1994,186.0						
8	7/6/1994,186.0						
9	8/6/1994,188.0						
10	9/6/1994,193.0						
11	10/6/1994,193.0						
12	13/6/1994,187.0						
13	14/6/1994,188.0						
14	15/6/1994,188.0						
15	16/6/1994,191.0						
16	17/6/1994,189.5						
17	20/6/1994,185.5						
18	21/6/1994,185.0						
19	22/6/1994,187.0						
20	23/6/1994,190.0						
21	24/6/1994,186.5						
22	27/6/1994,179.0						
23	28/6/1994,176.0						
24	29/6/1994,180.0						
25	30/6/1994,176.0						
26	1/7/1994,177.0						
27	4/7/1994,175.0						
28	5/7/1994,170.0						
29	6/7/1994,189.0						
30	7/7/1994,185.0						
31	8/7/1994,188.0						
32	11/7/1994,187.0						
33	12/7/1994,186.0						
34	13/7/1994,186.0						
35	14/7/1994,186.0						
36	15/7/1994,189.5						
37	18/7/1994,184.0						
38	19/7/1994,188.0						
39	20/7/1994,187.0						
40	21/7/1994,185.0						
41	22/7/1994,184.0						
42	25/7/1994,183.0						
43	26/7/1994,183.0						
44	27/7/1994,185.0						
45	28/7/1994,184.0						
46	29/7/1994,183.0						
47	1/8/1994,186.0						
48	2/8/1994,192.0						

Sometimes having an actual list of share prices is more useful than seeing the same data in the form of a chart. For example, to work out approximate capital gains tax liabilities, you need to know the price of an investment on the particular day you bought or sold it.

Market-Eye *(con't)*

http://www.market-eye.co.uk/scripts//Equity.dll?HandleForex

A list of the Bid and Offer (Ask) prices for the major currencies against Sterling and the Dollar can be obtained by clicking on the 'Forex' icon at the top of the screen shown below.

Fig 1.26 *The real bid/offer spread for currencies is a fraction of one percent.*

Market-Eye **Investor Prices**

PRICES | NEWS | SITE INFO | EYE-TO-EYE | TRADING FLOOR | World Equities | DataDownload | Home

Equities | Derivatives | Indices | Sectors | Forex | Key Pages | Biggest Movers

All data delayed by 20 minutes

Page timestamped at : 15:58:17 Tuesday, May 25, 1999

	Sterling (£)		US Dollar ($)	
	Bid	Ask	Bid	Ask
US Dollar	1.6021	1.6031		
EURO	1.5084	1.5104	0.9412	0.9435
Japanese Yen	196.31	196.75	122.54	122.74
Swiss Franc	2.4030	2.4057	1.5000	1.5010
Hong Kong Dollar	12.4130	12.4230	7.7535	7.7545
Australian Dollar	2.4347	2.4418	0.6564	0.6579
New Zealand Dollar	2.9437	2.9511	0.5430	0.5440
Canadian Dollar	2.3373	2.3412	1.4588	1.4603
German Mark	2.9483	2.9517	1.8398	1.8408
French Franc	9.8860	9.9015	6.1691	6.1749
Spanish Peseta	250.63	251.27	156.40	156.70
Belgian Franc	60.80	60.89	37.94	37.97
Dutch Guilder	3.3212	3.3265	2.0725	2.0745
Italian Lira	2917.13	2923.76	1820.36	1823.36
Irish Punt	1.1853	1.1904	1.3470	1.3520
Danish Krone	11.1938	11.2328	6.9852	7.0052
Norwegian Krone	12.4224	12.4943	7.7519	7.7919
Swedish Krona	13.5338	13.6002	8.4454	8.4816

It is quite rare to find an internet site which displays bid and offer prices for currencies. Many sites just display the mid price. It is interesting to note that the difference between the bid and the offer price for a currency is actually only a fraction of one percent. Compare that to the 15-20% spreads charged by travel agents or high street Banks!!

Market Eye *(con't)*

http://www.market-eye.co.uk/scripts/search/DerivRes.asp?Service=Investor

Fig 1.27 *Clicking on the 'Derivatives' icon gives access to Options Prices.*

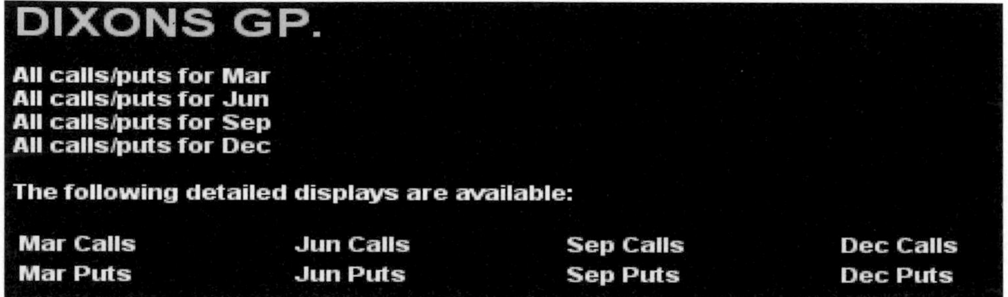

DIXONS GP.
All calls/puts for Mar
All calls/puts for Jun
All calls/puts for Sep
All calls/puts for Dec
The following detailed displays are available:
Mar Calls
Mar Puts
Jun Calls
Jun Puts
Sep Calls
Sep Puts
Dec Calls
Dec Puts

Fig 1.28 *A complete list of 'All calls/puts for June' for Dixons Group PLC.*

Jun for DIXONS GP.

TIME	LAST	BSIZE	BID	ASK	ASIZE	SERIES	VOLUME	OPEN INT	PREV SET
						460		0	700
						500		0	660
						550		0	610.5
						600		0	560.5
						650		13	510.5
						700		1	461
						750		12	411
						800		55	361.5
						850		6	312.5
						900		42	264.5
						950		0	217
						1000		13	173.5
						1050		7	134.5
						1100		15	100
						1150		16	69
09:55	37					1200	8	72	47
						1250		126	30
09:50	15					1300	3	145	19
						1350		64	11.5
						1400		54	6
						1450		170	3.5
						1500		503	2
						1600		93	0.5
						1700		1	0
						1800		14	0

Clicking on the 'Indices' icon at the top of Figure 1.2, displays the daily changes for individual sectors of the UK market. A further click on a sector will graphically display the performance over the last month (see Chapter 2). The 'World Equities' icon gives you access to over 32,000 international equity prices via the Datastream site which is fully described later in this Chapter.

E*Trade

http://research.etrade.co.uk/free/stock.cgi/

UK-iNvest have already established themselves as one of the largest and most successful online brokers in America and their plan is to do the same in the UK. Much of the information formally on the Electronic Share Information (esi) site has been incorporated onto this site giving investors free access to accurate, up to date share price data. Once you have registered, the internet address at the top of this page will lead you straight to the 'Quotes and Research' section.

Fig 1.3 *'The 'Quotes and Research' section gives access to accurate share price data.*

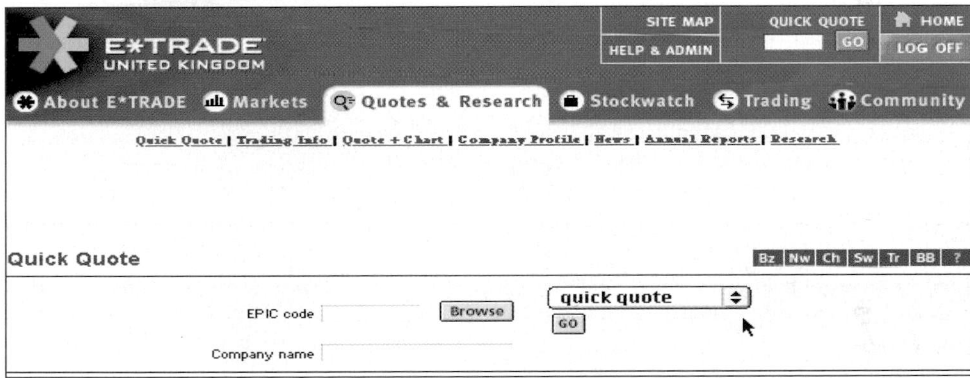

Clicking on the small arrows alongside the 'quick quote' heading in Figure 1.3, produces a drop down menu with five choices ranging from 'quick quote' to 'news archive' as shown below. To access the data select a heading from the menu, enter the name or Symbol (Epic Code) of a company in the box as shown below and click on 'Go'.

Fig 1.31 *You can choose to display share price information in 5 different formats.*

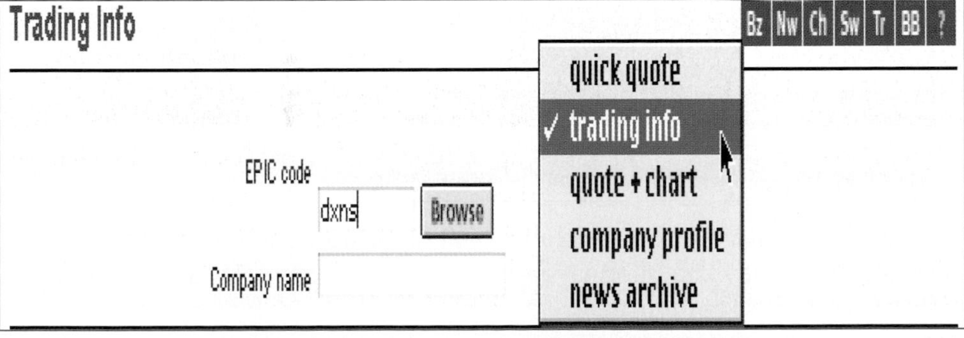

E*Trade *(con't)*

http://research.etrade.co.uk/free/stock.cgi/

The 'trading info' heading is particularly useful because a lot of relevant information is displayed on the same page. You can see at a glance the bid and offer price of a share, the size of the company, relevant financial statistics, whether the shares are ex dividend and any recent news headlines.

Fig 1.32 *The 'trading info' heading displays lots of useful share price data on one page.*

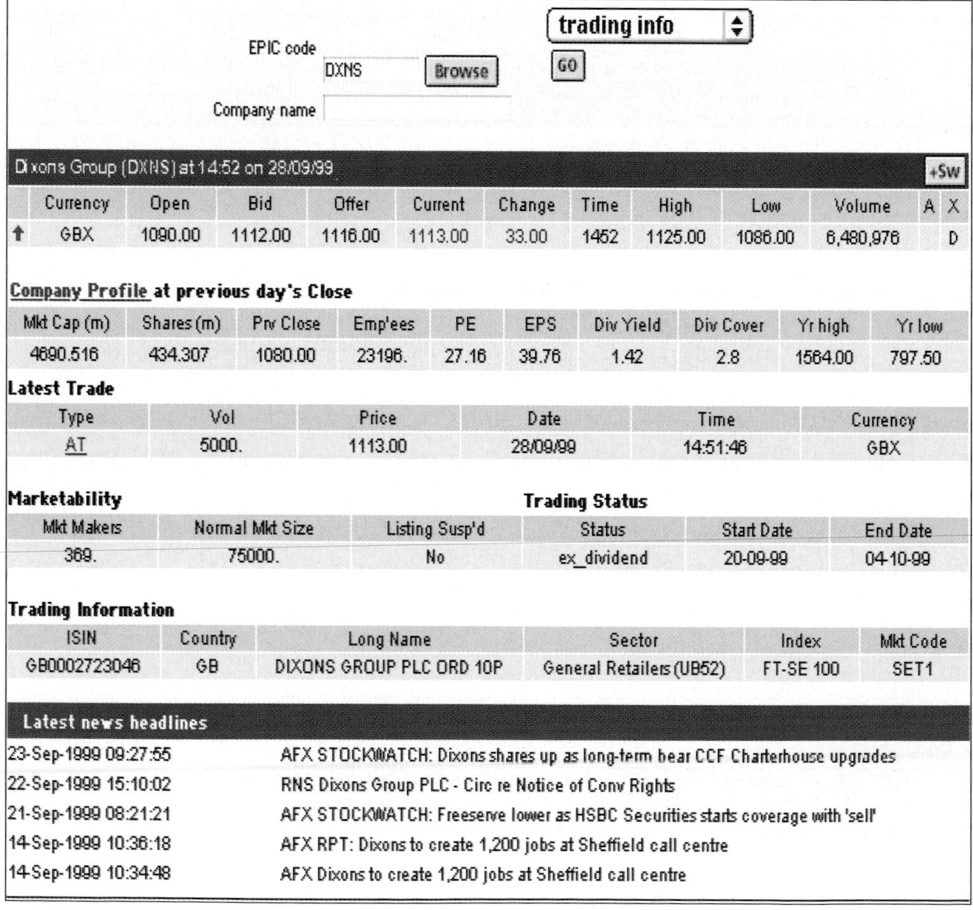

trading info

EPIC code DXNS Browse GO

Company name

Dixons Group (DXNS) at 14:52 on 28/09/99 +Sw

	Currency	Open	Bid	Offer	Current	Change	Time	High	Low	Volume	A	X
↑	GBX	1090.00	1112.00	1116.00	1113.00	33.00	1452	1125.00	1086.00	6,480,976		D

Company Profile at previous day's Close

Mkt Cap (m)	Shares (m)	Prv Close	Emp'ees	PE	EPS	Div Yield	Div Cover	Yr high	Yr low
4690.516	434.307	1080.00	23196.	27.16	39.76	1.42	2.8	1564.00	797.50

Latest Trade

Type	Vol	Price	Date	Time	Currency
AT	5000.	1113.00	28/09/99	14:51:46	GBX

Marketability / **Trading Status**

Mkt Makers	Normal Mkt Size	Listing Susp'd	Status	Start Date	End Date
369.	75000.	No	ex_dividend	20-09-99	04-10-99

Trading Information

ISIN	Country	Long Name	Sector	Index	Mkt Code
GB0002723046	GB	DIXONS GROUP PLC ORD 10P	General Retailers (UB52)	FT-SE 100	SET1

Latest news headlines

23-Sep-1999 09:27:55	AFX STOCKWATCH: Dixons shares up as long-term bear CCF Charterhouse upgrades
22-Sep-1999 15:10:02	RNS Dixons Group PLC - Circ re Notice of Conv Rights
21-Sep-1999 08:21:21	AFX STOCKWATCH: Freeserve lower as HSBC Securities starts coverage with 'sell'
14-Sep-1999 10:36:18	AFX RPT: Dixons to create 1,200 jobs at Sheffield call centre
14-Sep-1999 10:34:48	AFX Dixons to create 1,200 jobs at Sheffield call centre

You have to be a subscriber to view the full news stories although it is usually possible to get the same information for free by using the 'News' sources highlighted in Chapter 4 of this book.

E*Trade *(con't)*

http://research.etrade.co.uk/free/stock.cgi/

The 'company profile' option displays very useful dividend information including 'Amount per share', 'Announcement date', 'Ex dividend date' and 'Payment date'. The Registrars telephone number appears right at the bottom of the page. This is useful if you ever need to check how many shares you own following a capital reconstruction or take over bid for example.

Fig 1.33 *Dividend dates etc. can be displayed by selecting 'company profile'.*

Dixons Group PLC(DXNS) at 15:08 on 28/09/99 +Sw

	Currency	Open	Bid	Offer	Current	Change	Time	High	Low	Vol
↑	GBX	1090.00	1111.00	1116.00	1112.00	32.00	14:53	1125.00	1086.00	6,630,017

Fundamental Data

Activities in brief: Retail sale of consumer electronics, personal computers, domestic appliances, photographic equipment, communication products and related services; property development

Prev. Close	Shares/Issue (m)	Mkt Cap (m)	Employees	REM
1133.0000	434.307	4920.698	23,196	343.900

PE Ratio	EPS (Norm)	FRS3 EPS	Annual Div	Div Yield	Div Cover
28.5000	39.760	38.200	15.3000	1.3500	2.8000

Yr high (curr)	Yr low (curr)	Yr high (prev)	Yr low (prev)
1564.00	797.50	845.50	472.50

Key Dates

next AR year end	30 Apr 00	**int xd (2.90p)**	26 Jan 98
fin xd (9.80p)	20 Jul 98	**int results**	13 Jan 99
int xd (3.50p)	1 Mar 99	**year end**	1 May 99
annual report	7 Jul 99	**fin xd (11.8p)**	19 Jul 99
agm	8 Sep 99	**spdiv xd (7.50p)**	22 Nov 99

Last Dividend Announcement

Type	Amount per share	Announce. date	Ex Div	Payment date
	7.5000	08 Sep 1999	22 Nov 1999	13 Dec 1999

3 Year Financials

year ended 30 April	1997	1998	1999
turnover (£m)	2,443	2,792	3,156
pre tax profit (£m)	200	213	231

HEAD & REGISTERED OFFICE: Maylands Avenue, Hemel Hempstead, Hertfordshire, HP2 7TG
Tel: (01442) 353000 **Fax:** (01442) 233218

Registrar: IRG PLC, Ilford **Tel:** (0181) 639 2000

Currency	Sector	EPIC	NSIN	Segment	Nominal Value
GBP	General Retailers	DXNS	272304	SET1	0.1000

The 'quote + chart' and 'news archive' options shown in Figure 1.31 are fully described in Chapters 2 and 4 respectively. The 'quick quote' option displays the same information as the 'trading info' but without the news headlines.

Bloomberg Currency Calculator

http://www.bloomberg.com/markets/currency/fastcgi/currcalc.cgi/ukcurrcalc.html

This internet site has a very comprehensive list of over 200 currencies including everything from the Albanian 'Lek' to the Zambian 'Kwacha'. It is worth looking at the expanded currency list on this site, simply to increase your chances of answering the obscure currency questions in 'Trivial Pursuits'. What is particularly useful, is that the list has the stock market mnemonics alongside each currency, eg 'GBP' for the British Pound and 'THB' for the Thai Baht. These are useful when using the currency charting facilities described in Chapter 2.

Fig 1.4 *The 'Expanded List' consists of over 200 currencies.*

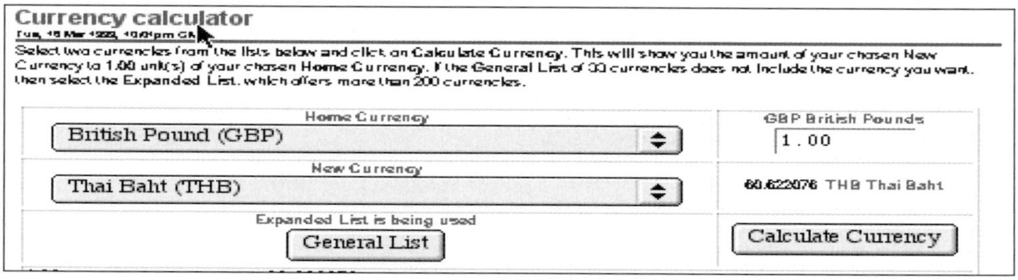

In addition to simply displaying currency exchange rates, this site also has a useful currency calculator. You can use this to quickly work out how much something costs in your home currency. For example, at the time of writing, a gallon of unleaded petrol in America cost $1.20. The currency calculator works this out to be equivalent to just under £0.74 at current exchange rates.

Fig 1.41 *The 'Currency Calculator' is good for calculating the cost of overseas goods.*

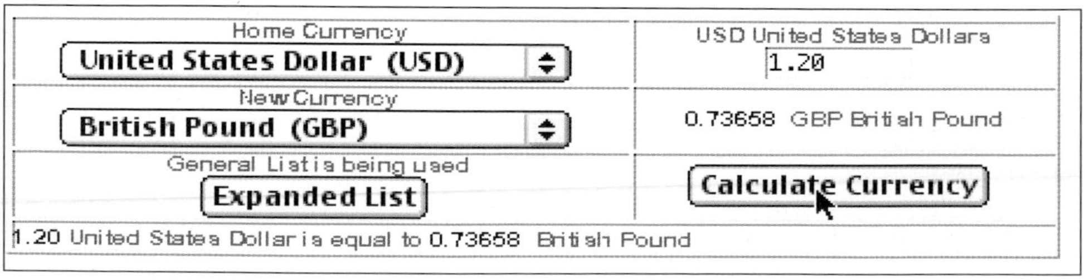

This site only displays the middle market currency exchange rates. Bid and offer prices for major currencies can be viewed under the 'Forex' section on the Market-Eye page. In the money markets, the difference between the buying and selling prices for major currencies is generally only a fraction of 1%. Compare this to the 10-20% bid/offer spreads quoted at your local travel agent or bank!

Datastream

http://www1.datastream.com/quotes/equity1.htm

Datastream has one of the largest financial data banks in the world and this site will provide end of day quotes for over 32,000 World Equities. When you first enter this site, change the setting to 'Datastream Company Name' as shown below unless you know the correct symbol (mnemonic).

Fig 1.5 *Over 32,000 international equity prices can be accessed at this site.*

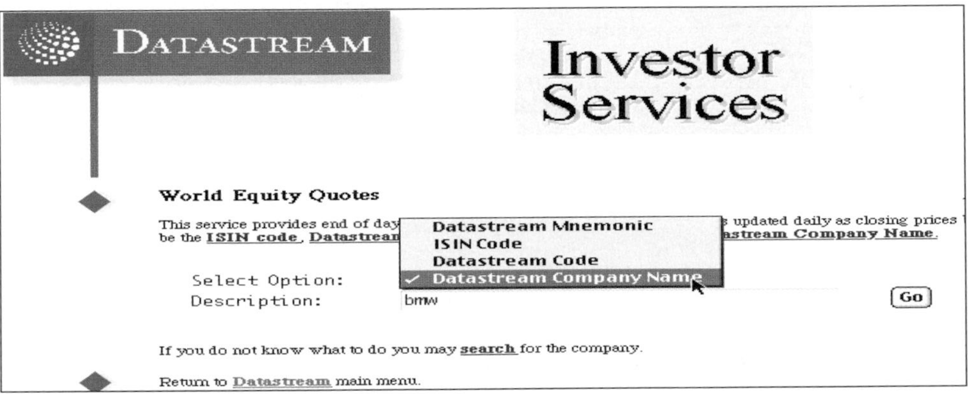

Fig 1.51 *Share price information for the German company 'BMW'.*

World Equity Quotes - Results

dd/mm/yy	Name	Location	Price	Price Earnings	Dividend Yield	Earnings per Share	Currency
16/03/99	BMW	BD	605	19.7	1.41	30.69	E

Return to ***World Equity Quotes*** *Page.*

Return to **Datastream** main menu.

Clicking on any of the headings in the Figure above, such as 'Dividend Yield', will take you to the Datastream glossary. Here you will find a full and comprehensive definition of the basis on which the information under that heading is derived. It is worth being aware of the fact that ratios like 'Earning per Share', may be calculated differently in other countries. If you are particularly interested in what online information is available for overseas investments, then the book 'Investing Online' by Stephen Eckett is worth reading.

Stock Point

http://www.stockpoint.com/retrieve.asp?mode=member

The Stock Point internet site has consistently been voted one of the best financial internet sites in America. An excellent feature of this site is that you can access 'real time quotes' for free. Most share prices on the internet are delayed by a minimum of 15 minutes. Once you have registered at this site and logged on, click on the 'Go' button alongside 'real time quotes' as shown below.

Fig 1.6 *This American internet site gives investors access to free 'real time quotes'.*

To display a 'real time quote' for a UK company, you have to remember to change the 'Country' to 'UK'. To do this, click on the small arrow below the 'Country' heading and select 'UK' from the drop down menu as shown in the figure below. The quickest way to display a price is to enter the correct share Symbol (eg dxns for Dixons PLC) and click on 'Go'. If you don't know the Symbol, you can enter all or part of the name of the company. The search will display a list of companies containing the letters you have entered, and you will need to click on the name of the company you are looking for.

Fig 1.61 *Change the 'Country' from 'US' to 'UK' before entering your share code.*

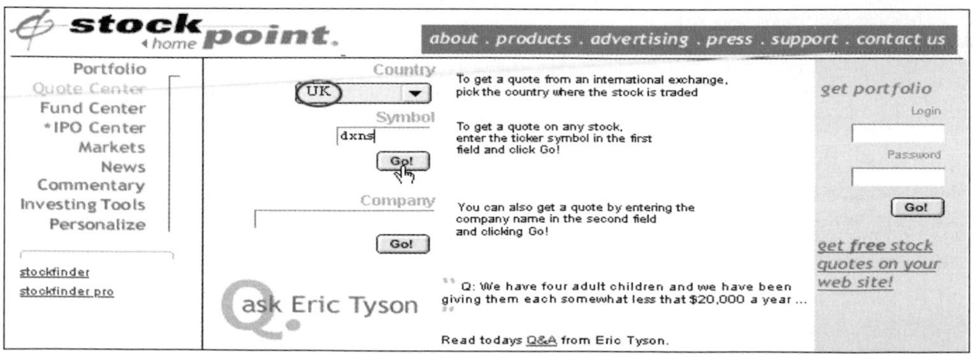

Stock Point *(con't)*

http://www.stockpoint.com/retrieve.asp?mode=member

Internet sites have to pay the London Stock Exchange a fee each time investors request a 'real time quote'. As a consequence, this internet site limits users to 50 'real time quotes' (RTQ's) per day. The top right hand corner of the screen shown in the figure below, tells you how many of your RTQ's you have used. The same page also displays other useful share price data such as the Earnings per Share, Price Earnings Ratio (P/E) and Market Capitalization. The volume of shares traded is also displayed together with the 52 Week High and Low price.

Fig 1.62 *Useful share price data is displayed alongside the 'real time quote'.*

[Quote Center] **real time quote**

Dixons Group Plc

You have selected 2 of your 50 RTQ's

As of Sep 28 12:26:00 PM (E.T.)

Last	1,121.00	Change	41.00
Open	1,115.00	% Change	3.80%
High	1,124.00	52 Week High	1,575.00
Low	1,080.00	52 Week Low	514.50
Volume	4.09M	Bid	1,120.00
Earnings P/Share	0.41	Ask	1,121.00
Shares Outstanding	434.26M	Bid Size	0
P/E Ratio	25.47	Ask Size	0
Bid Tick	N/A	Mkt Capitalization	4.55B
		Exchange	LSE

Another excellent feature of this site is the free charting function which allows you to select your own time period for share price charts. This feature is fully described in Chapter 2. Stock Point provide data to the UK-iNvest internet site This site is partially owned by the UK's largest internet service provider 'Freeserve PLC'.

2

Charts

There are a number of excellent FREE internet sites enabling you to display price charts for most types of investments. Some charts go back as far as 10 years, and allow you to compare investments against each other and also against relevant indices. In addition to prices, you can also display charts of other items such as dividends, earnings and currency movements.

UK companies which are covered by a US based internet site (usually via an ADR) tend to have even more comprehensive charting facilities. These include highlighting on the chart when major news stories have broken etc.

Hot Links

✍ 5 year charts with up to 2 stocks against various indices - *Interactive Investor*
✔ 3, 5 & 10 year share price charts relative to FTA All Share Index - *Hemscott*
✍ 1 & 5 year inv trust charts including net asset value & discount - *Trustnet*
✔ 1, 3 & 5 year charts for US listed stocks - *Quicken*
✔ 5 year charts of earnings, dividends and prices - *Wright Research Center*
✔ 1 year share price charts with a financial summary - *Datastream*
✍ 1 month chart for any sector of the UK market - *Market Eye*
✔ Currency charts - *Quote Watch*
✍ 1 year price chart of a UK share with news headlines - *E*Trade*
✔ 1 year user defined charts with multiple research tools - *Stock Point*
✔ 3 year interactive charts - *UK-iNvest*

A full list of UK stocks listed on the American stock market (eg ADR's) can be found in Appendix A at the back of this book. The definition of an ADR can be found in the Glossary which is also at the back of this book.

✍ Indicates that Registration is necessary to access information at this site.

III Interactive Investor

http://www.iii.co.uk/quotes/search

The charting facility on this site is one of the best free services available for UK stocks. In order to get a chart, you must first go to the 'Quotes' section of this site and select an investment. You can enter either all or part of the name, or the correct stock code. The example below shows how to display a share price chart for Dixons Group PLC for which the correct stock code is 'dxns'.

Fig 2.1 *Enter the stock code of the investment for which you wish to display a chart.*

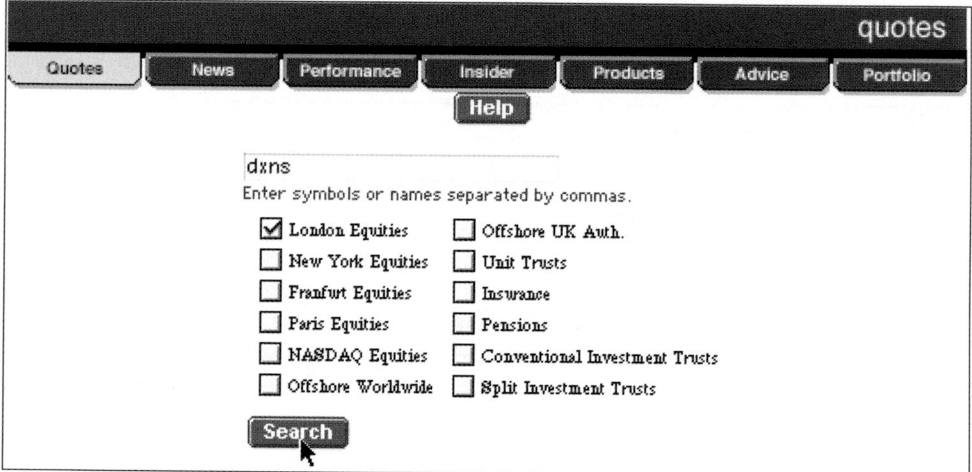

Once you have displayed a price quote, click on the small 'Graph' icon to the right of the screen as shown below.

Fig 2.11 *Click on the small 'Graph' icon to display a share price chart.*

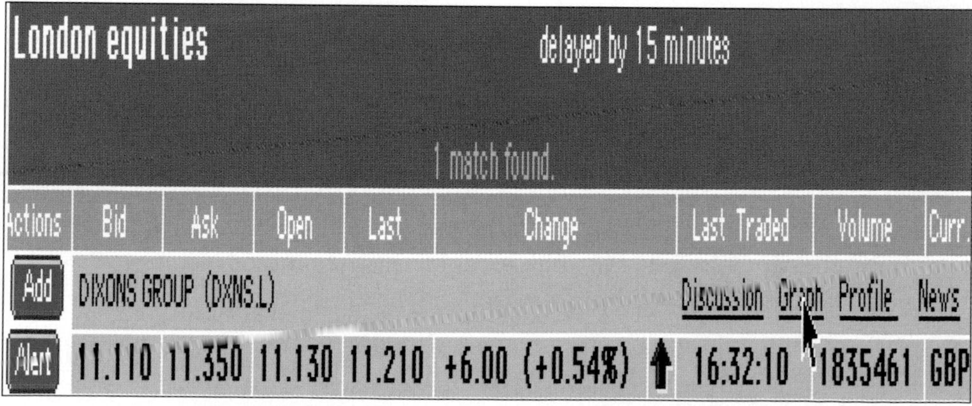

III Interactive Investor *(con't)*

http://www.iii.co.uk/quotes/search

Having entered the chart section, you can select one of 5 time periods ranging from 3 months to 5 years. Two stocks can be displayed on the same chart, and in the case of UK stocks, you can also choose to plot either the FT-SE 100, 250, 350 or FT-SE All Share Index on the same chart. The y-axis of the chart is set by the price of the first stock you plot which can be more useful than simply rebasing all the lines on the chart to 100 which often happens.

Fig 2.12 *You can compare different stocks on the same chart against different indices.*

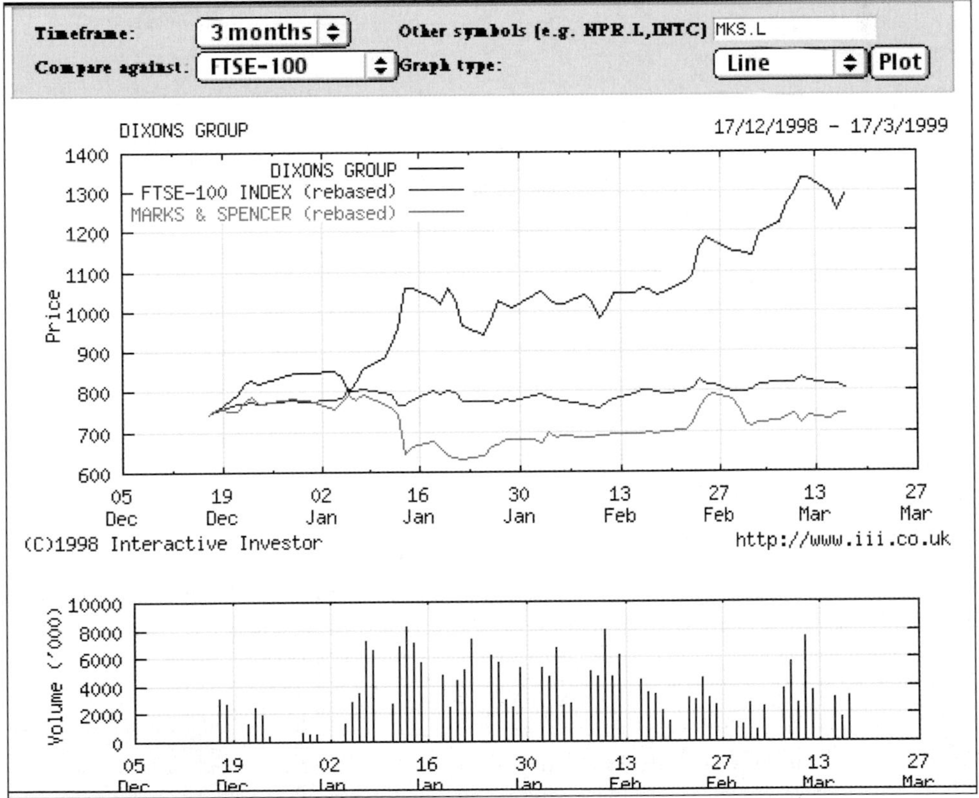

To display a second stock on the chart, you have to know the security code (ticker symbol) and remember to add the suffix '.L'. For example when searching for the first stock, it is sufficient to enter the stock symbol DXNS. If this was the second stock you wanted to display on the same chart, then you would enter DXNS.L, where the .L denotes that the stock is London listed.

III Interactive Investor *(con't)*

http://www.iii.co.uk/quotes/search

Rather than have a straight forward line plot, you can also opt to plot the highs and lows to get some idea of how volatile a price has been.

Fig 2.13 *The longer vertical lines, show greater volatility.*

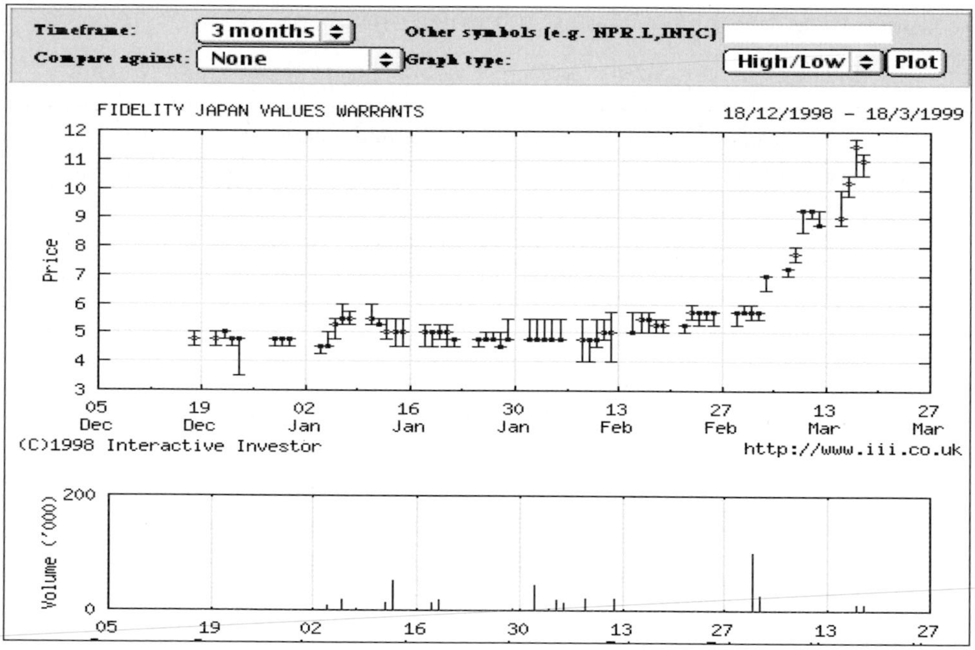

Other useful information which appears on the same page includes the current bid and offer prices, trading volume and the days high and low.

Fig 2.14 *The days high and low price and trading volume appear below the chart.*

Additional Information

Exchange:	ISE
Today's High:	0.458
Today's Low:	0.443
Trading Volume:	9806.690

III Interactive Investor *(con't)*

http://www.iii.co.uk/quotes/search

Fig 2.15 *Unit trust charts can be displayed over one of four periods.*

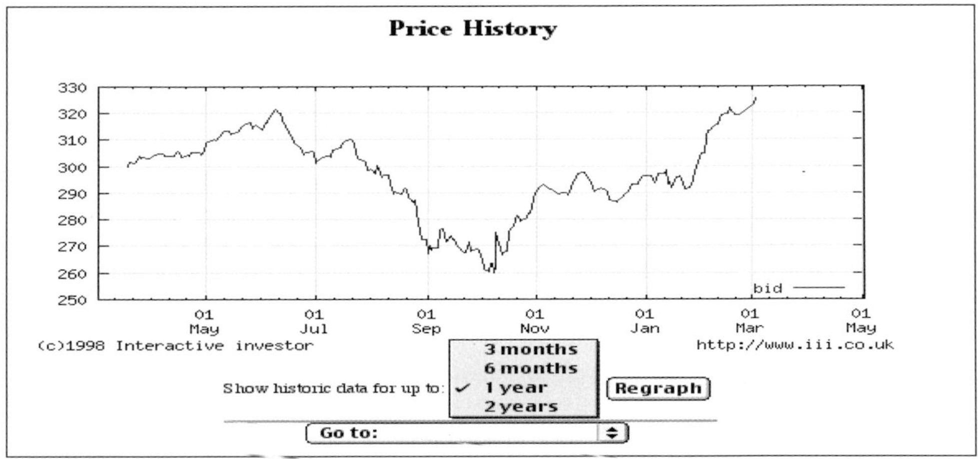

Fig 2.16 *A unit trust can be compared against a fund in the same sector and an index.*

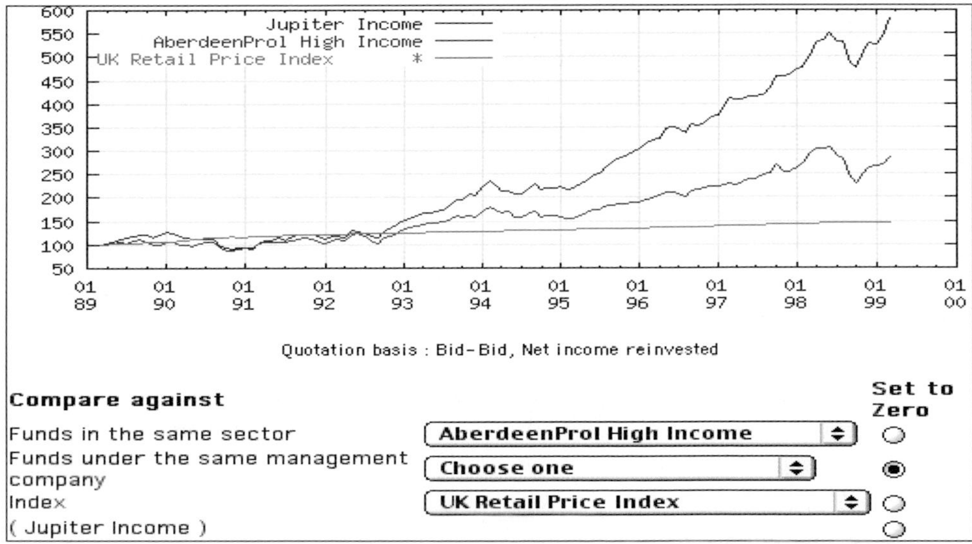

You can compare the performance of a unit trust against another fund in the same sector and one of the following indices: RPI, FT-SE All Share, Sector Average or the Micropal Average of all unit trusts. The time period automatically changes to 10 years when comparing a fund against something else.

III Interactive Investor *(con't)*

http://www.iii.co.uk/quotes/search

A very useful function in the unit trust charting section is the ability to set one of the chosen parameters to zero. This makes it very easy to see at a glance how the funds you have selected have performed relative to a chosen benchmark. In the example below, the 'UK Equity Income' index parameter has been set to zero. A line sloping upwards means the selected fund is outperforming.

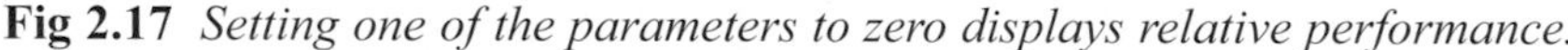

Fig 2.17 *Setting one of the parameters to zero displays relative performance.*

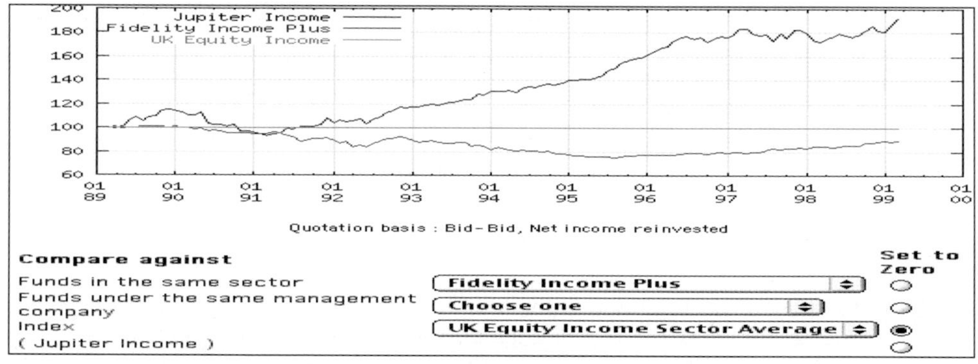

For unit trusts, you can choose whether to display performance cumulatively as in the chart above, or year by year in the form of a bar chart as shown in the Figure below. In both cases there is the option to show the results with either net or gross income reinvested. This site automatically displays the results numerically below the charts regardless of which format you have chosen.

Fig 2.18 *The 'Year by Year' chart indicates how consistent performance has been.*

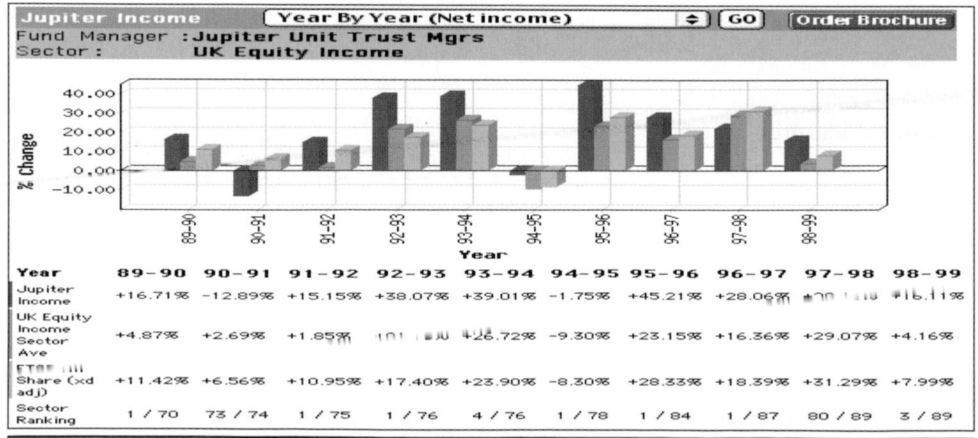

Year	89-90	90-91	91-92	92-93	93-94	94-95	95-96	96-97	97-98	98-99
Jupiter Income	+16.71%	-12.89%	+15.15%	+38.07%	+39.01%	-1.75%	+45.21%	+28.06%	[illegible]	+16.11%
UK Equity Income Sector Ave	+4.87%	+2.69%	+1.85%	[illegible]	+26.72%	-9.30%	+23.15%	+16.36%	+29.07%	+4.16%
FT[illegible] Share (xd adj)	+11.42%	+6.56%	+10.95%	+17.40%	+23.90%	-8.30%	+28.33%	+18.39%	+31.29%	+7.99%
Sector Ranking	1 / 70	73 / 74	1 / 75	1 / 76	4 / 76	1 / 78	1 / 84	1 / 87	80 / 89	3 / 89

Hemmington Scott

http://www.hemscott.com/EQUITIES/ATOZ.HTM

This site has recently been improved and now displays large clear graphs of shares and investment trusts plotted against both their respective sectors and the FT-SE All Share index. There are several steps you have to go through to access the charting function. The example below shows how to display a share price graph for Dixons Group PLC.

Fig 2.2 *Enter the name of a company in the box and click on 'Search'.*

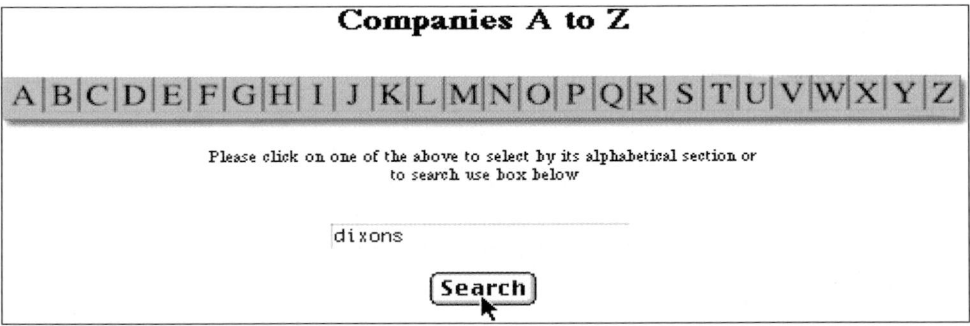

Clicking on one of the letters of the alphabet in the Figure above, simply displays an alphabetical list of shares beginning with that letter. Entering the correct name of a company and clicking on 'Search', usually displays just one result. If you enter a partial name such as 'Dixon', the screen would display all companies with those letters in the title such as 'Dixon Motors PLC' .

Fig 2.21 *Click on the name of the company to access share price data and a graph.*

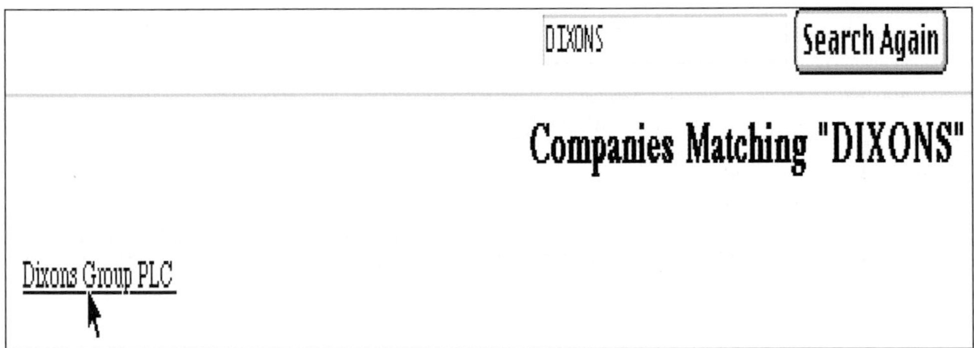

Hemmington Scott *(con't)*

http://www.hemscott.com/EQUITIES/ATOZ.HTM

Fig 2.22 *Click on 'Share Price Graph' in the left hand column of the screen.*

Dixons Group PLC

Summary Detail
5 Yr Summary P&L with Balance Sheet
Daily Share Price
15 Minute Delay Prices
Brokers' Consensus
Shareprice Graph
Advisers
Directors
Major Shareholders
Registrars
Contact Details
Key Dates

Dixons Group PLC

(Image)

ACTIVITIES: Retail sale of consumer electronics, personal computers, domestic appliances, photographic equipment, communication products and related services; property development

STATUS: Full; Lon option; ADR.

INDEX: FTSE 100

SECTOR: General Retailers

NO.EMP: 21,519 (19,019).

Eventually, you get to the charting function. You can choose between a 3, 5 or 10 year chart, and a useful feature is that the high and low price for each year is displayed under the chart. The information on this site tends to be very reliable and hence charts take account of share splits and other adjustments.

Fig 2.23 *10 year share price charts showing the FT-SE All Share index and the sector.*

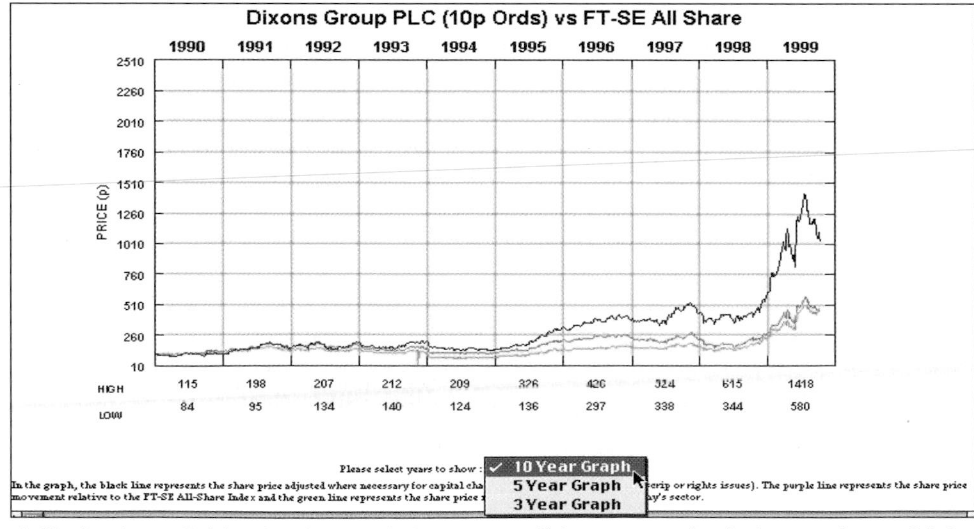

A limitation of this site, is that it is not possible to vary the index against which an investment is plotted, or to display more than one stock at a time. However, this is one of the few sites that currently offers free access to 10 year charts, and it is possible that there will be further upgrades in the future.

Trustnet

http://www.trustnet.co.uk/it/funds/list.asp

This is an excellent site for obtaining 1 and 5 year share price and discount charts of Investment Trust shares and other Closed-End funds. Initially an alphabetical list of funds is displayed. This site covers so many funds that the alphabet is split into 14 groupings as shown at the top of the Figure below. To display any of these alphabetical groupings, you need to click on the grouping, and then click on the 'Select' icon in the right hand corner of the screen.

Fig 2.3 *To display a chart, you need to click on the small 'Chart' icon as shown.*

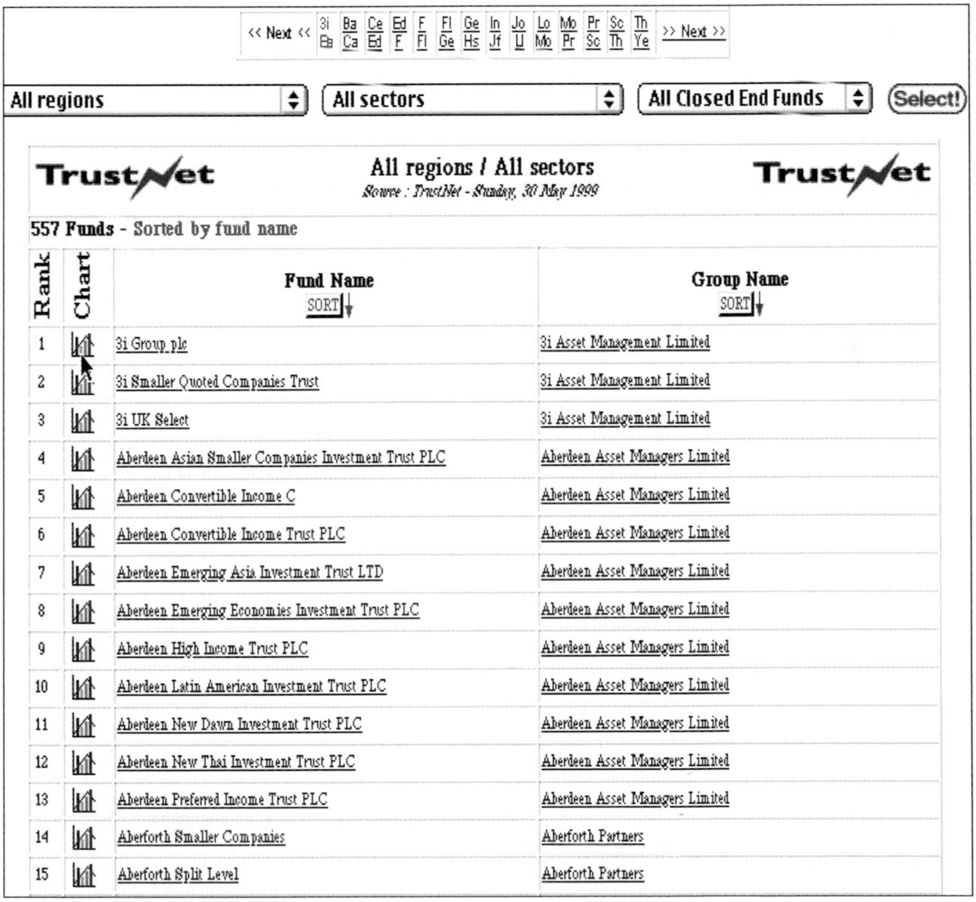

<< Next << 3i Ba Ce Ed F Fl Ge In Jo Lo Mo Pr Sc Th >> Next >>
Ba Ca Ed F Fl Ge Hs Jf Ll Mo Pr Sc Th Ye

All regions | All sectors | All Closed End Funds | Select!

TrustNet **All regions / All sectors** TrustNet
Source : TrustNet - Sunday, 30 May 1999

557 Funds - Sorted by fund name

Rank	Chart	Fund Name SORT	Group Name SORT
1		3i Group plc	3i Asset Management Limited
2		3i Smaller Quoted Companies Trust	3i Asset Management Limited
3		3i UK Select	3i Asset Management Limited
4		Aberdeen Asian Smaller Companies Investment Trust PLC	Aberdeen Asset Managers Limited
5		Aberdeen Convertible Income C	Aberdeen Asset Managers Limited
6		Aberdeen Convertible Income Trust PLC	Aberdeen Asset Managers Limited
7		Aberdeen Emerging Asia Investment Trust LTD	Aberdeen Asset Managers Limited
8		Aberdeen Emerging Economies Investment Trust PLC	Aberdeen Asset Managers Limited
9		Aberdeen High Income Trust PLC	Aberdeen Asset Managers Limited
10		Aberdeen Latin American Investment Trust PLC	Aberdeen Asset Managers Limited
11		Aberdeen New Dawn Investment Trust PLC	Aberdeen Asset Managers Limited
12		Aberdeen New Thai Investment Trust PLC	Aberdeen Asset Managers Limited
13		Aberdeen Preferred Income Trust PLC	Aberdeen Asset Managers Limited
14		Aberforth Smaller Companies	Aberforth Partners
15		Aberforth Split Level	Aberforth Partners

The list of funds which is displayed can be sorted alphabetically either by 'Fund Name' or 'Group Name'. To do this you need to click on the relevant 'Sort' icon under the Fund Name and 'Group Name' headings in the Figure above.

Trustnet *(con't)*

http://www.trustnet.co.uk/it/funds/list.asp

Both the share price and the net asset value are plotted against the FT-SE All Share index on the same chart. A separate chart of the Discount to Net Asset Value over 1 year, is displayed below on the same page. Although the charts only display 1 and 5 year data, a table is produced on the same page which lists the 'Price total return', 'Net Asset Value (NAV) total return' and the 'Relevant Comparative Index return' over 1, 3 and 5 years. The example below shows the 1 year chart for the Prolific Income investment trust.

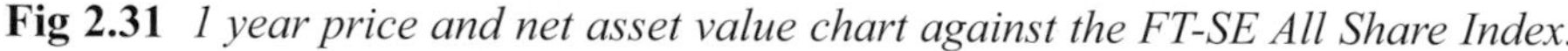

Fig 2.31 *1 year price and net asset value chart against the FT-SE All Share Index.*

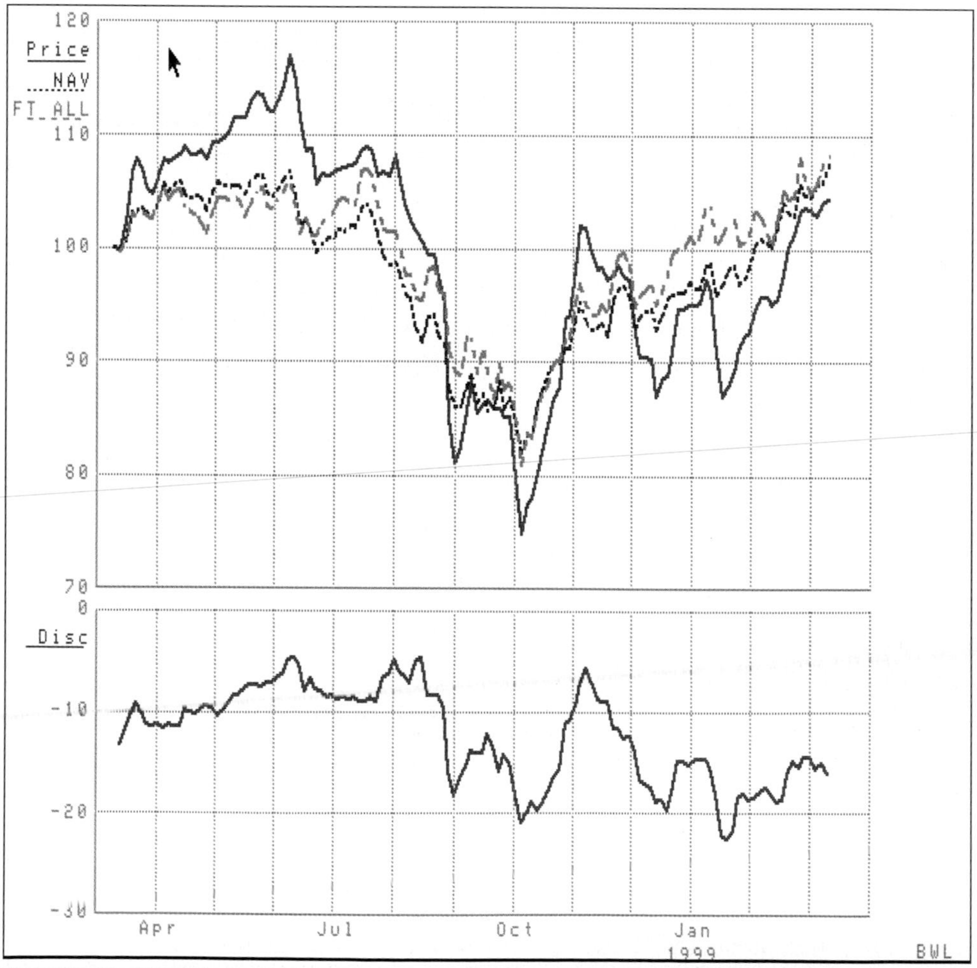

Trustnet *(con't)*

http://www.trustnet.co.uk/it/funds/list.asp

The performance table has a number of live links. These lead to an excellent bank of background information on that investment trust, together with peer group performance comparisons.

Fig 2.32 *A performance table is displayed below the graphs.*

TrustNet	Prolific Income PLC Source : TrustNet - Wednesday, 17 March 1999		TrustNet
Investment Company	Prolific Income PLC		
Management Group	Aberdeen Asset Managers Limited		
Peer Group Performance (Click to view tables)	Region: United Kingdom Sector: General Equity Region / Sector: United Kingdom / General Equity		
Price (17-Mar-99)	135.5 (GBX)	Discount to NAV (%)	-17.4
% Performance (Price total return in £)	+3.0 (1yr)	+38.8 (3yr)	n/a (5yr)
% Performance (NAV total return in £)	+7.9 (1yr)	+56.6 (3yr)	n/a (5yr)
Warburg Index FTSE All-Share Index	+5.6 (1yr)	+57.9 (3yr)	+74.9 (5yr)

A click on the 'Management Group' box will display useful information such as Gross Assets, other trusts managed by the same Management Company and the Web Site Address.

Fig 2.33 *Clicking on 'Management Group' displays more useful information.*

TrustNet	Aberdeen Asset Managers Limited Source : TrustNet - Wednesday, 17 March 1999	TrustNet
E-mail	Inv.trusts@aberdeen-asset.com	
Web Site	http://www.aberdeen-asset.com	
Address	One Bow Churchyard, Cheapside, London, EC4M 9HH	
Telephone	0171 463 6000	
Fax	0171 463 6001	
Unit Trusts & OEICs	Click here	
Year of Formation	1983	
Description of Group	Limited Company (Aberdeen Asset Management PLC, the holding company, is a public company)	
Ownership Details	Owned 100% by Aberdeen Asset Management PLC.	
Investment Activities	Investment Management.	
Investment Services	Investment Management Services.	
Total Gross Assets (of funds listed below)	£1,062.8m (GBP) $1,726.3m (USD)	
19 Investment Company(s) Performance Summary	Aberdeen Asian Smaller Companies Investment Trust PLC	
	Aberdeen Convertible Income C	
	Aberdeen Convertible Income Trust PLC	

Trustnet *(con't)*

http://www.trustnet.co.uk/it/funds/list.asp

Clicking on 'Investment Company' in the performance table will give you just about every thing you need to know about that investment trust. There is essential information about Gearing, Wind-Up Provisions, Capital Structure, Dividend Policy and Largest Holdings etc.

Fig 2.34 *Almost all the information you'll ever need to know about an investment trust.*

TrustNet	Prolific Income PLC Source : TrustNet - Wednesday, 17 March 1999 United Kingdom Registered Investment Trust		TrustNet
Management Group	Aberdeen Asset Managers Limited	**Fund Manager**	Neil Tyson
E-mail	Inv.trusts@aberdeen-asset.com	**Web Site**	http://www.aberdeen-asset.com
Registered Address	One Bow Churchyard, Cheapside, London, UK, EC4M 9HH		
Telephone	0171 463 6000	**Fax**	0171 463 6001
Investment Objectives	Above average growth in income and capital (relative to the FTSE All-Share)over the long term from a portfolio consisting predominantly of ordinary shares mainly in UK quoted companies. A proportion of the Company's assets, not to exceed twenty percent, may be invested in fixed interest instruments.		
PEP Status	£6,000	**Exchange / Domicile**	London / UK (1994)
Epic code: **Reuters code:**	PRI PRI.L	**Gross Assets** (Warburg estimate 16-Mar-99)	£92.1m $149.6m
Peer Group Performance (Click to view tables)	Region: Sector: Region / Sector:	United Kingdom General Equity United Kingdom / General Equity	
Performance Chart (1 year chart)		**Annual Accounts** (Order system)	n/a
Price (16-Mar-99)	135.5 (GBX)	**Discount to NAV (%)** (16-Mar-99)	-17.4
% Performance (Price total return in £)	+3.0 (1yr)	+38.8 (3yr)	n/a (5yr)
% Performance (NAV total return in £)	+7.9 (1yr)	+56.6 (3yr)	n/a (5yr)
Warburg Index FTSE All-Share Index	+5.6 (1yr)	+57.9 (3yr)	+74.9 (5yr)
Stockbroker(s)	HSBC		
Management Contract	The Manager will receive a monthly fee payable in arrears equal to one twelfth of 0.8% (plus VAT) of the value of the assets less current liabilities (excluding short term bank borrowings). The Manager will also provide secretarial services for a fee of £62,000 per annum (plus VAT) adjusted for the RPI. The agreement may be terminated by either party on 6 months notice given.		
Dividend Policy	Annualised starting gross yield of 4.5% and year on year growth in income thereafter.		
Dividends (Net annualised)	4.05 (GBX) ('96)	3.00 (GBX) ('95)	n/a
Gross Dividend Yield (%)	4.27 ('96)	3.64 ('95)	n/a
Borrowing Limit	Up to 20% of the share capital and reserves of the Company.		
Stated Gearing (%)	0.0	**Effective Gearing (%)**	-8.1
Last Accounts Date	July 31 1998	**Last Accounts Published**	September 15 1998
Last AGM	October 17 1997	**Next AGM**	October 19 1998
Borrowing Limit	n/a		
Continuation / Wind-up Provision	Ordinary resolution at the AGM in 2004 (and at every fifth subsequent AGM) that the Company should continue as an investment trust.		

Trustnet *(con't)*

http://www.trustnet.co.uk/it/funds/list.asp

The displayed list of information on an investment trust is enormous, but none the less very useful. At the end on the 'Investment Company' table, you will find details of 'Capital Structure', and 'Largest Holdings'.

Fig 2.35 *The table ends with details of Capital Structure and Major Portfolio Holdings.*

Capital Structure
Source : TrustNet - Wednesday, 17 March 1999

Share Type	Nominal Value		Authorised		Issued
Ordinary	5p		135,000,000		52,357,438
Warrant Type (Click on name for performance)	**Warrant Price**	**Expiry Date**	**Share Ratio**	**Exercise Price**	**Issued**
PROLIFIC INCOME	39.25 (GBX)(16-Mar-99)	Nov-2003	1.0 (ORD)	100.0 (GBX)	9,797,762

Source: TrustNet - Web: http://www.trustnet.co.uk E-mail: mail@trustnet.co.uk Tel: +44 (0)171 439 3160

Portfolio Summary
Source : TrustNet - Wednesday, 17 March 1999

Largest Holdings: (28-Feb-99)	(%)	Largest Regional Weightings: (n/a)	(%)	Largest Sector Weightings: (28-Feb-99)	(%)
British Telecom	3.6	n/a	n/a	UK Equities	86.4
Lloyds TSB	3.5	n/a	n/a	UK Convertibles	7.5
Glaxo Wellcome	3.4	n/a	n/a	Cash	3.8
National Westminster Bank	2.8	n/a	n/a	Overseas Equities	2.3
BP Amoco	2.7	n/a	n/a	n/a	n/a
SmithKline Beecham	2.5	n/a	n/a	n/a	n/a
Cattles	2.3	n/a	n/a	n/a	n/a
HSBC Holdings	2.3	n/a	n/a	n/a	n/a
Zeneca Group	2.3	n/a	n/a	n/a	n/a
Barclays	2.2	n/a	n/a	n/a	n/a

As if this was not enough, you can click on the 'Peer Group Performance' box in the middle of the left hand column of Figure 2.34, and display the performance over 1, 3 and 5 years of all the Investment Trusts in the same sector. This list can then be sorted in order of Discount to Net Asset Value or performance over a specified period (see Chapter 5). This site is maintained by one of the UK's premier institutional brokers and thus the information tends to be fairly up to date and accurate. A minor drawback to an otherwise excellent site, is that full information is not yet provided for all Investment Trusts.

Quicken

http://www.quicken.com/investments/charts

The information available on the internet for stocks listed in America, is at present far in excess of that available for UK listed stocks. Some UK companies have chosen to have a percentage of their shares listed in America through what are known as American Depository Receipts (ADRs). Quicken is one of the many excellent US based internet sites where investors can get in depth information on UK shares which have an ADR. A full list of UK stocks with an ADR is given in Appendix A. Enter the security code with upper case letters and click on 'Go' to display a chart.

Fig 2.4 *Enter the correct 'ADR' code in capital letters to display a chart.*

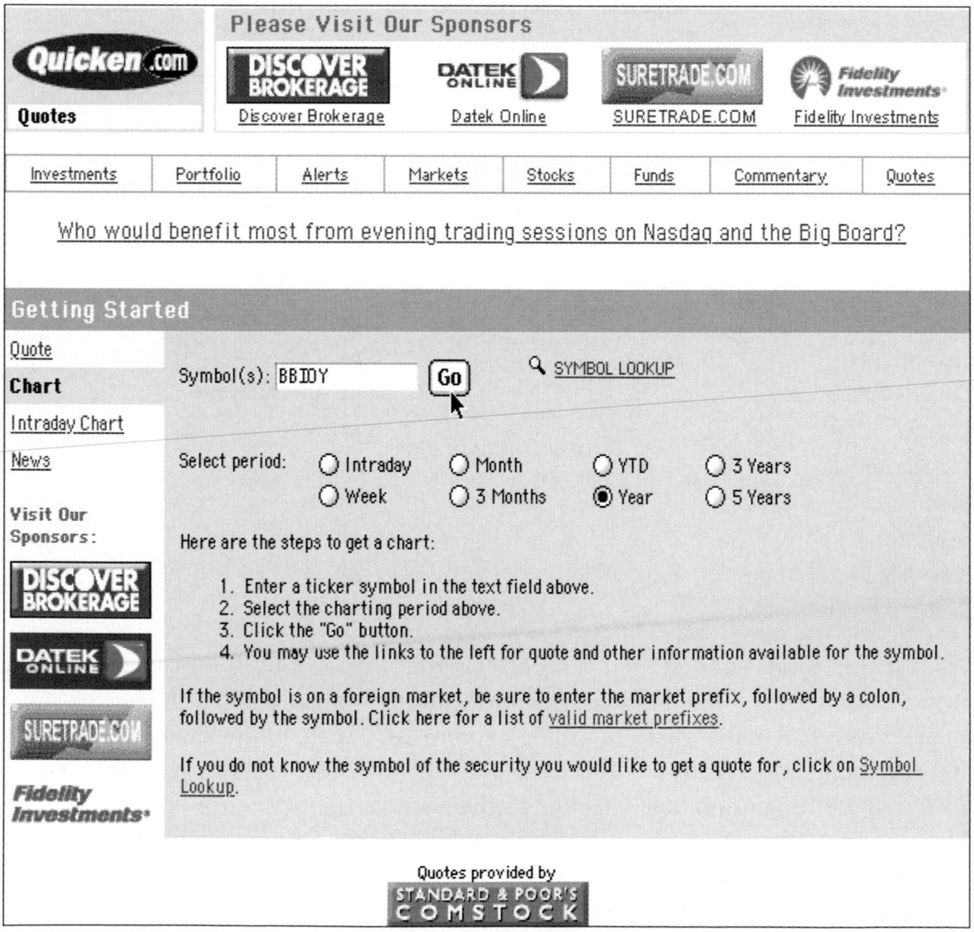

Quicken.com
Quotes

Please Visit Our Sponsors
DISCOVER BROKERAGE — Discover Brokerage
DATEK ONLINE — Datek Online
SURETRADE.COM — SURETRADE.COM
Fidelity Investments — Fidelity Investments

Investments | Portfolio | Alerts | Markets | Stocks | Funds | Commentary | Quotes

Who would benefit most from evening trading sessions on Nasdaq and the Big Board?

Getting Started

Quote
Chart
Intraday Chart
News

Visit Our Sponsors:
DISCOVER BROKERAGE
DATEK ONLINE
SURETRADE.COM
Fidelity Investments

Symbol(s): BBIDY Go SYMBOL LOOKUP

Select period: Intraday, Week, Month, 3 Months, YTD, Year, 3 Years, 5 Years

Here are the steps to get a chart:

1. Enter a ticker symbol in the text field above.
2. Select the charting period above.
3. Click the "Go" button.
4. You may use the links to the left for quote and other information available for the symbol.

If the symbol is on a foreign market, be sure to enter the market prefix, followed by a colon, followed by the symbol. Click here for a list of valid market prefixes.

If you do not know the symbol of the security you would like to get a quote for, click on Symbol Lookup.

Quotes provided by
STANDARD & POOR'S COMSTOCK

Quicken *(con't)*

http://www.quicken.com/investments/charts

The charting facility on this site offers just about everything you need to carry out basic research. You can select one of eight periods over which you would like the chart to be displayed, ranging from Intraday to 5 years. The example below shows a price chart for British Biotech whose ADR code is 'BBIOY'. Major news announcements are marked on the chart, and can be viewed by clicking on the 'News' icon in the left hand column of the page (not shown).

Fig 2.41 *Share price chart for British Biotech showing major news announcements.*

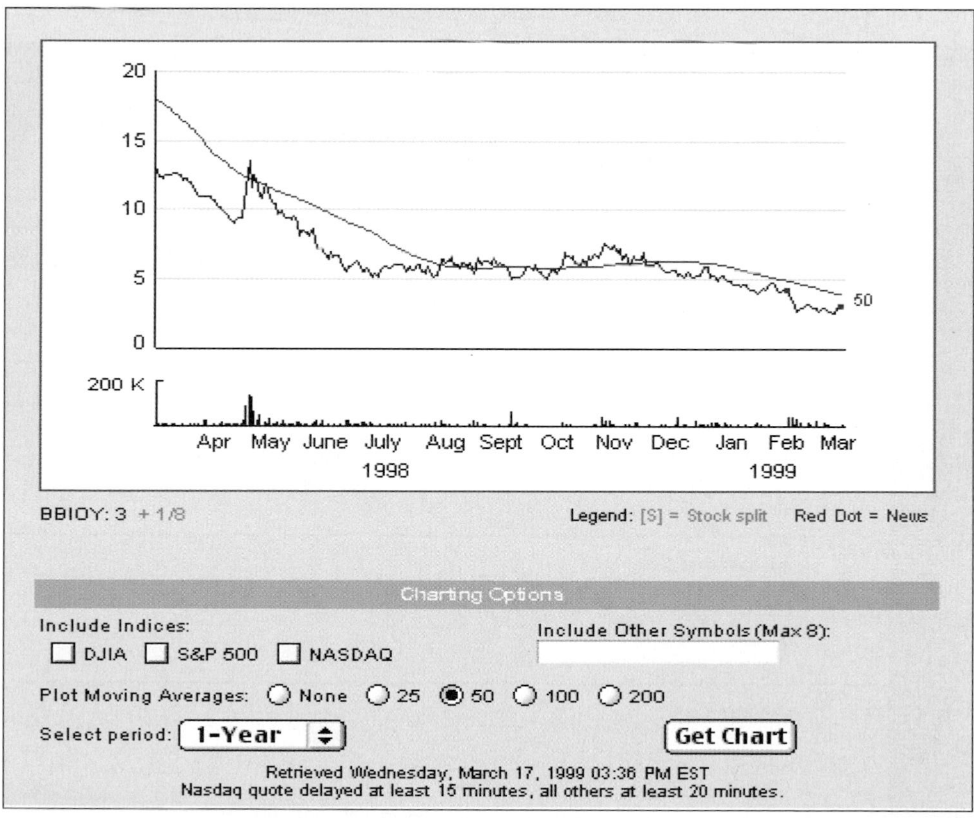

You can plot one of four preset 'Moving Average' lines, ranging between 25 and 200 days, and up to eight stocks can be plotted on the same chart. A small 'volume' chart is displayed below the main chart (not shown) which can be a useful indicator of why a share price is moving in a particular direction. A full list of UK stocks with ADR's is given in Appendix A.

Wright Research Center

http://profiles.wisi.com/profiles/Comsrch.htm

This is an American based internet site which offers free and detailed analysis on over 18,000 companies worldwide. Part of this analysis, includes a comprehensive charting facility which plots share price, earnings and dividend per share on the same chart. You can search for a stock either by entering the Company Name, the Ticker Symbol, using the Alphabetical List or the Country List. The quickest way to display a chart is to enter the correct Ticker Symbol and click on 'Search'.

Fig 2.5 *The quickest way to access a chart, is to enter the correct Ticker Symbol.*

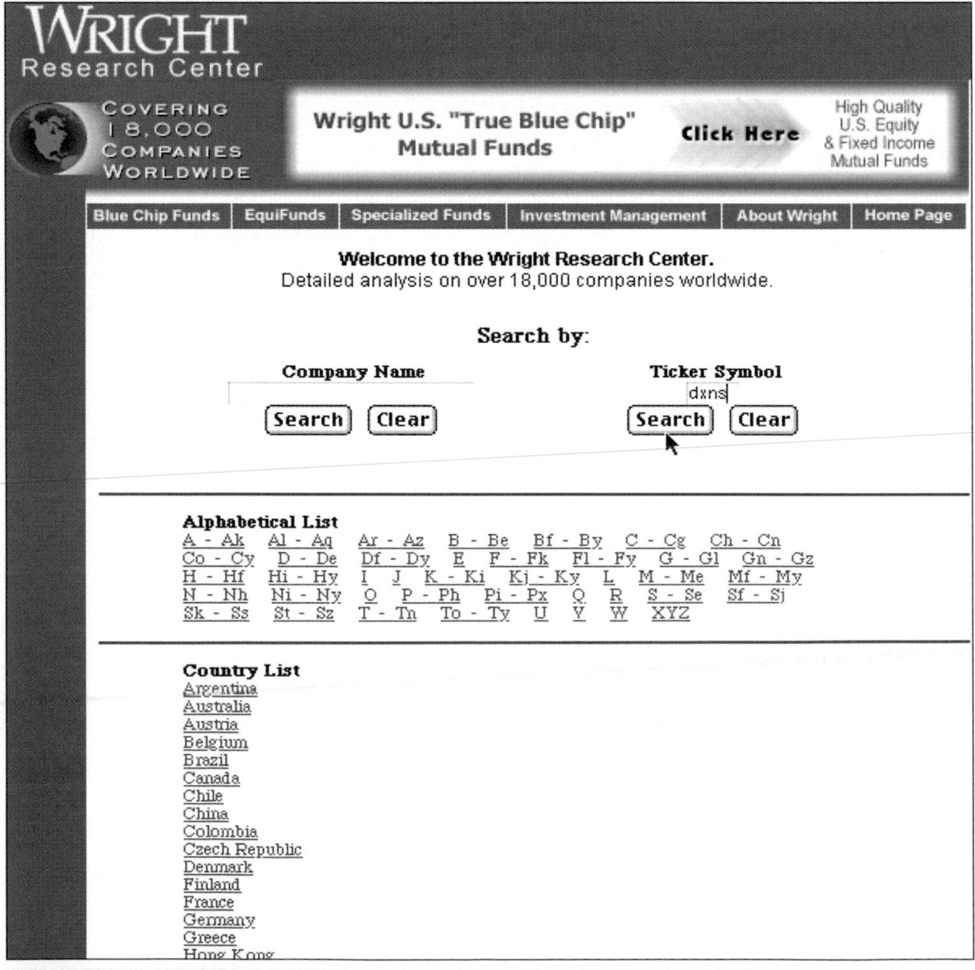

Wright Research Center *(con't)*

http://profiles.wisi.com/profiles/Comsrch.htm

The share price graph is unusual in that it shows both the 'average monthly price' (small black horizontal lines), together with the 'monthly share price range' (variable length black vertical lines). This latter feature gives a good indication as to how volatile a share price has been. The longer the vertical line, the more volatile a stock has been. The charts go back 5 years but it is not possible to vary either the time period or the information displayed.

Fig 2.51 *Five year earnings, dividends and share price shown on the same chart.*

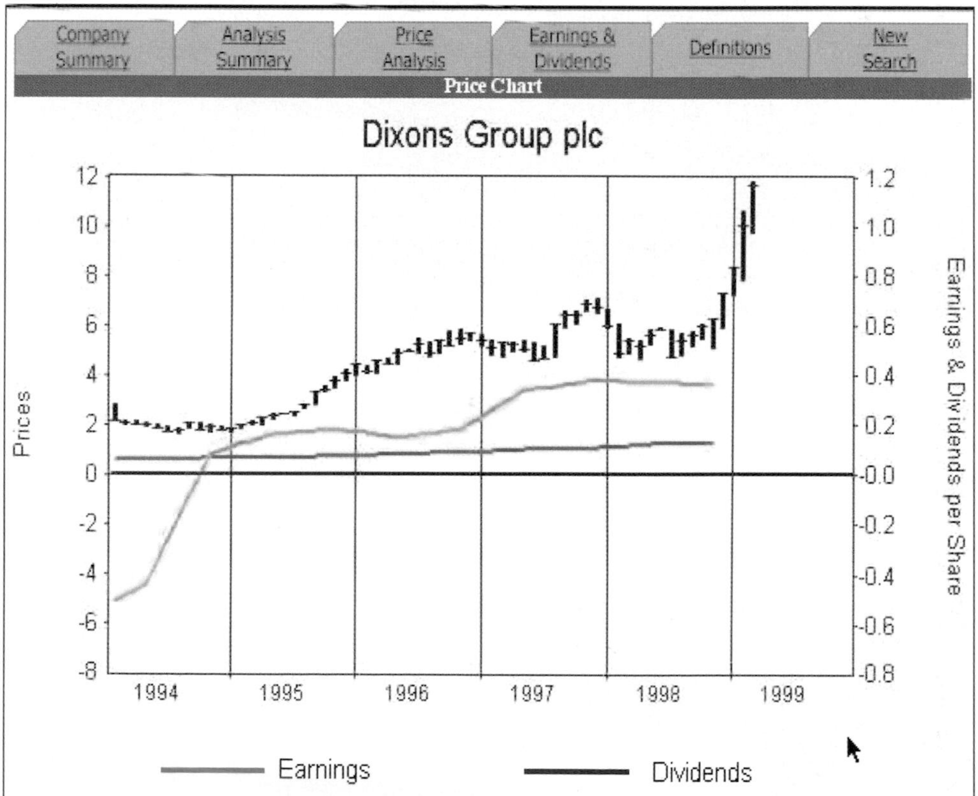

This is an excellent site which covers most UK shares and Investment Trusts. See Chapter 6 (Research) for an in depth description of the other free features available at this site. A whole host of useful information is displayed alongside the chart when you initially select a stock. The chart can be enlarged by clicking on a small icon which appears just below the graph (not shown).

Datastream

http://www.datastreaminsite.com/search.htm

Datastream are one of the largest suppliers of financial information in the world, and their information tends to be up to date and reliable. This site will display a one year price chart for shares and investment trusts. To display a chart you first need to search for that stock either by Name or Ticker Symbol.

Fig 2.6 *Enter the name or symbol of a stock and click on 'Search'.*

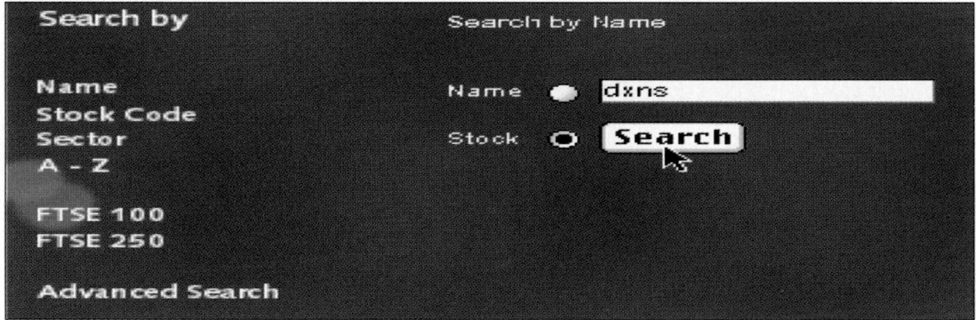

If you enter the correct ticker symbol such as 'dxns', then only one company will be displayed as shown in the Figure below. If you entered part of a company name, all companies with those letters in that order in the title would be displayed.

Fig 2.61 *Click on the company name to display a 1 year chart with other share data.*

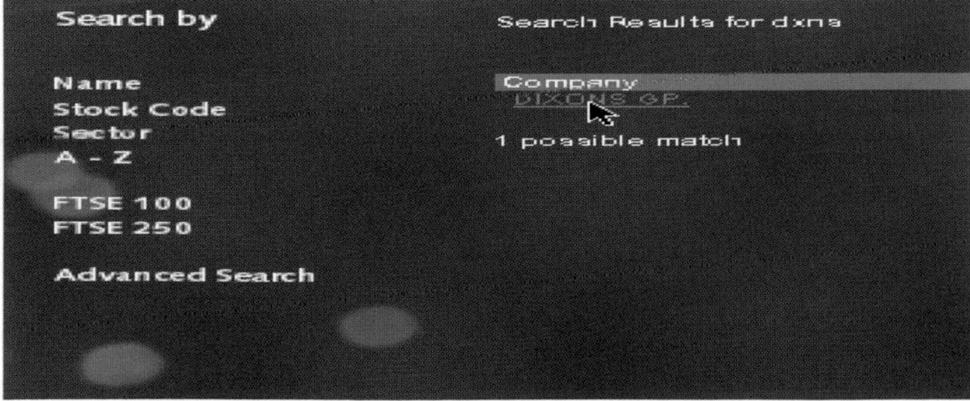

Datastream *(con't)*

http://www.datastreaminsite.com/search.htm

The latest news headline is shown above the chart and the full story can be accessed for free by clicking on the headline itself.

Fig 2.62 *Large 1 year charts are displayed, together with the latest news headline.*

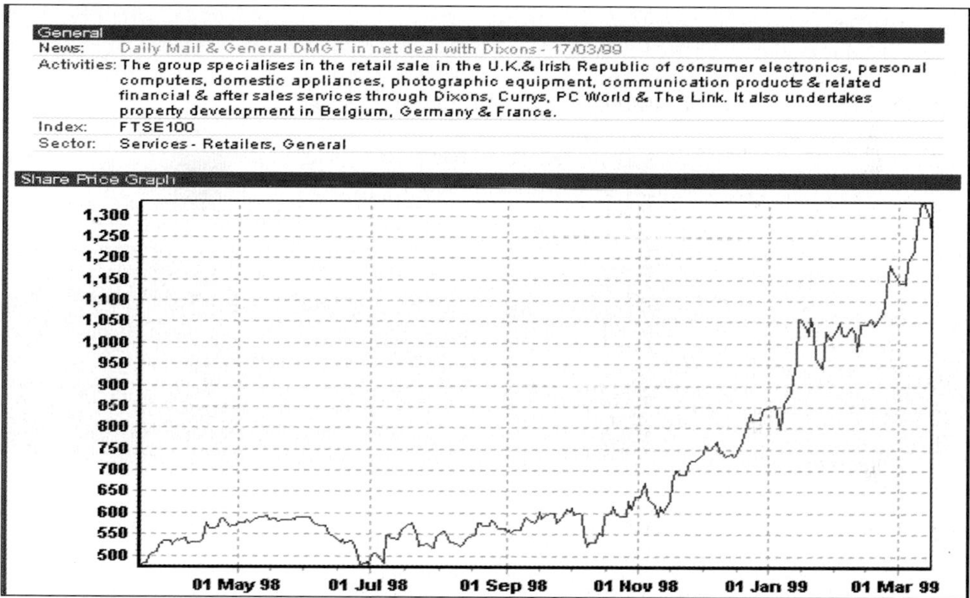

A whole host of other useful share data is displayed on the same page as the chart. This includes 5 year Pre Tax Profit figures, Total Debt & Turnover etc.

Fig 2.63 *Useful data on the selected company going back 5 years is also displayed.*

Key Share data

Share Price	Market cap	12-mnth div	PER	Dividend yield
1303	5431.05	12.7	33.2	1.33

Share Price and 12-mnth div are quoted in pence per share.
Market Cap is quoted in millions.
Price Earnings (PER) is a ratio.
Dividend Yield(DY) is a percentage.

Income Statement

	Pre-Tax Profit	Total Debt	Total Assets
5/98	218700	236400	1789800
5/97	200200	282600	1591600
4/96	101500	403100	1411500
4/95	100300	265000	1162500
4/94	-165200	386100	1167200
	Turnover	**Net Profit**	**Shareholder's Equity**
4/98	2774000	161100	583200
4/97	2443000	143400	444200
4/96	1920000	61300	283200
4/95	1647000	65800	247900
4/94	1921000	174000	207000

Income Statement data is quoted in thousands.

Share History

Floated	Last Capital Event	Description
30/12/64		

Market-Eye

http://www.market-eye.co.uk/scripts/Sectors.dll?HandleSectors

This section of the Market-Eye internet site enables you to see how a particular sector of the UK market has performed over the last month.

Fig 2.7 *The performance of each sector of the UK market is displayed at this site.*

Sector	Last	Change	Time	Open	High	Low	Close
MINING EXTRACTION							
Extract.Ind	3313.8	-46.8	16:30	3360.6	3360.6	3282.1	3360.6
Oil, Integ.	5493.2	+160.5	16:30	5332.7	5526.7	5332.7	5332.7
Oil, Explrtn.	1661.0	+70.9	16:30	1576.5	1686.7	1576.5	1590.1
GENERAL MANUFACTURERS							
Construction	1338.1	-4.1	16:30	1345.4	1345.5	1337.8	1342.2
Bldg Mtrls	1676.3	-18.8	16:30	1693.3	1704.9	1673.5	1695.1
Chemicals	1958.2	+12.4	16:30	1947.3	1960.8	1945.0	1945.8
Divfd.Indls.	1034.4	+12.4	16:30	1022.0	1034.4	1022.0	1022.0
Elnc&Elcl Eq	3218.1	-94.1	16:30	3309.4	3317.7	3207.2	3312.2
Engineering	2270.1	-23.1	16:30	2294.7	2295.1	2249.7	2293.2
Eng Vehicles	4457.6	-63.5	16:30	4520.5	4527.2	4413.9	4521.1
Paper & Pack	1635.5	+3.8	16:30	1624.9	1635.5	1617.9	1631.7
CONSUMER GOODS							
Alcoholic Beverages	3641.3	-156.3	16:30	3797.6	3797.6	3601.1	3797.6
Food Prodcrs	3377.7	+11.2	16:30	3366.9	3379.0	3347.7	3366.5
Hshld Goods	2331.0	-77.9	16:30	2408.9	2416.1	2207.0	2408.9
Health Care	2272.5	-26.9	16:30	2298.2	2298.2	2271.6	2299.4
Pharmaceutls	10521.7	-83.3	16:30	10604.6	10680.6	10341.3	10605.0
Tobacco	6677.0	+139.9	16:30	6537.1	6696.1	6525.7	6537.1

In order to access the graphs of sector performance, you simply need to click on the relevant sector name. The intraday movement for that sector is also displayed on the left hand side of the graph. Sometimes it is useful to know whether the performance of a share is as a result of a shift in sentiment towards its sector as a whole, or something specific to that share.

Fig 2.71 *You can see how a particular sector of the UK market has been performing.*

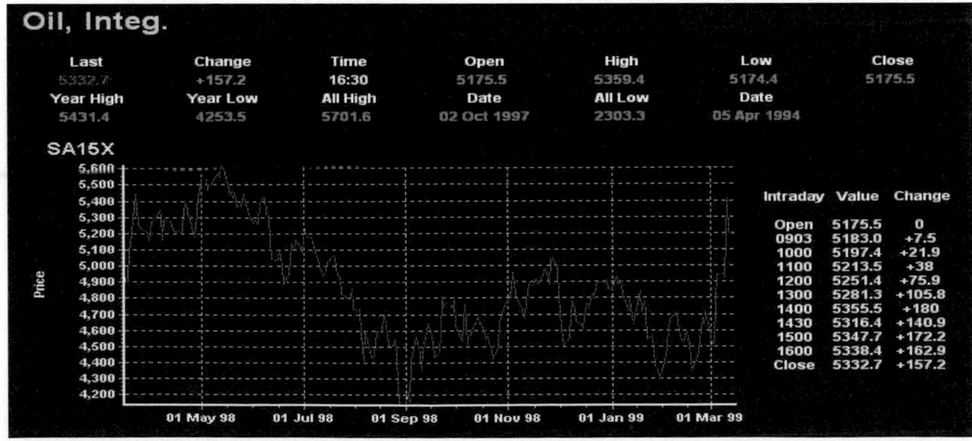

QuoteWatch

http://quotewatch.com

This is another excellent American based internet site where you can get a variety of free currency charts. To display a currency chart you need to enter either the correct symbol or part of the name of a currency. The example below shows how to display a chart of Sterling against the US dollar. The correct symbol (mnemonic) for this chart is 'GBPUS'. The Bloomberg currency page described in Chapter 1 has a useful list of currency mnemonics.

Fig 2.8 *Enter the correct currency mnemonic and click on 'Find'.*

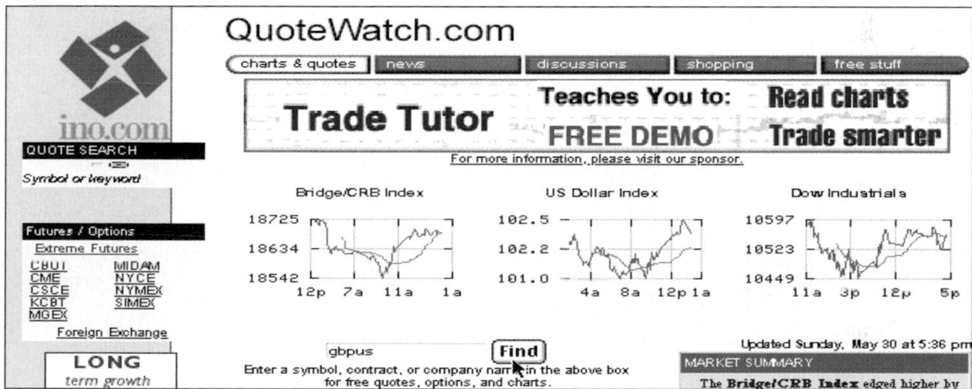

If you don't know the correct currency mnemonic, you could enter something like 'British Pound', and the search engine will display a list of contracts containing those words. Click on the currency contract and you will eventually get to the screen displayed in the Figure below.

Fig 2.81 *Select the time period over which to display the currency chart.*

QuoteWatch *(con't)*

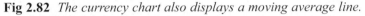

http://quotewatch.com

There is a choice of three time periods - Intraday, Daily and Weekly with a relevant 'moving average' line plotted on the same graph. In order to access a chart, you need to enter the appropriate currency code into the 'Find' box in the center of the screen in Figure 2.8. To display a chart of sterling versus the US dollar, you could either enter 'pound', or the correct mnemonic for sterling which is GBP. A comprehensive list of currency mnemonics is given on the Bloomberg currency page described in Chapter 1.

Fig 2.82 *The currency chart also displays a moving average line.*

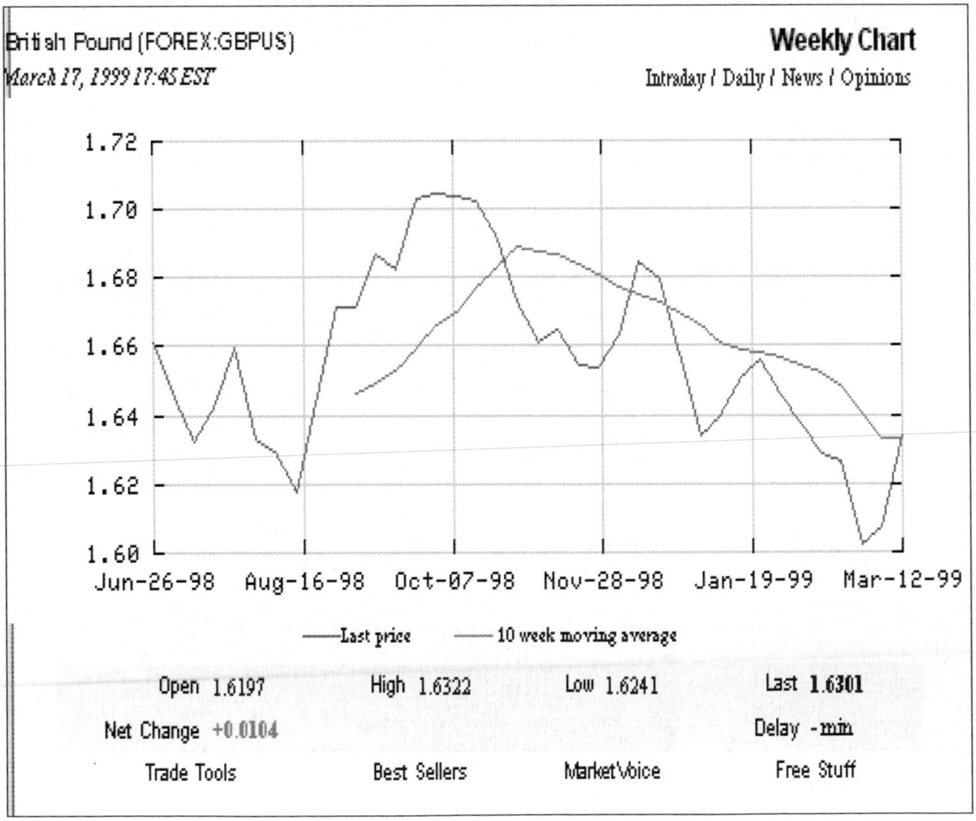

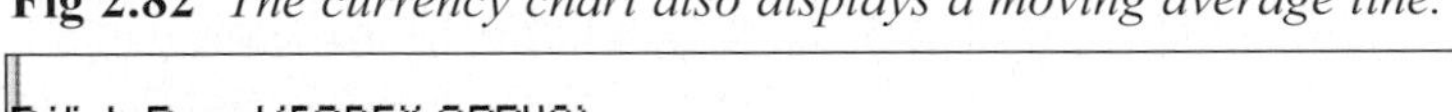

Unfortunately, as this a US based site, you can only plot currencies against the US dollar. The 'Intraday' chart will only display the movement for that day, whereas a 'Weekly' chart plots the movement over the previous few months.

E*Trade

http://research.etrade.co.uk/free/stock.cgi/

This site enables you to display large clear 1 year price charts on the same page as 'Bid and Offer' prices, 'Latest Trade' data and a list of 'Latest news headlines'. To display a chart, you first need to select the 'quote + chart' option in the drop down menu as shown below. Once you have done this, enter either the name or security code for an investment and click on 'Go'.

Fig 2.9 *To display a chart you need to change the default setting to 'quote + chart'.*

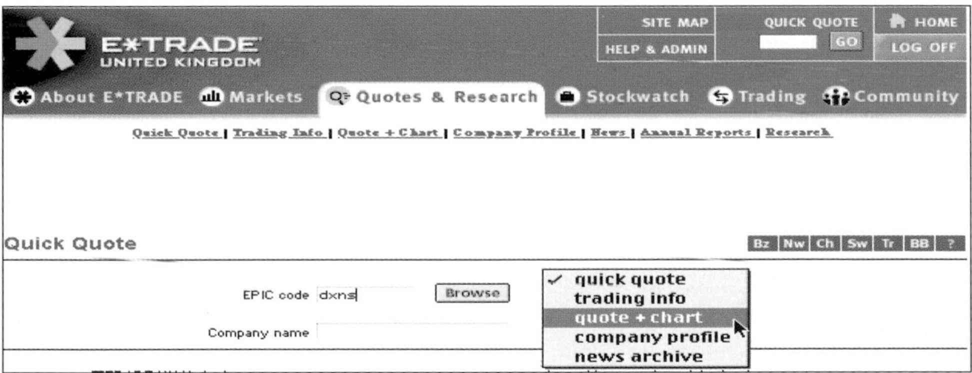

It is unusual to find a free internet site which displays 'Latest Trade' data. This information can sometimes help to explain why a share price has moved significantly despite any obvious news. Often the price of a relatively illiquid stock (such as a warrant), will change significantly due to a large sale or purchase.

Fig 2.91 *Share price data together with the 'Latest Trade' is displayed above the chart.*

Dixons Group (DXNS) at 14:52 on 28/09/99 +Sw

	Currency	Open	Bid	Offer	Current	Change	Time	High	Low	Volume	A	X
↑	GBX	1090.00	1112.00	1116.00	1113.00	33.00	1452	1125.00	1086.00	6,480,976		D

Latest Trade

Type	Vol	Price	Date	Time	Currency
AT	5000.	1113.00	28/09/99	14:51:46	GBX

E*Trade *(con't)*

http://research.etrade.co.uk/free/stock.cgi/

A large clear 1 year price chart is displayed together with a volume bar chart. It can be quite useful to have up to date news headlines displayed alongside a share price graph. Often these news headlines will give you a good insight as to why a price has been moving in a particular direction. Unfortunately you can't access the full news story for free at this site. However, the news sources highlighted in Chapter 4 will often enable you to view the full stories for free.

Fig 2.92 *It is useful to have 'Latest news headlines' displayed alongside the chart.*

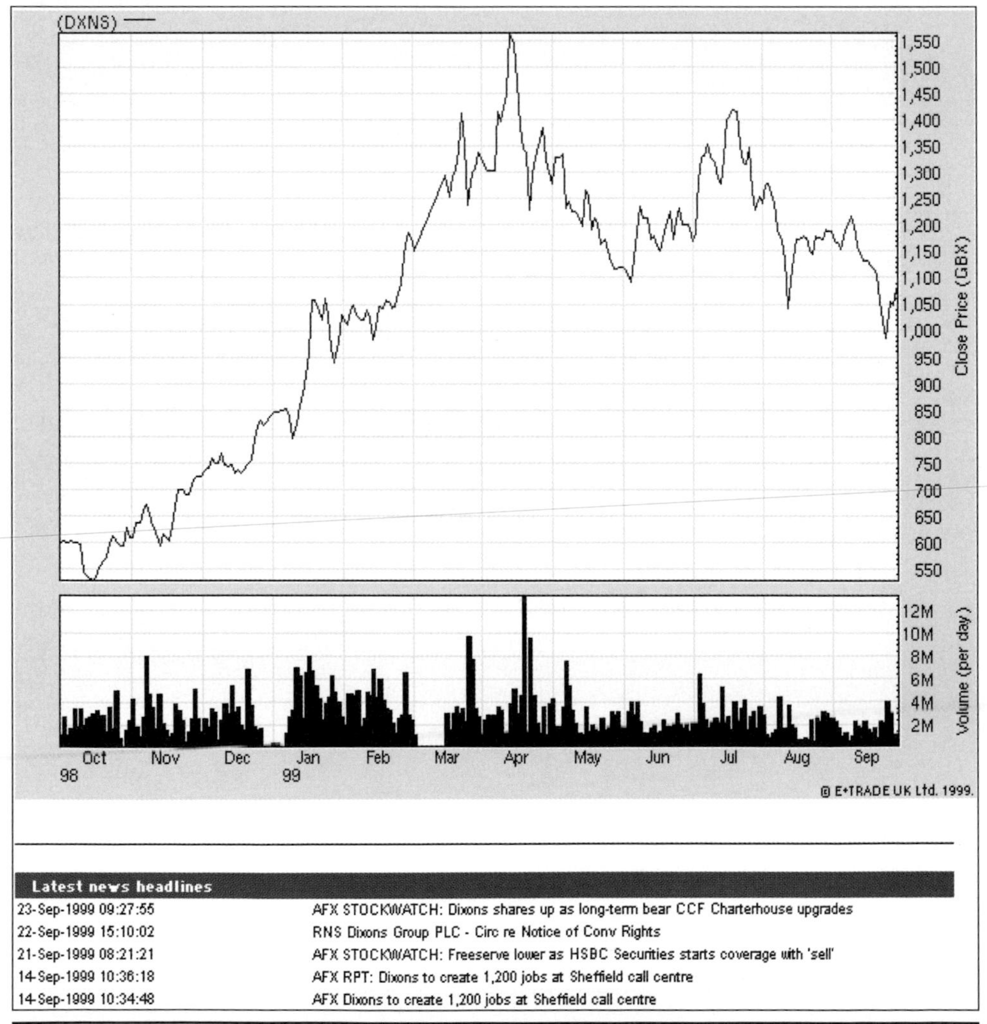

Stock Point

http://www.stockpoint.com/leftnav/stockinput.asp

Stock Point is an American based company which offers excellent free charting facilities covering UK stocks and indices. Most UK based internet sites charge investors for the privilege of accessing similar information. To display a chart, first change the 'Country' to UK as shown below. Enter a security symbol (eg dxns for Dixons PLC) and click on 'Go!'.

Fig 2.10.0 *Change the 'Country' setting to UK, and enter a stock code.*

A delayed share price quote is displayed, and the charting options are listed in the left hand column of the screen. The charting function is split into two main categories 'quick charts' and 'interactive charts'. The former enables investors to display up to 4 stocks (or indices) going back 5 years. The latter enables investors to specify an exact time period over which the chart is to be displayed.

Fig 2.10.1 *The charting functions are listed in the left hand column of the screen.*

stockpoint. home

about . products . advertising . press . support . contact us

Portfolio
Quote Center
Fund Center
*IPO Center
Markets
News
Commentary
Investing Tools
Personalize

quote
quick chart
interactive chart
option chain
SEC Filings:
edgar-online
help

[Quote Center] delayed quote

Dixons Group Plc

Real time quotes not available – Market Closed

As of Oct 2 3:30:00 PM (E.T.)

Last	1,069.00	Change	-13.00
Open	1,098.00	% Change	-1.20%
High	1,112.00	52 Week High	1,575.00
Low	1,033.00	52 Week Low	514.50
Volume	2.23M	Bid	1,070.00
Earnings P/Share	0.41	Ask	1,074.00
Shares Outstanding	434.26M	Mkt Capitalization	4.70B
P/E Ratio	26.33	Exchange	LSE

get quote
Country
UK
Symbol
dxns
Go!
or Company
Go!
get portfolio
Login

Stock Point *(con't)*

http://www.stockpoint.com/leftnav/stockinput.asp

Clicking on 'quick chart' displays a 1 year share price chart together with a volume bar chart.

Fig 2.10.2 *A 1 year share price chart for Dixons including a trading volume bar chart.*

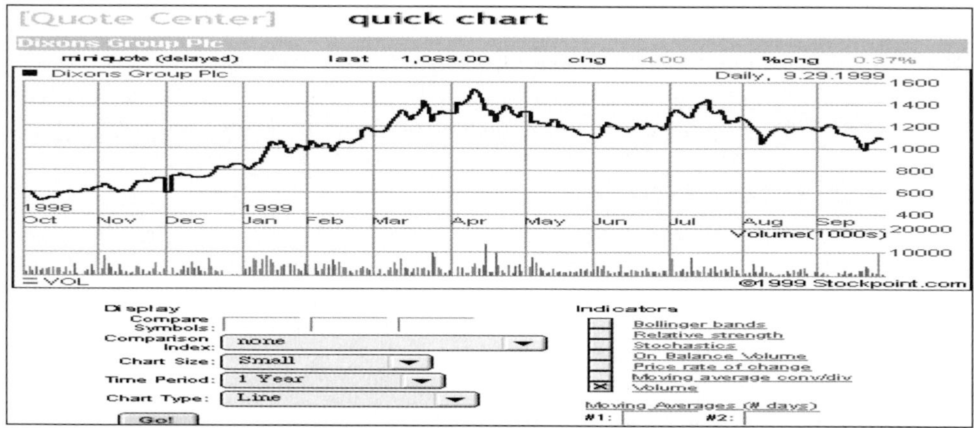

To compare other shares on the same chart, type in the appropriate share price codes in the 'Compare Symbols' and click on 'Go!'. The example below compares the share prices of Dixons (dxns), British Biotech (bbg), Marks & Spencer (mks) against the FT-SE All Share (asx) index. The stock symbols should be prefixed with 'ls:' as shown in the Figure below.

Fig 2.10.3 *Up to 4 shares or indices can be displayed on the same chart.*

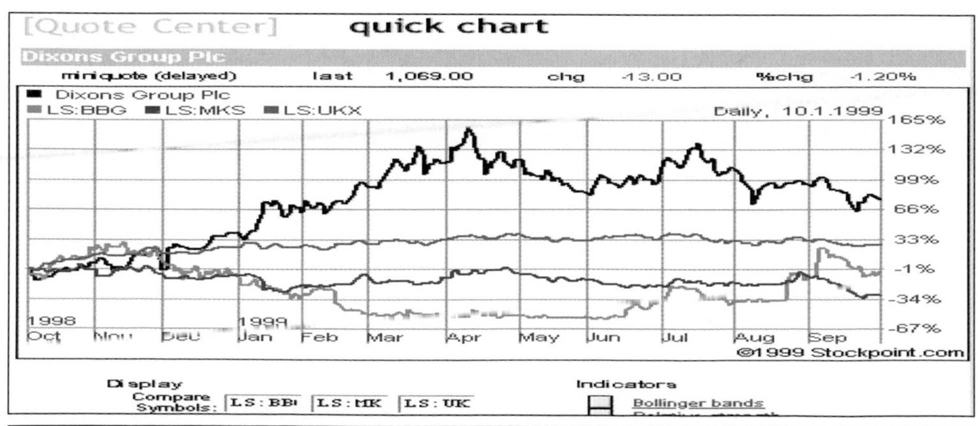

Stock Point *(con't)*

http://www.stockpoint.com/leftnav/stockinput.asp

Clicking on the 'Comparison Index' box displays a menu of indices against which a chosen share can be compared. Unfortunately these are all American indices although it is possible to display a variety of UK indices if you know the correct symbol. A list of all codes for all the FT-SE indices can be displayed by typing in the letters 'ft' in the 'Symbol' box (see Figure 2.10) and clicking 'Go!'

Fig 2.10.4 *Entering 'ft' displays a list of UK stock market index codes.*

Search Results

Companies beginning with ft'

Ftse 100 - UKX (LSE)
Ftse 100 Pre-Open - UKX2 (LSE)
Ftse 100(Train) Ftse 100 Trad - TRF1 (LSE)
Ftse 250 (Mid) - MCX (LSE)
Ftse 250 (Mid) ex. Its - MCIX (LSE)
Ftse 250 (Mid) ex. Its Pre-O - MCIX2 (LSE)
Ftse 250 (Mid) Pre-Open - MCX2 (LSE)
Ftse 350 - NMX (LSE)
Ftse 350 Exclt - NMIX (LSE)
Ftse 350 Exclt Pre Open - NMIX2 (LSE)
Ftse 350 Pre-Open - NMX2 (LSE)
Ftse Aim - AXX (LSE)
Ftse Aim Pre-Open - AXX2 (LSE)
Ftse All Sh Exclt - ASXX (LSE)
Ftse All Sh Exclt Pre Open - ASXX2 (LSE)
Ftse All Share - ASX (LSE)
Ftse All Share Pre-Open - ASX2 (LSE)
Ftse Eurotrack Eire Dm - IEP (LSE)
Ftse Higher Yield - HIX (LSE)
Ftse Higher Yield Pre-Open - HIX2 (LSE)
Ftse Lower Yield - LIX (LSE)
Ftse Lower Yield Pre-Open - LIX2 (LSE)
Ftse New Sm.Co. - NSX (LSE)
Ftse New Sm.Co. ex.Its - NSIX (LSE)
Ftse New Sm.Co. ex.Its Pre-O - NSIX2 (LSE)
Ftse New Sm.Co. Pre-Open - NSX2 (LSE)
Ftse Small Cap. - SMX (LSE)
Ftse Small Cap. ex Its - SMXX (LSE)
Ftse Small Cap. ex Its Pre-O - SMXX2 (LSE)
Ftse Small Cap. Pre-Open - SMX2 (LSE)

Entering one or more of these index codes into the 'Compare Symbols' box, enables you to compare stocks against various indices. It is also possible to compare different UK indices against each other as shown below.

Fig 2.10.5 *Chart showing the FT-SE Higher Yielding Index versus the FT-SE 100 Index.*

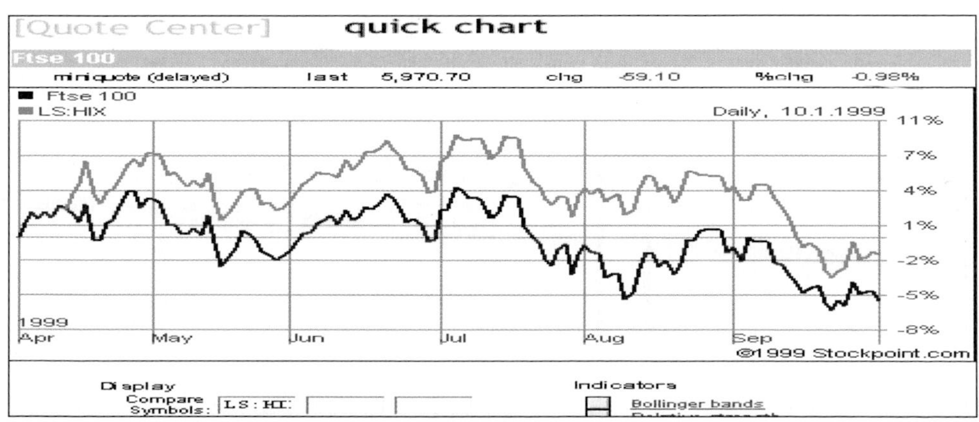

Stock Point *(con't)*

http://www.stockpoint.com/leftnav/stockinput.asp

The 'quick chart' function enables you to display charts over 8 different periods as shown below. To change the time period, click on the small black arrow alongside the 'Time Period' box. Choose one of the periods from the drop down menu which appears, and click on 'Go!' to display the chart.

Fig 2.10.6 *The 'quick charts' function offers a choice of 8 different time periods.*

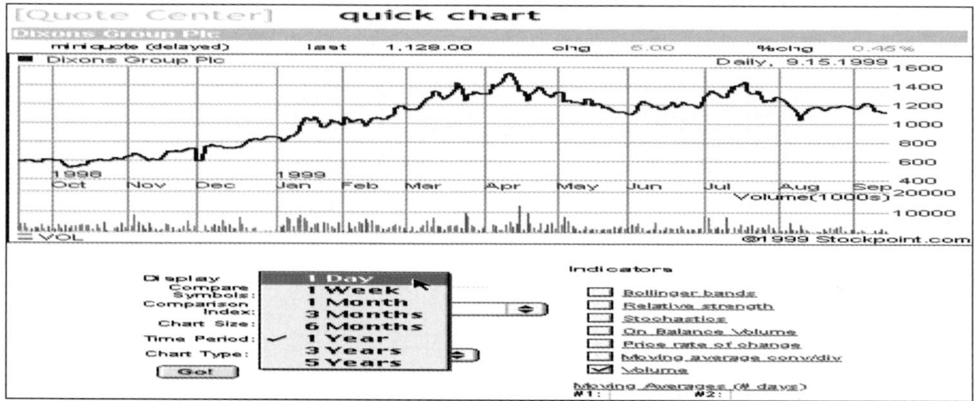

It is very rare to find a free charting function which enables charts to be displayed over short periods such as 1 day and 1 week. Sometimes it can be useful to get an idea of short term price movements prior to buying or selling shares.

Fig 2.10.7 *A 1 day chart of Dixons shares shows how volatile this share price can be.*

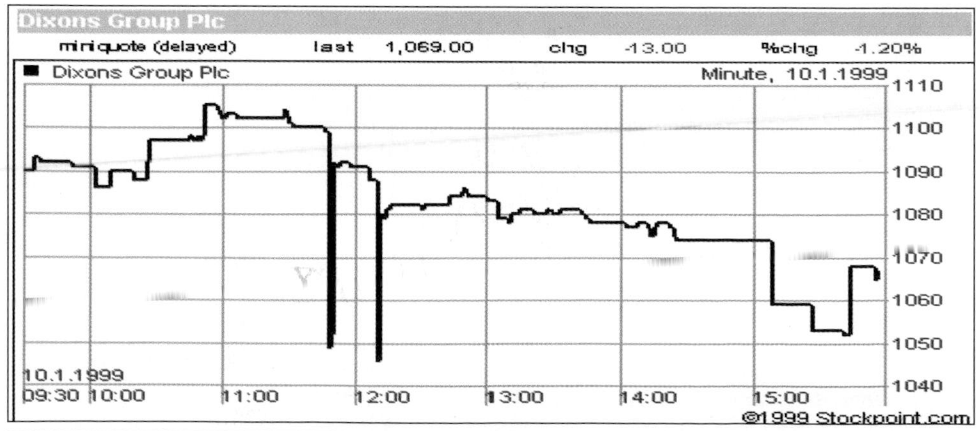

Stock Point *(con't)*

http://www.stockpoint.com/leftnav/stockinput.asp

A number of different technical 'Indicators' ranging from 'Bollinger bands' to 'Moving Averages' can be displayed with the chart. Some stock market traders use these technical indicators to ascertain whether it is a good time to buy or sell a particular share. To include one or more technical indicators on the chart, click in the boxes alongside the appropriate indicator so that a black cross appears in the box as shown below. To display the chart, click on 'Go!'.

Fig 2.10.8 *A share price chart of Dixons including 'Bollinger Bands' and 'Stochastics'.*

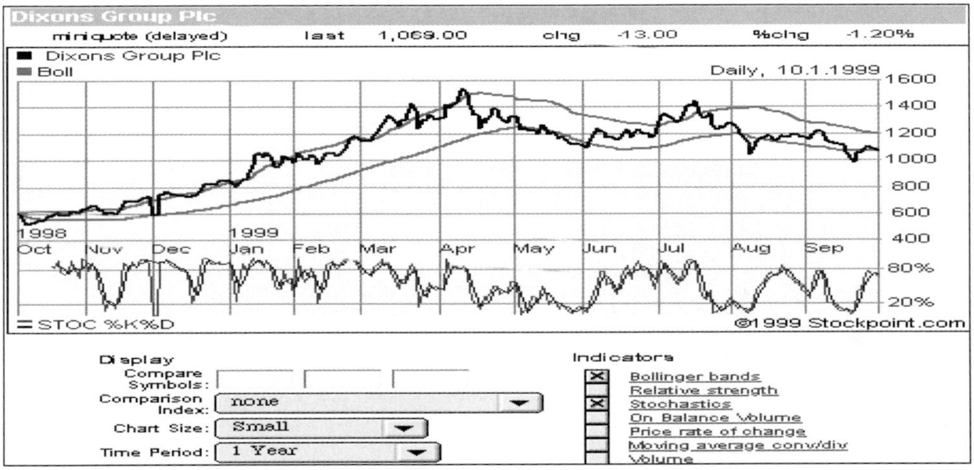

To find out more about what the various technical indicators mean, you can Click on the name of one of the technical indicators to display a brief description.

Fig 2.10.9 *Click on 'Bollinger Bands' to display a description of that technical indica-*

Bollinger Bands

Select this toggle to display Bollinger bands. These bands mark one standard deviation above and below the 30-day price average. The bands represent an envelope of support and resistance levels.

A few general behaviors John Bollinger identified in regards to Bollinger bands are:

- Sharp moves tend to occur after the bands tighten to the average.
- A move outside the bands calls for a continuation of the trend.
- Tops and bottoms made outside the bands, which are followed by tops and bottoms made inside the bands, indicate a trend reversal.
- A move originating at one band tends to go to the other band.

Stock Point *(con't)*

http://www.stockpoint.com/leftnav/stockinput.asp

One of the really excellent features at the Stock Point internet site is the 'interactive charts' function. The chart is initially displayed over 1 year together with a trading volume bar chart. Underneath the bar chart, the dates over which the chart is displayed are shown together with the share price on each date and the percentage change over that period. In the example below, Dixons shares were 584p on the 15th September 1998 and 1123p on the 16th September 1999. The price rise over that period was 92.25%. To display a chart, click on 'interactive chart' in the left hand column of Figure 2.101.

Fig 2.10.10 *The 'interactive chart' function initially displays a 1 year share price chart.*

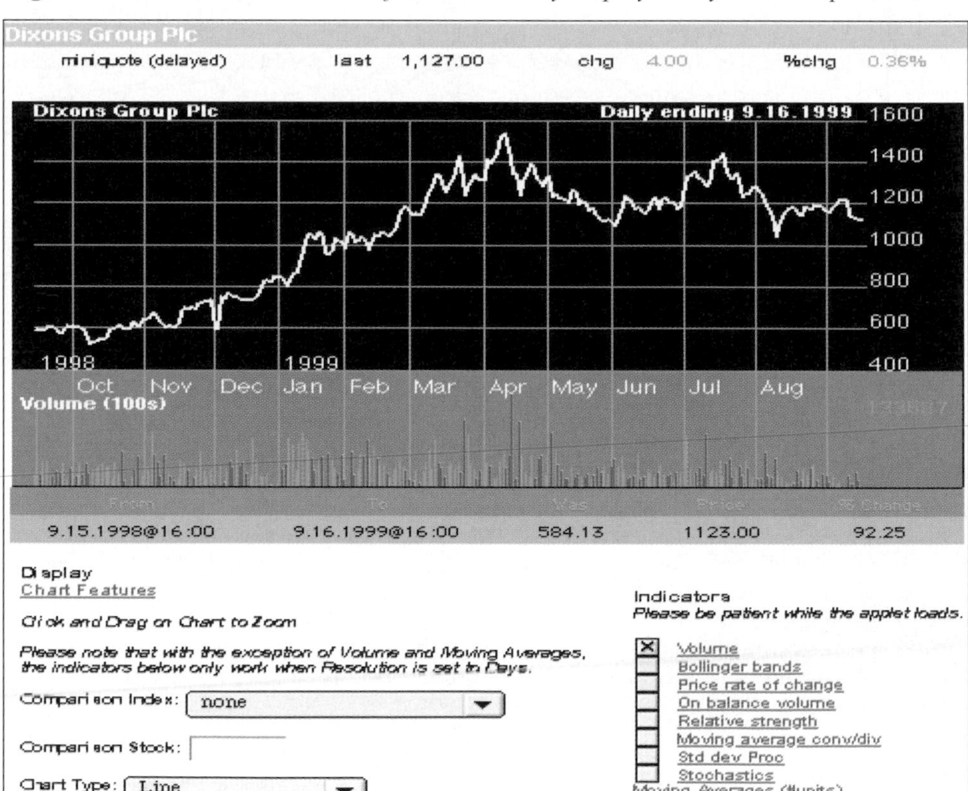

Note that in America dates are back to front so that 9.15.1998 actually means 15.9.1998, eg the 15th of September. At the time of writing, the 'interactive chart' function only worked with the Netscape browser when using a Macintosh computer.

Stock Point *(con't)*

http://www.stockpoint.com/leftnav/stockinput.asp

One of the unique features of the 'interactive chart' function is that you can click anywhere on the chart and display the share price on that day. In the example below, the mouse was moved to the 6th April and clicked once. The figures below the chart change to show that on the 6th April, the share price of Dixons was 1414p. The percentage change figure has also changed to show that between 6th April 1999 and 16 October 1999 the share price fell by 26.03%.

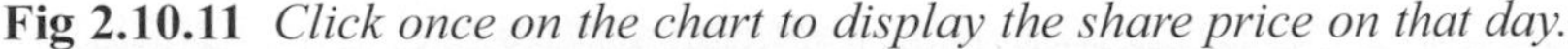

Fig 2.10.11 *Click once on the chart to display the share price on that day.*

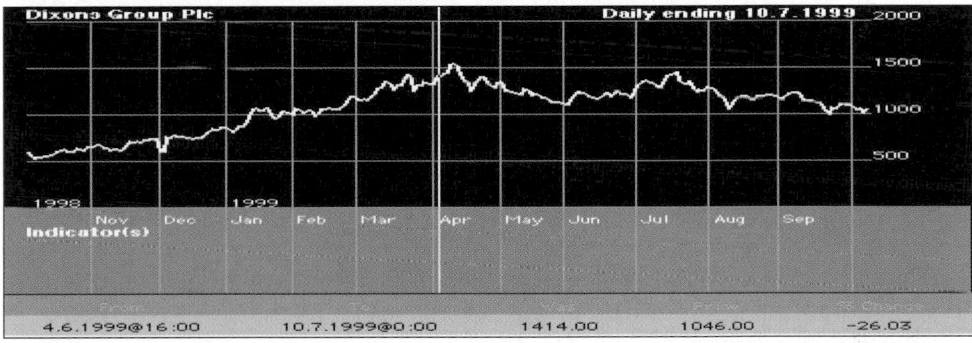

If you click on the chart and hold down the mouse button, you can move the mouse and change the 'To' date and price. As you roll the mouse towards the right hand side of the chart, you will see the 'To' date and the 'Price' changing. The '% Change' figure also changes to reflect the change in price between the 'To' and 'From' date you have selected.

Fig 2.10.12 *Click and hold down the mouse button to change the end date of the chart.*

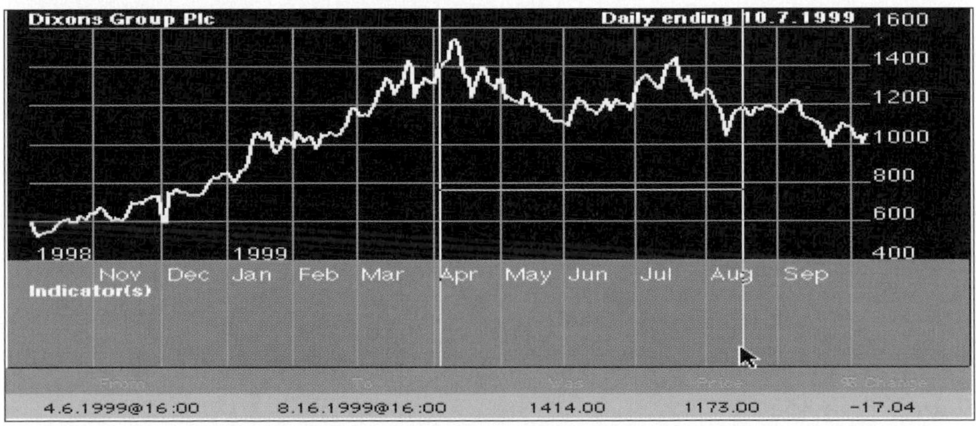

Stock Point *(con't)*

http://www.stockpoint.com/leftnav/stockinput.asp

When you release the mouse button, a chart is displayed over the period you have chosen. In the example below, the mouse was first clicked on 6th April 1999 (see Figure 2.1011), scrolled across the chart to the 17th August 1999 (Figure 2.1012) and released. To return back to the 1 year chart, click on 'UNZOOM' in the top right hand corner of the chart as shown below.

Fig 2.10.13 *You can choose the exact period over which to display a chart.*

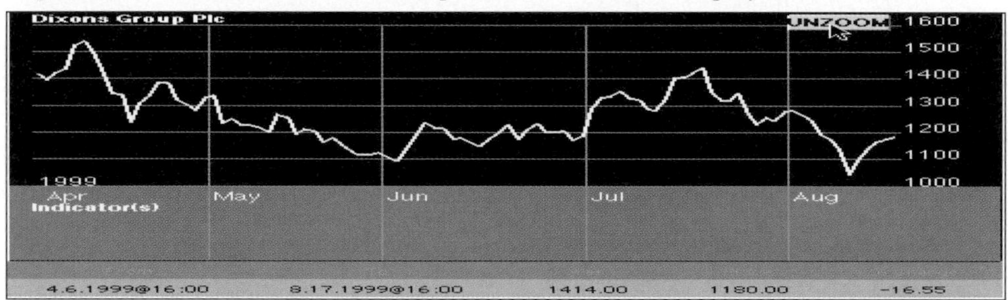

The 'interactive charts' function allows you to display two stocks or indices on the chart at the same time. The second stock can be an overseas stock which enables you to compare UK and US companies on the same chart. An interesting use of this function is to compare the performance of a UK stock such as Dixons (dxns) with that of its American ADR listing (dxngy). A list of UK stocks with an ADR listing is given in Appendix A.

Fig 2.10.14 *Performance of the UK listing of Dixons compared with Dixons US ADR.*

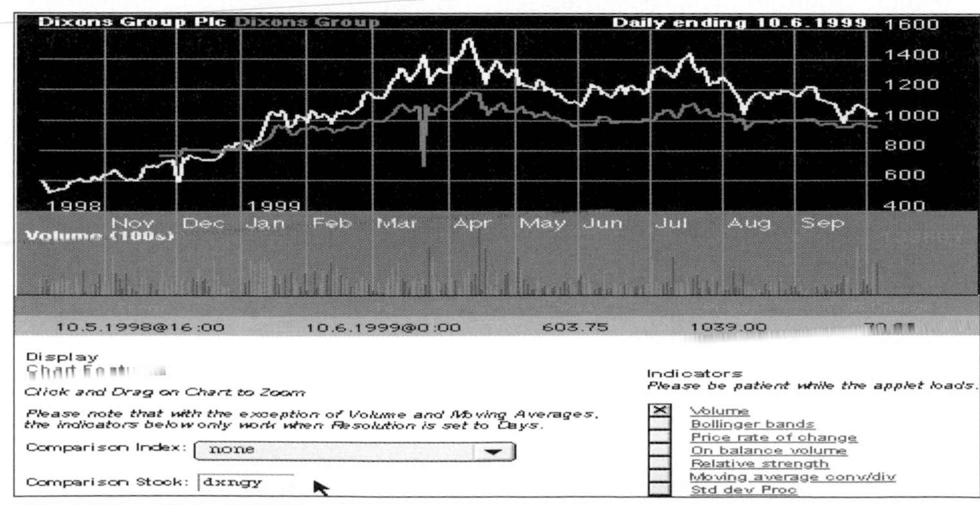

UK-iNvest

http://sites.stockpoint.com/ukinvest/quote.asp?Mode=COMPANYLIST

The prices and charts on the UK-iNvest site are supplied by the American company Stock Point. The UK-iNvest internet site allows investors to display interactive (Java) Charts over a 3 year period as opposed to just 1 year at the Stock Point site. The free charting functions on the UK-iNvest site and the Stock Point site are almost identical. On the UK-iNvest site, the 'interactive charts' described under Stock Point heading earlier in this Chapter, are referred to as 'Javacharts'. To display a chart, you need to enter either the name or stock code of a share, and click on 'Get Quote' as shown below.

Fig 2.11.0 *To display a chart, first enter a stock code and click on 'Get Quote'.*

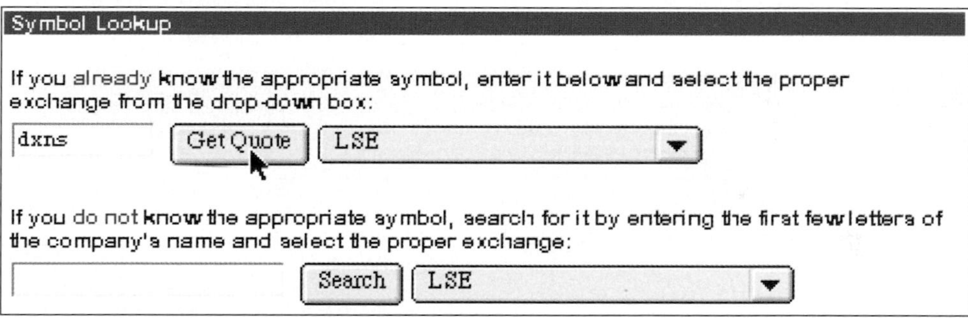

The 'Chart' heading in the Figure below takes you to the equivalent of 'quick charts' on the Stock Point internet site. Clicking on the 'Javachart' heading leads to the equivalent of the 'interactive charts' section of the Stock Point site.

Fig 2.11.1 *Click on the 'Javachart' heading to display a 1 year interactive chart.*

Get Quote | Chart | Javachart | Live Quotes | Profile

Dixons Group Plc (DXNS)

Delayed Quote — AS OF OCT 5, 1999 3:31:00 PM (B.S.T.)

Last	1,035.0p	Change	9.0p
Open	1,067.0p	% Change	0.88 %
High	1,067.0p	Low	1,022.0p
Bid	1,033.0p	Ask	1,036.0p
Volume	1.96M	Market Capitalization	4.64B
52 Week High	1,575.0	52 Week Low	514.5
Earnings Per Share	0.41	Shares Outstanding	434.26M
P/E Ratio	26.01	Exchange	LSE

UK-iNvest *(con't)*

http://sites.stockpoint.com/ukinvest/quote.asp?Mode=COMPANYLIST

When you click on the 'Javachart' heading, a 1 year interactive chart is initially displayed. It can take a little time to download the chart depending on the speed of your computer, and how busy the internet is at the time. To display an interactive (Java) chart over 3 years, click on the 'Time Period' box and select 'Weeks' from the drop down menu as shown below. Once again, you can click anywhere on the chart and the 'From' date and price will change to the date you have selected. This function is particularly useful if you want to find out the price of a share or level of an index on a particular day.

Fig 2.11.2 *The UK-iNvest site allows a 3 year interactive (Java) chart to be displayed.*

The interactive charting function doesn't appear to work with some versions of the Internet Explorer browser such as version 4.01. If you find that your computer doesn't display interactive charts, you can download a later version of Internet Explorer from the internet. Alternatively you can use version 4.0 (or higher) of the Netscape Navigator browser.

3

Portfolios Online

A good way to keep track of your existing portfolio and monitor new investments, is to set up an online portfolio. You will be able to obtain up to date valuations and have instant access to a variety of useful information about your investments. Some internet sites have advanced features such as 'news alerts' which will notify you via e-mail when shares in your portfolio reach a certain level. Other internet sites allow you to customise your portfolio to display the information you feel is most relevant to you. All the online portfolio services described in this Chapter require you to register. See Chapter 7 for further details on Registration.

Hot Links

✍ Shares, unit trusts, offshore funds, insurance bonds etc - *Interactive Investor*
✍ Shares, investment trusts & warrants with up to date trading data - *E*Trade*
✍ Investment trusts sortable by past performance and discounts - *Trustnet*
✍ Shares and investment trusts with customising facility - *Quicken*
✍ RESEARCH MASTER - quotes, charts, news and research - *ScottITonline*

The RESEARCH MASTER is potentially a very powerful research tool. You can avoid wasting valuable online time by creating a customised portfolio. This will enable you to go directly to stock specific information and thus avoid spending time (and money!) downloading pages of information which may not be particularly useful to you. Details of how to create your own free web site and customised online portfolio are given in Appendix C and D.

✍ *Indicates that Registration is necessary to access information at this site.*

III Interactive Investor

http://www.iii.co.uk/portfolio

This internet site has one of the best free online portfolio management services. A portfolio can include most types of investments including shares, unit trusts and investment trusts. To set up a portfolio online, you must first register and choose a login name and password. The registration procedure is very simple and is fully covered in Chapter 7.

Fig 3.1 *Enter your login name and password to access the online portfolio section.*

Enter Your Name And Password

Enter username for Interactive Investor Registered Users at www.iii.co.uk:

Name: your login name goes here

Password: ••••••••••

Cancel OK

To display an investment, enter either the name or the correct security code and click on the 'Search' icon at the bottom of the screen shown below. To add this investment to your online portfolio, click on the small 'Add' icon in the top left hand corner of the screen below.

Fig 3.11 *Enter a stock code or name and click on 'Search'.*

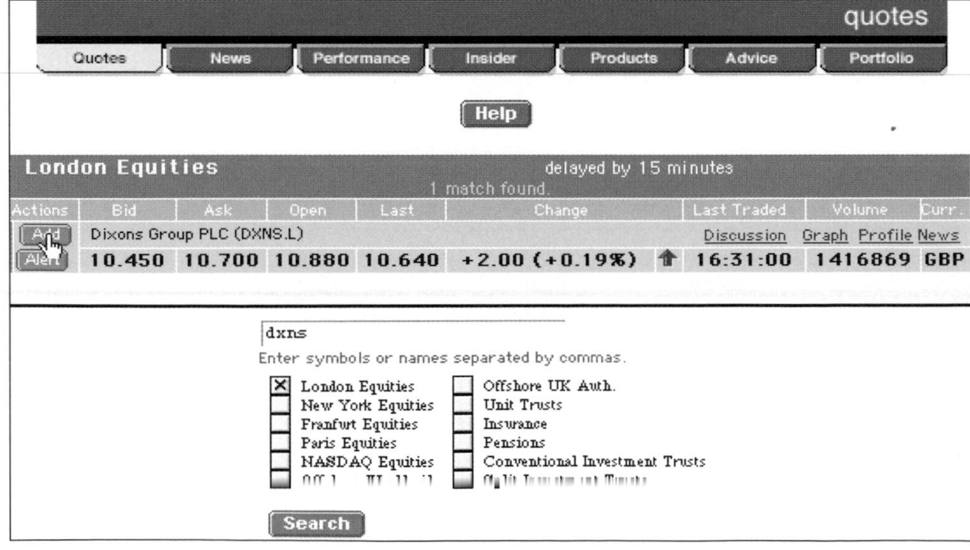

III Interactive Investor *(con't)*

http://www.iii.co.uk/portfolio

When you click on the 'Add' icon, the screen below is displayed. If you simply click on the 'Submit' button, the investment you have chosen, is automatically added to a default portfolio entitled 'Myportfolio'. To add the investment to a new or different portfolio, click in the 'Add to new Portfolio' box so that a small black circle appears as shown below. Type in a name for the new portfolio and click on the 'Submit' button at the bottom of the screen. In the example below, the portfolio has been named 'bookexample'.

Fig 3.12 *Add 1000 Dixons shares to a new portfolio called 'bookexample'.*

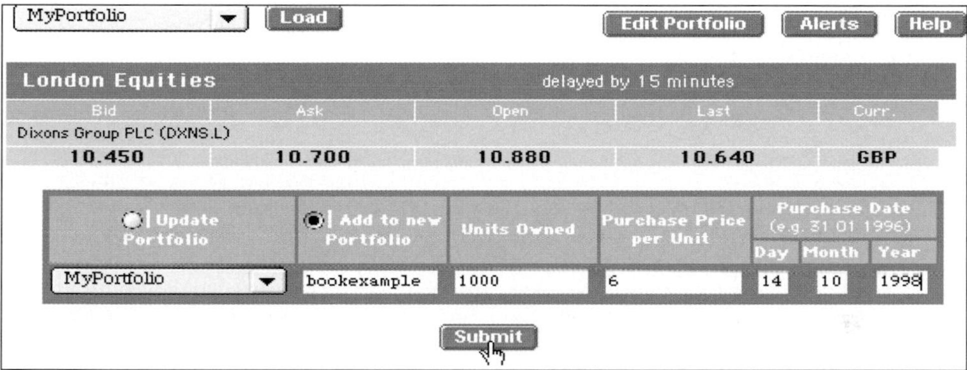

If you actually own the investment, you can complete the 'Units Owned', 'Purchase Price' and 'Purchase Date' boxes as in the example above. If you don't enter this information, the investment appears in your portfolio, but is not included in the valuation. The purchase price should be entered in pounds and not in pence (eg 6 pounds and not 600p).

Fig 3.13 *The portfolio displays an up to date valuation with profit and loss figures.*

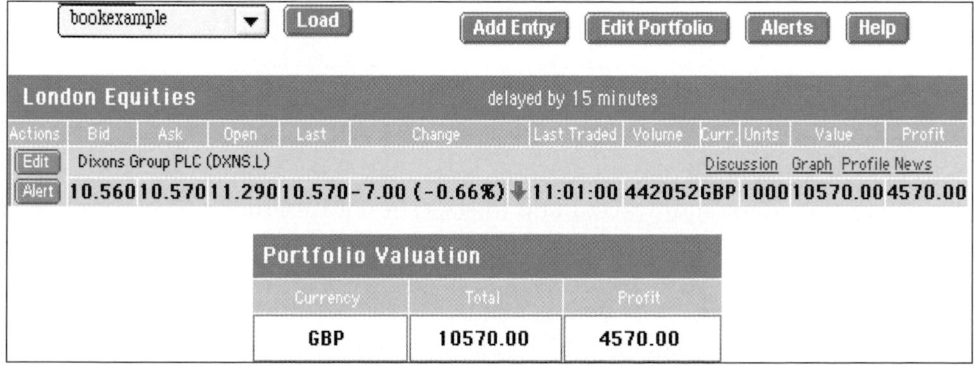

III Interactive Investor *(con't)*

http://www.iii.co.uk/portfolio

Portfolios can contain a wide range of different types of investment, including equities listed on the following exchanges: London, New York, Frankfurt, Paris NASDAQ. In addition to equities, you can also include Investment Trusts, Unit Trusts, Offshore Worldwide Funds, Offshore UK Authorized Funds, Insurance Bonds, Pension Funds and OIECS. Any combination of the investment vehicles listed above can be include in a portfolio. Once your portfolio is set up you can add additional stocks by clicking on the 'Add Entry' icon shown at the top of the Figure below.

Fig 3.14 *Portfolios can contain a variety of different types of investments.*

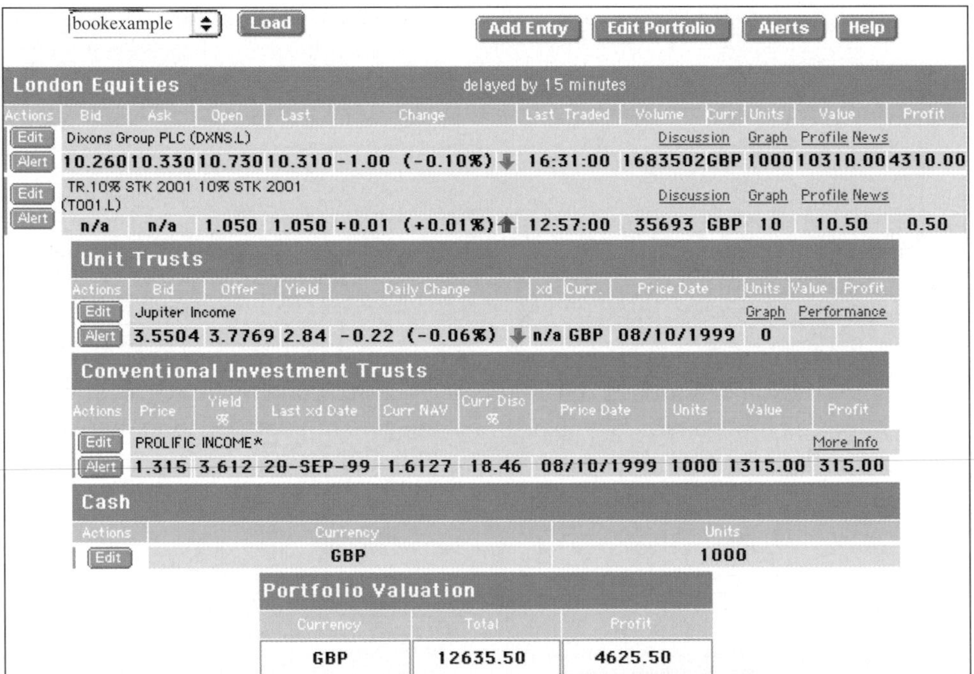

The information displayed for each different type of investment varies, as does the data you can access directly from the portfolio. For example, bid and offer prices are shown for equities and unit trusts, (but not for gilts) whereas middle market prices are displayed for investment trusts. For a full description of the additional information you can get from this page, see the Interactive Investor 'Prices' page in Chapter 1. A unique and useful feature of this site is the ability to include a 'Cash' investment which can be in either pounds or US dollars.

III Interactive Investor *(con't)*

http://www.iii.co.uk/portfolio

The 'Edit Portfolio' button at the top of Figure 3.14, can be used to 'Delete' stocks from an existing portfolio. Alternatively, you can use this button to copy stocks to a new or existing portfolio. First select the investment you want to edit so that a black tick appears as shown below. When you have made the necessary changes, click on 'Submit' in the bottom left hand corner of the screen.

Fig 3.15 *Click in the 'Select' box to copy a stock to a new portfolio.*

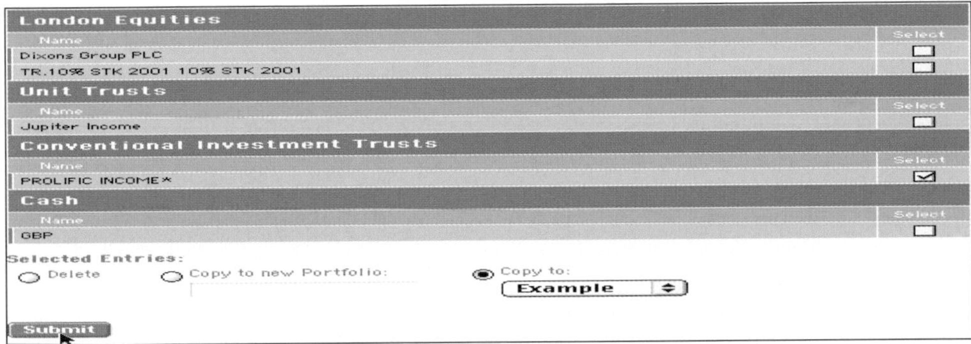

In this example, 'prolific income' has been copied from the portfolio shown in Figure 3.14 to another portfolio called 'Example'. This portfolio consists of three other income investment trusts. You can set up multiple portfolios to monitor different sectors of the market. To display a different portfolio, click on the small arrows at the end of the name box in the top left hand corner of the screen shown below. A window will appear which lists all your portfolios. Highlight the portfolio you wish to display and then click on 'Load'.

Fig 3.16 *To display other portfolios you need to change the name and click on 'Load'.*

Example | Load | Add Entry | Edit Portfolio | Alerts | Help

Conventional Investment Trusts

Actions	Price	Yield %	Last xd Date	Curr NAV	Curr Disc %	Price Date	Units	Value	Profit
Edit	G T INCOME GROWTH								More Info
Alert	1.365	2.564	14-JUN-99	1.5373	11.21	08/10/1999	0		
Edit	JUPITER SPLIT UNIT								More Info
Alert	80	2.69	23-AUG-99	89.3993	10.51	08/10/1999	0		
Edit	PROLIFIC INCOME*								More Info
Alert	1.315	3.612	20-SEP-99	1.6127	18.46	08/10/1999	0		
Edit	VALUE AND INCOME								More Info
Alert	1.305	3.985	07-JUN-99	1.6872	22.65	08/10/1999	0		

E*Trade

http://research.etrade.co.uk/free/share.cgi

This is a good site for monitoring portfolios of shares, investment trusts and warrants. Data at this site tends to be accurate and is set out in a useful and easy to understand format. Unfortunately, it is not yet possible to include other types of investments such as unit trusts in the portfolio. Before you can set up an online portfolio, you must register to obtain a user ID and password. Chapter 7 gives more details about registration. When you have been allocated your user ID and password, enter them in the relevant boxes as shown below.

Fig 3.2 *You need to register to obtain an E*Trade User ID and Password.*

To access the free online portfolio management service click on the 'Stockwatch' heading. At the time of writing, the 'Stockwatch' function only worked with Netscape and not Explorer when a Macintosh computer was used. On some internet sites, the Netscape browser works better than the Explorer browser and vice versa.

Fig 3.21 *Click on 'Stockwatch' to access the online portfolio section of this internet site.*

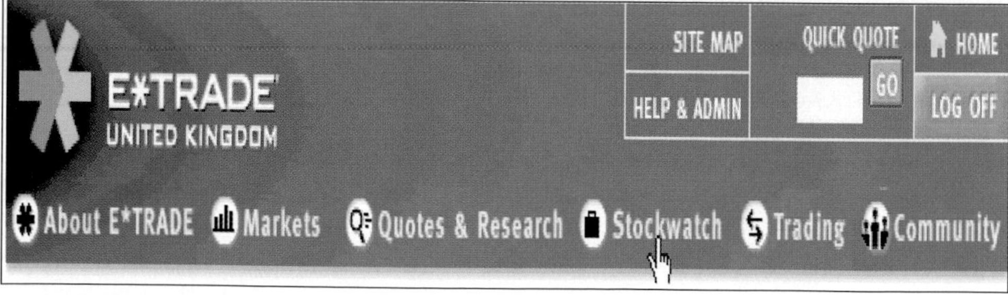

E*Trade *(con't)*

http://research.etrade.co.uk/free/share.cgi

To add a stock to your portfolio, enter the correct stock code (EPIC code) or company name, and click on the 'Add' icon as shown below. If you do not know the correct stock code, click on the 'Browse' button to display an alphabetical list of stocks and shares.

Fig 3.22 *To include stocks in the portfolio, enter the stock code and click on 'Add'.*

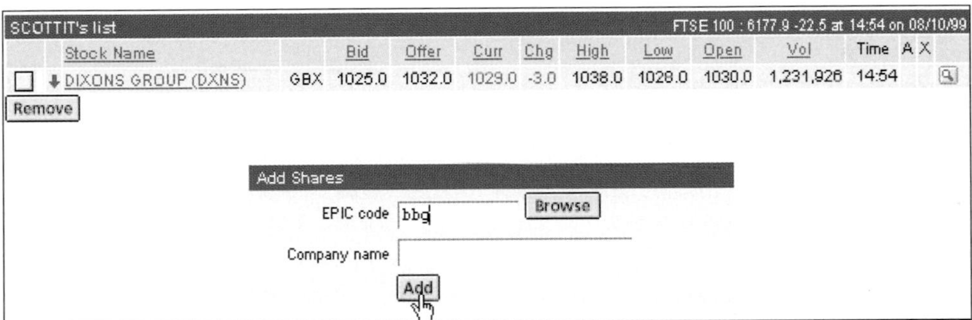

SCOTTIT's list — FTSE 100 : 6177.9 -22.5 at 14:54 on 08/10/99

	Stock Name		Bid	Offer	Curr	Chg	High	Low	Open	Vol	Time	A	X
☐	DIXONS GROUP (DXNS)	GBX	1025.0	1032.0	1029.0	-3.0	1038.0	1028.0	1030.0	1,231,926	14:54		

Remove

Add Shares

EPIC code bbg Browse

Company name

Add

The level of the FT-SE 100 index is displayed in the top right hand corner of the screen. If there has been an announcement that day or a stock in the portfolio is trading 'ex dividend', this will be shown in the end column under 'A' and 'X' respectively. If you click on any headings such as 'Chg' the portfolio will be sorted so that the stock with the biggest change appears first. This feature can be quite useful for monitoring specific sectors of the market. For example, you could set up a portfolio consisting purely of internet related stocks. At a glance, you could see which stock in that sector was performing the best or worst on a given day.

Fig 3.23 *The portfolio can be sorted by clicking on any of the headings.*

SCOTTIT's list — FTSE 100 : 6166.3 -34.1 at 15:05 on 08/10/99

	Stock Name		Bid	Offer	Curr	Chg	High	Low	Open	Vol	Time	A	X
☐	BR.BIOTECH (BBG)	GBX	32.5	33.0	33.0	+0.75	33.0	32.5	33.0	1,761,300	15:05		
☐	BULGIN 'A' (BGNA)	GBX	9.75	10.5	10.25	+0.0	10.25	10.0	10.0		15:05		
☐	PROLIFIC INC.WT (PRIW)	GBX	41.0	43.0	42.0	+0.0	42.0	41.5	41.5		15:05		
☐	DIXONS GROUP (DXNS)	GBX	1025.0	1030.0	1029.0	-3.0	1038.0	1028.0	1030.0	1,231,926	15:05		

Remove

E*Trade *(con't)*

http://research.etrade.co.uk/free/share.cgi

You can display useful information about a stock in the portfolios by clicking on the small magnifying glass icon to the far right of the stock. The magnifying icon is shown in Figure 3.22. This screen effectively takes you to the 'Quotes and Research' section of the site which is fully described in Chapters 1 and 2.

Fig 3.24 *A detailed company profile on any stock in the portfolio can be displayed.*

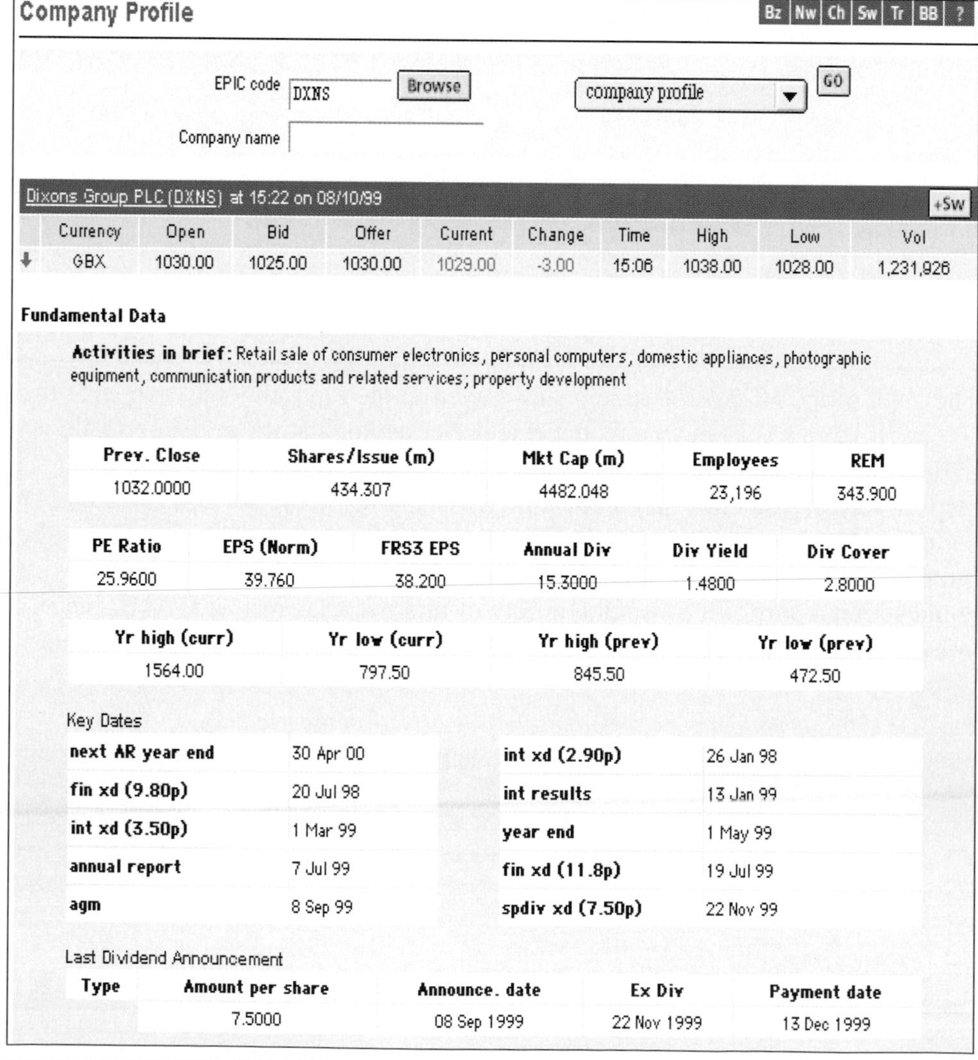

Company Profile

Bz Nw Ch Sw Tr BB ?

EPIC code DXNS Browse

Company name

company profile GO

Dixons Group PLC (DXNS) at 15:22 on 08/10/99 +Sw

	Currency	Open	Bid	Offer	Current	Change	Time	High	Low	Vol
↓	GBX	1030.00	1025.00	1030.00	1029.00	-3.00	15:06	1038.00	1028.00	1,231,926

Fundamental Data

Activities in brief: Retail sale of consumer electronics, personal computers, domestic appliances, photographic equipment, communication products and related services; property development

Prev. Close	Shares/Issue (m)	Mkt Cap (m)	Employees	REM
1032.0000	434.307	4482.048	23,196	343.900

PE Ratio	EPS (Norm)	FRS3 EPS	Annual Div	Div Yield	Div Cover
25.9600	39.760	38.200	15.3000	1.4800	2.8000

Yr high (curr)	Yr low (curr)	Yr high (prev)	Yr low (prev)
1564.00	797.50	845.50	472.50

Key Dates

next AR year end	30 Apr 00	int xd (2.90p)	26 Jan 98
fin xd (9.80p)	20 Jul 98	int results	13 Jan 99
int xd (3.50p)	1 Mar 99	year end	1 May 99
annual report	7 Jul 99	fin xd (11.8p)	19 Jul 99
agm	8 Sep 99	spdiv xd (7.50p)	22 Nov 99

Last Dividend Announcement

Type	Amount per share	Announce. date	Ex Div	Payment date
	7.5000	08 Sep 1999	22 Nov 1999	13 Dec 1999

Trustnet

http://www.trustnet.co.uk/it/portfolio/login.asp

This is one of the best online portfolio management services for monitoring or managing a portfolio of Investment Trusts. To gain access to the online portfolio section, it is necessary to register. Chapter 7 gives more details about the registration procedure. Once you have been allocated your 'Login name' and 'Password', enter them as shown and click on the 'Login!' button.

Fig 3.3 *Enter your 'Login name' and 'Password' and click on the 'Login' button.*

When you click on 'Login!' the screen shown below should appear. The same screen can be accessed by clicking on the 'Custom' button (not shown) which is always located in the top right hand corner of the screen. To access the list of funds which can be included in your portfolio, click on the 'Add Funds!' button as shown below.

Fig 3.31 *To display a list of funds which can be added click on the 'Add Funds!' button.*

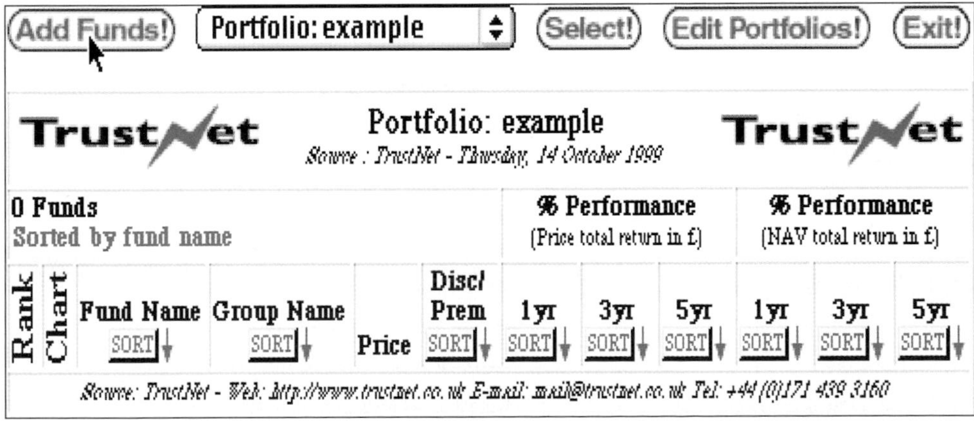

Trustnet *(con't)*

http://www.trustnet.co.uk/it/portfolio/login.asp

The funds which can be added to you portfolio are listed in alphabetical order. Initially funds from '3i to Ba' are listed. To display a different list of funds, you need to click on one of the alphabetical groupings at the top of the screen. For example, to add the fund 'Prolific Income' to your portfolio, you would first click on the alphabetical grouping 'Mu to Sa'.

Fig 3.32 *Initially an alphabetical list of funds is displayed starting with '3i to Ba'.*

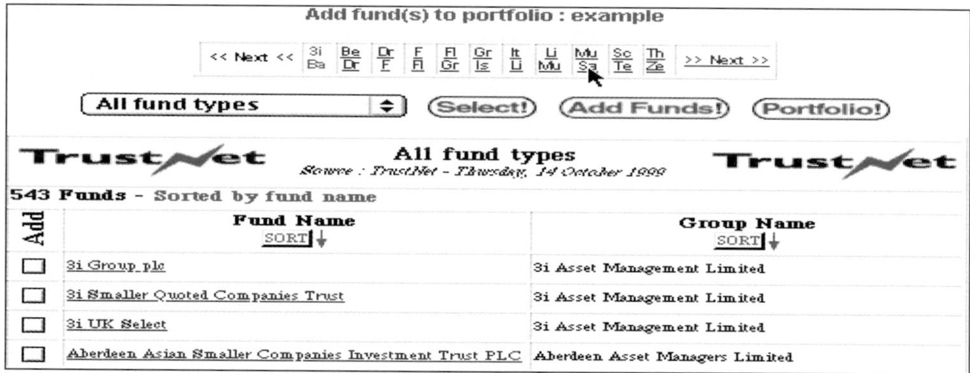

Add	Fund Name	Group Name
☐	3i Group plc	3i Asset Management Limited
☐	3i Smaller Quoted Companies Trust	3i Asset Management Limited
☐	3i UK Select	3i Asset Management Limited
☐	Aberdeen Asian Smaller Companies Investment Trust PLC	Aberdeen Asset Managers Limited

This site covers a huge number of funds and it is generally necessary to use the scroll bars at the side of your screen to display the fund you are looking for. Once you have found your chosen fund, click in the box alongside it so that a tick appears as shown below. To actually add this fund to your portfolio, you need to scroll back to the top of the screen (or right to the end) and click on the 'Add Funds!' button. This button is shown in the Figure above, between the 'Select!' and the 'Portfolio!' buttons.

Fig 3.33 *Click in the box alongside the fund you want to add so that a tick appears.*

☐	Perpetual Japanese	Perpetual Portfolio Management Limited
☐	Perpetual UK Smaller Companies	Perpetual Portfolio Management Limited
☐	Personal Assets Trust	Independently Managed
☐	Portugal Fund Inc	Credit Suisse Asset Management
☑	Prolific Income PLC	Aberdeen Asset Managers Limited
☐	Prospect Japan Fund Limited	Prospect Asset Management Inc
☐	Ptarmigan International Capital Trust	Stewart Ivory & Company Limited
☐	Radiotrust	Aberdeen Asset Managers Limited
☐	Red Tiger Investment Co Ltd	Regent Fund Management Limited

Trustnet *(con't)*

http://www.trustnet.co.uk/it/portfolio/login.asp

Once you have set up your portfolio, there is an excellent sorting facility which enables you to sort the portfolio alphabetically by either 'Fund/Group Name' or by 'Discount to Net Asset Value'. Alternatively, you can sort by the percentage 'Performance' of either 'Price' or 'Net Asset Value'. A useful research tool would be to set up multiple portfolios covering the sectors you are interested in. You could have one portfolio for Japanese Investments Trusts, one for UK High Income Trusts etc.

Fig 3.34 *Portfolio of UK income Investment Trusts sorted alphabetically by Fund Name.*

TrustNet — Portfolio: scottitonline — *Source: TrustNet - Friday, 19 March 1999* — TrustNet

10 Funds Sorted by fund name						% Performance (Price total return in £)			% Performance (NAV total return in £)		
Rank	Chart	Fund Name SORT	Group Name SORT	Price	Disc/Prem SORT	1yr SORT	3yr SORT	5yr SORT	1yr SORT	3yr SORT	5yr SORT
1		CITY OF LONDON INV TST	HENDINVEST	264.0 (GBX)	-0.7	+2.4	+81.6	+112.3	+3.9	+80.3	+116.9
2		DUNEDIN INC GROWTH	EFM	220.25 (GBX)	-8.5	+13.1	+86.1	+91.5	+9.6	+80.7	+107.8
3		GT INCOME GROWTH	GT MGT	132.0 (GBX)	-13.4	-3.4	n/a	n/a	+3.6	n/a	n/a
4		JUPITER SPLIT PACKAGE	JUP ASSMAN	7950.0 (GBX)	-7.4	+19.4	+47.6	n/a	+5.5	+57.2	n/a
5		MERCHANTS	DRESDRCMGI	419.0 (GBX)	-4.5	+8.7	+75.4	+93.3	+5.8	+75.4	+108.9
6		MOR GREN EQU INCOME	MG INV MGT	205.0 (GBX)	-9.0	+8.9	+46.5	+72.9	+8.3	+62.6	+90.9
7		PERPETUAL INC & GWTH	PERPETUAL	130.25 (GBX)	-8.1	-6.7	n/a	n/a	+4.3	n/a	n/a
8		PROLIFIC INCOME	ABERDEEN	133.0 (GBX)	-17.7	-3.6	+36.2	n/a	+4.4	+53.8	n/a
9		SCHRODER INCOME GROWTH	SCHRODR IM	136.5 (GBX)	-8.4	-8.9	+39.7	n/a	-1.4	+53.3	n/a
10		VALUE & INCOME	OLIM	118.5 (GBX)	-23.1	-17.3	+9.5	+27.9	-1.4	+40.5	+79.5

You can use this internet site to create tailor made sectors consisting only of the funds you might consider buying. At the time of writing, the sector categorisations on this site are not particularly accurate and do not always include all the relevant funds. For example, when comparing UK Income Investment Trusts you might find it relevant to include the packaged units of split level funds such as Jupiter Split Packaged Units. These trusts are often overlooked by investors.

Trustnet *(con't)*

http://www.trustnet.co.uk/it/portfolio/login.asp

Fig 3.35 *A sample of UK Income Investment Trusts sorted by 1 year price performance.*

10 Funds 1yr price performance						% Performance (Price total return in £)			% Performance (NAV total return in £)		
Rank	Chart	Fund Name SORT	Group Name SORT	Price	Disc/ Prem SORT	1yr SORT	3yr SORT	5yr SORT	1yr SORT	3yr SORT	5yr SORT
1		JUPITER SPLIT PACKAGE	JUP ASSMAN	7950.0 (GBX)	-7.4	+19.4	+47.6	n/a	+5.5	+57.2	n/a
2		DUNEDIN INC GROWTH	EFM	220.25 (GBX)	-8.5	+13.1	+86.1	+91.5	+9.6	+80.7	+107.8
3		MOR GREN EQU INCOME	MG INV MGT	205.0 (GBX)	-9.0	+8.9	+46.5	+72.9	+8.3	+62.6	+90.9
4		MERCHANTS	DRESDRCMGI	419.0 (GBX)	-4.5	+8.7	+75.4	+93.3	+5.8	+75.4	+108.9
5		CITY OF LONDON INV TST	HENDINVEST	264.0 (GBX)	-0.7	+2.4	+81.6	+112.3	+3.9	+80.3	+116.9
6		GT INCOME GROWTH	GT MGT	132.0 (GBX)	-13.4	-3.4	n/a	n/a	+3.6	n/a	n/a
7		PROLIFIC INCOME	ABERDEEN	133.0 (GBX)	-17.7	-3.6	+36.2	n/a	+4.4	+53.8	n/a
8		PERPETUAL INC & GWTH	PERPETUAL	130.25 (GBX)	-8.1	-6.7	n/a	n/a	+4.3	n/a	n/a
9		SCHRODER INCOME GROWTH	SCHRODR IM	136.5 (GBX)	-8.4	-8.9	+39.7	n/a	-1.4	+53.3	n/a
10		VALUE & INCOME	OLIM	118.5 (GBX)	-23.1	-17.3	+9.5	+27.9	-1.4	+40.5	+79.5

Fig 3.36 *The same funds sorted by Discount to Net Asset Value.*

10 Funds Sorted by discount (-) to NAV						% Performance (Price total return in £)			% Performance (NAV total return in £)		
Rank	Chart	Fund Name SORT	Group Name SORT	Price	Disc/ Prem SORT	1yr SORT	3yr SORT	5yr SORT	1yr SORT	3yr SORT	5yr SORT
1		VALUE & INCOME	OLIM	118.5 (GBX)	-23.1	-17.3	+9.5	+27.9	-1.4	+40.5	+79.5
2		PROLIFIC INCOME	ABERDEEN	133.0 (GBX)	-17.7	-3.6	+36.2	n/a	+4.4	+53.8	n/a
3		GT INCOME GROWTH	GT MGT	132.0 (GBX)	-13.4	-3.4	n/a	n/a	+3.6	n/a	n/a
4		MOR GREN EQU INCOME	MG INV MGT	205.0 (GBX)	-9.0	+8.9	+46.5	+72.9	+8.3	+62.6	+90.9
5		DUNEDIN INC GROWTH	EFM	220.25 (GBX)	-8.5	+13.1	+86.1	+91.5	+9.6	+80.7	+107.8
6		SCHRODER INCOME GROWTH	SCHRODR IM	136.5 (GBX)	-8.4	-8.9	+39.7	n/a	-1.4	+53.3	n/a
7		PERPETUAL INC & GWTH	PERPETUAL	130.25 (GBX)	-8.1	-6.7	n/a	n/a	+4.3	n/a	n/a
8		JUPITER SPLIT PACKAGE	JUP ASSMAN	7950.0 (GBX)	-7.4	+19.4	+47.6	n/a	+5.5	+57.2	n/a
9		MERCHANTS	DRESDRCMGI	419.0 (GBX)	-4.5	+8.7	+75.4	+93.3	+5.8	+75.4	+108.9
10		CITY OF LONDON INV TST	HENDINVEST	264.0 (GBX)	-0.7	+2.4	+81.6	+112.3	+3.9	+80.3	+116.9

See Chapter 1 for a full description of the information which can be accessed directly from this site by clicking on the various live icons. Unfortunately, you cannot include warrants when you create a customised portfolio.

Quicken

http://www.quicken.co.uk/investment/portfolio

This free online portfolio service is unusual because it allows you to customise the data which is displayed. You have to register and obtain a password before you can set up a portfolio. Enter your e-mail address and password as shown below, and click on 'Get My Portfolio' to access the online portfolio section.

Fig 3.4 *Enter your e-mail address and password to access your portfolio.*

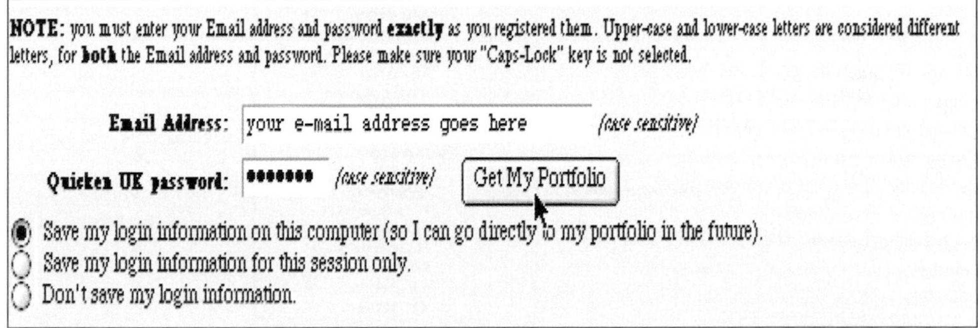
NOTE: you must enter your Email address and password exactly as you registered them. Upper-case and lower-case letters are considered different letters, for both the Email address and password. Please make sure your "Caps-Lock" key is not selected.
Email Address: your e-mail address goes here (case sensitive)
Quicken UK password: (case sensitive)
Get My Portfolio
Save my login information on this computer (so I can go directly to my portfolio in the future).
Save my login information for this session only.
Don't save my login information.

When you first access the portfolio section at this site, a 'Default Portfolio' is displayed which consists of a selection of well known UK shares. You can either choose to delete this portfolio, or alternatively modify it to suit your own needs. Click on 'Create New Portfolio' on the left hand side of the screen shown below to set up your own online portfolio.

Fig 3.41 *Initially the 'Default Portfolio' is displayed which you can delete or modify.*

Investments | Portfolio | Quotes | Managed Fund Service | Top Stories | FT Guides

Enter symbol(s): United Kingdom [Get Quotes]
Share Symbol

Create New Portfolio — Update Prices — View for Printing

Default Portfolio — Add Symbols — Remove Symbols — Adjust Shares — Customise Display

Symbol	Currency	Current Price	Today's Change	% Change	Volume	Day Range	More Information	Time
BP.	GBP / Pence	924.50	+27.00	+3.01%	0	0.00 - 0.00		Jan 4
BT.A	GBP / Pence	982.00	+10.00	+1.03%	10,683,851	955.50 - 1008.00		4:26PM
GLXO	GBP / Pence	1728.00	-52.00	-2.92%	6,253,090	1728.00 - 1804.00		4:43PM
LLOY	GBP / Pence	768.50	-11.50	-1.47%	17,366,896	765.50 - 786.50		4:27PM
SB.	GBP / Pence	774.00	-6.50	-0.83%	10,472,672	767.50 - 788.00		4:27PM
SHEL	GBP / Pence	450.00	-3.50	-0.77%	25,404,517	446.50 - 477.50		4:28PM
UKX	GBP / Pence	6039.70	-73.70	-1.21%	0	6038.10 - 6131.60		4:25PM

Last updated: 14. Oktober 1999, 06: 57 PM—All data delayed at least 20 minutes

Quicken *(con't)*

http://www.quicken.co.uk/investment/portfolio

Choose a name for your portfolio and type it in the box alongside 'Portfolio Name'. In the Figure below, the portfolio has been named 'example'. Enter the stock codes of the investments you want to include in the portfolio such as 'dxns' for Dixons PLC.

Fig 3.42 *Choose a name for your portfolio, and enter the correct stock codes.*

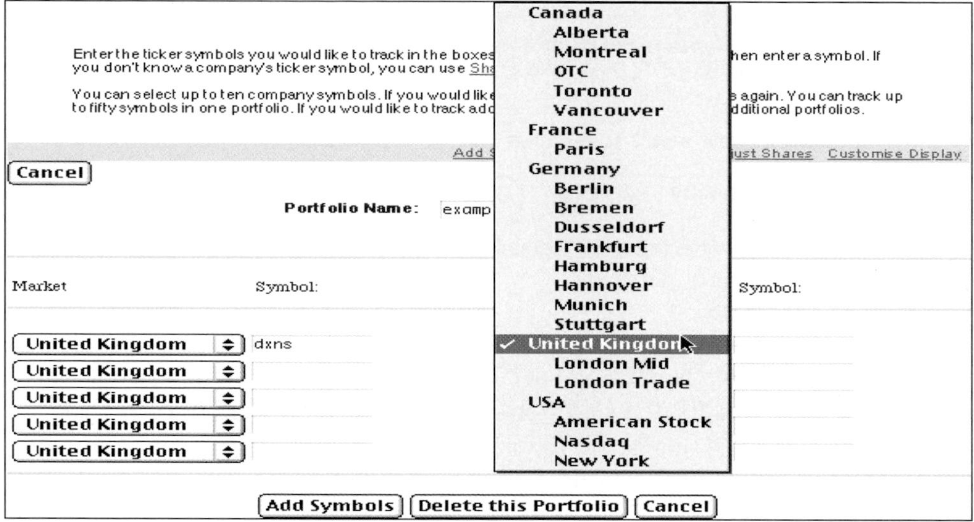

This free online portfolio service allows you to create customised portfolios which can consist of equities listed in Canada, France, Germany, UK and America. The 'default' portfolio setting displays the middle market price together with the percentage price change, trading volume and the day's price range.

Fig 3.43 *Portfolio initially displays mid price, % change, volume and the day's range.*

Create New Portfolio Update Prices View for Printing

example Hide Add Symbols Remove Symbols Adjust Shares Customise Display

Symbol	Currency	Current Price	Today's Change	% Change	Volume	Day Range	More Information	Time
DXNS	GBP / Pence	1064.00	+2.00	+0.19%	952,675	1054.00 - 1100.00		4:27PM

Last updated: 14. Oktober 1999, 06:58 PM – All data delayed at least 20 minutes

Quicken *(con't)*

http://www.quicken.co.uk/investment/portfolio

To add stocks to your portfolio click on 'Add Symbols' at the top of the screen. Portfolios can contain shares, investment trusts, warrants, gilts and certain overseas stocks.

Fig 3.44 *Portfolios can contain a variety of different types of stocks including gilts.*

Example Hide — Add Symbols Remove Symbols Adjust Shares Customise Display

Symbol	Current Price	Today's Change	% Change	Volume	Day Range	More Information	Time
DXNS	1349.00	+46.00	+3.53%	1,018,124	1302.00 - 1358.00		1:31PM
PRI	134.25	+1.25	+0.94%	27,997	132.50 - 134.25		1:22PM
T001	109.37	-0.03	-0.03%	46,467	109.37 - 109.39		10:24AM
FRANKT:BMW	661.00	+26.00	+4.09%	8,528	638.00 - 673.00		1:16PM

Clicking on 'Customize Display' in the top right hand corner of the Figure above gives access to four different 'Predefined Column Lists'. In the Figure below, the 'Default' option is displayed initially but this can be changed to either 'Holding Summary', 'Price Performance', 'Valuation' or 'Equity Fundamentals'.You also have the option to display up to 12 customised columns of data. Some data on the 'Custom Column List' is only available for US listed shares.

Fig 3.45 *Choose either a 'Predefined Column List' or design your own.*

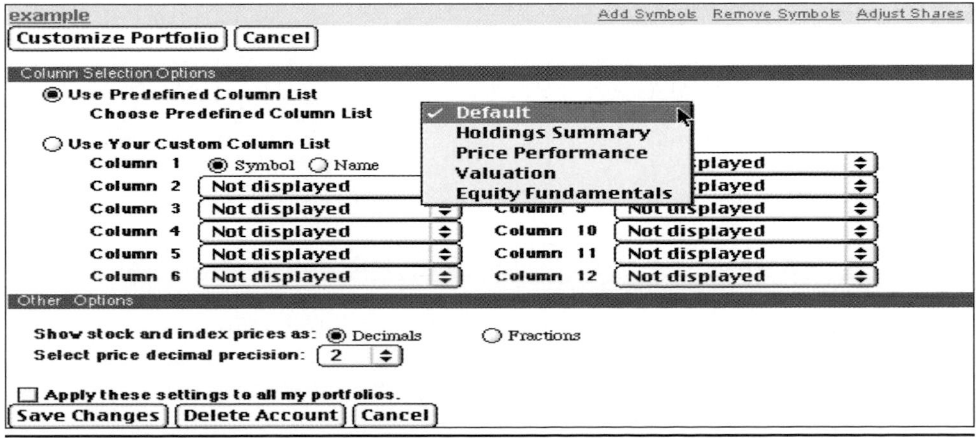

Quicken *(con't)*

http://www.quicken.co.uk/investment/portfolio

Choosing the 'Holdings Summary' in the 'Predefined Column List', displays additional information about the holdings in your portfolio. This includes the 'Average Purchase Price', 'Number of Shares' and 'Current Value'. The 'Trading Volume' and 'Day Range' are no longer displayed.

Fig 3.46 *Choosing the 'Holdings Summary' setting, gives a portfolio valuation.*

Example Hide — Add Symbols Remove Symbols Adjust Shares Customise Display

Symbol	Avg Purchase Price	Shares	Current Price	Today's Change	% Change	Current Value	Gain/Loss	More Information
DXNS	600.000	1,000.000	1349.00	+46.00	+3.53%	13,490.00	+7,490.00	
PRI	30.000	1,000.000	134.25	+1.25	+0.94%	1,342.50	+1,042.50	
T001	100.000	1,000.000	109.37	-0.03	-0.03%	1,093.70	+93.70	
Total					+3.06%	15,926.20	+8,626.20	

Choosing the 'Price Performance' in the Predefined Column List', displays most of the information in the 'Default' setting. In addition, the previous day's 'Closing Price' and the 'Opening Price' is also displayed. The day's 'High' and 'Low' price is actually the same as the 'Day Range' in the default setting.

Fig 3.47 *The 'Price Performance' setting, displays the 'Opening' and 'Closing' price.*

Example Hide — Add Symbols Remove Symbols Adjust Shares Customise Display

Symbol	Current Price	Time	Today's Change	% Change	Volume	Open	High	Low	Close	52 Week Low	52 Week High	More Information
DXNS	1349.00	1:31PM	+46.00	+3.53%	1,018,124	1313.00	1358.00	1302.00	1303.00			
PRI	134.25	1:22PM	+1.25	+0.94%	27,997	132.50	134.25	132.50	133.00			
T001	109.37	10:24AM	-0.03	-0.03%	46,467	109.39	109.39	109.37	109.40			
FRANKF:BMW	661.00	1:16PM	+26.00	+4.09%	8,528	638.00	673.00	638.00	635.00			

Quicken *(con't)*

http://www.quicken.co.uk/investment/portfolio

Choosing the 'Valuation' setting from the 'Predefined Column List' displays the same information as the 'Holdings Summary' except that 'Total Purchase Value' is shown instead of the price change.

Fig 3.48 *The 'Valuation' setting displays the 'Total Purchase Value' of each holding.*

Example Hide — Add Symbols Remove Symbols Adjust Shares Customise Display

Symbol	Avg Purchase Price	Shares	Current Price	Total Purchase Value	Current Value	Gain/Loss	More Information
DXNS	600.000	1,000.000	1349.00	6,000.00	13,490.00	+7,490.00	
PRI	30.000	1,000.000	134.25	300.00	1,342.50	+1,042.50	
T001	100.000	1,000.000	109.37	1,000.00	1,093.70	+93.70	
Total				7,300.00	15,926.20	+8,626.20	

The last setting in the 'Predefined Column List' is the 'Equity Fundamentals' setting which only displays any useful information for US listed shares.

Fig 3.49 *The 'Equity Fundamentals' setting is only useful for US equities.*

Example Hide — Add Symbols Remove Symbols Adjust Shares Customise Display

Symbol	Name	Market	P/E Ratio	Latest Dividend	52 Week Low	52 Week High	Ex-Dividend Date	Dividend Yield	More Information
DXNS	DXNS			0.00				0.00	
PRI	PRI			0.00				0.00	
T001	T001			0.00				0.00	

Last updated: 19. March 1999, 03:21 PM – All data delayed at least 20 minutes

There is an extensive list of share data which can be displayed using the 'Customized Column List' although much of it is only available for US listed equities.

Research Master

http://www.freeyellow.com/members5/scott2b/page6.html

If you have your own web site, it can be extremely useful to set up a custom made web page to display your portfolio. In this way you can include all the links to the sites you are interested in on one page. Ultimately this will save a lot of time and give you a much greater degree of flexibility. In the example below, many of the best sites described in this book have been included on the same web page for Dixons shares. When you click on one of the links in this page, you will go directly to the relevant information for Dixons shares. For example, clicking on the 'E*Trade' link, gives you the share price quote for Dixons straight away with you first having to enter the stock code.

Fig 3.5 *A custom made web page which allows you to display exactly what you want.*

RESEARCH MASTER

PORTFOLIO NAME: *ScottIT online*

Top gainers and losers
FT LEX | Tips in the weekend press
UK Market & Business News
Currency charts | Blomberg news

Company	Price Quotes	Charts	Company News in the UK and US	UK Bulletin Boards	Stock Monitor
Dixons [DXNS]	Real Time Schwab Market Eye Intraday	1yr with news 5yr vs FTSE Up to 10yrs Interactive 1yr	News Review | MM Telegraph | Reuter s AFX | Bloomberg Datastr eam and ICV	Market Eye Hemmington Scott UK Shares Fool UK	III Portfolio Technical Analysis Trustnet Portfolio Quicken Portfolio

You can include as many investments as you like on your web page, and have different links set up for different types of investment. You can also include general market data on the same page. For example, clicking on the 'UK Market & Business News' link, will display the day's business news headlines. Clicking on 'Portfolio Monitor' displays a portfolio of stocks set up using the 'III Interactive Investor' internet site described previously in this Chapter. Appendix C lists the computer code to create your own 'Research Master'.

News and Company Announcements

4

The financial news services available over the internet broadly fall into two categories - general news affecting markets and the economy, and stock specific news. There are many different news sources available, and you could spend hours trawling through them all. The news services highlighted here are some of the best FREE sites. Each site generally has a search facility which enables you to quickly find news items on specific stocks and themes.

Hot Links

✍ Latest up to date news story on a stock - *Market-Eye/ICV*
✔ Bloomberg's UK Business and Financial news - *Bloomberg*
✔ Reuters (via Yahoo) UK Business and company news - *Reuters/PA*
✍ AFX news stories - *Freequotes*
✔ News stories in the Daily Telegraph - *Daily Telegraph*
✔ CNN financial news with stock search facility - *CNN*
✔ News for UK stocks with an American (ADR) listing - *Quicken*
✔ News stories from the weekend press - *News Review*
✍ Lex Column and the Financial Times 30 day archive - *FT*
✔ List of all UK online newspapers - *RI Index*
✍ RNS and AFX news headlines - *E*Trade*

If you are trying to find news on a particular share, check Appendix A to see if that share is listed in America via an ADR. Sometimes American based internet sites give access to news stories which are almost impossible to obtain for free at a UK based internet site. You may see the suffix 'RNS' alongside some company announcements. RNS stands for 'Regulatory News Service' and most internet sites charge to access the full announcement. Some excellent sources of news have been omitted in the interests of brevity.

✍ *Indicates that Registration is necessary to access information at this site.*

Market-Eye

http://www.market-eye.co.uk/scripts/News.dll?SearchNews

The Market-Eye site will display the latest news headline on that day for a particular stock. The source of the news is Datastream/ICV, which tends to pick up most of the important company announcements. For this reason, it is a good place to access a news story that you might have to pay for elsewhere. When you initially enter the site via the address above, you are presented with a screen which offers a variety of options. If you don't know the correct stock code, then you can simply enter the name of the investment in the 'Symbol/Keyword' box, and click on 'Submit'. It is almost always quicker to enter the correct stock code rather than search by name. On some sites such as this one, you have to remember to change the 'Search Type' from 'Keyword' to 'Symbol'. To do this, click in the white circle to the right of the word 'Symbol'. Keep the 'Source' as 'All News' for the best results.

Fig 4.1 *A good place to search for and access a full news story for free.*

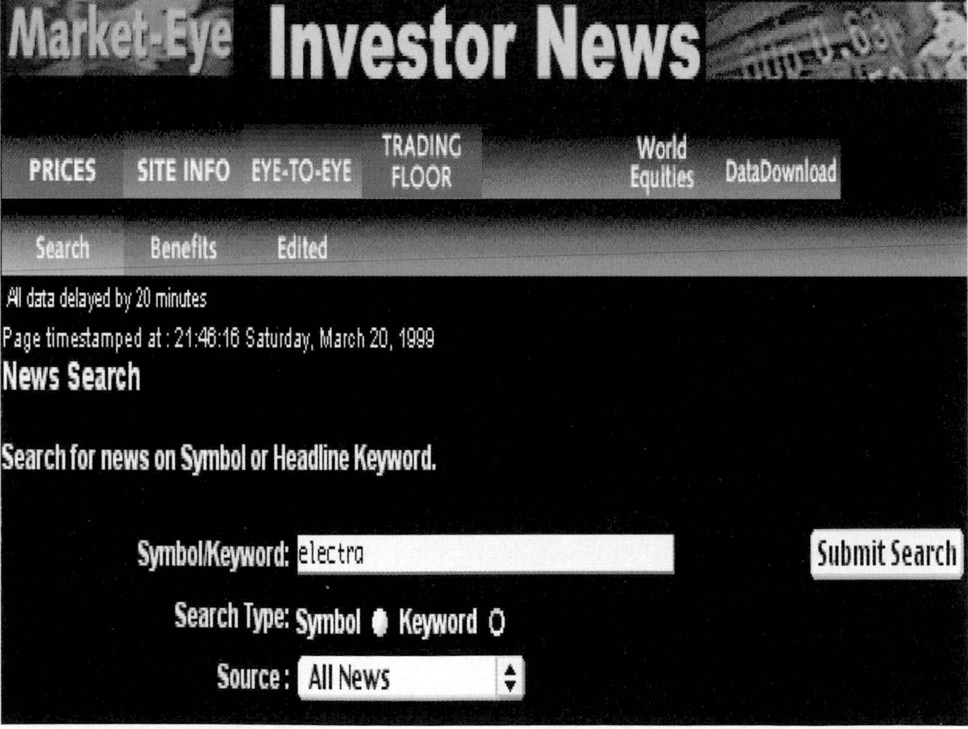

Market-Eye *(con't)*

http://www.market-eye.co.uk/scripts/News.dll?SearchNews

One of the big advantages of this particular search engine, is that it only tends to display relevant headlines. Some search engines display every single story which might contain the keyword you entered. The headlines have the date and time alongside them. To access the full story, simply click on the headline.

Fig 4.11 *This site displays very up to date news headlines.*

PRICES | SITE INFO | EYE-TO-EYE | TRADING FLOOR | World Equities | DataDownload

Search | Benefits | Edited

All data delayed by 20 minutes

Page timestamped at : 21:47:28 Saturday, March 20, 1999

Search result for keyword electra

Electra Inv Trust, 3i response to Electra	19/03/1999 17:53:50
Electra Inv Trust, Take no action on 3i bid	19/03/1999 12:55:19
Electra Inv.Trust, Offer by 3i Group	19/03/1999 08:33:09
Electra Inv.Trust, £1.25bn/725p offer by 3i	19/03/1999 08:16:11

On this site, you can only access free news stories on the day they appear. For example, if a company makes an announcement on a Tuesday, you would not be able to access that story for free on Wednesday. To get the best out of this site, use it in conjunction with other sites which display a comprehensive list of free headlines, but which have a charge to view the full story.

Fig 4.12 *You can access the full story for free by clicking on the headline.*

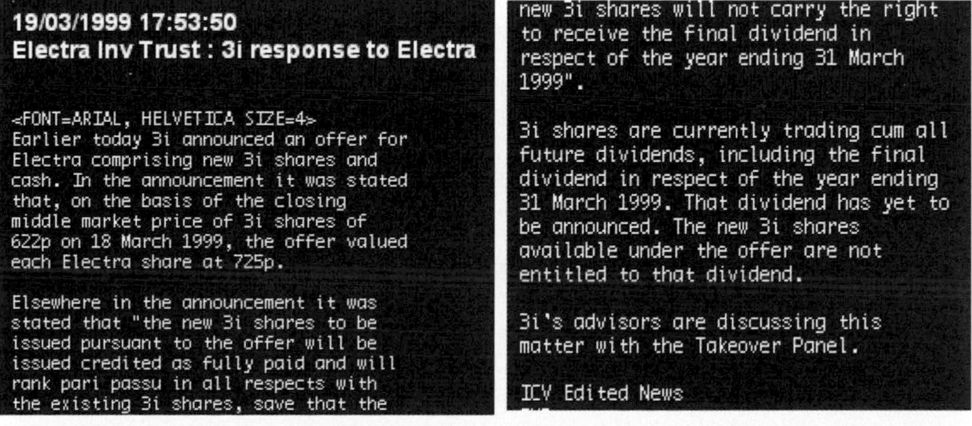

19/03/1999 17:53:50
Electra Inv Trust : 3i response to Electra

<FONT=ARIAL, HELVETICA SIZE=4>
Earlier today 3i announced an offer for Electra comprising new 3i shares and cash. In the announcement it was stated that, on the basis of the closing middle market price of 3i shares of 622p on 18 March 1999, the offer valued each Electra share at 725p.

Elsewhere in the announcement it was stated that "the new 3i shares to be issued pursuant to the offer will be issued credited as fully paid and will rank pari passu in all respects with the existing 3i shares, save that the new 3i shares will not carry the right to receive the final dividend in respect of the year ending 31 March 1999".

3i shares are currently trading cum all future dividends, including the final dividend in respect of the year ending 31 March 1999. That dividend has yet to be announced. The new 3i shares available under the offer are not entitled to that dividend.

3i's advisors are discussing this matter with the Takeover Panel.

ICV Edited News

Bloomberg

http://www.bloomberg.com/uk/markets/index.html

A good daily summary of how the main financial markets have performed is provided by Bloomberg. Charts of the FT-SE 100, Dow Jones and the Hang Seng indices, give a useful visual representation of how these markets have moved during the trading day. A summary of the main currency movements is shown, and from this page you can go directly to the Bloomberg Currency Calculator detailed in Chapter 1. The screen also displays the top six share gainers or losers at a given point during the trading day. Being aware of stocks which have risen or fallen sharply can be a good source of investment ideas.

Fig 4.2 *Bloomberg provides a good visual summary of the day's financial news.*

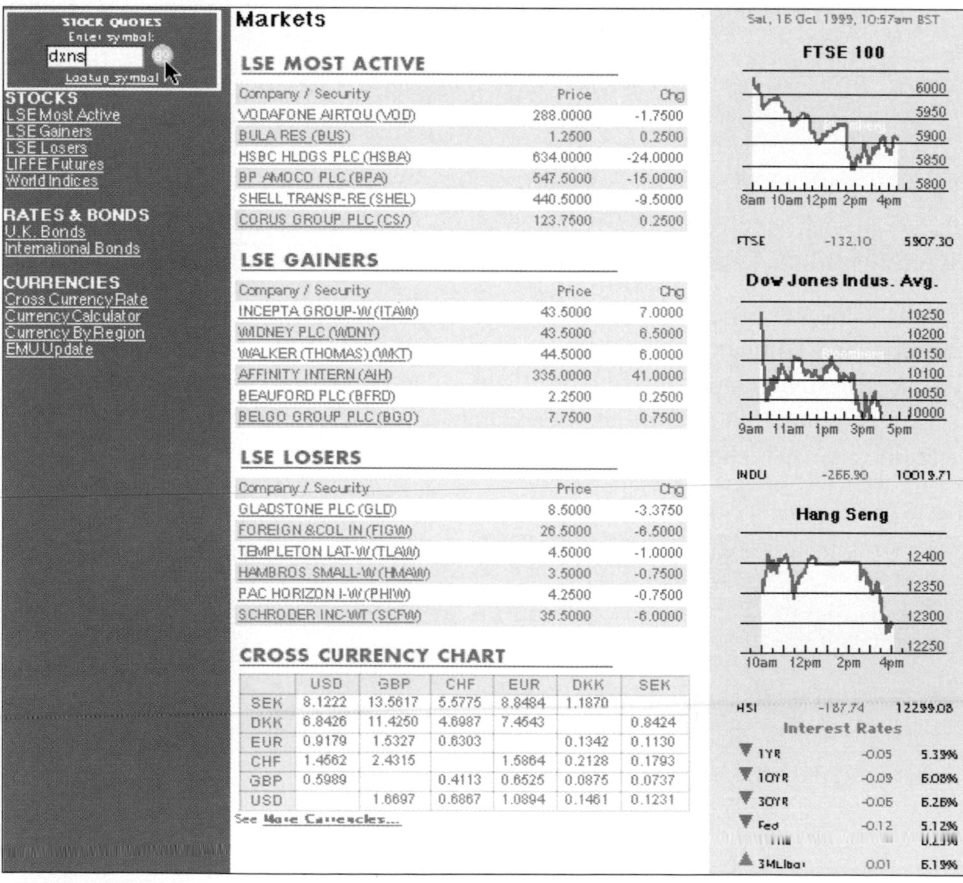

LSE MOST ACTIVE

Company / Security	Price	Chg
VODAFONE AIRTOU (VOD)	288.0000	-1.7500
BULA RES (BUS)	1.2500	0.2500
HSBC HLDGS PLC (HSBA)	634.0000	-24.0000
BP AMOCO PLC (BPA)	547.5000	-15.0000
SHELL TRANSP-RE (SHEL)	440.5000	-9.5000
CORUS GROUP PLC (CS/)	123.7500	0.2500

LSE GAINERS

Company / Security	Price	Chg
INCEPTA GROUP-W (ITAW)	43.5000	7.0000
WIDNEY PLC (WDNY)	43.5000	6.5000
WALKER (THOMAS) (WKT)	44.5000	6.0000
AFFINITY INTERN (AIH)	335.0000	41.0000
BEAUFORD PLC (BFRD)	2.2500	0.2500
BELGO GROUP PLC (BGO)	7.7500	0.7500

LSE LOSERS

Company / Security	Price	Chg
GLADSTONE PLC (GLD)	8.5000	-3.3750
FOREIGN &COL IN (FIGW)	26.5000	-6.5000
TEMPLETON LAT-W (TLAW)	4.5000	-1.0000
HAMBROS SMALL-W (HMAW)	3.5000	-0.7500
PAC HORIZON I-W (PHIW)	4.2500	-0.7500
SCHRODER INC-WT (SCFW)	35.5000	-6.0000

CROSS CURRENCY CHART

	USD	GBP	CHF	EUR	DKK	SEK
SEK	8.1222	13.5617	5.5775	8.8484	1.1870	
DKK	6.8426	11.4250	4.6987	7.4643		0.8424
EUR	0.9179	1.5327	0.6303		0.1342	0.1130
CHF	1.4562	2.4315		1.5864	0.2128	0.1793
GBP	0.5989		0.4113	0.6525	0.0875	0.0737
USD		1.6697	0.6867	1.0894	0.1461	0.1231

To access investment information on a specific stock, enter the correct stock code in the left hand column of the page, and click on 'go'.

Bloomberg *(con't)*

http://www.bloomberg.com/uk/markets/index.html

Fig 4.21 *Click on the stock symbol as shown to access up to date news stories.*

Click symbol for news, charts & more

DXNS Dixons Group

Last	Change	% Change	Bid / Ask	Hi / Low	Open	Vol
1035.0000	-29.0000	-2.73	1033.0000 / 1035.0000	1129.0000 / 1007.0000	1129.0000	1883869

Last Trade: 10/15 16:30

Fig 4.22 *Bloomberg gives free access to a comprehensive list of recent news stories.*

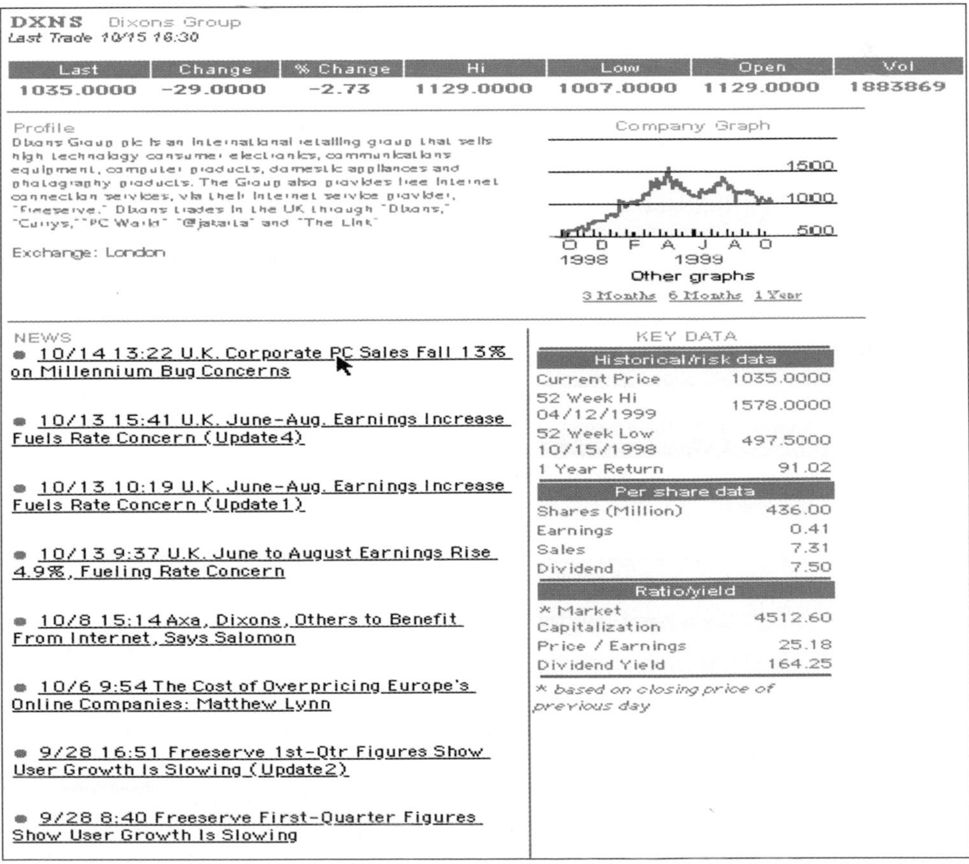

The full news story can be displayed by clicking on the appropriate headline. This page also displays useful share data including the '52 Week High and Low Price', '1 Year Return' and the 'Market Capitalization'. The only minor drawback of an otherwise excellent site is the small size of the graph.

Yahoo

http://www.yahoo.co.uk/headlines/business

Yahoo provides one of the best sites for up to date general UK business and financial news. This service is one of the few that gives free access to full news stories from Reuters and the Press Association (PA). The 'Business' section of this site, displays a list of the recent business news headlines relating to UK shares, together with a brief summary of the story .

Fig 4.3 *Up to date Business news stories from Reuters and the Press Association.*

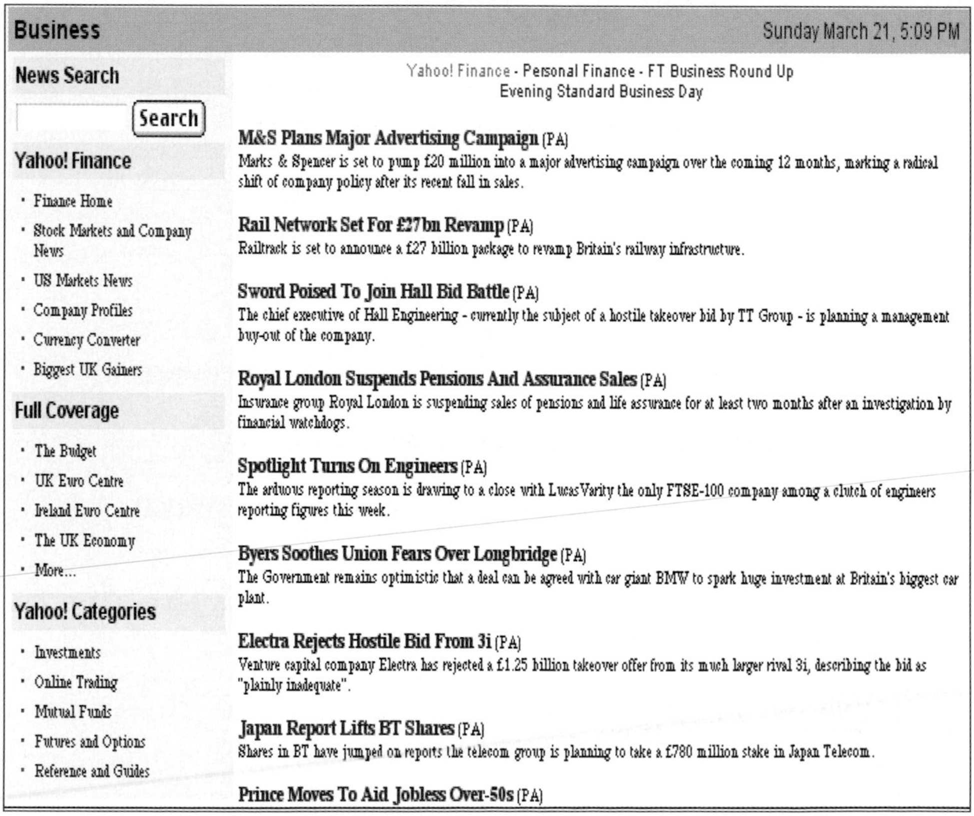

Business Sunday March 21, 5:09 PM

News Search

Search

Yahoo! Finance

- Finance Home
- Stock Markets and Company News
- US Markets News
- Company Profiles
- Currency Converter
- Biggest UK Gainers

Full Coverage

- The Budget
- UK Euro Centre
- Ireland Euro Centre
- The UK Economy
- More...

Yahoo! Categories

- Investments
- Online Trading
- Mutual Funds
- Futures and Options
- Reference and Guides

Yahoo! Finance - Personal Finance - FT Business Round Up
Evening Standard Business Day

M&S Plans Major Advertising Campaign (PA)
Marks & Spencer is set to pump £20 million into a major advertising campaign over the coming 12 months, marking a radical shift of company policy after its recent fall in sales.

Rail Network Set For £27bn Revamp (PA)
Railtrack is set to announce a £27 billion package to revamp Britain's railway infrastructure.

Sword Poised To Join Hall Bid Battle (PA)
The chief executive of Hall Engineering - currently the subject of a hostile takeover bid by TT Group - is planning a management buy-out of the company.

Royal London Suspends Pensions And Assurance Sales (PA)
Insurance group Royal London is suspending sales of pensions and life assurance for at least two months after an investigation by financial watchdogs.

Spotlight Turns On Engineers (PA)
The arduous reporting season is drawing to a close with LucasVarity the only FTSE-100 company among a clutch of engineers reporting figures this week.

Byers Soothes Union Fears Over Longbridge (PA)
The Government remains optimistic that a deal can be agreed with car giant BMW to spark huge investment at Britain's biggest car plant.

Electra Rejects Hostile Bid From 3i (PA)
Venture capital company Electra has rejected a £1.25 billion takeover offer from its much larger rival 3i, describing the bid as "plainly inadequate".

Japan Report Lifts BT Shares (PA)
Shares in BT have jumped on reports the telecom group is planning to take a £780 million stake in Japan Telecom.

Prince Moves To Aid Jobless Over-50s (PA)

The full story can be accessed by clicking on the relevant news headline. At the bottom of the page you can click on the day's 'Earlier Stories', or if desired, view the business headlines from the previous two weeks. From this page you can also search for news on a specific stock. To do this, enter the appropriate name in the 'News Search' box in the top left hand corner of the screen above, and click on 'Search'.

Yahoo *(con't)*

http://www.yahoo.co.uk/headlines/business

When you enter the name of a stock such as 'Dixons', a list of headlines which contain the word 'Dixons' will be displayed. Unfortunately, many of the stories will not be related to the company 'Dixons'. The search does not seem to pick up all the relevant stories for a given investment, and generally, better results are obtained on other sites for stock specific news searches.

Fig 4.31 *Many unrelated news stories are displayed with this search engine.*

Yahoo! UK & Ireland Headline Matches (1 - 5 of 5)

Supermarket bites at price of computers
PC launch comes as high street computer prices are being investigated by the Office of Fair Trading
-Mar 16 1:25 PM

Zimbabwe paper says U.S. suspects not tortured
HARARE, March 19 - Government-employed doctors who examined three Americans held in Zimbabwe on terrorism, sabotage and espionage charges say they saw no evidence that they were tortured, the official Herald newspaper reported on Friday.
-Mar 19 9:55 AM

Assembly Chiefs Lead Wave Of Condemnation
CHURCH leaders, politicians and community leaders have all added their voices to a chorus of condemnation across Northern Ireland following the murder of Rosemary Nelson
-Mar 16 2:48 PM

Keep peace process going, urges Blair
By Colin Brown, Chief Political Correspondent
-Mar 16 3:40 AM

Car bomb attack kills mother of three
A leading woman civil rights lawyer died in hospital today after losing both her legs when a terrorist bomb ripped her car apart in Northern Ireland.
-Mar 15 5:01 PM

The full news story can be accessed by clicking on the appropriate headline. At the top of the page, you will be able to see the original source of the story. In the example below, this was 'The Scotsman' newspaper.

Fig 4.32 *The full story can be accessed by clicking on the appropriate headline.*

Yahoo! The Scotsman **Headlines**

Tuesday March 16, 1:24 PM

Supermarket bites at price of computers

TWO of the United Kingdom's leading supermarket chains yesterday stepped up the pressure on the high street by launching own-brand personal computers and plans to sell cut-price mopeds.

Asda said it was challenging "overpriced" electrical retailers with its range of own-brand PCs and Tesco revealed it is planning to sell cut-price scooters as part of campaign against alleged monopoly trading byretailers.

More than half of Asda's 226 stores, including 24 in Scotland, will now stock the PC, which the supermarket chain claims is up to £200 cheaper than the equivalent brands on sale in the high street.

Tesco will begin selling thousands of the 50cc mopeds, bought on the so-called grey market in the Far East, from June.

The Fun 50 scooters will cost £1,200, including delivery,licence plates, road tax, registration and an introductory driving session. The supermarket claims the deal will save shoppers about £600.

Tesco's announcement follows a ban on grey market imports which come from outside the European Union without manufacturers' consent. The supermarket aims to capitalise on the burgeoning popularity of scooters in the UK, which last year saw sales soar by 84 per cent.

Asda's PC launch comes as high street computer prices are being investigated by the Office of Fair Trading.

Earlier this year Intel, the world's biggest computer chip manufacturer, accused Dixons of driving down PC sales in the UK by charging "ridiculous margins".

While Dixons denies the allegation, there is considerable evidence that PC prices are generally higher in the UK than abroad.

A recent study showed equivalent PCs cost about a third less in the United States and Germany. A home computer priced at £1,125 in the UK costs £748 in the US and £741 in Germany.

The Asda Targa Pro 400 computer, priced at £599, is manufactured in the UK and has a colour monitor, software and a modem for internet access.

Yahoo *(con't)*

http://uk.biz.yahoo.com/news.html

Differentiating between the various news services on this site, can be quite an ordeal. Clicking on 'Stock Markets and Company News' in the left hand column of the page (under 'Yahoo! Finance' in Figure 4.3), displays a list of international news headlines. These are specifically related to individual investments and stock markets. There is a brief summary of the story behind the headline, which makes it easier to decide whether its worth spending time downloading and reading the full story.

Fig 4.33 *International Business News Headlines can be accessed at this site.*

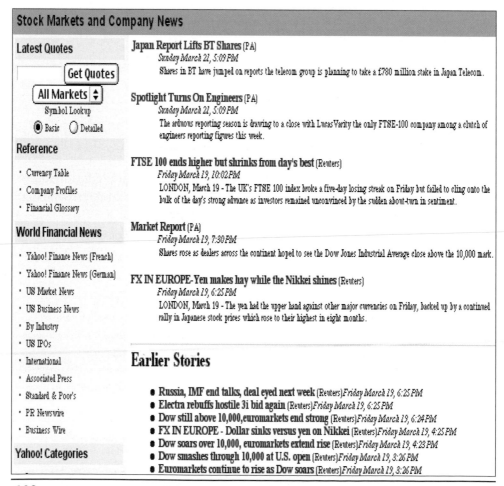

Stock Markets and Company News

Latest Quotes

Get Quotes

All Markets

Symbol Lookup

Basic Detailed

Reference

- Currency Table
- Company Profiles
- Financial Glossary

World Financial News

- Yahoo! Finance News (French)
- Yahoo! Finance News (German)
- US Market News
- US Business News
- By Industry
- US IPOs
- International
- Associated Press
- Standard & Poor's
- PR Newswire
- Business Wire

Yahoo! Categories

Japan Report Lifts BT Shares (PA)
Sunday March 21, 5:09 PM
Shares in BT have jumped on reports the telecom group is planning to take a £780 million stake in Japan Telecom.

Spotlight Turns On Engineers (PA)
Sunday March 21, 5:09 PM
The arduous reporting season is drawing to a close with LucasVarity the only FTSE-100 company among a clutch of engineers reporting figures this week.

FTSE 100 ends higher but shrinks from day's best (Reuters)
Friday March 19, 10:02 PM
LONDON, March 19 - The UK's FTSE 100 index broke a five-day losing streak on Friday but failed to cling onto the bulk of the day's strong advance as investors remained unconvinced by the sudden about-turn in sentiment.

Market Report (PA)
Friday March 19, 7:30 PM
Shares rose as dealers across the continent hoped to see the Dow Jones Industrial Average close above the 10,000 mark.

FX IN EUROPE-Yen makes hay while the Nikkei shines (Reuters)
Friday March 19, 6:25 PM
LONDON, March 19 - The yen had the upper hand against other major currencies on Friday, backed up by a continued rally in Japanese stock prices which rose to their highest in eight months.

Earlier Stories

- **Russia, IMF end talks, deal eyed next week** (Reuters) *Friday March 19, 6:25 PM*
- **Electra rebuffs hostile 3i bid again** (Reuters) *Friday March 19, 6:25 PM*
- **Dow still above 10,000,euromarkets end strong** (Reuters) *Friday March 19, 6:24 PM*
- **FX IN EUROPE - Dollar sinks versus yen on Nikkei** (Reuters) *Friday March 19, 4:25 PM*
- **Dow soars over 10,000, euromarkets extend rise** (Reuters) *Friday March 19, 4:23 PM*
- **Dow smashes through 10,000 at U.S. open** (Reuters) *Friday March 19, 3:26 PM*
- **Euromarkets continue to rise as Dow soars** (Reuters) *Friday March 19, 3:26 PM*

Freequotes

http://www.freequotes.co.uk/axl-dlls/frameset.tpl

This is a relatively new internet site which gives free access to real time quotes and AFX news stories. The AFX news service is a financial news wire compiled by FT journalists and is used by analysts and traders in the City.

Fig 4.4 *Enter a 'Stock Code', click on 'Select' and scroll down to 'News'.*

The most recent news stories appear automatically when you release the mouse button. If there is just one news story in the last week, the full story will appear on the screen immediately. In the example below, there have been several announcements, and in order to display the full story, you need to click on the appropriate headline as shown below.

Fig 4.41 *A list of recent announcements is displayed for Prolific Income PLC.*

Please select a headline to view an article
Hits from 09/10/1999 to 16/10/1999
(Displaying matches 1 to 3 of 3)

Date	Time	Service	Headline	Priority
15/10/1999	16:55:04	AFR	Prolific Income PLC - Net Asset Value	3
14/10/1999	15:57:12	AFR	Prolific Income PLC - Net Asset Value	3
13/10/1999	17:19:24	AFR	Prolific Income PLC - Net Asset Value	3

Freequotes *(con't)*

http://www.freequotes.co.uk/axl-dlls/frameset.tpl

Several investment trust companies (such as Prolific Income PLC) calculate their net asset value daily. The figure is released to the stock market via the AFX and RNS news services. Most net asset value figures you see published in the press or on the internet are estimates. Sometimes there can be quite a large difference between the estimated figures and the actual figure which can lead to sudden price movements. This is one of the few internet sites which enables you to access the actual net asset value figures for certain investment trusts for free. Most internet sites charge a monthly subscription fee to access full AFX news stories and announcements.

Fig 4.42 *The full announcement can be accessed for free at this internet site.*

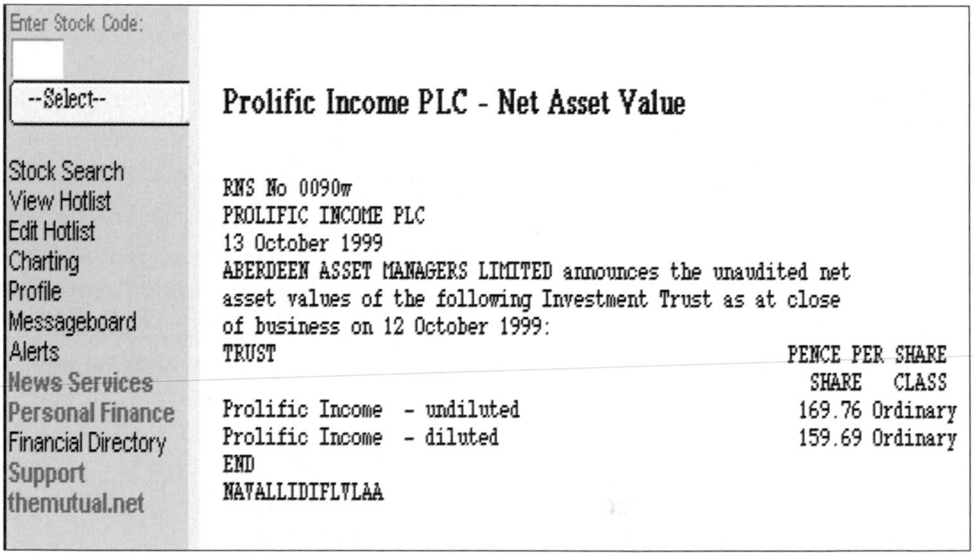

Enter Stock Code:

--Select--

Stock Search
View Hotlist
Edit Hotlist
Charting
Profile
Messageboard
Alerts
News Services
Personal Finance
Financial Directory
Support
themutual.net

Prolific Income PLC - Net Asset Value

RNS No 0090w
PROLIFIC INCOME PLC
13 October 1999
ABERDEEN ASSET MANAGERS LIMITED announces the unaudited net asset values of the following Investment Trust as at close of business on 12 October 1999:

TRUST	PENCE PER SHARE	SHARE CLASS
Prolific Income - undiluted	169.76	Ordinary
Prolific Income - diluted	159.69	Ordinary

END
NAVALLIDIFLVLAA

At the time of writing, the 'Freequotes' internet site was very much under development and in the process of being modified. This site also gives free access to an unlimited number of real time price quote. There is an online portfolio service which is quite useful as it has direct access to real time news and price quotes and a basic charting function. Unfortunately, the online portfolio only works with Netscape if you are using a Macintosh computer.

Daily Telegraph

http://www.telegraph.co.uk/ixcity.html

The Daily Telegraph has a particularly good Business Section and an excellent internet site. The search facility on this page is very comprehensive which ultimately reduces the time taken to find a particular story. You can confine your search to certain sections of the paper (eg Business Section), and to a particular time period or a specific date. The news archive of a daily newspaper is potentially huge, so it saves time if the search engine allows you to be specific. To access a particular story, simply click on the relevant headline.

Fig 4.5 *The Business news headlines for that day are displayed when you enter the site.*

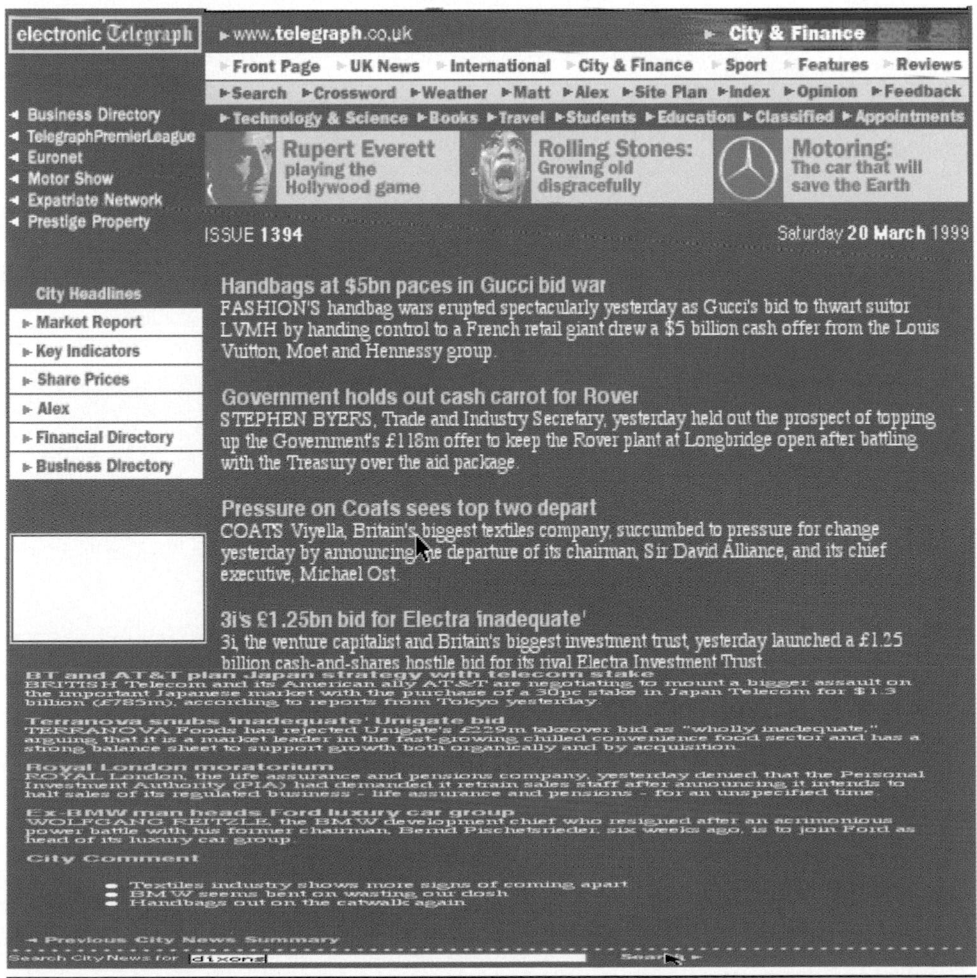

electronic Telegraph ▸ www.telegraph.co.uk ▸ City & Finance

▸ Front Page ▸ UK News ▸ International ▸ City & Finance ▸ Sport ▸ Features ▸ Reviews

▸ Search ▸ Crossword ▸ Weather ▸ Matt ▸ Alex ▸ Site Plan ▸ Index ▸ Opinion ▸ Feedback

▸ Technology & Science ▸ Books ▸ Travel ▸ Students ▸ Education ▸ Classified ▸ Appointments

◂ Business Directory
◂ TelegraphPremierLeague
◂ Euronet
◂ Motor Show
◂ Expatriate Network
◂ Prestige Property

Rupert Everett playing the Hollywood game

Rolling Stones: Growing old disgracefully

Motoring: The car that will save the Earth

ISSUE 1394 — Saturday 20 March 1999

City Headlines
▸ Market Report
▸ Key Indicators
▸ Share Prices
▸ Alex
▸ Financial Directory
▸ Business Directory

Handbags at $5bn paces in Gucci bid war
FASHION'S handbag wars erupted spectacularly yesterday as Gucci's bid to thwart suitor LVMH by handing control to a French retail giant drew a $5 billion cash offer from the Louis Vuitton, Moet and Hennessy group.

Government holds out cash carrot for Rover
STEPHEN BYERS, Trade and Industry Secretary, yesterday held out the prospect of topping up the Government's £118m offer to keep the Rover plant at Longbridge open after battling with the Treasury over the aid package.

Pressure on Coats sees top two depart
COATS Viyella, Britain's biggest textiles company, succumbed to pressure for change yesterday by announcing the departure of its chairman, Sir David Alliance, and its chief executive, Michael Ost.

3i's £1.25bn bid for Electra inadequate'
3i, the venture capitalist and Britain's biggest investment trust, yesterday launched a £1.25 billion cash-and-shares hostile bid for its rival Electra Investment Trust.

BT and AT&T plan Japan strategy with telecom stake
BRITISH Telecom and its American ally AT&T are negotiating to mount a bigger assault on the important Japanese market with the purchase of a 30pc stake in Japan Telecom for $1.3 billion (£785m), according to reports from Tokyo yesterday.

Terranova snubs 'inadequate' Unigate bid
TERRANOVA Foods has rejected Unigate's £229m takeover bid as "wholly inadequate," arguing that it is a market leader in the fast-growing chilled convenience food sector and has a strong balance sheet to support growth both organically and by acquisition.

Royal London moratorium
ROYAL London, the life assurance and pensions company, yesterday denied that the Personal Investment Authority (PIA) had demanded it retrain sales staff after announcing it intends to halt sales of its regulated business - life assurance and pensions - for an unspecified time.

Ex-BMW man heads Ford luxury car group
WOLFGANG REITZLE, the BMW development chief who resigned after an acrimonious power battle with his former chairman, Bernd Pischetsrieder, six weeks ago, is to join Ford as head of its luxury car group.

City Comment

- Textiles industry shows more signs of coming apart
- BMW seems bent on wasting our dosh
- Handbags out on the catwalk again

◂ Previous City News Summary

Search City News for dixons Search ▸

Daily Telegraph *(con't)*

http://www.telegraph.co.uk/ixcity.html

You can also use this site to get specific news headlines on a particular stock. Enter the name of a company (eg dixons), in the search box at the bottom of the page. The page will display the recent news headlines for 'dixons'. Once again you can limit your search to specific time periods. The full story can be accessed simply by clicking on the relevant headline.

Fig 4.51 *The search engine is excellent and enables you to search for specific articles.*

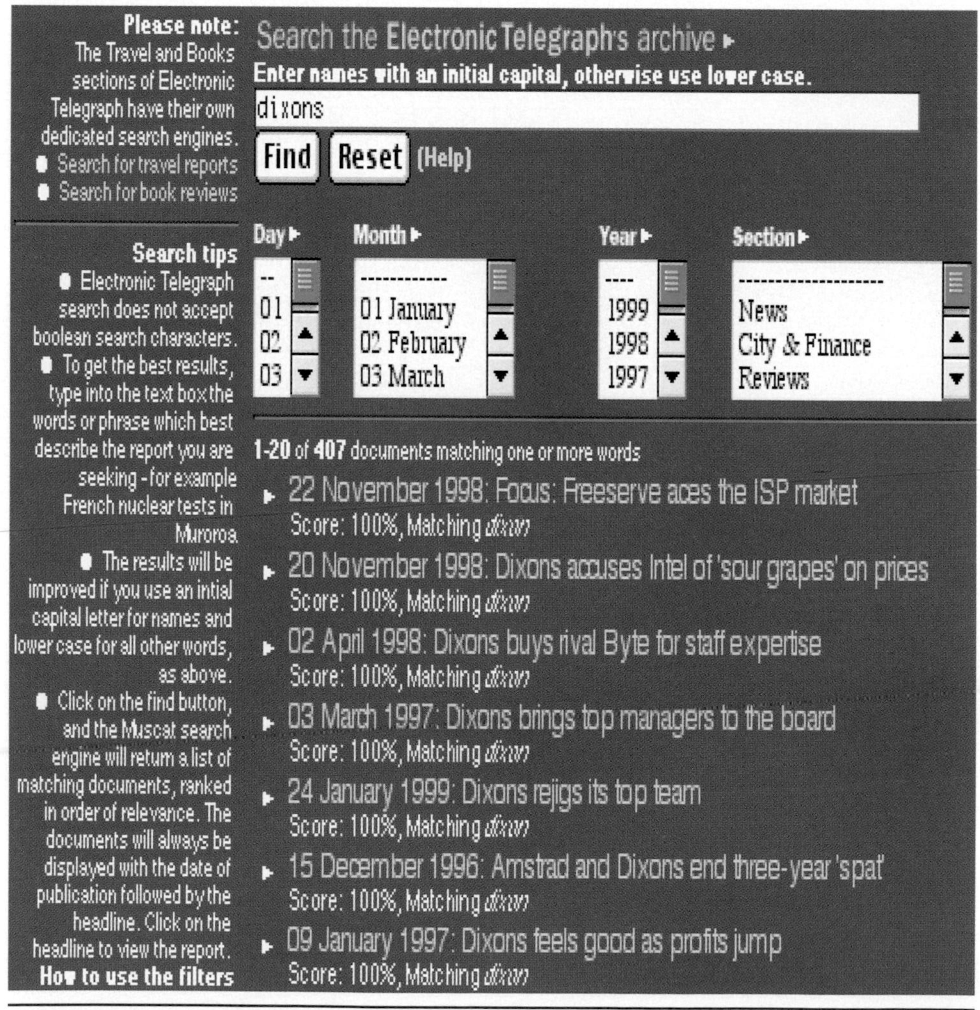

CNN

http://search.cnnfn.com/

This is an American based site which will sometimes have useful news stories on UK based companies. Enter the name of the company you are interested in and click on 'seek'.

Fig 4.6 *It is sometimes worth checking to see whether CNN have a particular story.*

There is a summary of the full story accompanying the headline which is useful. The full story can be accessed by clicking on the relevant headline. Sometimes the full story contains reams of text and it is not always easy to find where the reference to the stock you are searching for appears.

Fig 4.61 *An extensive list, but often important company announcements are omitted.*

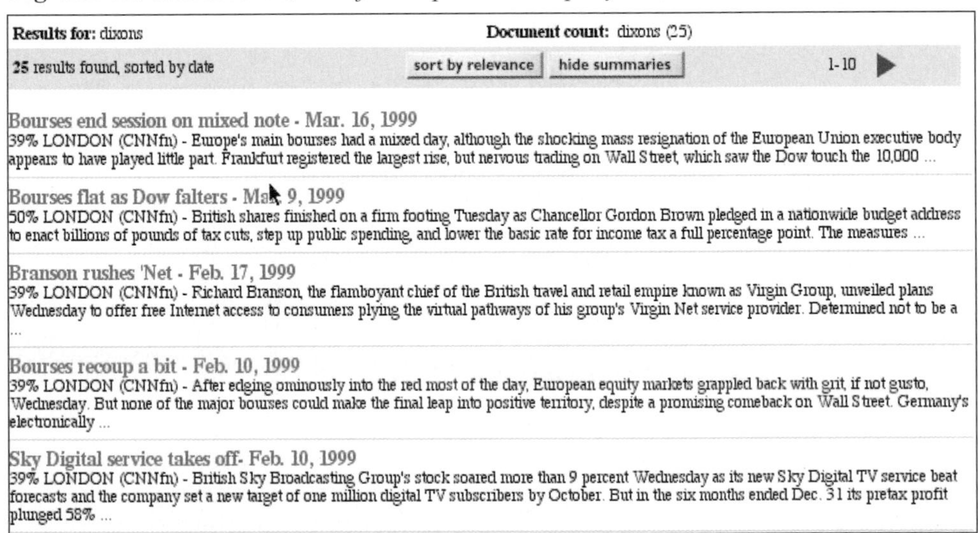

Quicken

http://www.quicken.com:80/investments/news

This is a US based web site which can be a good source of news for UK stocks listed in America via an ADR. A full list of UK stocks with ADR's is given in Appendix A. You can save time by entering the stock symbol directly. Make sure you have selected 'Headline News' in the box to the right of the 'Symbol' box. Click on 'Go' to display the news headlines for that stock.

Fig 4.7 *You can save time, by looking up the stock symbol and entering it directly.*

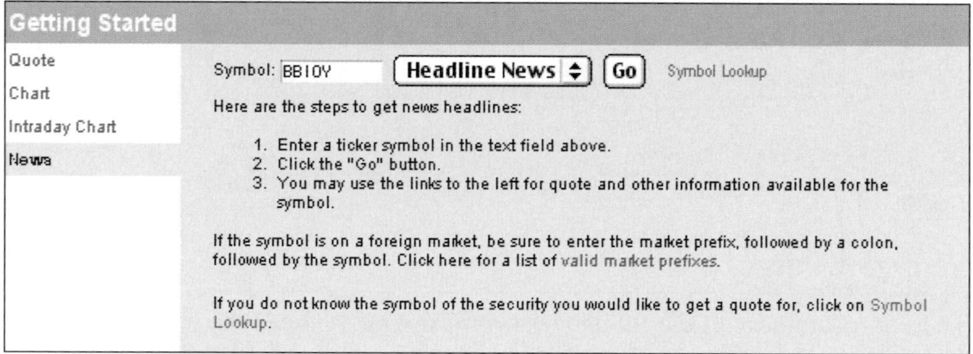

US based web sites tend to offer more comprehensive free facilities than their UK counterparts. On this site, you can click on the 'Article Archive' icon in the left hand column, and display a whole host of additional stories and articles. Most of these publications would be very difficult to get hold of in the UK, and would, for the most part, certainly not be available free as they are on this site.

Fig 4.71 *Up to date headlines with the back to front date format used in America.*

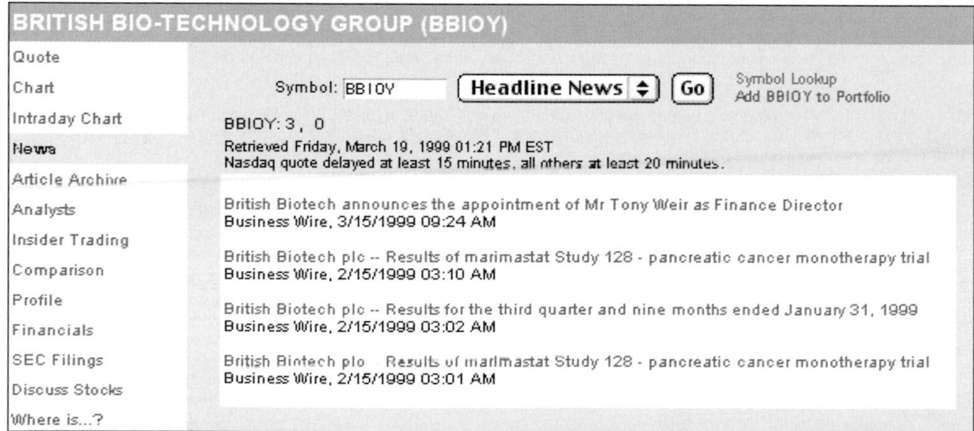

Quicken *(con't)*

http://www.quicken.com:80/investments/news

A novel feature of this site is the ability to automatically e-mail a given news story to a friend. This could be useful if you knew somebody was interested in a stock, but not necessarily monitoring it as closely as you were.

Fig 4.72 *You can automatically e-mail News stories from this site to a friend.*

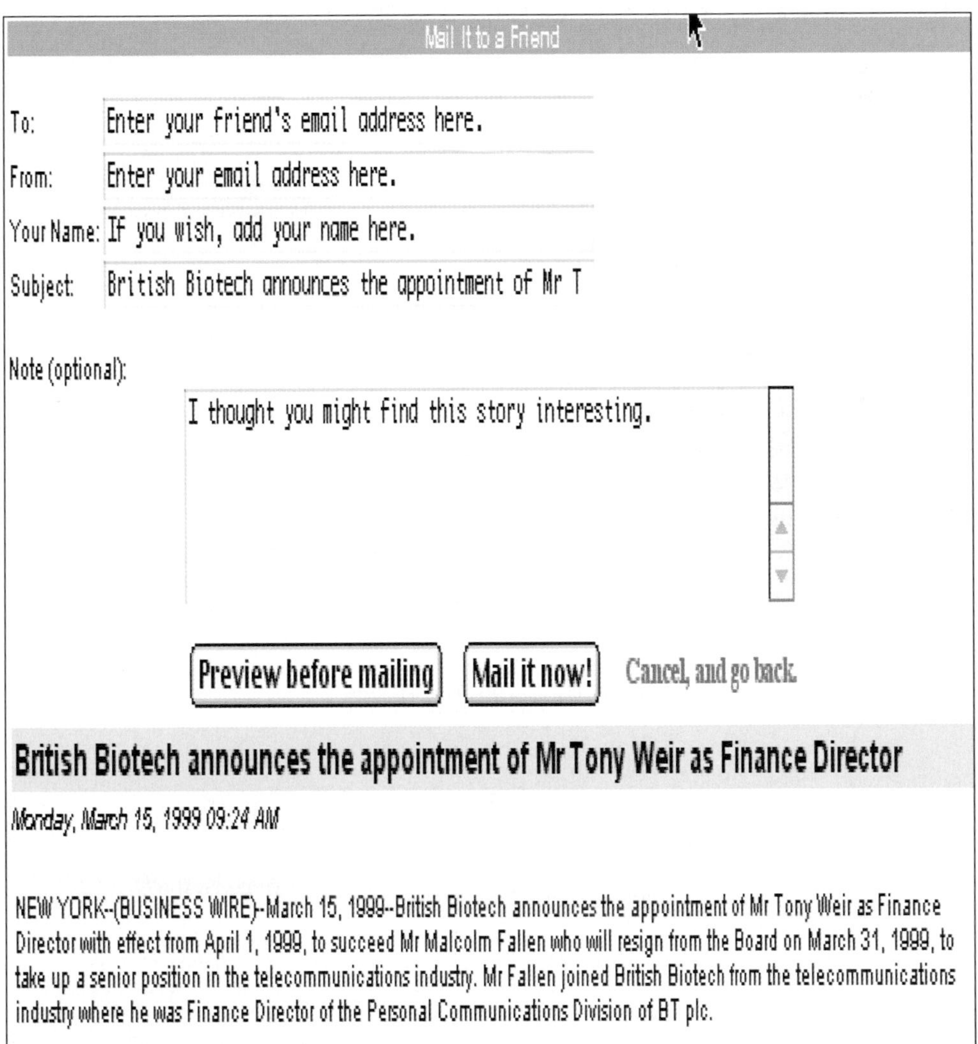

British Biotech announces the appointment of Mr Tony Weir as Finance Director

Monday, March 15, 1999 09:24 AM

NEW YORK--(BUSINESS WIRE)--March 15, 1999--British Biotech announces the appointment of Mr Tony Weir as Finance Director with effect from April 1, 1999, to succeed Mr Malcolm Fallen who will resign from the Board on March 31, 1999, to take up a senior position in the telecommunications industry. Mr Fallen joined British Biotech from the telecommunications industry where he was Finance Director of the Personal Communications Division of BT plc.

News Review

http://www.news-review.co.uk/reg/home.html

This site allows you to search the weekend papers for stories on a particular stock. You can choose to search over specific time periods if you know when an article appeared.

Fig 4.8 *An excellent site for searching all the Sunday Newspapers.*

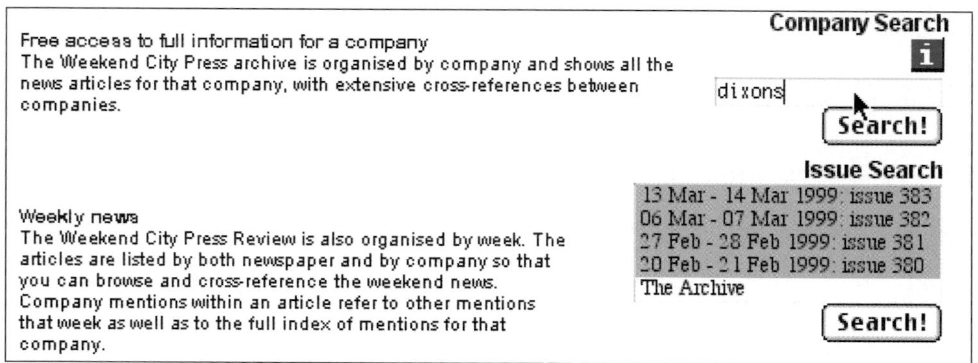

Once you have entered a company name in the search box and clicked on 'Search', the screen will display how many articles have been found, and the date of the most recent article. A useful feature of this search facility, is that if you enter a word like 'dixons' for example, you will only get a list of stories related to companies with the word 'dixons' in them. Many search engines will return a list of news articles with the word 'dixons' in them, some of which may not be relevant.

Fig 4.81 *The search only produces a list of companies with the chosen word in them.*

Companies matching 'dixons'

Company	Articles	Most Recent
Dixons Group PLC	227	13 Mar - 14 Mar 1999
Dixon Motors PLC	21	13 Feb - 14 Feb 1999
Dixon Motors PLC		

News Review *(con't)*

http://www.news-review.co.uk/reg/home.html

You can display a list of headlines for the company you are interested in, by clicking on the relevant company name. The same page will also display a company profile supplied by Hemmington Scott.

Fig 4.82 *A company profile from Hemmington Scott is shown alongside the headlines.*

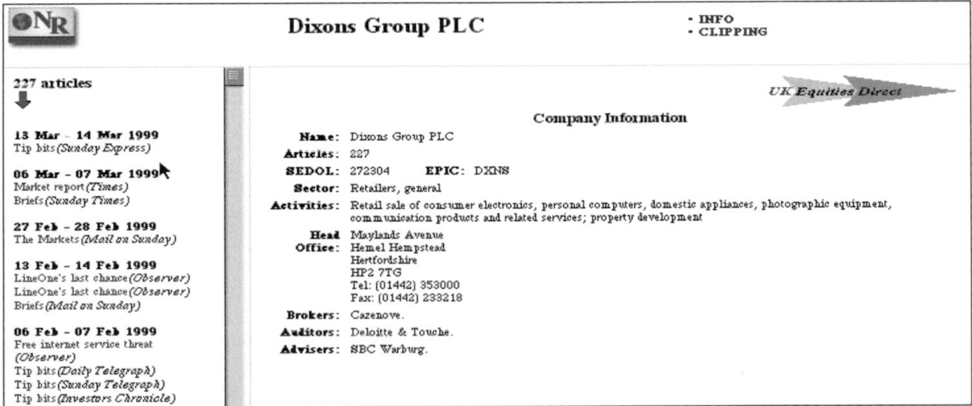

The full story can be accessed for free simply by clicking on the appropriate headline. A particularly good feature of this search engine, is that it highlights the word you are searching for in the article. With long general articles, it can sometimes be frustrating to have to read a whole article, only to find that the reference to the stock you are interested in is not really that relevant.

Fig 4.83 *The company you are looking for is highlighted in red.*

Tip bits

BUY: Polypipe, 136.5p, which is on the acquisition trail and has seen profits forecasts rise.

Geest, 383.5p, which is out of bananas and should see profits around £28m from its growing chilled food business.

WSP, 185.5p, the engineering consultancy with a full order book and an acquisition strategy.

Granada, 1332.5p, where strong trading and disposals will free cash for strategic acquisitions.

HOLD: Dixons, 1334.5p, which should benefit from the computer-friendly budget but is looking toppy.

Financial Times - Lex column

http://www.ft.com/hippocampus/lex.htm

The Lex column on the back page of the Financial Times, is one of the most widely read columns in the business and financial community. The column appears daily during the week, and usually contains a useful insight into a diverse range of subjects. There are generally four or five topics covered, and to access a full story, you simply need to click on the appropriate headline. You can also access the Lex column for the previous few days from this internet page. The exact internet address for this page is scheduled to change so try http://www.ft.com if you experience any problems.

Fig 4.9 *The Lex column is one of the most widely read in the UK business community.*

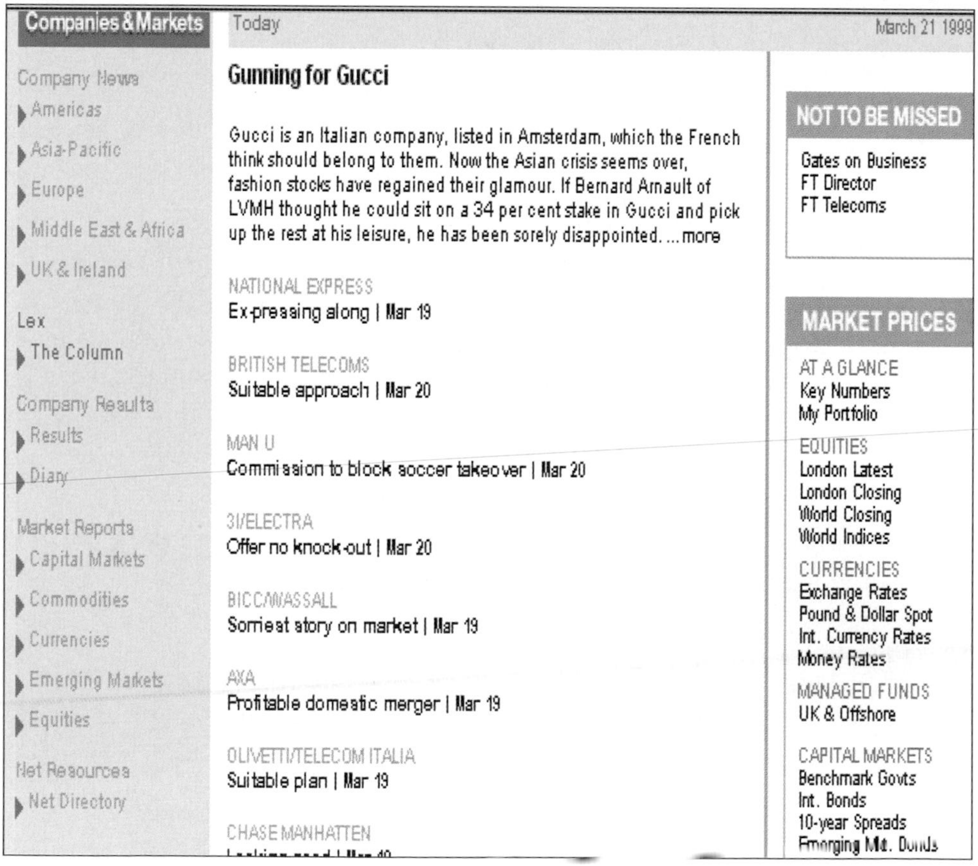

Companies & Markets

Company News
- Americas
- Asia-Pacific
- Europe
- Middle East & Africa
- UK & Ireland

Lex
- The Column

Company Results
- Results
- Diary

Market Reports
- Capital Markets
- Commodities
- Currencies
- Emerging Markets
- Equities

Net Resources
- Net Directory

Today — March 21 1999

Gunning for Gucci

Gucci is an Italian company, listed in Amsterdam, which the French think should belong to them. Now the Asian crisis seems over, fashion stocks have regained their glamour. If Bernard Arnault of LVMH thought he could sit on a 34 per cent stake in Gucci and pick up the rest at his leisure, he has been sorely disappointed. ...more

NATIONAL EXPRESS
Ex-pressing along | Mar 19

BRITISH TELECOMS
Suitable approach | Mar 20

MAN U
Commission to block soccer takeover | Mar 20

3I/ELECTRA
Offer no knock-out | Mar 20

BICC/WASSALL
Sorriest story on market | Mar 19

AXA
Profitable domestic merger | Mar 19

OLIVETTI/TELECOM ITALIA
Suitable plan | Mar 19

CHASE MANHATTEN

NOT TO BE MISSED
- Gates on Business
- FT Director
- FT Telecoms

MARKET PRICES

AT A GLANCE
- Key Numbers
- My Portfolio

EQUITIES
- London Latest
- London Closing
- World Closing
- World Indices

CURRENCIES
- Exchange Rates
- Pound & Dollar Spot
- Int. Currency Rates
- Money Rates

MANAGED FUNDS
- UK & Offshore

CAPITAL MARKETS
- Benchmark Govts
- Int. Bonds
- 10-year Spreads
- Emerging Mkt. Bonds

The Financial Times site is huge and you could literally spend hours exploring all the various online pages.

Financial Times -Lex *(con't)*

http://www.ft.com/hippocampus/lex.htm

At the bottom of the Lex page you can enter the name of a company (eg dixons), to search the FT 30 day archive for stories containing that word.

Fig 4.91 *More up to date news stories can often be found on other internet sites.*

Search Results

Your query "dixons" matched 24 documents out of 4586.

1 - 10 of 24 documents found.

Article Title	Score
February 24 1999: BUSINESS: Freeserve hooks window shoppers	0.93
February 15 1999: DIXONS: Freeserve float considered	0.92
February 16 1999: INTERNET: Providers poised for overhaul	0.82
WEB REVOLUTION: Brave few take the plunge	0.82
February 25 1999: ELECTRONICS BOUTIQUE: Talks with Game proceed	0.80
February 17 1999: RETAIL: Taking stock of better service	0.80
February 10 1999: BSkyB links with AOL as interim profits halve	0.80
July 2 1997: Market reaction: Sterling hits five-year high	0.78
March 4 1999: TELECOM ITALIA: Non-voting Olivetti shares for shareholders	0.78
March 4 1999: OLIVETTI: Chinese boxes may hold key	0.78

The Financial Times web site is well laid out and allows you to easily access other online pages. The information you can access at this site tends to be quite detailed and specific. Sometimes investors will be better served buying the actual newspaper, rather than spending time and money browsing online. There are some features that you won't get in the newspaper such as the 'Analysts Estimates' link which enables you to get a feel for how a share is viewed in the market. This feature is outlined in Chapter 6 which covers Research.

Research Index

http://www.thedataindex.co.uk/research/newspaper.htm

This is a particularly useful site as it gives access to most of the online newspapers in the UK. There is also a search engine on this site which will carry out a comprehensive search of all these newspapers. If your English is a little rusty, you can switch to one of five other European languages by clicking on the appropriate flag.

Fig 4.10.0 *A very useful site giving access to a whole host of online publications.*

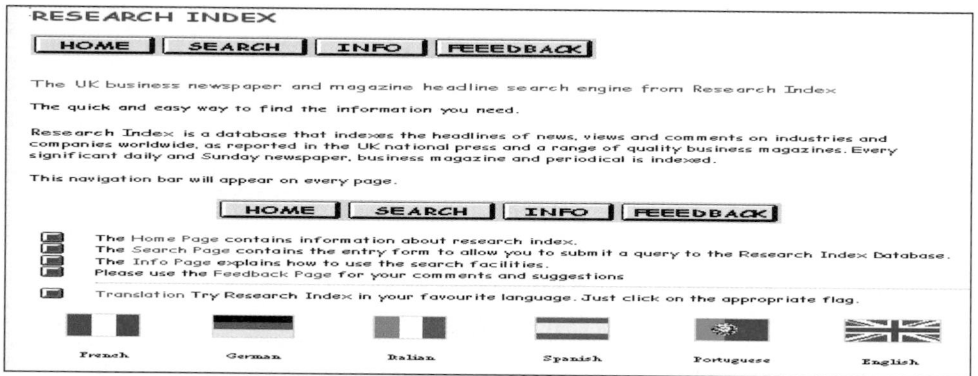

To search the site, you need to click on the 'Search' icon at the top of the page. You can either search by 'Company' (eg Dixons) or by 'Industry' (eg electrical retailers). A useful feature is the ability to decide whether to enact a search where your chosen word appears at the 'Start of Text' or in the 'Body of Text'. When you have made your selection, click on 'Start Search' in the Figure below.

Fig 4.10.1 *When you have made your selection, click on 'Start Search'.*

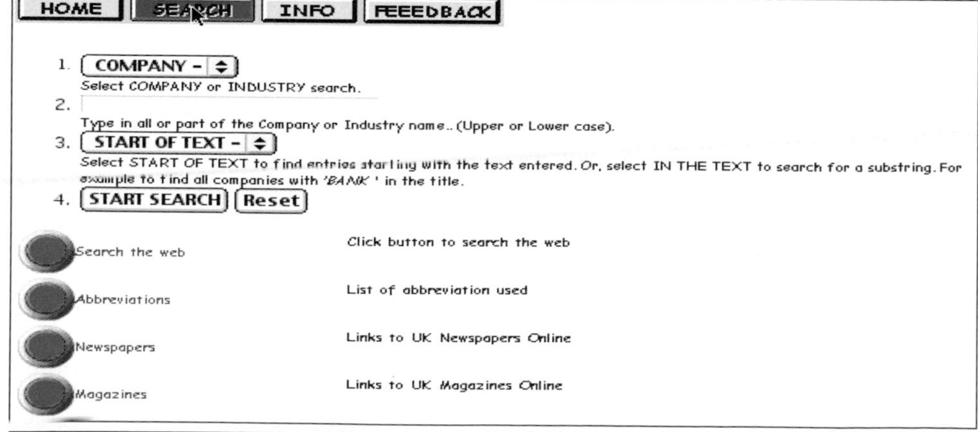

Research Index *(con't)*

http://www.thedataindex.co.uk/research/newspaper.htm

The page which appears after clicking on the 'Start Search' icon summarises your search criteria and displays the total number of entries found. The list of news headlines can be displayed by clicking on the red button below the flags.

Fig 4.10.2 *Initially a summary of the search results is displayed.*

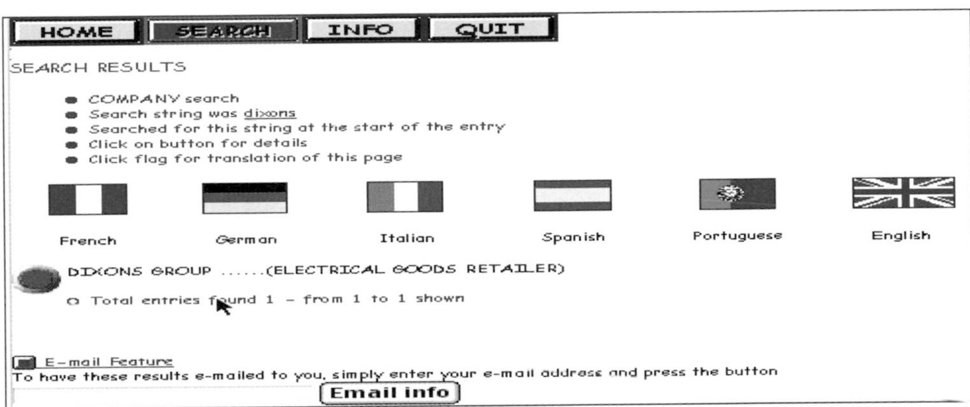

A search on this site produces a detailed set of news headlines from most newspapers in the UK. Only news stories pertaining to the company 'Dixons' are displayed as opposed to every article which contains the word 'dixons'. Unfortunately you can't access the full news stories directly from this page.

Fig 4.10.3 *The search produces a comprehensive list of relevant news headlines.*

DIXONS GROUP ......(ELECTRICAL GOODS RETAILER)

- 07-MAR-99 DIXONS 'CLEARED OF OVERCHARGING' (S. TIMES p:B3.2)
- 26-FEB-99 GERMAN NET LINK-UP SENDS DIXONS SOARING (TIMES p:34)
- 26-FEB-99 DIFFICULTIES WITH DIXONS' INTERNET PHENOMENON (INVEST. CHR. p:22)
- 25-FEB-99 DIXON'S INTERNET LINK WITH BERTELSMANN (SCOTSMAN p:25)
- 25-FEB-99 ONLINE LIFT FOR DIXONS (TIMES p:30)
- 25-FEB-99 DIXONS NETS BIG GAINS (F.T. p:56)
- 15-FEB-99 DIXONS MAY CONSIDER FLOATING INTERNET SERVICE (F.T. p:21)
- 14-FEB-99 FASTER NET PROFITS ON LINE FOR DIXONS (MAIL ON SUNDAY p:FM:7)
- 02-FEB-99 DIXONS STEPS UP BATTLE WITH TESCO ON THE NET (INDEPENDENT p:14)
- 28-JAN-99 ROOM AT THE TOP AFTER DIXONS REJIG (MARKTG. WK. p:6)
- 28-JAN-99 THE DANGER OF FOLLOWING DIXONS INTO FREE ISP (MARKTG. WK. p:36)
- 26-JAN-99 DIXONS OVERHAULS ITS STRUCTURE TO REFLECT BUSINESS CHANGES (W.S.J.E. p:14)
- 26-JAN-99 FREESERVE RESTRUCTURE (TIMES p:28)
- 26-JAN-99 DIXONS ANNOUNCES COMPANY SHAKE-UP (TELEGRAPH p:29)
- 26-JAN-99 DIXONS TURNS FOCUS ON CURRYS (SCOTSMAN p:22)
- 26-JAN-99 DIXONS MAY FLOAT INTERNET SERVICE (D. EXPRESS p:51)
- 24-JAN-99 REJIGS ITS TOP TEAM (S. TELEGRAPH p:B;3)
- 19-JAN-99 DIXONS NET FINDS A FRESH MARKET (TELEGRAPH p:31)
- 17-JAN-99 INTERNET IS NO FREE RIDE FOR DIXONS, THE RETAILER (OBSERVER p:B6)
- 15-JAN-99 WITH FOCUS ON FREESERVE, SHARES JUMP 9.8% (W.S.J.E. p:3)
- 15-JAN-99 COMPANY RESULTS (INVEST. CHR. p:70)
- 01-JAN-99 475,000 NEW USERS IN 6 WEEKS (REVOLUTION p:31)
- 12-DEC-98 DIXONS SOARS IN CYBERSPACE (TELEGRAPH p:B2)
- 11-DEC-98 ICL TOYS WITH DIXON'S REGAINED BLUE-CHIP STATUS (INVEST. CHR. p:9)
- 06-DEC-98 DIXONS HITS BACK OVER PRICING WAR (MAIL ON SUNDAY p:FM:5)
- 03-DEC-98 DIXONS IN THE DOCK (MARKTG. WK. p:26*)

Total entries found 104 - from 1 to 26 shown

Research Index *(con't)*

http://www.thedataindex.co.uk/research/newspaper.htm

Fig 4.10.4 *Clicking on the 'Newspapers' icon in Figure 4.10.1 lists online newspapers.*

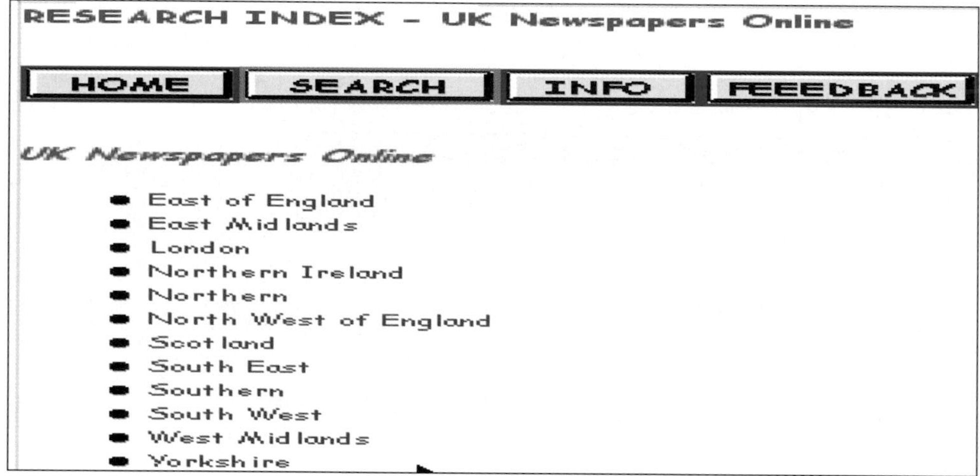

Fig 4.10.5 *Click on a region to see the list of online newspapers in that area.*

Newspapers - London

- Financial Mail on Sunday - London
- Financial Times - London
- Hampstead & Highgate Express - London
- London Evening Standard - London
- Newsquest London Newspapers - London
- The Daily Mail - London
- The Daily Telegraph - London
- The Guardian / Observer - London
- The Guardian Weekly - London
- The Independent - London
- The Mirror - London
- The Times - London
- Weekend City Press Review - London

The online newspapers can be accessed directly from this site by clicking on the relevant newspaper title.

Research Index *(con't)*

http://www.thedataindex.co.uk/research/newspaper.htm

Fig 4.10.6 *The 'Electronic Telegraph' can be accessed directly from 'Research Index'*

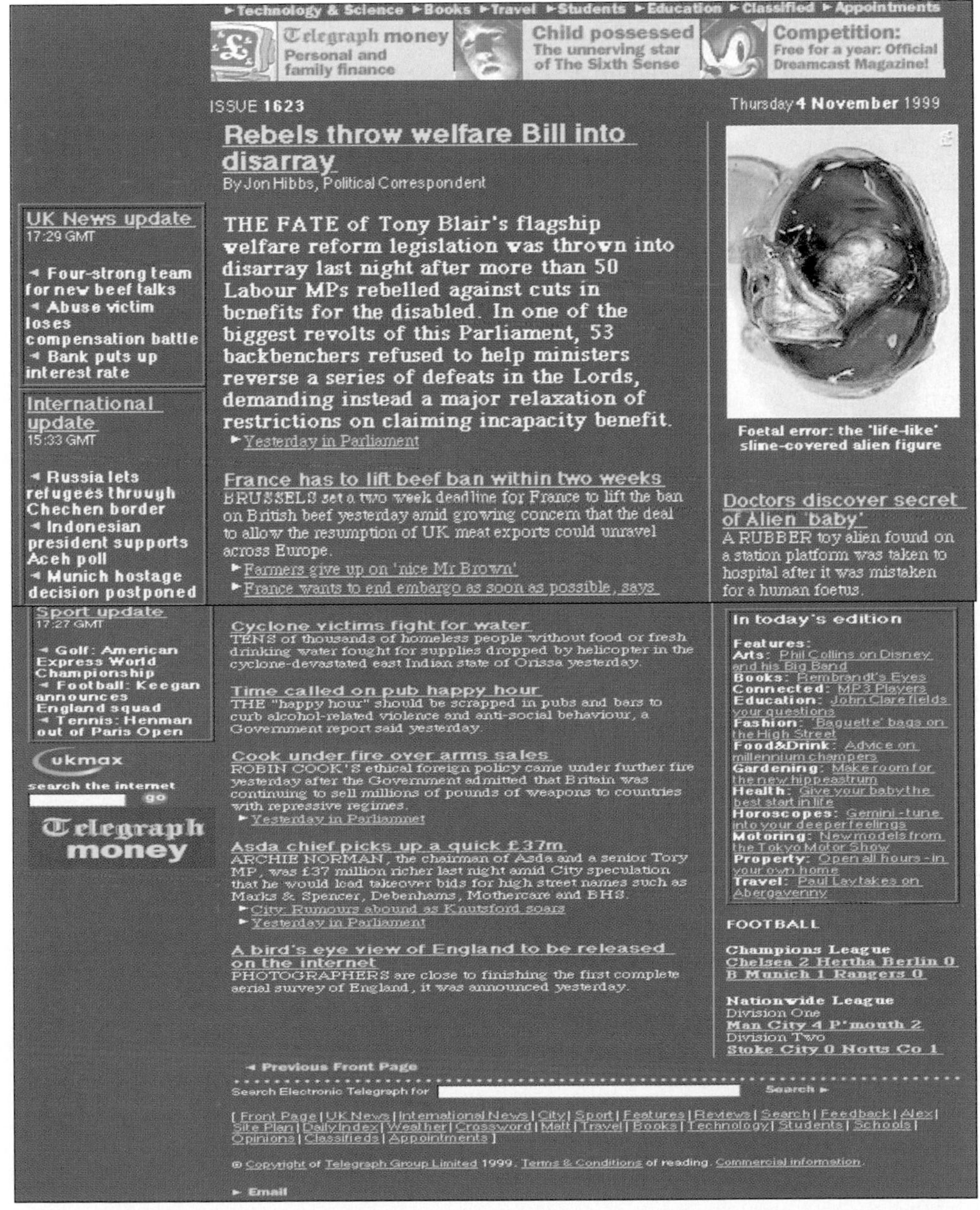

▸Technology & Science ▸Books ▸Travel ▸Students ▸Education ▸Classified ▸Appointments

Telegraph money
Personal and family finance

Child possessed
The unnerving star of The Sixth Sense

Competition:
Free for a year: Official Dreamcast Magazine!

ISSUE **1623**

Thursday **4 November** 1999

Rebels throw welfare Bill into disarray

By Jon Hibbs, Political Correspondent

THE FATE of Tony Blair's flagship welfare reform legislation was thrown into disarray last night after more than 50 Labour MPs rebelled against cuts in benefits for the disabled. In one of the biggest revolts of this Parliament, 53 backbenchers refused to help ministers reverse a series of defeats in the Lords, demanding instead a major relaxation of restrictions on claiming incapacity benefit.

▸ Yesterday in Parliament

France has to lift beef ban within two weeks
BRUSSELS set a two week deadline for France to lift the ban on British beef yesterday amid growing concern that the deal to allow the resumption of UK meat exports could unravel across Europe.

▸ Farmers give up on 'nice Mr Brown'
▸ France wants to end embargo as soon as possible, says

UK News update
17:29 GMT

◂ Four-strong team for new beef talks
◂ Abuse victim loses compensation battle
◂ Bank puts up interest rate

International update
15:33 GMT

◂ Russia lets refugees through Chechen border
◂ Indonesian president supports Aceh poll
◂ Munich hostage decision postponed

Sport update
17:27 GMT

◂ Golf: American Express World Championship
◂ Football: Keegan announces England squad
◂ Tennis: Henman out of Paris Open

ukmax
search the internet
go

Telegraph money

Foetal error: the 'life-like' slime-covered alien figure

Doctors discover secret of Alien 'baby'
A RUBBER toy alien found on a station platform was taken to hospital after it was mistaken for a human foetus.

Cyclone victims fight for water
TENS of thousands of homeless people without food or fresh drinking water fought for supplies dropped by helicopter in the cyclone-devastated east Indian state of Orissa yesterday.

Time called on pub happy hour
THE "happy hour" should be scrapped in pubs and bars to curb alcohol-related violence and anti-social behaviour, a Government report said yesterday.

Cook under fire over arms sales
ROBIN COOK'S ethical foreign policy came under further fire yesterday after the Government admitted that Britain was continuing to sell millions of pounds of weapons to countries with repressive regimes.
▸ Yesterday in Parliamnet

Asda chief picks up a quick £37m
ARCHIE NORMAN, the chairman of Asda and a senior Tory MP, was £37 million richer last night amid City speculation that he would lead takeover bids for high street names such as Marks & Spencer, Debenhams, Mothercare and BHS.
▸ City: Rumours abound as Knutsford soars
▸ Yesterday in Parliament

A bird's eye view of England to be released on the internet
PHOTOGRAPHERS are close to finishing the first complete aerial survey of England, it was announced yesterday.

In today's edition

Features:
Arts: Phil Collins on Disney and his Big Band
Books: Rembrandt's Eyes
Connected: MP3 Players
Education: John Clare fields your questions
Fashion: 'Baguette' bags on the High Street
Food&Drink: Advice on millennium champers
Gardening: Make room for the new hippeastrum
Health: Give your baby the best start in life
Horoscopes: Gemini - tune into your deeper feelings
Motoring: New models from the Tokyo Motor Show
Property: Open all hours - in your own home
Travel: Paul Lay takes on Abergavenny

FOOTBALL

Champions League
Chelsea 2 Hertha Berlin 0
B Munich 1 Rangers 0

Nationwide League
Division One
Man City 4 P'mouth 2
Division Two
Stoke City 0 Notts Co 1

◂ Previous Front Page

Search Electronic Telegraph for Search ▸

[Front Page | UK News | International News | City | Sport | Features | Reviews | Search | Feedback | Alex | Site Plan | Daily Index | Weather | Crossword | Matt | Travel | Books | Technology | Students | Schools | Opinions | Classifieds | Appointments]

© Copyright of Telegraph Group Limited 1999. Terms & Conditions of reading. Commercial information.

▸ Email

E*Trade

http://research.etrade.co.uk/free/qq.cgi

This site enables you to display a comprehensive list of news headlines for a stock. The news comes from AFX and RNS which are the two premier sources of business news. To access news headlines for a specific stock, you need to change the heading in the menu box from 'quick quote' to 'news archive' as shown below.

Fig 4.12.0 *Change the heading to 'news archive', enter a stock code and click on 'GO'.*

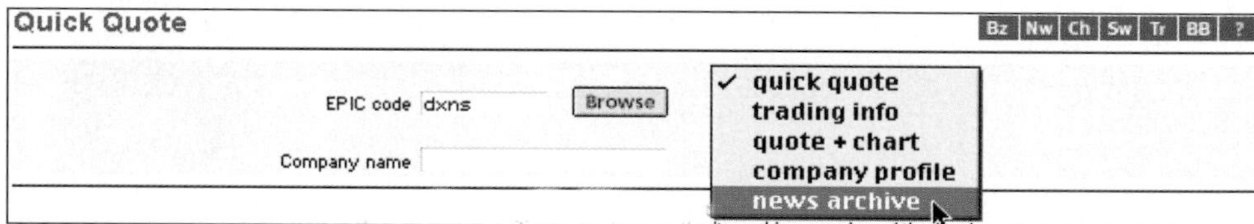

This site has an excellent feature which enables you to display specific categories of news as shown below. For example, instead of simply displaying 'all news for this company' you could change the menu setting to one of the other five settings such as 'earnings and dividends'.

Fig 4.12.1 *You can choose which category of headlines you wish to display.*

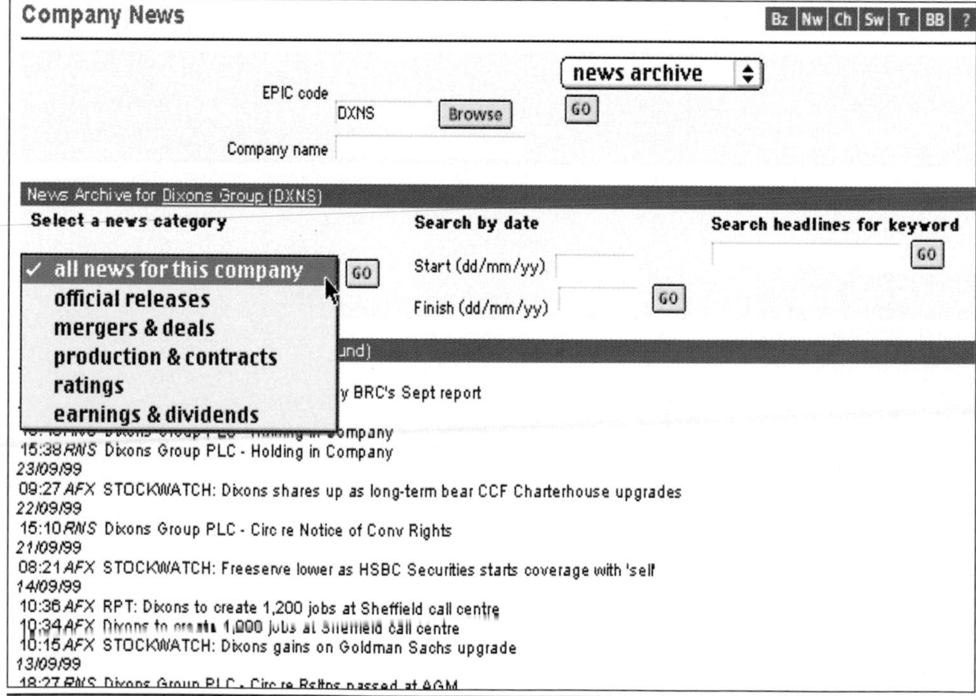

E*Trade *(con't)*

http://research.etrade.co.uk/free/qq.cgi

A particularly good feature of the news function at this site, is the ability to search the headlines for a specific word. The example below displays the results of searching the Dixons headlines for the word 'Freeserve'. You could use this function to search for very specific news headlines using such words as 'dividend' or 'chairman' etc. You can also use the search function to look for a headline made between specific dates.

Fig 4.12.2 *A comprehensive list of news headlines is displayed for Freeserve PLC.*

Search results for "freeserve". (62 stories found)

21/09/99
08:21 AFX STOCKWATCH: Freeserve lower as HSBC Securities starts coverage with 'sell'
24/08/99
09:18 AFX STOCKWATCH: Freeserve ease as Goldman Sachs sets downside price target of 200p
29/07/99
09:07 AFX CSFB exercises over-allotment option on Freeserve shares
26/07/99
17:48 AFX ROUNDUP: Freeserve shares surge to 37 pct premium on first day of trading
15:04 AFX Freeserve -- 2 (ADS' open at 32-1/4 usd)
14:35 AFX Freeserve shares open at 220 pence in huge volume
11:10 AFX STOCKWATCH: Freeserve rated 'sell' by Credit Lyonnais; worth 1 stg
09:52 AFX STOCKWATCH: Dixons' Freeserve shares seen opening up to 50 pct higher
08:07 AFX Dixons says Freeserve flotation price 150p/shr; unit valued at 1.51 bln stg
07:31 RNS Dixons Group PLC - Freeserve Flotation Shr.Price
25/07/99
18:32 AFX Freeserve issue reportedly 20 times oversubscribed
23/07/99
11:12 AFX Freeserve grey market price 203-210p/share
07:29 AFX RPT: Dixons' Freeserve flotation reportedly 10 times oversubscribed
07:12 AFX Dixon's Freeserve flotation reportedly 10 times oversubscribed
22/07/99
06:48 AFX Freeserve shares reportedly quoted at 189-197p in 'grey market' dealings
21/07/99
06:59 AFX Dixons' Freeserve applicants reportedly face shortage of shares
19/07/99
10:49 AFX STOCKWATCH: WestLB says 'avoid' Freeserve post-float, fair value 60 p/shr
06:45 AFX AOL seen launching UK competitor to Dixons' Freeserve
16/07/99
13:29 AFX RPT: IG Index quotes 189-195p for Dixons unit Freeserve's first day trading
13:27 AFX IG Index quotes 189-195p for Dixon unit Freeserve's first day trading
14/07/99
14:25 AFX STOCKWATCH: Dixons higher as investors anticipate Freeserve boost
12/07/99
12:41 AFX STOCKWATCH: Dixons lower as Freeserve valuation falls short of market view
08:33 AFX Dixons says Freeserve flotation range 130-150p/share; value 1.31-1.51 bln stg
08:17 AFX Freeserve buys Babyworld for 3.7 mln stg; to launch internet-based credit card
07:32 RNS Dixons Group PLC - Re Freeserve Flotation
07:31 RNS Dixons Group PLC - Re Freeserve Credit Card
07:03 AFX Freeserve share discount reportedly could value group at 1.3 bln stg
06/07/99
12:28 AFX Dixons' Freeserve signs web-based email deal with World Telecom
05/07/99
11:49 RNS Dixons Group PLC - Re Freeserve Directorate
02/07/99
12:45 AFX STOCKWATCH: Dixons up ahead of Freeserve presentation
30/06/99
13:05 AFX CRRCT: Dixons' Freeserve loses customers to rival with 'free share' offer
07:06 AFX RPT: Dixons' Freeserve loses customers to rival with 'free share' offer
07:04 AFX Dixon's Freeserve loses customers to rival with 'free share' offer
29/06/99
09:46 AFX STOCKWATCH: Goldman Sachs cautious on Dixons' Freeserve valuations
28/06/99
15:23 RNS Dixons Group PLC - Re Freeserve ADSs
13:06 AFX FOCUS: Freeserve's longer term prospects in question
08:55 AFX Dixons/Freeserve -- 2 (details of retail offering)
08:30 RNS Dixons Group PLC - Re Flotation of Freeserve
08:28 AFX Dixons to float up to 18.25 pct of Freeserve
25/06/99
16:32 AFX Dixons' Freeserve invests 10 mln usd in TelePost
16:14 RNS Dixons Group PLC - Re Investment by Freeserve

Unfortunately, it is not possible to access the full stories at this site for free, although the headlines in themselves are often useful to know. In many cases the full story can be accessed for free at other sites described in this Chapter.

5

Past Performance

It can be a useful research tool to examine the past performance of an investment against its peer group or a relevant index. The free past performance statistics on the internet are excellent and information can be displayed in a variety of different formats. Some sites display information as a set of figures, whereas others show a price chart. The performance of investments which make up individual sectors of the market can be sorted into either ascending or descending order. You can also customise your own group of investments and sort it. Some sites display year on year past performance (as opposed to cumulative), which can be a good way of checking how consistent past performance has been.

Hot Links

✔ Top and bottom performing investments over 1, 3 & 5 years - *Hindsight*
✔ Unit trusts, Investment Trusts and Offshore funds - *Micropal*
✍ Investment Trusts and Warrants - *Trustnet*
✍ Stock Market indices over 1, 3 & 5 years - *Trustnet*
✍ Currencies over 1, 3 & 5 years - *Trustnet*
✍ Unit trusts to Pensions, year on year bar charts - *Interactive Investor*

The past performance information available at some internet sites is enormous. There is not enough space in this book to describe what is available for each type of investment so the examples have concentrated on Shares, Unit Trusts and Investment Trusts. These tend to be the most widely held type of investments.

Hindsight

http://www.moneyworld.co.uk/funds/

Hindsight provides past performance statistics on a whole host of different types of investments including Unit Trusts, Investment Trusts, Life Funds, Offshore Funds and Pensions. The Hindsight past performance statistics can be accessed indirectly via the Money World internet site at the internet address given above. Initially the full range of investment categories is displayed on the screen.

Fig 5.1 *Hindsight has past performance statistics on most types of investments.*

Unit Trusts:
Sectors A-Z or PowerSearch

Investment Trusts:
Sectors A-Z or PowerSearch

Life Funds:
Sectors A-Z or PowerSearch

Pension Funds:

You can choose to display the past performance of the investments in a given category in one of two ways. If you click on the 'Sectors A-Z' option, a list of all the sectors in that category will be displayed. For example, clicking on 'Sectors A-Z' in the 'Investment Trusts' category would generate an alphabetical list of different sectors within the Investment Trust sector as shown below.

Fig 5.11 *Clicking on 'Sectors A-Z' will display an alphabetical list of sectors.*

- Smaller Companies UK
- Split - Capital
- Split - Capital Indexed
- Split - Inc & Resid Cap
- Split - Income
- Split - Stepped Prefs
- Split - Zero Dividend
- UK Capital Growth
- UK General
- UK Income Growth
- Venture & Develop't Cap
- Warrants

Hindsight *(con't)*

http://www.moneyworld.co.uk/funds/invtrusts/503.htm

You can click on any of these sectors to display an alphabetical list of individual investments which make up that sector. The performance of each investment in that sector is displayed over 1, 3 and 5 years together with its sector ranking.

Fig 5.12 *Percentage performance over 1, 3 & 5 years is displayed together with rank.*

Investment Trust Performance (UK Income Growth)

Close to Close performance calculated 1/3/5 years to 1st March. Results assume net income has been reinvested.

Fund Name	**1 year**	**Rank**	**3 year**	**Rank**	**5 year**	**Rank**
City of London	4.11	9	73.56	2	91.05	1
Dumyat Cnv Annual Dividend	6.70	6	13.74	15		
Dumyat Cnv Monthly Dividend	-3.88	15	8.87	16		
Dunedin Income Growth	12.80	3	72.95	3	77.74	5
Fleming Income & Capital Units	14.19	2	71.32	4	81.73	2
Foreign & Col Income Growth	4.10	10	22.01	14		
Gartmore Brit Inc & Gth Units	17.03	1	76.62	1		
GT Income Growth	-3.89	16				
Guinness Flight Extra Inc Unit	11.49	4	64.19	7		
Investors Capital Units	2.01	12	57.59	8	67.07	8
Lowland	-4.20	17	7.36	17	23.38	10
M&G Income Units	2.22	11	51.74	9	70.16	6
Merchants	7.79	5	66.92	5	80.76	3
Morgan Grenfell Equity Income	6.45	7	42.92	10	67.41	7
Murray Income	-3.85	14	30.32	12	45.71	9
Perpetual Income & Growth	-8.06	19				
Prolific Income	-0.44	13	36.32	11		
Schroder Income Growth	-7.45	18	28.17	13		
Temple Bar	5.21	8	64.33	6	78.81	4
Value and Income	-23.19	20	-0.09	18	9.80	11
Averages / Totals	**1.96**	**20**	**43.82**	**18**	**63.06**	**11**

Clicking on the 'PowerSearch' option shown in Figure 5.1 gives you a choice over what is displayed in the past performance table. You can choose to list either 10, 20, 50 or All of the best or worst funds, over either 1, 3 or 5 years.

Fig 5.13 *Clicking on the 'PowerSearch' option displays a menu of choices.*

Hindsight *(con't)*

http://www.moneyworld.co.uk/powersearch/simple_search?fundid=IT

The 'PowerSearch' option is a very useful tool because it enables you to display just the past performance information which is relevant to you. For example, if you wanted to just display the best ten performing UK Income Investment Trusts over one year, you would enter the criteria exactly as shown in Figure 5.13. The following performance table would then be displayed.

Fig 5.14 *A 'PowerSearch' allows you to customise the past performance statistics.*

Rank	Fund Name	Growth	Fund / Sector
1.	Gartmore Brit Inc & Gth Units	17.03 %	Investment Trust / UK Income Growth
2.	Fleming Income & Capital Units	14.19 %	Investment Trust / UK Income Growth
3.	Dunedin Income Growth	12.80 %	Investment Trust / UK Income Growth
4.	Guinness Flight Extra Inc Unit	11.49 %	Investment Trust / UK Income Growth
5.	Merchants	7.79 %	Investment Trust / UK Income Growth
6.	Dumyat Cnv Annual Dividend	6.70 %	Investment Trust / UK Income Growth
7.	Morgan Grenfell Equity Income	6.45 %	Investment Trust / UK Income Growth
8.	Temple Bar	5.21 %	Investment Trust / UK Income Growth
9.	City of London	4.11 %	Investment Trust / UK Income Growth
10.	Foreign & Col Income Growth	4.10 %	Investment Trust / UK Income Growth

The information displayed using the 'PowerSearch' option, is quite basic. The table shows the name of the fund and its percentage growth (with net income reinvested). The investment category (Investment Trusts in this example) and the sector within that category (UK Income Growth) are also shown alongside each investment. More comprehensive past performance statistics are available at some of the other internet sites described in this Chapter.

Micropal

http://www.micropal.com/index2.htm

Micropal has an extremely comprehensive bank of free past performance statistics covering practically every type of investment fund. There are excellent searching and sorting facilities at this site, and the only drawback is that there are almost too many options for investors. The first thing to do when you enter this site is to decide which type of investment you wish to analyze.

Fig 5.2 *Micropal offers past performance statistics on a huge range of different funds.*

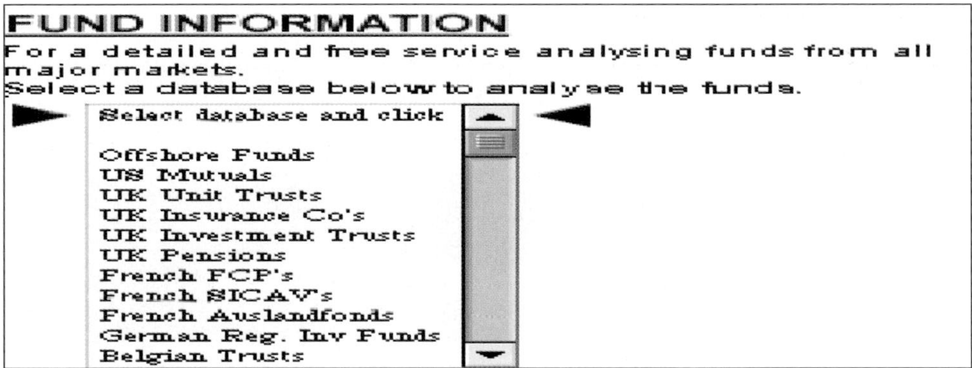

If you clicked on 'UK Unit Trusts' for example, the screen in Figure 5.21 would be displayed. You can click on any of the headings from 'Database Summary' to 'Fund Selector' to access different parts of the Micropal database. Clicking on the 'Click here' icon in the bottom left hand corner of the screen has the same effect as clicking on 'Database Summary'.

Fig 5.21 *The opening screen for each investment category offers a range of options.*

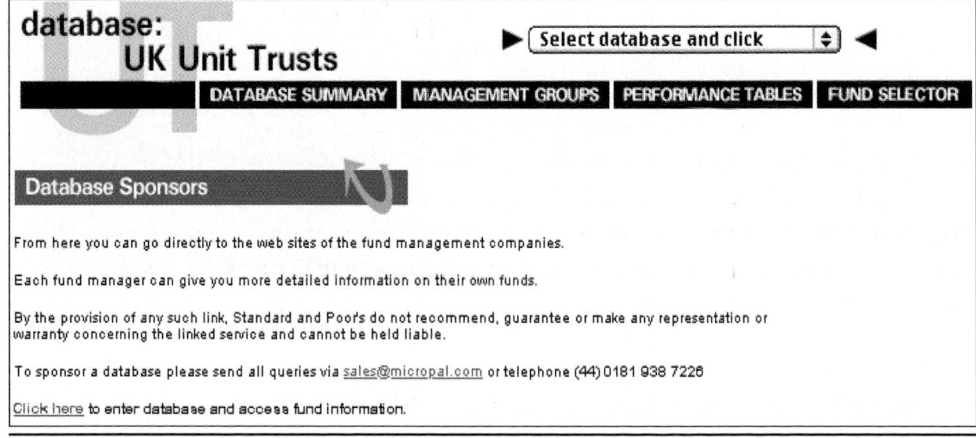

Micropal *(con't)*

http://www.micropal.com/analystv3/mainbody.cfm

Clicking on 'Database Summary', produces a box which enables you to get past performance data on a specific fund by entering the exact name or sedol number of the fund. The sedol number is a unique number code which identifies that investment. If you are not sure of the exact name of a fund, then you can enter a word and all the funds with that word in their name will be displayed.

Fig 5.22 *Use this table to get past performance data on a specific fund.*

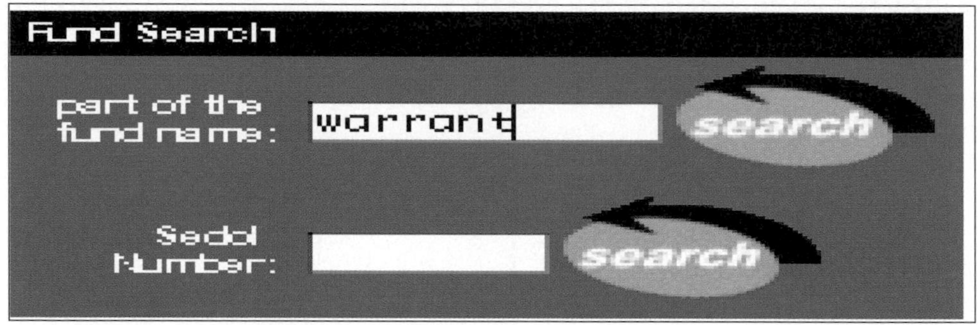

For example, you could display past performance data on all the unit trusts with the word 'warrant' in the title. To do this, you would simply type in the word 'warrant' as shown above. You can change the time frame within the performance table from '1 - 10 years' to '1 to 6 months', by clicking on the 'Tables Over 6 Months' icon at the bottom of the each performance table.

Fig 5.23 *The 6 month performance of all unit trusts with the word 'warrant' in the title.*

Mgmt Group	Fact Sheet	Web Link	Fund Name	Currency	Fund Size (Calculated in Millions)	3 Yr Volatility	Star Ranking	Invested Over a number of months & Sector Ranking at 19-Apr-99					
								1mth sort	2mth sort	3mth sort	4mth sort	5mth sort	6mth sort
		-	Exeter Warrant	GBP	3.70	6.43		2.25 106	7.79 75	13.54 21	20.99 17	23.02 28	37.40 17
		-	HL Warrant Ptfl	GBP	10.00	11.52		6.41 11	16.59 7	22.27 1	28.45 8	21.64 34	38.77 15

Save Table | Tables Over 10 Years | Printable Version | Export to Excel

Micropal *(con't)*

http://www.micropal.com/analystv3/mainbody.cfm

Clicking on 'Database Summary' also displays a table which shows how that investment category is made up. For Unit Trusts, there are six main categories ranging from 'Asset Allocation' to 'Other'. Each of these categories is then broken down further. You can see from the table below, that the largest category is 'Equity' which consists of 13 sub sectors and 1184 individual unit trusts.

Fig 5.24 *Clicking on 'Database Summary' gives a breakdown of the Unit Trust sector.*

DATABASE SUMMARY (22-Mar-1999)

(Geographical Sectors)

Main Categories	No of Sectors	No of Funds	Month's Best Fund % Growth	Month's Worst Fund % Growth
Asset Allocation	5	215	8.54	-1.20
Commodity	1	9	6.96	-0.81
Equity	13	1184	28.68	-4.72
Fixed Income	3	166	4.63	-2.37
Money Market	1	33	0.46	-2.08
Other	2	17	8.38	-6.50

● From the table above you can access the Sector Summary tables and the Fact Sheets of the funds which have achieved this month's highest and lowest percentage(%) growth.

Source: Standard & Poor's Micropal

Clicking on 'Equity' under the 'Main Categories' heading, displays the past performance of each of the thirteen sectors within that category. The table shows the size of each sector in millions of pounds, and its 3 year Volatility.

Fig 5.25 *Performance of the thirteen sectors which make up the 'Equity' category.*

Performance Table	Top Ten 3yrs	Bot Ten 3yrs	Sector Name	Sector Fund Size (Calculated in Millions)	3 Yr Volatility	Invested Over a number of years & No. of funds at 22-Mar-99				
						1yr sort	2yrs sort	3yrs sort	5yrs sort	10yrs sort
			Emerging Markets	26.27	9.88	-23.32 47	-29.26 37	-25.84 31	-45.51 19	72.05 3
			Europe	182.04	5.53	8.86 131	45.75 125	70.69 117	111.37 112	333.74 81
			Far East Excluding Japan	44.65	8.39	-9.67 81	-35.50 81	-37.10 73	-34.00 61	137.78 26
			Far East Including Japan	32.87	6.55	2.35 31	-20.86 31	-27.43 31	-29.29 30	53.05 24
			International Equity Growth	100.52	4.67	8.88 152	31.07 137	39.97 130	60.19 113	219.84 85
	-	-	International Equity Income	133.20	3.42	7.65 4	39.68 3	52.58 3	74.61 3	255.64 3
			Japan	42.20	6.44	24.53 91	3.59 87	-22.28 84	-28.72 76	-3.76 58
			North America	89.24	5.20	13.86 118	50.62 112	69.41 111	126.27 107	424.81 87
	-	-	Property	72.00	1.69	2.44 4	19.06 4	38.00 4	32.71 3	
			UK Equity Growth	169.49	3.91	2.11 155	35.40 146	58.74 135	82.86 118	198.41 92
			UK Equity Income	196.02	3.47	0.93 90	37.87 90	58.85 88	77.23 79	201.62 70
			UK Growth & Income	232.50	3.71	2.67 150	40.09 141	62.36 133	87.39 112	214.11 82
			UK Smaller Companies	100.28	4.53	-3.86 76	12.08 74	32.32 69	47.75 60	117.61 39

Micropal *(con't)*

http://www.micropal.com/analystv3/mainbody.cfm

The performance of individual funds within each sector can be accessed directly from the table in Figure 5.25. To do this, click on the vertical 'Performance Table' heading in the left hand column, alongside the sector you wish to display. An alphabetical list of the individual funds which comprise that sector is dis-

Fig 5.26 *Alphabetical list of funds in the 'UK Equity Income' sector.*

Mgmt Group	Fact Sheet	Web Link	Fund Name	Currency	Fund Size (Calculated in Millions)	3 Yr Volatility	Star Ranking	Invested Over a number of years & Sector Ranking at 22-Mar-99				
								1yr sort	2yrs sort	3yrs sort	5yrs sort	10yrs sort
		-	Abbey General	GBP	129.80	3.51	μ	-5.34 145	24.45 129	34.07 125	61.58 103	153.24 75
		-	Abbey Natl UK Growth	GBP	1453.00	3.76	μμμμ	3.51 65	44.08 47	70.43 33		
		-	AberdeenProl UK Blue Chip	GBP	339.90	3.84	μμμμμ	7.70 11	48.65 26	79.81 11	115.41 8	
		-	ABN AMRO Growth & Income	GBP	7.64	3.70	μ	-5.99 146	11.09 141	20.93 133	38.92 110	148.22 78
		-	AES UK General	GBP	31.20	3.74	μμμ	2.98 85	37.70 101	64.73 65	94.46 32	
		-	Avon Equity	GBP	87.80	3.56	μμμ	2.80 89	44.39 44	67.91 41	102.11 17	269.96 11
		-	AXA Equity&Law General	GBP	186.74	3.67	μμ	3.06 82	40.74 81	59.08 96	85.86 68	271.26 10
		-	AXA Equity&Law UK Growth	GBP	432.03	3.69	μμ	2.67 92	38.73 96	60.17 91	87.59 64	247.32 20
		-	AXA Sun Life UK Income	GBP	10.42	3.78	μμ	-0.88 134	37.81 100	61.63 85	76.57 91	152.98 76

Individual funds which make up a sector, can be sorted in order of performance. Below, the 'UK Equity Income' sector has been sorted in order of 3 year performance, by clicking on the small 'sort' icon under the 3 years heading. In this example Jupiter Income was the best performing fund with a gain of 89.14%.

Fig 5.27 *'UK Equity Income' sector sorted by 3 year performance.*

Mgmt Group	Fact Sheet	Web Link	Fund Name	Currency	Fund Size (Calculated in Millions)	3 Yr Volatility	Star Ranking	Invested Over a number of years & Sector Ranking at 22-Mar-99				
								1yr sort	2yrs sort	3yrs sort	5yrs sort	10yrs sort
		-	Jupiter Income	GBP	904.14	3.30	μμμμ	14.94 1	48.90 6	89.14 1	169.85 1	506.34 1
		-	BWD UK Equity Income	GBP	45.93	3.41	μμμμμ	7.64 6	52.79 3	86.42 2	122.27 2	258.93 12
		-	Fidelity Income Plus	GBP	256.60	3.35	μμμμμ	6.69 7	54.13 2	82.77 3	92.78 10	167.97 51
			Newton Higher Income	GBP	204.83	3.83	μμμμμ	5.59 10	56.49 1	81.64 4	107.31 4	274.39 6
		-	NPI Global Care Income Inst	GBP	24.70	3.06	μμμμ	12.51 2	47.13 8	81.55 5		
		-	NPI Global Care Income Rtl	GBP	31.00	3.05	μμμμ	12.37 3	46.94 9	81.31 6		
		-	Guinness Right Income Share	GBP	46.50	3.99	μμμμ	6.62 8	45.31 12	78.12 7		
		-	Dresdner RCM High Yield	GBP	184.13	3.96	μμμμμ	5.18 13	49.05 5	75.96 8	88.97 19	221.14 18
		-	Britannia Higher Yield	GBP	277.40	3.35	μμμμμ	5.38 11	45.07 14	72.48 9	108.41 3	345.98 2
		-	Premier Dividend	GBP	28.38	3.56	μμμμ	2.33 28	49.30 4	71.99 10	105.10 5	113.36 68
	-	-	SECTOR AVERAGE	-	196.02	3.47	-	0.93 90	37.87 90	58.85 88	77.23 79	201.62 70

Micropal *(con't)*

http://www.micropal.com/analystv3/mainbody.cfm

On the left hand side of the table shown in Figure 5.25, there are two headings entitled 'Top 10 3yrs' and 'Bot 10 3yrs'. Rather than displaying the performance of all the funds in a sector, you can click on one of these icons to display just the 10 best or worst funds over a 3 year period. In the example below, the 10 best funds in the 'UK Growth & Income' sector were selected.

Fig 5.28 *Just the top or bottom 10 funds in a sector over 3 years can be displayed.*

Mgmt Group	Fact Sheet	Web Link	Fund Name	Currency	Fund Size (Calculated in Millions)	3 Yr Volatility	Star Ranking	Invested Over a number of years & Sector Ranking at 22-Mar-99				
								1yr sort	2yrs sort	3yrs sort	5yrs sort	10yrs sort
		-	Govett Geared UK Index	GBP	3.31	6.52		- 11.49 150	52.31 8	97.13 1	135.23 1	
		-	Laurence Keen Income & Growth	GBP	24.20	3.73		6.09 15	49.57 22	89.93 2	111.13 12	
		-	Fleming Select UK Income	GBP	36.90	3.81		4.97 24	55.94 3	88.34 3	124.71 2	241.93 23
			Newton Income	GBP	568.95	3.50		13.08 1	62.64 1	85.87 4	113.64 9	386.39 1
		-	Johnson Fry UK Income	GBP	9.96	4.13		9.54 6	61.05 2	84.46 5		
		-	Five Arrows UK Major Cos B	GBP	31.29	4.18		10.61 5	51.98 9	83.48 6	112.11 10	275.07 6
		-	Family Asset Trust	GBP	51.82	3.86		11.54 2	55.27 6	83.41 7	101.41 19	
		-	Five Arrows UK Major Cos A	GBP	31.29	4.23		10.73 3	51.45 10	82.84 8	111.37 11	273.77 8
		-	River & Mercantile Top 100	GBP	60.50	3.94		4.69 30	50.85 11	80.75 9		
		-	Fidelity MoneyBuilder Index	GBP	131.80	4.11		4.96 25	52.57 7	80.54 10		
	-	-	SECTOR AVERAGE	-	232.50	3.71	-	2.67 150	40.09 141	62.36 133	87.39 112	214.11 82

When the performance of individual funds is displayed, you will notice that a new range of headings appear on the left hand side of the table. In the example above, you can see that the 'Newton Income' fund has an arrow next to it under the heading of 'Web Link'. This signifies that Newton has its own internet site which you can access directly by clicking on this arrow. The next section deals with what information is available under the headings of 'Mgmt Group' and 'Fact Sheet'. This information can either be accessed from a performance table like the one above, or from the opening screen shown in Figure 5.21.

Micropal *(con't)*

http://www.micropal.com/analystv3/Managers/ManagersSearch.cfm

Information about a Management Group can be accessed from the opening screen shown in Figure 5.21 by clicking on the heading entitled 'Management Groups'. If you want details on an 'Individual Management Group', you need to click on the arrow at the end of the box, select a name from the list that appears, and click on 'Search'. The screen in Figure 5.2.11 will be displayed.

Fig 5.29 *Clicking on the 'Management Group' heading gives you three search options.*

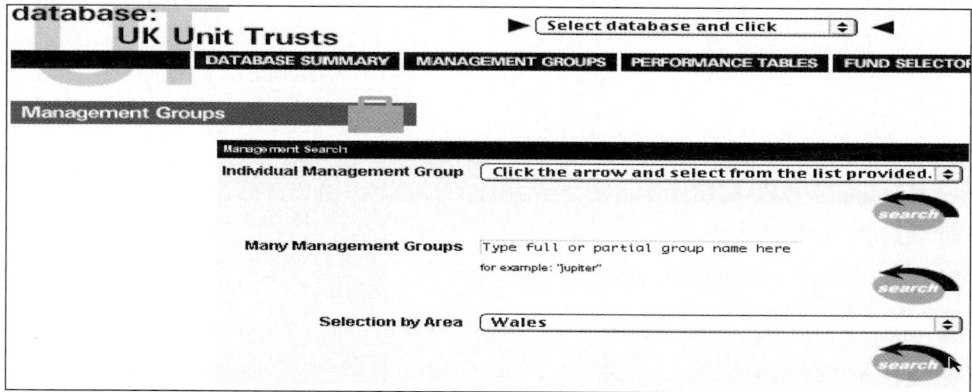

The 'Selection by Area' option at the bottom of this screen, allows you to list contact details for Fund Management Groups in either Wales, Scotland or England. If, for example, you entered 'Wales' as an option, only contact details for the group 'Legal & General' are displayed indicating that they are the only group based in Wales. The same screen is displayed by typing in Legal & General in the 'Many Management Groups' box and clicking on 'Search'.

Fig 5.2.10 *A handy place to quickly get contact details for a Management Group.*

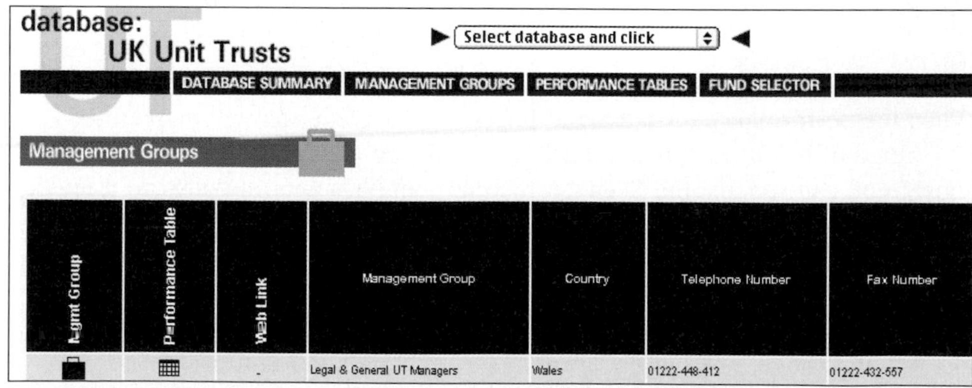

Micropal *(con't)*

http://www.micropal.com/analystv3/Managers/ManagersSearch.cfm

When you make a selection using the 'Individual Management Group' option, full contact details are displayed including the address. The example below shows what is displayed when the Management Group 'Lazard' is selected. This screen gives you access to the past performances of all the funds managed by that group, together with detailed fact sheets on each fund.

Fig 5.2.11 *This screen enables you to display information about the funds of a Group.*

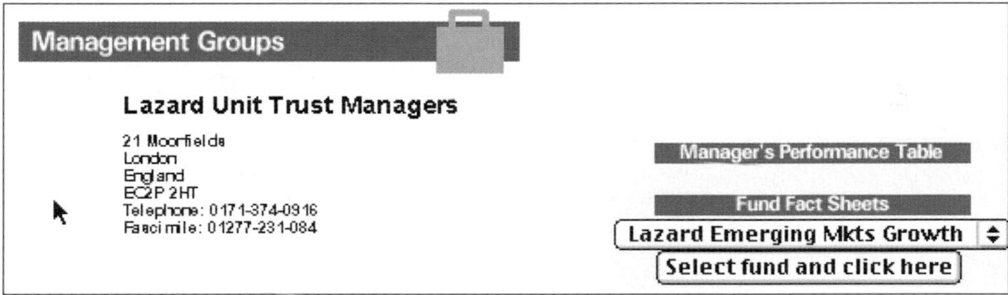

Clicking on the 'Managers Performance Table' heading will display a table showing the past performances of all the funds managed by that group.

Fig 5.2.12 *Past Performance of all the Lazard unit trusts displayed in one table.*

Mgmt Group	Fact Sheet	Web Link	Fund Name	Currency	Fund Size (Calculated in Millio	3 Yr Volatility	Star Ranking	Invested Over a number of years & Sector Ranking at 22-Mar-99				
								1yr sort	2yrs sort	3yrs sort	5yrs sort	10yrs sort
		-	Lazard Emerging Mkts Growth	GBP	3.64	-	-	-21.47 13				
		-	Lazard European Growth	GBP	167.54	5.70	µµ	13.35 25	50.55 48	65.98 79	116.15 37	446.31 8
		-	Lazard Growth Portfolio	GBP	12.12	3.25	µ	-0.58 41	18.97 35	27.70 33	43.56 26	
		-	Lazard Income Portfolio	GBP	19.00	3.25	µµµµ	1.73 54	32.45 10	47.53 6	61.15 9	
		-	Lazard International Equity	GBP	140.94	-	-	12.56 38				
		-	Lazard Japan Growth	GBP	5.35	5.75	µµµ	24.76 32	11.17 22	-20.95 35		
		-	Lazard North American Growth	GBP	32.46	4.91	µµ	15.18 63	45.96 69	62.77 65	136.56 46	320.66 67
		-	Lazard Pacific Growth	GBP	1.96	9.20	µ	-11.81 51	-52.38 80	-56.38 72		
		-	Lazard UK Capital	GBP	36.21	4.26	µµ	-0.60 115	31.89 93	52.31 93	85.31 60	201.10 46
		-	Lazard UK Income	GBP	218.03	3.94	µµ	-1.91 75	30.58 78	56.96 51	91.35 13	259.36 11
		-	Lazard UK Income & Growth	GBP	50.89	3.77	µµ	1.03 114	36.47 106	59.76 93	92.26 45	221.23 36
		-	Lazard UK Smaller Cos Growth	GBP	93.34	4.25	µµµ	-5.13 40	9.31 36	30.37 30	38.70 32	139.54 15
		-	Lazard Worldwide Portfolio	GBP	10.01	3.94	µ	4.64 22	18.66 49	17.72 58	30.08 31	

Micropal *(con't)*

http://www.micropal.com/analystv3/Managers/ManagersSearch.cfm

Under the 'Fund Fact Sheets' heading in Figure 5.2.11, you can select a fund, and display a very detailed Fact Sheet relating to that fund. Just about every thing you need to know about a fund is displayed on the same page.

Fig 5.2.13 *Detailed Fact Sheet for the Lazard European unit trust.*

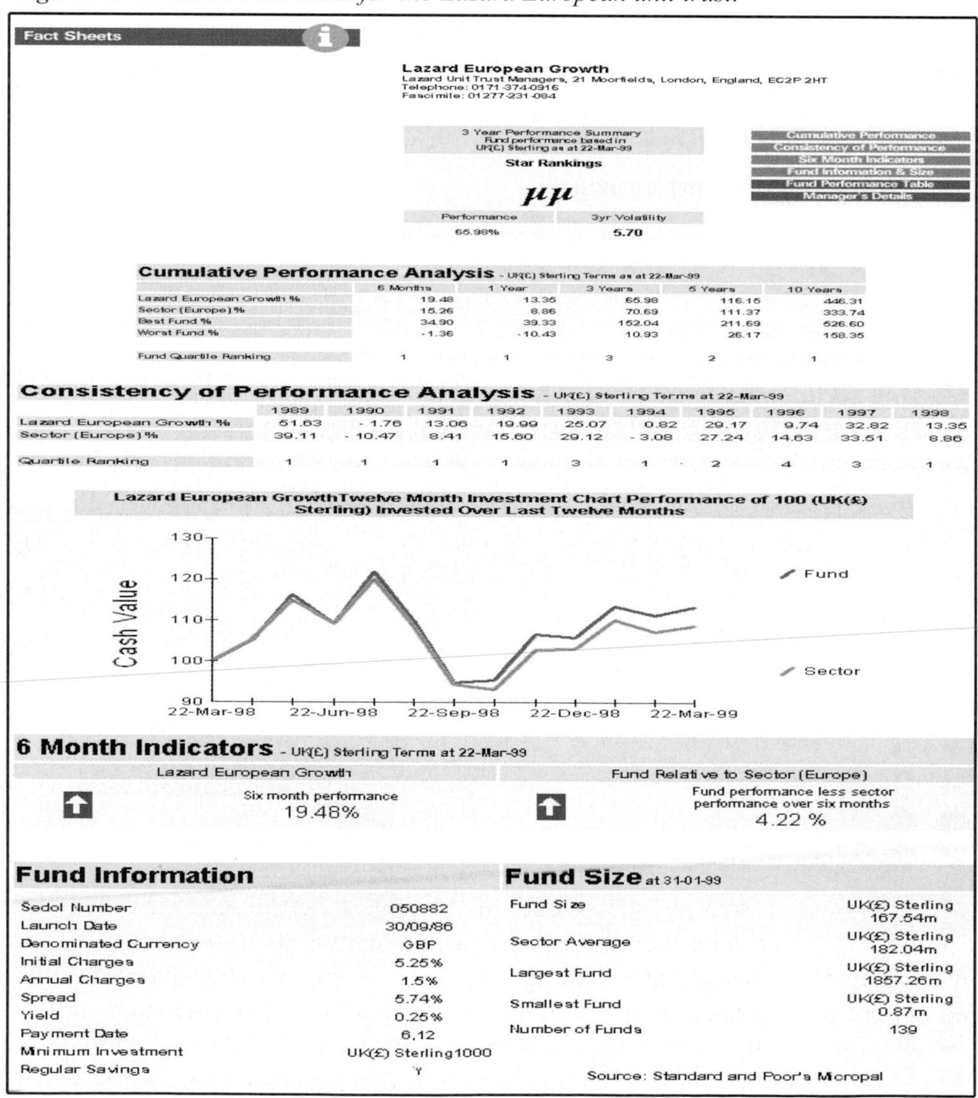

Fact Sheets

Lazard European Growth
Lazard Unit Trust Managers, 21 Moorfields, London, England, EC2P 2HT
Telephone: 0171-374-0916
Fascimile: 01277-231-084

3 Year Performance Summary
Fund performance based in
UK(£) Sterling as at 22-Mar-99

Star Rankings

μμ

Performance	3yr Volatility
65.98%	**5.70**

Cumulative Performance
Consistency of Performance
Six Month Indicators
Fund Information & Size
Fund Performance Table
Manager's Details

Cumulative Performance Analysis - UK(£) Sterling Terms as at 22-Mar-99

	6 Months	1 Year	3 Years	5 Years	10 Years
Lazard European Growth %	19.48	13.35	65.98	116.15	446.31
Sector (Europe) %	15.26	8.86	70.69	111.37	333.74
Best Fund %	34.90	39.33	152.04	211.69	526.60
Worst Fund %	-1.36	-10.43	10.93	26.17	158.35
Fund Quartile Ranking	1	1	3	2	1

Consistency of Performance Analysis - UK(£) Sterling Terms at 22-Mar-99

	1989	1990	1991	1992	1993	1994	1995	1996	1997	1998
Lazard European Growth %	51.63	- 1.76	13.06	19.99	25.07	0.82	29.17	9.74	32.82	13.35
Sector (Europe) %	39.11	- 10.47	8.41	15.60	29.12	- 3.08	27.24	14.63	33.51	8.86
Quartile Ranking	1	1	1	1	3	1	2	4	3	1

6 Month Indicators - UK(£) Sterling Terms at 22-Mar-99

Lazard European Growth	Fund Relative to Sector (Europe)
Six month performance 19.48%	Fund performance less sector performance over six months 4.22 %

Fund Information

Sedol Number	050882
Launch Date	30/09/86
Denominated Currency	GBP
Initial Charges	5.25%
Annual Charges	1.5%
Spread	5.74%
Yield	0.25%
Payment Date	6.12
Minimum Investment	UK(£) Sterling1000
Regular Savings	Y

Fund Size at 31-01-99

Fund Size	UK(£) Sterling 167.54m
Sector Average	UK(£) Sterling 182.04m
Largest Fund	UK(£) Sterling 1857.26m
Smallest Fund	UK(£) Sterling 0.87m
Number of Funds	139

Source: Standard and Poor's Micropal

Micropal *(con't)*

http://www.micropal.com/analystv3/Tables/Main.cfm

The table shown below is displayed when you click on the heading of 'Performance Tables' in Figure 5.21. In this example, the best performing sector over 1 year was the 'Fixed Income' sector with a gain of 10.36%. The number just below the average gain figure, shows the number of funds in that sector.

Fig 5.2.14 *Average performance of the sectors which make up UK Unit Trust category.*

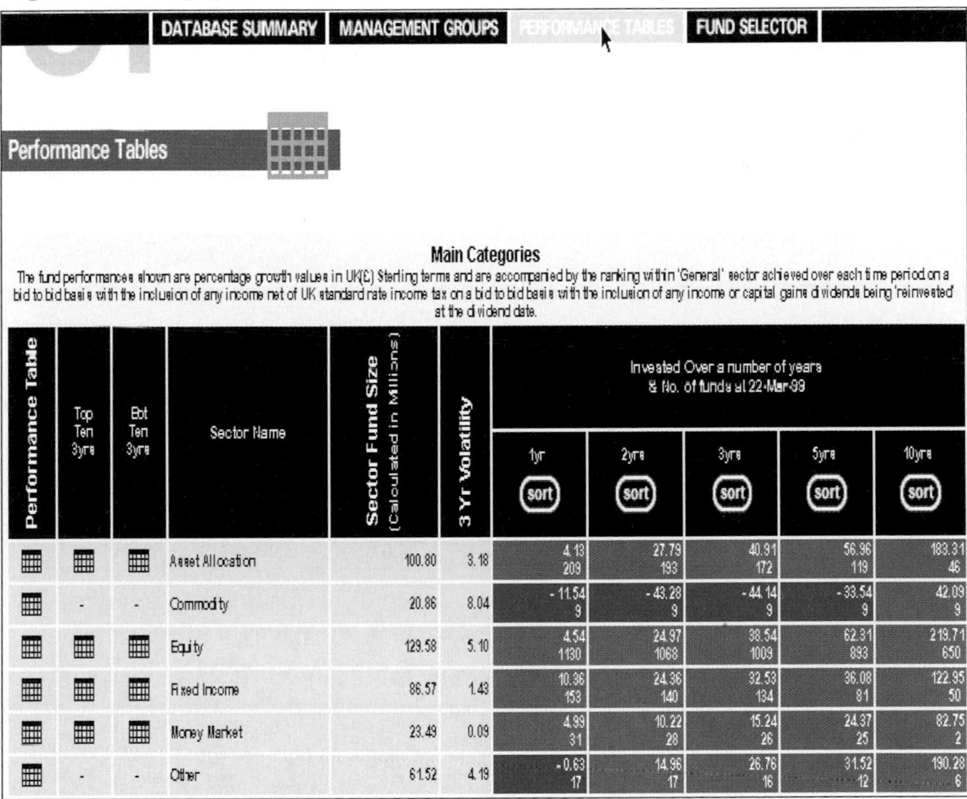

DATABASE SUMMARY | MANAGEMENT GROUPS | PERFORMANCE TABLES | FUND SELECTOR

Performance Tables

Main Categories

The fund performances shown are percentage growth values in UK(£) Sterling terms and are accompanied by the ranking within 'General' sector achieved over each time period on a bid to bid basis with the inclusion of any income net of UK standard rate income tax on a bid to bid basis with the inclusion of any income or capital gains dividends being 'reinvested' at the dividend date.

Performance Table	Top Ten 3yrs	Bot Ten 3yrs	Sector Name	Sector Fund Size (Calculated in Millions)	3 Yr Volatility	Invested Over a number of years & No. of funds at 22-Mar-99				
						1yr sort	2yrs sort	3yrs sort	5yrs sort	10yrs sort
			Asset Allocation	100.80	3.18	4.13 209	27.79 193	40.91 172	56.96 119	183.31 46
	-	-	Commodity	20.86	8.04	-11.54 9	-43.28 9	-44.14 9	-33.54 9	42.09 9
			Equity	129.58	5.10	4.54 1130	24.97 1068	38.54 1009	62.31 893	219.71 650
			Fixed Income	86.57	1.43	10.36 153	24.36 140	32.53 134	36.08 81	122.95 50
			Money Market	23.49	0.09	4.99 31	10.22 28	15.24 26	24.37 25	82.75 2
	-	-	Other	61.52	4.19	-0.63 17	14.96 17	26.76 16	31.52 12	190.28 6

The number of funds in a sector, can be a useful indicator of how popular a sector has been. For example, the number of 'Money Market' Funds has grown from 2 to 51 over the last 10 years, whereas the number of 'Commodity' funds has remained unchanged at 8. Falling inflation over the last 10 years has resulted in poor performance from commodity stocks and there has been no demand for new funds in this sector. Money Market funds have capitalised on falling interest rates by offering slightly higher returns than standard Bank and Building Society accounts.

Micropal *(con't)*

http://www.micropal.com/analystv3/Selector/Selectorut.html

Last but not least, there is the heading of 'Fund Selector' in Figure 5.21. Clicking on this heading gives you access to the extremely powerful fund selection menu shown below. Here you can set very specific search criteria so that only the funds matching those criteria will be displayed. Once you have selected your criteria, click on 'Generate Table' to display the results.

Fig 5.2.15 *You can choose to display only those funds which meet certain criteria.*

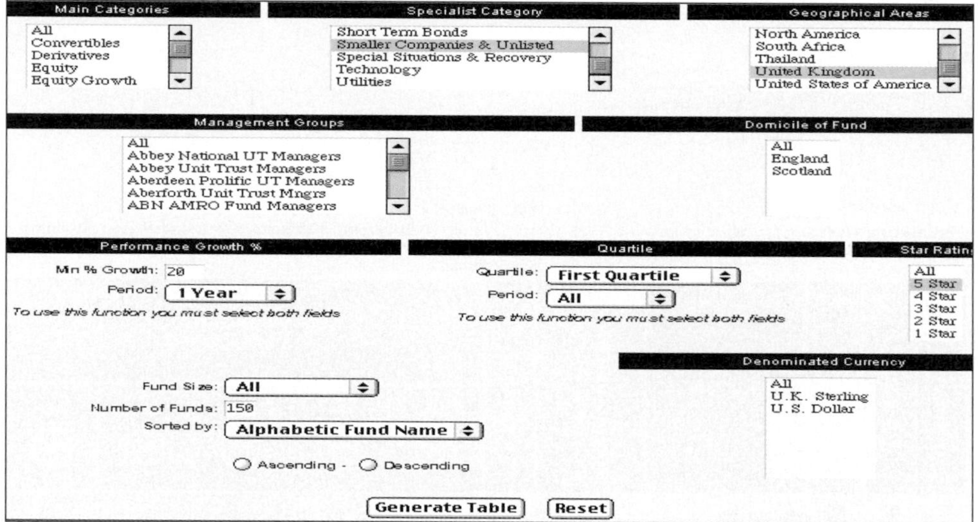

Micropal awards each fund a 'Star Rating' denoted by the Greek symbol mu. The ratings are based on all sorts of things such as consistency of performance, volatility etc. and a five star rating is the best. For example, the performance table below was produced by selecting 'Smaller Company' funds in the 'United Kingdom' which have generated a 'Minimum Growth of 20%' over '1 year', have a 5 star rating, and have been 'First Quartile' over 'All' periods.

Fig 5.2.16 *Only the GT UK Smaller Companies fund meets the selected criteria.*

Mgmt Group	Fact Sheet	Web Link	Fund Name	Currency	Fund Size (Calculated in Millions)	3 Yr Volatility	Star Ranking	Invested Over a number of years & Sector Ranking at 19-Apr-99				
								1yr sort	2yrs sort	3yrs sort	5yrs sort	10yrs sort
			GT UK Smaller Companies ACC	GBP	9.91	4.38	μμμμμ	24.97 1	72.39 1	100.25 1	104.59 8	

Trustnet - Closed End Funds

http://www.trustnet.co.uk/it/funds/perf.asp

This is an excellent site for obtaining comprehensive past performance statistics on most types of closed ended funds including investment trusts and investment trust warrants. There is also a section listing the past performance of major currencies and stock markets which is extremely useful. When you first enter this site via the internet address given above, an alphabetical list of all closed ended funds is displayed. The alphabet is broken down into different sections in a box at the top of the table, and you will need to click on the appropriate section to display a particular fund.

Fig 5.3 *The Share Price and the NAV performance is displayed over 1, 3 & 5 years.*

Unit Trusts & OEICs | Investment Trusts
Search | Indices | Rates | Disclaimer | Feedback | Home | Help
Funds | Performance | Groups | Forum | Custom

<< Next << 3i Ag | At Br | Br Cz | De Em | Em Fi | Fi Fl | Fl Ge | Ge He | He Is | It La | La Me | Me Ol | Ol Ri | Ro Sh | Sh Th | Th Wa | Wh Wo >> Next >>

All regions | All sectors | All Closed End Funds | Select!

TrustNet **All regions / All sectors** (ex splits) TrustNet

Source : TrustNet - Saturday, 27 March 1999

484 Funds
Sorted by fund name

Rank	Chart	Fund Name SORT	Group Name SORT	Price	Disc/ Prem SORT	% Performance (Price total return in £) 1yr SORT	3yr SORT	5yr SORT	% Performance (NAV total return in £) 1yr SORT	3yr SORT	5yr SORT
1		3I GROUP	3I PLC	611.5 (GBX)	+1.9	+5.8	+54.7	+149.1	+8.8	+63.9	+113.3
2		3I SMALLER QUOTED COS	3I PLC	180.0 (GBX)	-13.6	+0.9	+30.0	n/a	-1.5	+36.4	n/a
3		ABERDEEN ASIAN SMALLER	ABERDEEN	52.0 (GBX)	-21.6	+2.3	-44.1	n/a	-2.9	-32.0	n/a
4		ABERDEEN CONV INC C	ABERDEEN	105.0 (GBX)	-0.9	n/a	n/a	n/a	n/a	n/a	n/a
5		ABERDEEN CONV INCOME	ABERDEEN	110.5 (GBX)	+3.5	+2.9	+92.4	+39.2	-3.6	+54.4	+52.9
6		ABERDEEN EMER ASIA	ABERDEEN	23.5 (GBX)	-17.8	-21.7	-68.1	-67.2	-22.9	-65.3	-63.8
7		ABERDEEN EMER ECON	ABERDEEN	43.5 (GBX)	-26.1	-32.0	-49.1	-48.9	-27.9	-37.3	-40.2
8		ABERDEEN HIGH INCOME	ABERDEEN	125.25 (GBX)	+8.3	+13.7	+162.4	+104.3	+5.7	+112.0	+96.4
9		ABERDEEN LAT AMERICAN	ABERDEEN	43.0 (GBX)	-27.1	-46.6	-35.9	n/a	-40.7	-26.5	n/a
10		ABERDEEN NEW DAWN	ABERDEEN	110.75 (GBX)	-16.2	-10.3	-50.6	-46.4	-10.7	-45.7	-41.0
11		ABERDEEN NEW THAI	ABERDEEN	44.75 (GBX)	-3.2	-14.7	-71.2	-58.6	-10.9	-75.3	-60.3
12		ABERFORTH SMALLER	ABERFORTH	219.5 (GBX)	-17.3	-2.6	+16.0	+30.1	+5.6	+40.0	+71.5
13		ABERFORTH SPLIT UNIT	ABERFORTH	324.5 (GBX)	-18.2	-3.2	+18.3	+30.3	+3.1	+31.4	+62.5
14		ABTRUST SCOTLAND	ABERDEEN	48.0 (GBX)	-21.1	-6.2	+35.1	+47.6	-0.2	+27.5	+67.2
15		ADVANCE DEVELOPING MKT	PROGRDEV	87.0 (GBX)	-10.6	n/a	n/a	n/a	n/a	n/a	n/a

The discount to Net Asset Value (NAV) is displayed for each trust together with share price and the NAV performance over 1, 3 & 5 years. A particularly good feature is that all these parameters are sortable into ascending or descending order, so you can quickly see which trusts have the widest discounts or have been the best performers.

Trustnet - Closed End Funds *(con't)*

http://www.trustnet.co.uk/it/funds/perf.asp

At the top of the table in Figure 5.3 there are three boxes with the headings 'All Regions', 'All Sectors' and 'All Closed End Funds'. You can click on these boxes, and select other parameters from the list which appears. This enables you to just display the past performance of specific sectors or types of fund. In the example below, the parameters have been changed to display 'United Kingdom' 'High Income' and 'UK Investment Trusts'. Once you have made your selection, you need to click on 'Select !' to display the table.

Fig 5.31 *Performance Table for UK High Income Investment Trusts*

United Kingdom | High Income | UK Investment Trusts | Select!

TrustNet — United Kingdom / High Income — TrustNet

Source : TrustNet - Saturday, 27 March 1999

14 Funds
Sorted by fund name

Rank	Chart	Fund Name SORT	Group Name SORT	Price	Disc/ Prem SORT	% Performance (Price total return in £) 1yr SORT	3yr SORT	5yr SORT	% Performance (NAV total return in £) 1yr SORT	3yr SORT	5yr SORT
1		ABERDEEN CONV INC C	ABERDEEN	105.0 (GBX)	-0.9	n/a	n/a	n/a	n/a	n/a	n/a
2		ABERDEEN CONV INCOME	ABERDEEN	110.5 (GBX)	+3.5	+2.9	+92.4	+39.2	-3.6	+54.4	+52.9
3		ABERDEEN HIGH INCOME	ABERDEEN	125.25 (GBX)	+8.3	+13.7	+162.4	+104.3	+5.7	+112.0	+96.4
4		CITY MERCHANTS HI YD	INVESCO	193.0 (GBX)	+9.9	+11.2	+83.1	+94.0	+1.9	+47.5	+78.7
5		FLEMING INC&CAP UNIT	FLEM INV	192.0 (GBX)	-9.0	+6.2	+76.9	+90.6	+5.0	+72.1	+115.3
6		GARTMORE BRIT INC UNIT	GARTMORE	345.0 (GBX)	+0.1	+16.8	+90.6	+103.9	+3.3	+69.4	+114.1
7		GLASGOW INCOME	GLASGOW	75.25 (GBX)	-3.9	+4.6	+111.8	+114.0	+4.7	+86.7	+110.9
8		GUINNESS FL EXTRA UTS	GUIN FL	282.5 (GBX)	-8.6	+8.3	+69.2	n/a	+3.6	+73.2	n/a
9		HENDERSON HIGH INCOME	HENDINVEST	168.0 (GBX)	-6.9	+3.4	+53.2	+75.5	+1.7	+63.2	+90.6
10		INVESCO CONVERTIBLE	INVESCO	119.5 (GBX)	-14.6	+5.7	+58.1	n/a	+10.7	+64.7	n/a
11		INVESTORS CAP PKG UNIT	FRNDS I&S	196.0 (GBX)	-11.6	-3.3	+70.0	+75.6	+0.6	+57.2	+88.0
12		MARTIN CURRIE HIGH INC	MAR CURRIE	99.0 (GBX)	+16.7	n/a	n/a	n/a	n/a	n/a	n/a
13		OLIM CONVERTIBLE UTS	OLIM	655.0 (GBX)	-7.4	-9.1	+15.2	n/a	-7.4	+22.8	n/a
14		SHIRES INCOME	GLASGOW	445.5 (GBX)	-3.1	+11.5	+116.2	+98.6	+6.9	+87.0	+120.5

The table is initially displayed in alphabetical order, but once again, you can click on any of the 'SORT' icons to change the format. To the left of each fund name, there is a small chart icon which you can click on to display a 1 year chart of the share price and Discount to NAV versus the FTA All Share Index. The charting facility on this site is more fully described in Chapter 2.

Trustnet - Closed End Funds *(con't)*

http://www.trustnet.co.uk/it/funds/warrants.asp

The Trustnet site is one of the few places where you can get reliable past performance data for Investment Trust Warrants. When you first enter the site via the address given above, an alphabetical list of all Closed End fund warrants is displayed. Once again, you can change the parameters at the top of the table top and just display a particular category of warrant. In the example below, the parameters have been changed to display Japanese warrants of UK listed Investment Trusts.

Fig 5.32 *A past performance table of Japanese Investment Trust warrants.*

Japan | All sectors | UK Investment Trusts

TrustNet — Japan / All sectors — TrustNet

Source : TrustNet - Saturday, 27 March 1999

12 Warrants
Sorted by warrant name

% Performance
(Warrant price in £)

Rank	Warrant Name SORT	Warrant Price	Share Price	Date SORT	Share Ratio	Ex. Price	1wk SORT	1mth SORT	1yr SORT	3yr SORT	5yr SORT
1	ATLANTIS JAPAN GROWTH	0.32 (USD)	6.3	Apr-2001	1.0 (ORD)	10.0	-3.0	+162.1	-28.5	n/a	n/a
2	B G SHIN NIPPON 05	20.25 (GBX)	82.0	Apr-2005	1.0 (ORD)	200.0	+1.3	+32.8	+153.1	-56.0	n/a
3	EDINBURGH JAPAN	44.25 (GBX)	96.0	Oct-2005	1.0 (ORD)	100.0	+4.7	+22.9	+26.4	-57.7	-67.7
4	FIDELITY JAPANESE VAL	11.5 (GBX)	47.5	Apr-2004	1.0 (ORD)	100.0	+4.5	+100.0	+70.4	-54.0	-80.2
5	FLEMING JAPANESE	0.05 (GBX)	176.8	Feb-1999	1.0 (ORD)	192.0	-37.5	-88.0	-99.4	-99.9	-100.0
6	GARTMORE SELECT JAPAN	12.25 (GBX)	49.8	Jun-2003	1.0 (ORD)	100.0	+11.4	+58.1	+25.6	n/a	n/a
7	HTR JAPANESE SMALLER	6.75 (GBX)	43.5	Nov-2002	1.0 (ORD)	100.0	+28.6	+58.8	+8.0	-81.3	-90.2
8	INVESCO JAPAN	15.25 (GBX)	50.5	Aug-2004	1.0 (ORD)	100.0	+22.0	+74.3	+90.6	-50.8	n/a
9	INVESCO TOKYO	10.75 (GBX)	31.3	Sep-2004	1.0 (ORD)	55.0	+10.3	+59.3	+38.7	-53.3	n/a
10	MARTIN CURRIE JAPAN	29.5 (GBX)	93.0	Sep-2002	1.0 (ORD)	100.0	+9.3	+53.2	+59.5	-26.3	n/a
11	PERPETUAL JAPANESE	6.0 (GBX)	43.8	Nov-2000	1.0 (ORD)	100.0	0.0	+100.0	+4.3	-79.7	-91.4
12	SCHRODER JAPAN	21.25 (GBX)	71.0	Nov-2004	1.0 (ORD)	100.0	+1.2	+54.5	+80.9	-37.5	n/a

In the case of Warrants, the past performance is displayed over 1 week and 1 month and over 1, 3 & 5 years. It is also worth mentioning that you can sort the warrants into expiry date order. This feature is extremely useful as it is often the case that warrants nearing the end of their life will exhibit very large price swings. This often makes the cumulative past performance rather meaningless.

Trustnet - Closed End Funds *(con't)*

http://www.trustnet.co.uk/it/funds/perf.asp

At the time of writing, not all investment trusts were included in the correct category. For example, if you change the selection parameters at the top of the table to 'United Kingdom' 'Income Growth' and 'UK Investment Trusts', only one fund is displayed which is not very helpful. The way round this problem is to use the 'Customised Portfolio' function described in Chapter 3.

Fig 5.33 *Only F&C Income Growth is categorised under 'UK Income Growth'!!!*

United Kingdom | Income Growth | UK Investment Trusts | Select!

TrustNet — United Kingdom / Income Growth — TrustNet

Source : TrustNet - Saturday, 27 March 1999

1 Funds Sorted by fund name						% Performance (Price total return in £)			% Performance (NAV total return in £)		
Rank	Chart	Fund Name SORT	Group Name SORT	Price	Disc/ Prem SORT	1yr SORT	3yr SORT	5yr SORT	1yr SORT	3yr SORT	5yr SORT
1		F & C INC GROWTH	F&C MGMT	109.0 (GBX)	-19.5	-7.8	+23.0	+36.3	-0.9	+44.5	+67.2

More accurate sector categorisations can be obtained from the Micropal site described earlier in this Chapter. You can look at the complete list of funds which should appear in a sector and then choose which of these to include in your customised portfolio. The example below is a customised portfolio which includes a selection on Income Growth Investment Trusts sorted by discount.

Fig 5.34 *Use the 'Customise' function to create more useful past performance tables.*

TrustNet — Portfolio: scottitonline — TrustNet

Source : TrustNet - Friday, 23 April 1999

11 Funds Sorted by fund name						% Performance (Price total return in £)			% Performance (NAV total return in £)		
Rank	Chart	Fund Name SORT	Group Name SORT	Price	Disc/ Prem SORT	1yr SORT	3yr SORT	5yr SORT	1yr SORT	3yr SORT	5yr SORT
1		CITY OF LONDON INV TST	HENDINVEST	270.0 (GBX)	-4.2	+2.0	+78.9	+116.6	+9.2	+83.7	+135.0
2		DUNEDIN INC GROWTH	EFM	217.5 (GBX)	-13.9	+5.0	+72.9	+93.9	+11.0	+75.7	+126.7
3		GT INCOME GROWTH	GT MGT	131.0 (GBX)	-19.0	-6.3	+49.1	n/a	+8.9	+71.9	n/a
4		JUPITER SPLIT PACKAGE	JUP ASSMAN	8100.0 (GBX)	-8.1	+15.7	+55.8	n/a	+6.4	+55.6	n/a
5		MERCHANTS	DRESDRCMGI	439.5 (GBX)	-6.1	+9.1	+82.6	+109.1	+10.7	+77.6	+126.4
6		MOR GREN EQU INCOME	MG INV MGT	209.5 (GBX)	-10.4	+13.8	+39.5	+78.6	+11.8	+61.8	+104.9
7		PERPETUAL INC & GWTH	PERPETUAL	132.5 (GBX)	-11.9	-4.3	+53.3	n/a	+8.7	+83.9	n/a
8		PROLIFIC INCOME	ABERDEEN	142.5 (GBX)	-16.5	+2.2	+28.1	n/a	[illegible]	[illegible]	n/a
9		SCHRODER INCOME GROWTH	[illegible]	138.5 (GBX)	-11.2	-11.0	+30.4	n/a	+3.3	+53.8	n/a
10		TEMPLE BAR	IGFITM	620.5 (GBX)	-5.4	+9.2	+90.7	+120.9	+9.4	+80.6	+127.1
11		VALUE & INCOME	OLIM	131.5 (GBX)	-23.7	-14.4	+15.1	+42.5	+5.5	+50.9	+92.9

Trustnet - Indices

http://www.trustnet.co.uk/general/indices.asp

The Trustnet site has excellent past performance data on over 100 different stock market indices. The past performance is quoted over 1 month and 1, 3 & 5 years in Sterling and in Local currency terms. Performance can be sorted over any of these periods so that it easy to see which have been the best performing stock markets. Initially, an alphabetical list of all 109 indices is displayed.

Fig 5.4 *Trustnet has past performance data on over 100 different stock market indices.*

<< Next << Af Fr Fr If If Mu Na Wa >> Next >>

All Select!

TrustNet All Indices TrustNet

Source : TrustNet - Saturday, 27 March 1999

106 Indices Sorted by index name			% Performance (Sterling)				% Performance (Local Currency)				
Rank	Index Name SORT	Index Value	1mth SORT	1yr SORT	3yr SORT	5yr SORT	1mth SORT	1yr SORT	3yr SORT	5yr SORT	Date
1	Affarsvarlden Weighted All SHR (SEK)	3414.65	-4.3	-6.7	+32.7	+107.9	-0.8	-5.1	+77.3	+137.4	25-Mar-99
2	Argentina Merval (ARP)	399.44	+4.1	-41.7	-29.4	-38.0	+6.6	-42.8	-23.9	-32.0	24-Mar-99
3	Athens SE General (GRD)	3471.48	-1.0	+98.1	+164.0	+145.9	+3.0	+80.5	+249.9	+227.8	25-Mar-99
4	Australia All Industrials (AUD)	5355.4	+2.0	+9.1	+22.6	+34.8	+2.0	+11.9	+59.4	+64.2	25-Mar-99
5	Australian All Ord (AUD)	2996.6	+2.8	+4.7	+1.8	+14.0	+2.8	+7.4	+32.4	+38.8	25-Mar-99
6	Austria Traded ATX (EUR)	1165.9	-4.1	-18.5	-14.8	-12.2	-0.9	-21.7	+9.1	+2.9	25-Mar-99
7	Bangkok SET (THB)	365.7	+7.7	-20.3	-82.4	-82.4	+9.9	-23.8	-72.0	-71.4	25-Mar-99
8	Bangladesh Index (BTK)	515.71	-5.5	-23.9	n/a	n/a	-3.2	-21.8	n/a	n/a	24-Mar-99
9	Baring Emerg Mkts Europe (USD)	112.11	+0.9	-19.8	-19.0	-3.9	+2.6	-22.0	-13.4	+4.7	25-Mar-99
10	Baring Emerging Markets (USD)	123.04	+6.4	-19.6	-26.6	-28.6	+8.2	-21.7	-21.5	-22.2	25-Mar-99
11	Baring Emerging Mkts Asia (USD)	114.08	+7.4	-5.1	-50.8	-42.2	+9.3	-7.6	-47.4	-37.0	25-Mar-99
12	Baring Emg Markets Lat.Am (USD)	128.79	+11.2	-30.1	-7.3	-23.0	+13.1	-31.9	-0.8	-16.1	25-Mar-99
13	Baring Pan Europe Index (USD)	113.36	-1.2	-21.9	+0.7	n/a	+1.2	-23.4	+8.5	n/a	24-Mar-99
14	Bombay SE National 100 (INR)	1619.85	+10.5	-9.3	-18.9	-38.8	+12.0	-5.2	+7.8	-9.8	25-Mar-99
15	Bombay Sensitive (INR)	3682.69	+10.5	-10.3	-14.1	-32.0	+12.0	-6.2	+14.2	+0.1	25-Mar-99
16	Brazil Bovespa Index (BRC)	10429.0	+30.0	-44.2	+3.1	n/a	+20.2	-11.3	+107.3	n/a	24-Mar-99
17	Budapest (BUX) Index (HUF)	5457.5	-7.4	-42.5	+31.0	+16.7	-3.6	-37.7	+128.2	+189.6	25-Mar-99
18	Budapest SE (HUF)	5295.23	-10.1	-44.6	+26.2	+15.4	-5.7	-39.6	+121.4	+188.5	24-Mar-99
19	Cairo SE General Index (EGP)	446.51	-0.9	+18.0	n/a	n/a	+1.3	+15.5	n/a	n/a	24-Mar-99

The alphabet is split up into four blocks in a box above the table. You need to click on the appropriate alphabetical block to display the other indices.

Trustnet - Indices *(con't)*

http://www.trustnet.co.uk/general/indices.asp

A very useful feature of this site, is the ability to select which indices are displayed. This is done by clicking on the small box above the table which initially has 'All' in it. A list of options appears and you simply pick the indices you are interested in and click on 'Select' to display them.

Fig 5.41 *Selecting 'UK' enables you to compare different sectors of the UK market.*

UK | Select!

TrustNet — UK Indices — Source : TrustNet - Saturday, 27 March 1999 — TrustNet

12 Indices Sorted by index name			% Performance (Sterling)				% Performance (Local Currency)				
Rank	Index Name SORT	Index Value	1mth SORT	1yr SORT	3yr SORT	5yr SORT	1mth SORT	1yr SORT	3yr SORT	5yr SORT	Date
1	FT-SE 100 Index (GBX)	6084.99	-2.0	+2.0	+65.3	+94.5	-2.0	+2.0	+65.3	+94.5	25-Mar-99
2	FT-SE 350 Index (GBX)	2905.7	-1.0	+1.3	+56.7	+82.9	-1.0	+1.3	+56.7	+82.9	25-Mar-99
3	FT-SE AIM Index (GBX)	854.9	+4.1	-19.3	-13.4	n/a	+4.1	-19.3	-13.4	n/a	25-Mar-99
4	FT-SE Mid 250 Index (GBX)	5462.5	+4.5	-1.5	+27.1	+44.7	+4.5	-1.5	+27.1	+44.7	25-Mar-99
5	FT-SE Small Cos Index (GBX)	2388.0	+5.1	-9.1	+14.5	+22.9	+5.1	-9.1	+14.5	+22.9	25-Mar-99
6	FT-SE Small Ex-IT Index (GBX)	2361.5	+5.5	-9.8	+14.0	+23.0	+5.5	-9.8	+14.0	+23.0	25-Mar-99
7	FTA Insurance (GBX)	2228.14	-4.7	-20.1	+61.9	+63.8	-4.7	-20.0	+61.9	+63.8	25-Mar-99
8	FTA Pharmaceuticals (GBX)	10445.81	-6.8	+11.8	+113.9	+259.8	-6.8	+11.8	+113.9	+259.8	25-Mar-99
9	FTA Property (GBX)	1882.87	+3.9	-20.5	+29.4	+16.1	+3.9	-20.5	+29.4	+16.1	25-Mar-99
10	FTA Utilities (GBX)	3856.98	-3.7	+0.1	+57.7	+64.5	-3.7	+0.1	+57.7	+64.5	25-Mar-99
11	FTSE All-Share Index (GBX)	2815.34	-0.7	+0.7	+53.5	+78.1	-0.7	+0.7	+53.5	+78.0	25-Mar-99
12	FTSE Fledgling X Inv Tsts. (GBX)	1306.8	+4.3	-8.8	+11.3	n/a	+4.3	-8.8	+11.3	n/a	25-Mar-99

For UK Indices, the Sterling and Local Currency performance is obviously the same. For overseas stock markets, there can be big differences in performance depending on whether the local currency has been strong or weak against Sterling. In the example below, the French stock market is up 106.5% in local terms over 3 years, but up only 65.1% in Sterling terms.

Fig 5.42 *Currency movements have a significant effect on stock market performance.*

TrustNet — European Indices — Source : TrustNet - Saturday, 27 March 1999 — TrustNet

17 Indices 1yr £ performance			% Performance (Sterling)				% Performance (Local Currency)				
Rank	Index Name SORT	Index Value	1mth SORT	1yr SORT	3yr SORT	5yr SORT	1mth SORT	1yr SORT	3yr SORT	5yr SORT	Date
1	France CAC-40 (EUR)	4137.01	-3.7	+12.8	+61.1	+65.2	-0.4	+8.3	+106.5	+93.6	25-Mar-99
2	France SBF 120 (EUR)	2778.09	-3.7	+11.7	+54.3	+59.1	-0.5	+7.2	+97.7	+86.5	25-Mar-99
3	France SBF 250 (EUR)	2619.14	-3.4	+11.3	+49.3	+54.4	-0.1	+0.8	+91.4	+80.9	25-Mar-99
4	Milan Comit (EUR)	1545.92	-1.7	+6.2	+106.1	+96.9	+1.6	+2.0	+164.1	+130.8	25-Mar-99
5	MSCI Europe (USD)	1275.57	-4.6	+3.5	+57.8	+91.8	-2.9	+0.7	+68.9	+109.0	25-Mar-99
6	FTA Wrld Europe X UK (USD)	320.22	-3.1	+3.4	+57.6	+96.7	-1.5	+0.7	+68.6	+114.4	25-Mar-99
7	FTA Europe (USD)	350.09	-2.5	+2.9	+58.3	+92.5	-0.8	+0.2	+69.4	+109.8	25-Mar-99
8	Swiss SPI General Index (CHF)	408.1	-3.1	-0.0	+40.1	+102.7	+0.4	-4.3	+84.6	+128.6	25-Mar-99
9	France Agefi Second Market (EUR)	537.76	-0.1	-0.3	+1.9	+14.9	+1.7	-3.5	+28.0	+30.2	10-Mar-99
10	Germany DAX (DEM)	4897.81	-5.2	-0.5	+48.6	+94.2	-2.0	-4.6	+93.6	+128.2	25-Mar-99
11	Germany FAZ (DEM)	1551.24	-7.0	-2.1	+33.8	+60.9	-3.8	-6.2	+74.2	+89.1	25-Mar-99
12	HSBC Smaller Europe (Ex.Uk) (USD)	140.71	-3.3	-5.6	+28.6	+38.9	-1.6	-8.1	+37.6	+51.3	25-Mar-99
13	Affarsvarlden Weighted All SHR (SEK)	3414.65	-4.3	-6.7	+32.7	+107.9	-0.8	-5.1	+77.3	+137.4	25-Mar-99
14	Irish General (EUR)	3752.8	-5.8	-9.0	+29.1	+71.0	-2.6	-12.7	+65.4	+100.5	25-Mar-99
15	Austria Traded ATX (EUR)	1165.9	-4.1	-18.5	-14.8	-12.2	-0.9	-21.7	+9.1	+2.9	25-Mar-99
16	Baring Pan Europe Index (USD)	113.36	-1.2	-21.9	+0.7	n/a	+1.2	-23.4	+8.5	n/a	24-Mar-99
17	Central European Stock Index (USD)	1083.35	-4.4	-30.8	n/a	n/a	-2.1	-32.2	n/a	n/a	24-Mar-99

Trustnet - Currencies

http://www.trustnet.co.uk/general/rates.asp

The Trustnet site also has past performance data on over 30 major currencies. If you are looking at the past performance of overseas investments, it is as well to be aware of how much of the performance is made up of currency movement. If a currency moves against you, it doesn't matter whether you picked the best performing investment on the stock market, you still have the potential to lose money. Currencies are listed alphabetically, and performance is shown against both Sterling and the US Dollar over 1 month and 1, 3 & 5 years. The exchange rate for each currency is also shown, which is useful.

Fig 5.5 *The Trustnet site has performance data on over 30 major currencies.*

TrustNet — **Exchange Rates** — TrustNet

Source : TrustNet - Saturday, 27 March 1999

37 Exchange Rates Sorted by currency			% Performance (Sterling)					% Performance (Dollar)				
Rank	Currency Name SORT	£ Rate	1mth SORT	1yr SORT	3yr SORT	5yr SORT	$ Rate	1mth SORT	1yr SORT	3yr SORT	5yr SORT	Date
1	Australia Dollar (AUD)	2.56	-0.0	-2.5	-23.1	-17.9	1.56	+1.7	-5.1	-17.8	-10.5	25-Mar-99
2	Austria Schilling (ATS)	20.65	-3.3	+4.8	-23.3	-15.1	12.6	-1.6	+1.5	-17.9	-7.5	25-Mar-99
3	Belgium Financial Franc (BEF)	60.54	-3.3	+4.3	-23.5	-15.0	36.94	-1.6	+1.6	-18.2	-7.3	25-Mar-99
4	Brazil Real (BRC)	2.94	+11.3	-35.3	-48.8	n/a	1.84	+13.2	-37.0	-45.2	n/a	25-Mar-99
5	Canadian Dollar (CAD)	2.46	-2.1	-3.9	-15.7	-16.5	1.5	-0.4	-6.5	-9.8	-9.0	25-Mar-99
6	Chile Peso (CLP)	793.93	+0.7	-4.7	-20.9	-19.2	489.75	+2.5	-7.3	-15.4	-12.0	25-Mar-99
7	China Renminbi Yuan (CNY)	13.51	-1.7	+2.7	-5.3	-4.1	8.28	-0.0	0.0	+1.3	+4.5	25-Mar-99
8	Colombia Peso (COP)	2503.1	+0.6	-8.6	-35.8	-51.2	1541.75	+2.4	-11.1	-31.3	-46.8	25-Mar-99
9	Euro (EUR)	1.5	-3.3	+4.2	-22.0	-14.7	0.92	-1.6	+1.4	-16.5	-7.0	25-Mar-99
10	French Franc (FRF)	9.84	-3.3	+4.2	-21.7	-13.1	6.01	-1.6	+1.5	-16.2	-5.3	25-Mar-99
11	German Mark (DEM)	2.94	-3.3	+4.3	-23.2	-14.9	1.79	-1.6	+1.5	-17.9	-7.3	25-Mar-99
12	Greece Drachma (GRD)	486.9	-3.9	+9.7	-24.6	-25.0	297.05	-2.2	+6.8	-19.3	-18.2	25-Mar-99
13	Hong Kong Dollar (HKD)	12.64	-1.7	+2.7	-6.7	-8.5	7.75	0.0	-0.0	-0.2	-0.3	25-Mar-99
14	India Rupee (INR)	69.19	-1.4	-4.3	-24.8	-32.1	42.4	+0.4	-6.8	-19.5	-26.0	25-Mar-99
15	Indonesian Rupiah (IDR)	14461.39	-2.6	-2.9	-75.3	-77.7	8845.01	-0.9	-5.5	-73.6	-75.7	25-Mar-99
16	Ireland Punt (IEP)	1.18	-3.3	+3.0	-17.9	-12.1	0.72	-1.6	+0.2	-12.2	-4.2	25-Mar-99
17	Israel Shekel (ISL)	6.64	-2.2	-9.5	-28.9	-33.2	4.04	-0.5	-11.9	-24.0	-27.3	25-Mar-99
18	Italian Lira (ITL)	2905.96	-3.3	+3.9	-18.1	-15.0	1772.98	-1.6	+1.1	-12.4	-7.4	25-Mar-99
19	Japanese Yen (JPY)	192.76	-0.1	+12.1	-16.0	-18.6	117.6	+1.7	+9.2	-10.2	-11.3	25-Mar-99
20	Malaysian Ringit (MYR)	8.86	-1.7	-32.1	-56.2	-54.1	5.43	0.0	-33.9	-53.2	-50.0	25-Mar-99
21	Mexico Peso (MXP)	15.74	+1.7	-9.2	-26.9	-68.1	9.68	+3.4	-11.6	-21.8	-65.2	25-Mar-99
22	Netherlands Guilder (NLG)	3.31	-3.3	+4.3	-23.8	-15.1	2.02	-1.6	+1.6	-18.4	-7.5	25-Mar-99
23	New Zealand Dollar (NZD)	3.03	+0.4	-1.9	-26.9	-12.8	1.85	+2.2	-4.5	-21.8	-5.0	25-Mar-99
24	Peru New Sol (PEI)	5.51	-0.0	-14.4	-35.0	-41.5	3.39	+1.7	-16.7	-30.4	-36.3	25-Mar-99
25	Philippine Peso (PHP)	63.15	-0.8	-1.7	-36.7	-35.7	38.7	+0.9	-4.3	-32.3	-29.9	25-Mar-99
26	Poland Zloty (POZ)	6.44	-2.9	-10.6	-38.9	-49.1	3.97	-1.2	-13.0	-34.6	-44.5	25-Mar-99
27	Portugal Escudo (PTE)	300.88	-3.3	+4.2	-22.6	-14.2	183.57	-1.6	+1.5	-17.2	-6.5	25-Mar-99
28	RSA Rand (ZAR)	10.13	-2.2	-17.7	-40.8	-49.1	6.2	-0.5	-19.9	-36.6	-44.5	25-Mar-99

Trustnet - Currencies *(con't)*

http://www.trustnet.co.uk/general/rates.asp

Once again, the currencies can be sorted in order of past performance. This makes it easy to see at a glance which have been the best and worst performing currencies over a selected time period. In the example below, the currencies have been sorted in their 3 year performance relative to Sterling. The table clearly shows what a powerful effect the strength of sterling has had on overseas investments. For example, the Swiss Franc - often thought of as a safe haven - has lost a quarter of its value against sterling over the last 3 years.

Fig 5.51 *Over 3 years, Sterling has been the strongest major currency.*

TrustNet — **Exchange Rates** — *Source : TrustNet - Saturday, 27 March 1999* — TrustNet

37 Exchange Rates 3yr £ performance		% Performance (Sterling)					% Performance (Dollar)					
Rank	Currency Name SORT	£ Rate	1mth SORT	1yr SORT	3yr SORT	5yr SORT	$ Rate	1mth SORT	1yr SORT	3yr SORT	5yr SORT	Date
1	China Renminbi Yuan (CNY)	13.51	-1.7	+2.7	-5.3	-4.1	8.28	-0.0	0.0	+1.3	+4.5	25-Mar-99
2	United States Dollar (USD)	1.63	-1.7	+2.7	-6.5	-8.2	1.0	0.0	0.0	0.0	0.0	25-Mar-99
3	Hong Kong Dollar (HKD)	12.64	-1.7	+2.7	-6.7	-8.5	7.75	0.0	-0.0	-0.2	-0.3	25-Mar-99
4	Canadian Dollar (CAD)	2.46	-2.1	-3.9	-15.7	-16.5	1.5	-0.4	-6.5	-9.8	-9.0	25-Mar-99
5	Japanese Yen (JPY)	192.76	-0.1	+12.1	-16.0	-18.6	117.6	+1.7	+9.2	-10.2	-11.3	25-Mar-99
6	Ireland Punt (IEP)	1.18	-3.3	+3.0	-17.9	-12.1	0.72	-1.6	+0.2	-12.2	-4.2	25-Mar-99
7	Italian Lira (ITL)	2905.96	-3.3	+3.9	-18.1	-15.0	1772.98	-1.6	+1.1	-12.4	-7.4	25-Mar-99
8	Chile Peso (CLP)	793.93	+0.7	-4.7	-20.9	-19.2	489.75	+2.5	-7.3	-15.4	-12.0	25-Mar-99
9	French Franc (FRF)	9.84	-3.3	+4.2	-21.7	-13.1	6.01	-1.6	+1.5	-16.2	-5.3	25-Mar-99
10	Euro (EUR)	1.5	-3.3	+4.2	-22.0	-14.7	0.92	-1.6	+1.4	-16.5	-7.0	25-Mar-99
11	Portugal Escudo (PTE)	300.88	-3.3	+4.2	-22.6	-14.2	183.57	-1.6	+1.5	-17.2	-6.5	25-Mar-99
12	Taiwan Dollar (new) (TWD)	54.05	-1.8	+1.3	-23.1	-26.8	33.1	-0.1	-1.4	-17.7	-20.3	25-Mar-99
13	Australia Dollar (AUD)	2.56	-0.0	-2.5	-23.1	-17.9	1.56	+1.7	-5.1	-17.8	-10.5	25-Mar-99
14	German Mark (DEM)	2.94	-3.3	+4.3	-23.2	-14.9	1.79	-1.6	+1.5	-17.9	-7.3	25-Mar-99
15	Austria Schilling (ATS)	20.65	-3.3	+4.3	-23.3	-15.1	12.6	-1.6	+1.5	-17.9	-7.5	25-Mar-99
16	Belgium Financial Franc (BEF)	60.54	-3.3	+4.3	-23.5	-15.0	36.94	-1.6	+1.6	-18.2	-7.3	25-Mar-99
17	Netherlands Guilder (NLG)	3.31	-3.3	+4.3	-23.8	-15.1	2.02	-1.6	+1.6	-18.4	-7.5	25-Mar-99
18	Singapore Dollar (SGD)	2.82	-1.8	-4.9	-23.9	-16.2	1.73	-0.1	-7.4	-18.5	-8.6	25-Mar-99
19	Swiss Franc (CHF)	2.4	-3.5	+4.5	-24.1	-11.3	1.46	-1.8	+1.7	-18.8	-3.4	25-Mar-99
20	Spanish Peseta (ESP)	249.71	-3.3	+4.0	-24.2	-17.7	152.35	-1.6	+1.3	-18.8	-10.3	25-Mar-99
21	Greece Drachma (GRD)	486.9	-3.9	+9.7	-24.6	-25.0	297.05	-2.2	+6.8	-19.3	-18.2	25-Mar-99
22	India Rupee (INR)	69.19	-1.4	-4.3	-24.8	-32.1	42.4	+0.4	-6.8	-19.5	-26.0	25-Mar-99
23	New Zealand Dollar (NZD)	3.03	+0.4	-1.9	-26.9	-12.8	1.85	+2.2	-4.5	-21.8	-5.0	25-Mar-99
24	Mexico Peso (MXP)	15.74	+1.7	-9.2	-26.9	-68.1	9.68	+3.4	-11.6	-21.8	-65.2	25-Mar-99
25	Israel Shekel (ISL)	6.64	-2.2	0.5	-28.9	-33.2	4.04	-0.5	-11.9	-24.0	-27.3	25-Mar-99
26	Peru New Sol (PEI)	5.51	-0.0	-14.4	-35.0	-41.5	3.39	+1.7	-16.7	-30.4	-36.3	25-Mar-99
27	Colombia Peso (COP)	2503.1	+0.6	-8.6	-35.8	-51.2	1541.75	+2.4	-11.1	-31.3	-46.8	25-Mar-99

Interactive Investor

http://www.iii.co.uk/performance

The Interactive Investor site has comprehensive past performance statistics on most types of investments.To access data, you need to move the cursor over the bullet point alongside an investment category and click once.

Fig 5.6 *The Interactive Investor site has performance data for most types of investment.*

If you click on 'Unit Trusts', the best performing funds and sectors over 1, 3, 5 & 10 years are displayed. You can display a chart of any of these funds simply by clicking on the fund name. If you click on one of the top performing sectors, the top fund in that sector is displayed along with an alphabetical list of all the fund management groups with funds in that sector. See over the page.

Fig 5.61 *Initially an overview of the top performing funds and sectors is displayed.*

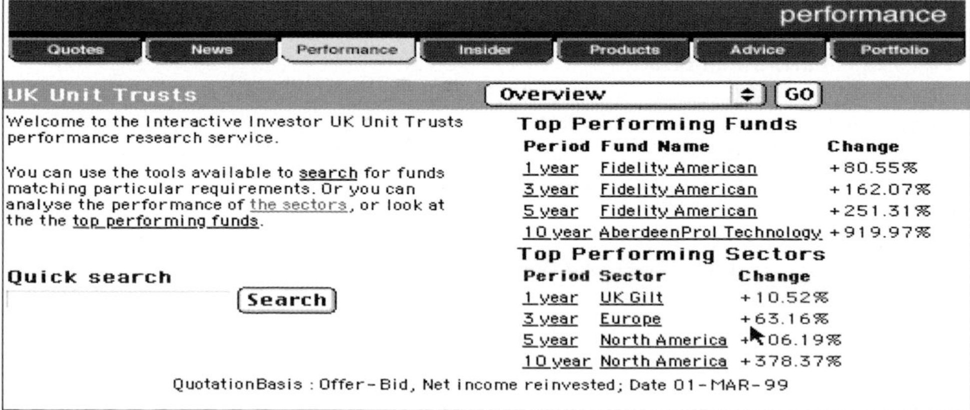

Interactive Investor *(con't)*

http://www.iii.co.uk/performance/micropal.epl?code=market:uu

The unit trust charting facility at the Interactive Investor site is very comprehensive and is fully described in Chapter 2.

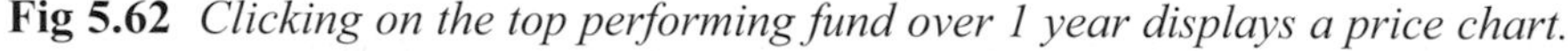

Fig 5.62 *Clicking on the top performing fund over 1 year displays a price chart.*

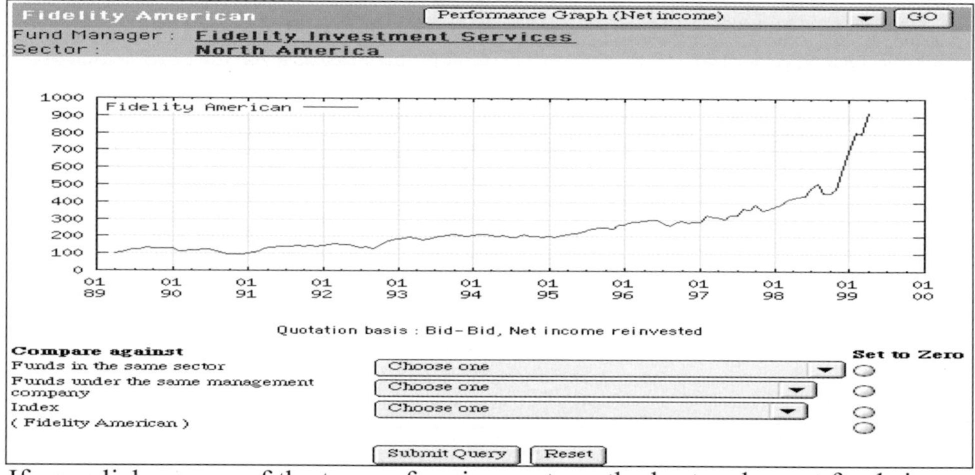

If you click on one of the top performing sectors, the best and worst funds in that sector over 1, 3, 5 & 10 years are displayed. Once again you can click on any of these funds to obtain a price chart. You can also click on any one of the fund management group names to display a price chart of their fund in that sector.

Fig 5.63 *Clicking on one of the top performing sectors, shows the best and worst funds.*

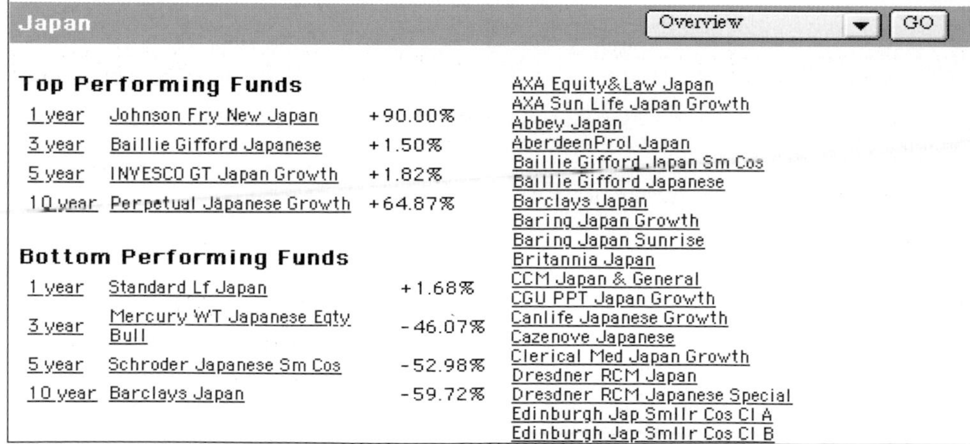

Japan | Overview | GO

Top Performing Funds

1 year	Johnson Fry New Japan	+90.00%
3 year	Baillie Gifford Japanese	+1.50%
5 year	INVESCO GT Japan Growth	+1.82%
10 year	Perpetual Japanese Growth	+64.87%

Bottom Performing Funds

1 year	Standard Lf Japan	+1.68%
3 year	Mercury WT Japanese Eqty Bull	-46.07%
5 year	Schroder Japanese Sm Cos	-52.98%
10 year	Barclays Japan	-59.72%

AXA Equity&Law Japan
AXA Sun Life Japan Growth
Abbey Japan
AberdeenProl Japan
Baillie Gifford Japan Sm Cos
Baillie Gifford Japanese
Barclays Japan
Baring Japan Growth
Baring Japan Sunrise
Britannia Japan
CCM Japan & General
CGU PPT Japan Growth
Canlife Japanese Growth
Cazenove Japanese
Clerical Med Japan Growth
Dresdner RCM Japan
Dresdner RCM Japanese Special
Edinburgh Jap Smllr Cos Cl A
Edinburgh Jap Smllr Cos Cl B

Interactive Investor *(con't)*

http://www.iii.co.uk/performance/micropal.epl?code=market:uu

If you want to display the performance of a specific fund, you need to click on the 'Search' box in Figure 5.61. A box appears, and you must type in part of the funds name and then click on 'Submit'.

Fig 5.64 *Submitting a search for funds with the word 'newton' in the title.*

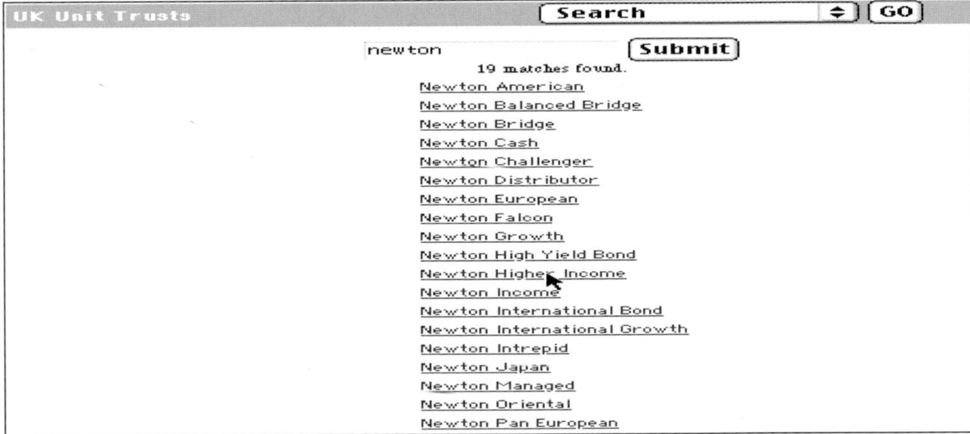

To display the past performance for one of these funds, click on the name of the fund. The price chart which appears gives you a number of options including the ability to compare other investments on the same chart and display a set of year on year figures. These options are more fully described in Chapter 2.

Fig 5.65 *Clicking on a fund such as 'Newton Higher Income' displays a price chart.*

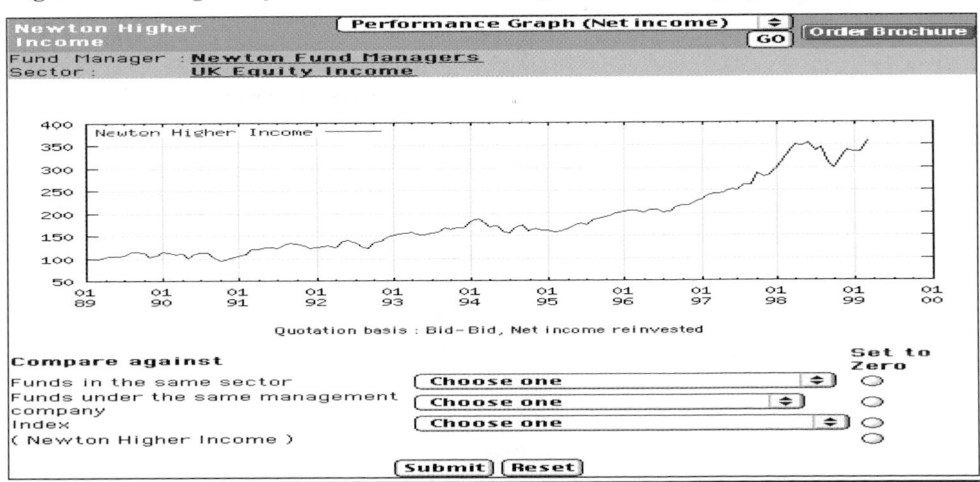

Interactive Investor *(con't)*

http://www.iii.co.uk/performance/micropal.epl?action=power_search&code=market%3Auu&=Go

On the screen shown in Figure 5.61, it is quite easy to miss the box at the top of the page initially entitled 'Overview'. Clicking on this box reveals a powerful list of additional options including 'Power Search', 'Top Funds', 'Sector Performance' and 'Fund Managers'. The Power Search option enables you to set certain criteria and display only the performance over 1, 3, 5 & 10 years of the ten best funds which meet those criteria. When you have set your criteria, you need to click on 'Go' to display the results. Once again you can click on any of the fund names to display the performance in the form of a price chart.

Fig 5.66 *A Power Search display of the top ten 'UK Equity Income' funds over '1 year'.*

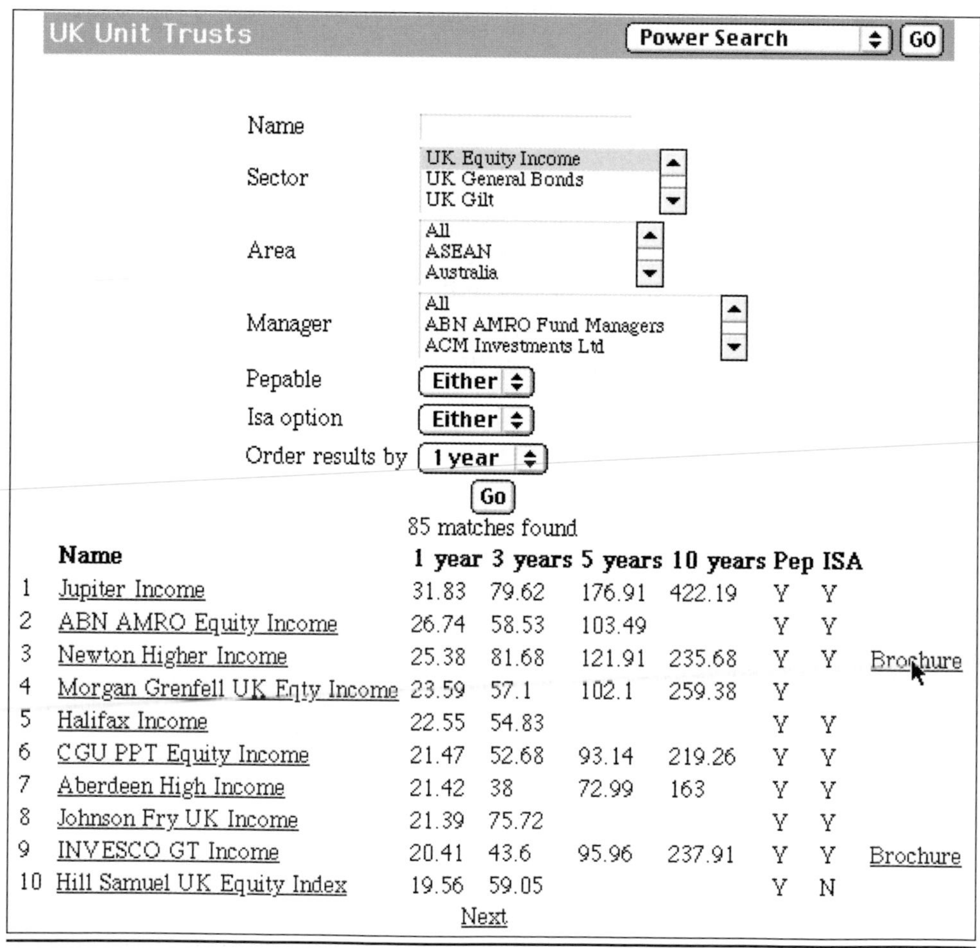

	Name	1 year	3 years	5 years	10 years	Pep	ISA	
1	Jupiter Income	31.83	79.62	176.91	422.19	Y	Y	
2	ABN AMRO Equity Income	26.74	58.53	103.49		Y	Y	
3	Newton Higher Income	25.38	81.68	121.91	235.68	Y	Y	Brochure
4	Morgan Grenfell UK Eqty Income	23.59	57.1	102.1	259.38	Y		
5	Halifax Income	22.55	54.83			Y	Y	
6	CGU PPT Equity Income	21.47	52.68	93.14	219.26	Y	Y	
7	Aberdeen High Income	21.42	38	72.99	163	Y	Y	
8	Johnson Fry UK Income	21.39	75.72			Y	Y	
9	INVESCO GT Income	20.41	43.6	95.96	237.91	Y	Y	Brochure
10	Hill Samuel UK Equity Index	19.56	59.05			Y	N	

Next

Interactive Investor *(con't)*

http://www.iii.co.uk/performance/micropal.epl?action=market_top_funds&code=market%3Auu&=GO

The 'Top Funds' option allows you to choose to display either 10, 20 or 50 of the best performing funds over either 1, 3, 5 or 10 years. Each time you have made your selection, you need to click on 'Go' to display the results.

Fig 5.67 *The 'Top 10 Funds' over 5 years.*

UK Unit Trusts — Top Funds — GO

Show top 10 funds over 5 years Go

Name	1 Year	3 Years	5 Years	10 Years
Fidelity American	+103.88%	+198.72%	+321.13%	+771.08%
AberdeenProl Technology	+50.98%	+84.52%	+282.11%	+921.17%
GA North American Growth	+26.06%	+101.74%	+277.23%	+787.56%
Edinburgh North American Cl B	+36.24%	+107.04%	+232.97%	+640.92%
Edinburgh North American Cl A	+35.95%	+106.60%	+232.26%	+639.36%
Fidelity American Special Sits	+36.49%	+92.28%	+217.18%	+489.94%
Threadneedle Amer Sel Gth 2	+36.34%	+100.19%	+213.28%	+509.42%
Threadneedle Amer Sel Gth 1	+30.70%	+98.74%	+211.02%	+505.02%
Jupiter UK Growth Exempt	+6.64%	+126.95%	+208.78%	N/A
Framlington American Growth	+38.24%	+110.82%	+203.23%	N/A

The 'Sector Performance' option displays the best performing fund within each sector. You can choose to display the sectors either alphabetically or ordered over 1, 3, 5 or 10 years. Clicking on any one of the sectors, will display the best performing funds in that sector.

Fig 5.68 *The best performing sectors over '3 years'.*

UK Unit Trusts — Sector Performance — GO

Order by 3 years Go

Name	1 Year	3 Years	5 Years	10 Years
North America	+9.86%	+58.71%	+123.84%	+377.54%
UK Growth & Income	+0.70%	+56.02%	+89.48%	+193.65%
Europe	-0.19%	+54.56%	+96.05%	+285.64%
UK Equity Income	-2.70%	+52.41%	+78.38%	+182.41%
UK Equity & Bond	-0.01%	+51.75%	+85.12%	+223.81%
UK Equity Growth	-1.12%	+50.56%	+84.63%	+178.64%
UK Equity & Bond Income	-0.56%	+44.92%	+63.41%	+142.35%
International Equity Income	+2.26%	+42.82%	+70.20%	+221.26%
Managed Fund	+1.74%	+37.24%	+59.34%	+175.44%
UK Fixed Interest	+6.12%	+36.57%	+49.18%	+119.05%
UK Gilt	+9.62%	+35.13%	+41.39%	+118.58%
Property	-2.94%	+31.15%	+30.60%	N/A
International Equity Growth	+3.36%	+30.74%	+57.69%	+193.16%
International Equity & Bond	+4.32%	+28.14%	+48.57%	+178.61%
Investment Trust Units	-7.50%	+26.45%	+43.28%	+160.67%
Fund of Funds	-1.87%	+24.64%	+44.70%	+154.43%
UK Smaller Companies	-9.76%	+21.54%	+46.87%	+98.79%
Money Market	+4.67%	+14.60%	+23.62%	+78.46%
International Fixed Interest	+4.12%	+6.05%	+15.94%	+90.51%
Japan	+24.80%	-26.85%	-29.90%	-6.75%
Emerging Markets	-25.63%	-28.23%	-41.83%	+50.55%
Far East Including Japan	-0.03%	-31.22%	-26.57%	+43.37%
Far East Excluding Japan	-11.79%	-40.13%	-29.85%	+110.82%
Index Bear	-9.08%	-41.52%	-52.07%	N/A

Interactive Investor *(con't)*

http://www.iii.co.uk/performance/micropal.epl?action=managers&code=market%3Auu&=GO

The 'Fund Managers' option enables you to display the performance of the four best and worst funds from that Management Group over 1, 3, 5, & 10 years. Type in the name of a Fund Management Group in the appropriate box and click on 'Go'. The complete list of funds managed by that group is displayed on the same page alongside the performance figures. Click on any of the fund names to display a price performance chart.

Fig 5.69 *The 'Fund Managers' option initially displays the four best and worst funds.*

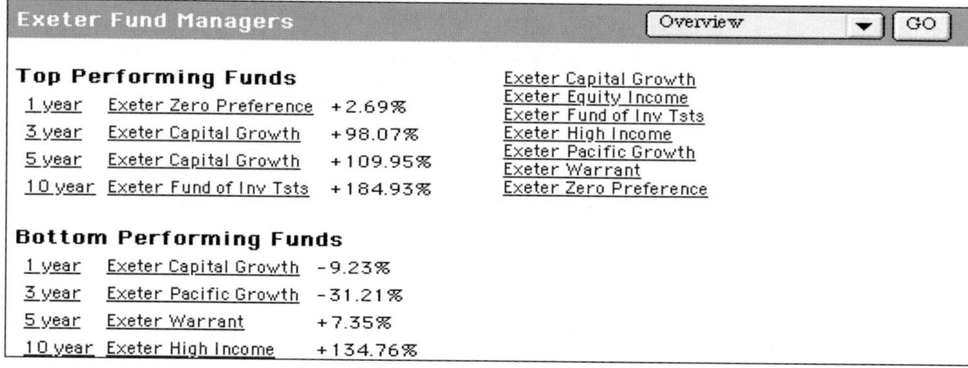

Exeter Fund Managers
Overview
GO
Top Performing Funds
1 year Exeter Zero Preference +2.69%
3 year Exeter Capital Growth +98.07%
5 year Exeter Capital Growth +109.95%
10 year Exeter Fund of Inv Tsts +184.93%
Bottom Performing Funds
1 year Exeter Capital Growth -9.23%
3 year Exeter Pacific Growth -31.21%
5 year Exeter Warrant +7.35%
10 year Exeter High Income +134.76%
Exeter Capital Growth
Exeter Equity Income
Exeter Fund of Inv Tsts
Exeter High Income
Exeter Pacific Growth
Exeter Warrant
Exeter Zero Preference

You can opt to display the 1, 3, 5, & 10 year performance of all the funds managed by a Group. To do this, click on the box in the top right hand corner of the screen entitled 'Overview', change it to 'Performance' and click 'Go'. The order in which the funds appear in the table, can be changed by clicking on the 'Order by' box and changing the selection from 1 year to either 3, 5 or 10 years.

Fig 5.6.10 *Change 'Overview' to 'Performance' to display the performance of all funds.*

Exeter Fund Managers — Performance — GO

Order by 1 year — Go

Name	1 Year	3 Years	5 Years	10 Years
Exeter Zero Preference	2.69	25.6	43.26	N/A
Exeter High Income	2.58	61.71	54.79	134.76
Exeter Warrant	-.37	20.33	7.35	N/A
Exeter Equity Income	-2.73	52.02	N/A	N/A
Exeter Pacific Growth	-6.12	-31.21	N/A	N/A
Exeter Fund of Inv Tsts	-9.13	23.24	42.33	184.93
Exeter Capital Growth	9.23	98.07	109.95	N/A

6

Research

Many investment decisions have three distinct phases. The initial idea, identifying investments which will benefit and researching those individual investments. An investment idea can come from a variety of sources such as news reports, your own experiences or a tip from a friend. Identifying investments which might benefit from certain conditions could involve looking at particular sectors of a market. Individual stock research would involve analyzing figures (profits, earnings growth etc.), looking at a price chart, and reading comments from other investors. All these parameters and variables are covered in this Chapter.

Hot Links

- ✔ Stock research - *Wright Research Center*
- ✔ Sorting stocks by dividend yield, earnings etc. - *Datastream*
- ✔ Stock tips in the Weekend Press - *Financial News Digest*
- ✔ Consensus of Brokers Earnings Estimates - *Hemscott*
- ✔ Consensus Recommendations and Analysts Forecasts - *Financial Times*
- ✔ The 10 best and worst UK stocks - *Automated City Analyst*
- ✔ Best savings and deposit rates - *Money Facts*
- ✍ UK Bulletin Boards - *Market-Eye, Hemscott, UK Shares & Interactive Inv*

Most research on individual stocks, has to be paid for although a few American internet sites do provide free research on some UK stocks. Over time, it is likely that an increasing number of UK brokers will allow investors free access to their Research. Meanwhile, many investors will find that there is sufficient information in other Chapters of this book, to allow them to conduct their own basic research. This Chapter also tells you where to find out which banks and building societies are offering the best saving rates on a variety of different savings accounts.

✍ *Indicates that Registration is necessary to access information at this site.*

Wright Research Center

http://profiles.wisi.com/

The Wright Research Center is an excellent internet site where investors can get free analysis on most UK shares. When you first enter this site via the address above, you are presented with a number of different ways to search for information on a particular share. The quickest way to access information, is to type in the correct 'Ticker Symbol' for that share and click on 'Search'. For example, to access information on the company Dixons, you would type in 'dxns'. If you simply type in 'dixons' in the 'Company Name' box and click on 'Search', a list of all companies and classes of share with the word 'dixons' in the title will be displayed. You can also use the 'Alphabetical List' to search for stocks, or alternatively click on one of the countries under the 'Country List'. The latter displays an alphabetical list of all the stocks in that country covered at this site.

Fig 6.1 *Wright Research Center has analysis on over 18,000 International companies.*

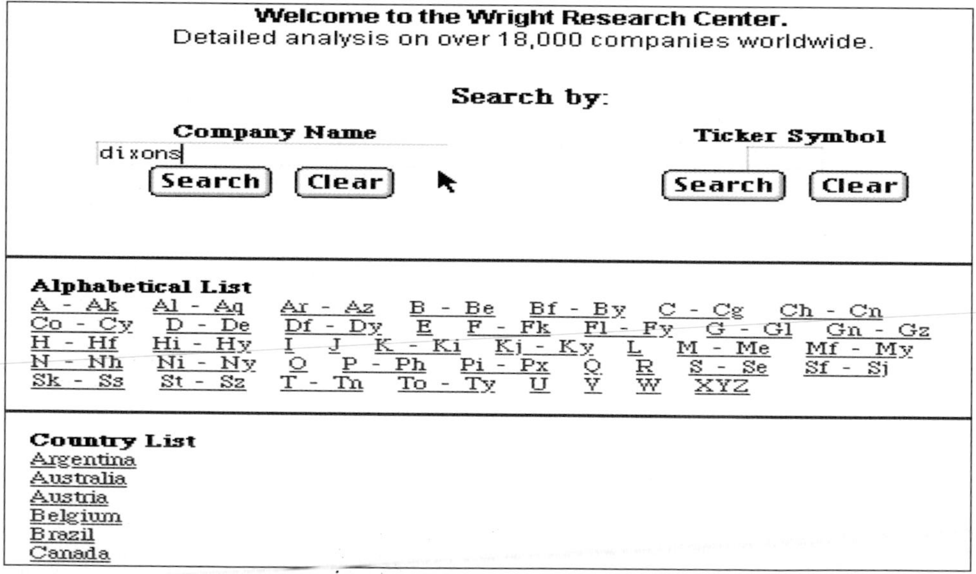

A surprisingly good feature of this American based site, is that it covers the majority of UK smaller companies. Many sites only have information on the top 100 or 250 UK companies. Another good feature is the ability to convert any of the displayed figures into another currency. This would be useful if you wanted to compare say an Argentinian Oil company's figures with a UK Oil company's figures. Some of the information at this site is only updated quarterly and may thus be a few months out of date at any one time.

Wright Research Center *(con't)*

http://profiles.wisi.com/

Once you have selected a share, the 'Company Analysis' will automatically be displayed. Each company is given a 'Wright Quality Rating' which appears at the top of the page just below the company name. This rates a company in terms of parameters such as liquidity, quality of earning etc. This rating is actually a very quick way of double checking the quality of a company in terms of its past history. A particularly poor rating might draw to your attention some potential problems with that company which you may have overlooked. The best possible rating is 'AAA20' and a full definition of what these figures mean is given in Figure 6.15.

Fig 6.11 *Company Summary for Dixons.*

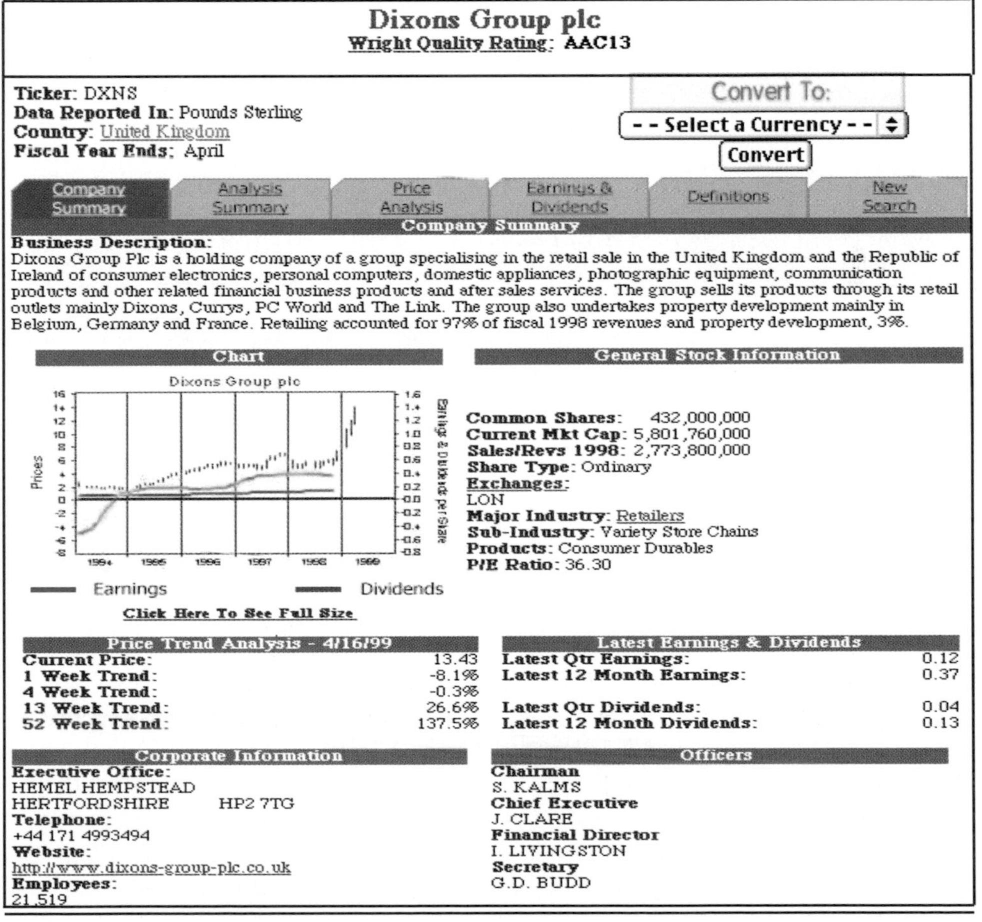

Dixons Group plc

Wright Quality Rating: AAC13

Ticker: DXNS
Data Reported In: Pounds Sterling
Country: United Kingdom
Fiscal Year Ends: April

Convert To:
- - Select a Currency - -
Convert

Company Summary | Analysis Summary | Price Analysis | Earnings & Dividends | Definitions | New Search

Company Summary

Business Description:
Dixons Group Plc is a holding company of a group specialising in the retail sale in the United Kingdom and the Republic of Ireland of consumer electronics, personal computers, domestic appliances, photographic equipment, communication products and other related financial business products and after sales services. The group sells its products through its retail outlets mainly Dixons, Currys, PC World and The Link. The group also undertakes property development mainly in Belgium, Germany and France. Retailing accounted for 97% of fiscal 1998 revenues and property development, 3%.

Chart

Click Here To See Full Size

General Stock Information

Common Shares: 432,000,000
Current Mkt Cap: 5,801,760,000
Sales/Revs 1998: 2,773,800,000
Share Type: Ordinary
Exchanges:
LON
Major Industry: Retailers
Sub-Industry: Variety Store Chains
Products: Consumer Durables
P/E Ratio: 36.30

Price Trend Analysis - 4/16/99	
Current Price:	13.43
1 Week Trend:	-8.1%
4 Week Trend:	-0.3%
13 Week Trend:	26.6%
52 Week Trend:	137.5%

Latest Earnings & Dividends	
Latest Qtr Earnings:	0.12
Latest 12 Month Earnings:	0.37
Latest Qtr Dividends:	0.04
Latest 12 Month Dividends:	0.13

Corporate Information

Executive Office:
HEMEL HEMPSTEAD
HERTFORDSHIRE HP2 7TG
Telephone:
+44 171 4993494
Website:
http://www.dixons-group-plc.co.uk
Employees:
21,519

Officers

Chairman
S. KALMS
Chief Executive
J. CLARE
Financial Director
I. LIVINGSTON
Secretary
G.D. BUDD

Wright Research Center *(con't)*

http://profiles.wisi.com/

Fig 6.12 *Clicking on 'Analysis Summary' displays a range of useful 10 year figures.*

Company Summary | Analysis Summary | Price Analysis | Earnings & Dividends | Definitions | New Search

Analysis Summary

	Market Price Last	Ratio Price To Earnings	Ratio Price To Equity	Equity Capital Earned Growth %	Equity Capital Profit Rate %	Equity Capital Book Value Begin Yr	Earnings Per Share Last 12 Mos	Earnings Per Share % Chg	Dividends Per Share Last 12 Mos	Dividends Per Share Yield Avg	Sales Revs mil
5 - 10 Year Averages											
89-93		d	2.5	3.8	11.3	0.75	0.08		0.06	3.0	1,805
94-98	3.89	d	9.6	-9.7	14.3	0.41	0.12		0.09	2.5	2,072
89-98	3.20	d	7.0	-3.0	12.8	0.58	0.10	18	0.07	2.7	1,939
Years Ended											
1989	1.45	12.5	0.0	11.3	19.0	0.61	D 0.12	-29	0.05	n.c.	1,755
1990c	1.20	9.5	0.0	9.7	17.5	0.72	AD 0.13	9	0.06	n.c.	1,771
1991	1.91	15.2	2.0	8.8	16.4	0.77	D 0.13	0	0.06	3.7	1,695
1992	2.56	26.9	2.7	4.3	11.6	0.82	AD 0.10	-25	0.06	2.7	1,863
1993c	2.16	d	2.8	-15.3	-7.8	0.83	ABDE -0.07	d	0.06	2.6	1,944
1994	2.07	d	9.2	-192	-167	0.26	ADE -0.44	d	0.07	2.7	1,578
1995	2.42	14.6	8.4	37.6	66.8	0.25	D 0.17	d	0.07	3.5	1,647
1996	4.94	32.3	10.6	18.6	43.5	0.35	AD 0.15	-8	0.09	2.4	1,920
1997c	5.22	15.2	12.3	55.0	79.3	0.43	AD 0.34	124	0.11	2.0	2,443
1998c	5.77	15.3	7.7	32.4	48.9	0.77	AD 0.38	10	0.13	2.2	2,774
1999		36.6	9.6			1.06	0.37		0.13	1.3	
4/16	13.43	36.6	11.8							1.0	

(A) *INCLUDES OR EXCLUDES EXTRAORDINARY CHARGE OR CREDIT* - INCLS NOM CR IN FIS 1998, INCLS 0.02 PRETAX CHG & 0.05 PRETAX CR IN FIS 97, INCLS 0.08 PRETAX CHG IN FIS 96, INCLS 0.11 PRETAX CR & 0.66 PRETAX CHG IN FIS 94, INCLS 0.01 PRETAX CR & 0.11 PRETAX CHG IN FIS 93, EXCLS 0.03 CHG IN FIS 92, EXCLS 0.03 CHG IN FIS 90
(B) *INCLUDES THE EFFECTS OF A CHANGE IN ACCOUNTING POLICIES OR TAX LAWS* - - ADOPTED FRS 3, REPORTING FINANCIAL PERFORMANCE IN FIS 93, EARNINGS IMPACT NOT SPECIFIED
(C) *ACQD* - BYTE COMPUTER SUPERSTORES LTD IN FIS 1998, GORDON PLUNKETT GROUP & DN COMPUTER SERVICES IN FIS 97, VISION TECHNOLOGY GROUP IN FIS 93, 23 FEDERATED GROUP STORES IN FIS 90
(D) *BASED ON AVERAGE SHARES OUTSTANDING* - - FULLY DILUTED EARNINGS FOR THE 12 MOS ENDED MAY 1998 WERE 0.354

Fig 6.13 *Clicking on 'Price Analysis' displays quarterly share price movements.*

Company Summary | Analysis Summary | Price Analysis | Earnings & Dividends | Definitions | New Search

Quarterly Price Analysis

	Qtr 1 - Jul High	Qtr 1 - Jul Low	Qtr 1 - Jul Last	Qtr 2 - Oct High	Qtr 2 - Oct Low	Qtr 2 - Oct Last	Qtr 3 - Jan High	Qtr 3 - Jan Low	Qtr 3 - Jan Last	Qtr 4 - Apr High	Qtr 4 - Apr Low	Qtr 4 - Apr Last
Years Ended												
1989			1.78			1.47			1.51			1.45
1990A			1.67			1.14			1.32	1.24	1.14	1.20
1991	1.56	1.18	1.41	1.56	1.15	1.45	1.58	1.30	1.45	1.99	1.50	1.97
1992	2.45	1.91	2.45	2.72	2.40	2.50	2.57	1.79	2.36	2.64	1.90	2.55
1993A	2.74	1.84	1.84	2.51	1.87	2.51	2.80	2.11	2.19	2.38	1.95	2.14
1994	2.37	1.92	2.33	2.85	2.23	2.70	2.92	2.07	2.15	2.15	1.87	1.89
1995	2.07	1.70	1.83	2.14	1.77	1.97	2.04	1.76	2.02	2.47	2.03	2.42
1996	2.88	2.36	2.88	3.99	2.87	3.83	4.49	3.84	4.16	5.06	4.14	4.93
1997A	5.52	4.76	4.95	5.87	4.96	5.49	5.73	4.88	5.17	5.48	4.79	5.06
1998A	6.64	4.67	6.51	7.16	6.14	6.75	6.73	4.80	5.44	5.93	4.72	5.87
1999	5.89	4.79	5.67	7.40	5.19	7.40	11.9	7.32	11.8	14.1	11.4	

Price on Friday, April 16, 1999: 13.43

(A) *ACQD* - BYTE COMPUTER SUPERSTORES LTD IN FIS 1998, GORDON PLUNKETT GROUP & DN COMPUTER SERVICES IN FIS 97, VISION TECHNOLOGY GROUP IN FIS 93, 23 FEDERATED GROUP STORES IN FIS 90

Analyzing the quarterly price movements can be a way of checking how volatile a share price has been. You can see that in the case of Dixons, the 'Qtr 4 - Apr High' figures have progressively increased over the last 10 years, indicating that Dixons share price has made steady upwards progress over this period.

Wright Research Center *(con't)*

http://profiles.wisi.com/

Fig 6.14 *'Earning & Dividends', displays quarterly figures going back 10 years.*

Company Summary	Analysis Summary	Price Analysis	Earnings & Dividends	Definitions	New Search

Earnings and Dividends

	Earnings Per Share					Dividends Per Share				
	Last 12 Mos	Qtr 1 Jul	Qtr 2 Oct	Qtr 3 Jan	Qtr 4 Apr	Last 12 Mos	Qtr 1 Jul	Qtr 2 Oct	Qtr 3 Jan	Qtr 4 Apr
5-10 Year Averages										
89-93	0.08	n.a.	0.03	n.a.	0.05	0.06	n.a.	0.02	n.a.	0.04
94-98	0.12	n.a.	-0.04	n.a.	0.16	0.09	n.a.	0.02	n.a.	0.07
89-98	0.10	n.a.	-0.00	n.a.	0.10	0.07	n.a.	0.02	n.a.	0.06
Years Ended										
1989	D 0.12	n.a.	0.06	n.a.	0.06	0.05	n.a.	0.01	n.a.	0.03
1990c 199119921993c	AD 0.13	n.a.	0.05	n.a.	0.08	0.06	n.a.	0.02	n.a.	0.04
	D 0.13	n.a.	0.03	n.a.	0.09	0.06	n.a.	0.02	n.a.	0.04
	AD 0.10	n.a.	0.02	n.a.	0.08	0.06	n.a.	0.02	n.a.	0.04
	ABDE -0.07	n.a.	0.01	n.a.	-0.08	0.06	n.a.	0.02	n.a.	0.05
1994	ADE -0.44	n.a.	-0.49	n.a.	0.05	0.07	n.a.	0.02	n.a.	0.05
199519961997c 1998c	D 0.17	n.a.	0.04	n.a.	0.13	0.07	n.a.	0.02	n.a.	0.05
	AD 0.15	n.a.	0.06	n.a.	0.09	0.09	n.a.	0.02	n.a.	0.07
	AD 0.34	n.a.	0.09	n.a.	0.25	0.11	n.a.	0.02	n.a.	0.08
	AD 0.38	n.a.	0.13	n.a.	0.25	0.13	n.a.	0.03	n.a.	0.10
1999	0.37	n.a.	0.12	n.a.	n.a.	0.13	n.a.	0.04	n.a.	n.a.

Fig 6.15 *Explanation of 'Wright Quality Rating' obtained by clicking on 'Definitions'.*

Wright Quality Rating:	Three letters and a numeral make up the Wright Quality Rating. The letters indicate (1) Investment Acceptance and Marketability, (2) Financial Strength, and (3) Profitability and Stability. Each of these letter ratings can b "A": Outstanding, "B": Excellent, "C": Good, "D": Fair, "L": Limited, "N": Not Rated, or "*": Indeterminable because of instability or recent or prospective developments which cannot yet be reliably evaluated. The "Not Rated" symbol is used whenever data is incomplete. When the Earnings Stability Index is less than 60%, the Profitability and Growth Rating is published with the letter note "z", indicating that reliability is limited. When earnings stability is less than 45%, an "*" is substituted for the growth rating. The numeral is a composite measure of the company's annual Corporate Growth Rate, based on Earnings and modified by the growth rates of equity, dividends, and the stability index and may vary from 0 to a high of 20.

Clicking on 'Definitions' displays an alphabetical list which explains all the terminology used at this site. The 'Wright Quality Rating' is a series of letters and numbers which appears under the name of each selected stock. (see Figure 6.1)

Datastream

http://www.datastreaminsite.com/insite.htm

This site provides basic financial information on all UK listed companies. When you first enter this site, you need to click on 'Search' at the top of the screen to access share information. The screen in Figure 6.2 appears and gives you a number of options. If you simply type in the name of a company as shown below and click on 'Search', you will access the basic financial information described in Chapter 2 under Datastream.

Fig 6.2 *Datastream's 'Advanced Search' function is useful for stock research.*

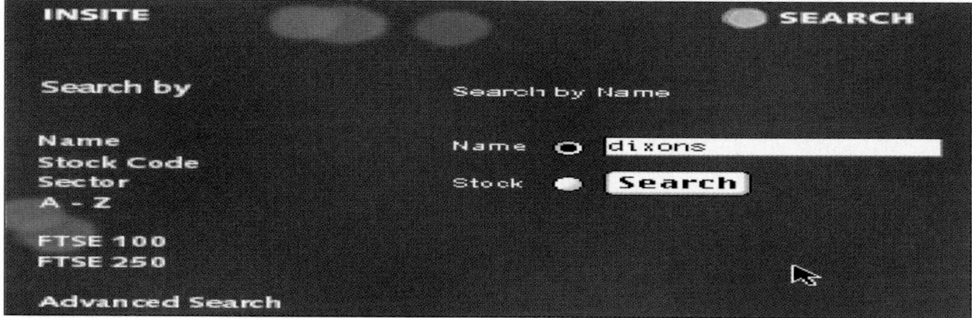

The 'Advanced Search' function on the left of the screen is particularly useful because you can identify stocks with particular financial characteristics. You can search for stocks with a specific 'Price Earning' ratio, 'Dividend Yield', 'Market Capitalization' and 'Return on Equity'. Each of these parameters has a number of settings. These can be accessed and changed by clicking on the small black arrows to the right of each parameter box as shown below.

Fig 6.21 *'Advanced Search' allows you to identify stocks with specific characteristics.*

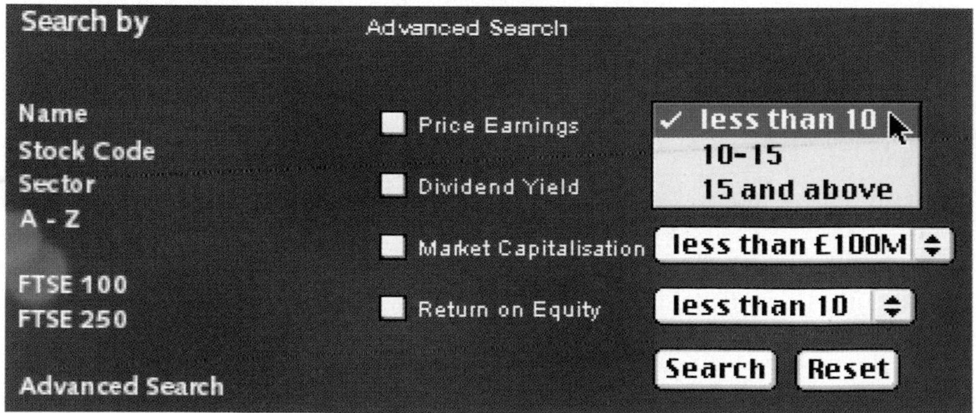

Datastream *(con't)*

http://www.datastreaminsite.com/insite.htm

In the example below, the parameters have been set to identify stocks with a Price Earnings ratio of 'less than 10', a Dividend Yield of '5.0% and above', a Market Capitalization of '1bn and above' and a Return on Equity of 'less than 10'. To display the results, you need to first click in the small white box alongside each parameter (so that a black tick appears) and then click on 'Search'.

Fig 6.22 *Make sure each parameter you have set, has a small black tick alongside it.*

In this example, the search reveals that only five Utility companies match these criteria. To get basic financial information on any of these companies, you need to click on the company name. The information is displayed in the format described in Chapter 2 under Datastream. The headings of 'FTSE100' and 'FTSE250' in the left hand column of the screen in Figure 6.22 give access to basic financial information of all the stocks which make up these two Indices.

Fig 6.23 *Only five 'Utility' companies match the criteria.*

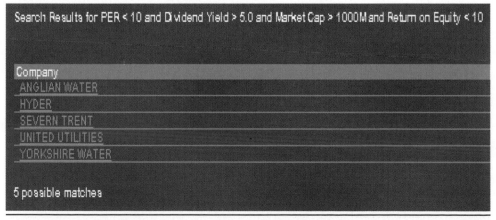

Search Results for PER < 10 and Dividend Yield > 5.0 and Market Cap > 1000M and Return on Equity < 10

Company
ANGLIAN WATER
HYDER
SEVERN TRENT
UNITED UTILITIES
YORKSHIRE WATER

5 possible matches

Financial News Digest

http://www.pigeon.co.uk

This is a really useful site which is privately maintained and updated. Here, you can read comments, tips and recommendations made on individual shares in all of the quality Sunday newspapers. The site is updated at the crack of dawn each Sunday and will display information from that Sundays newspapers for the rest of the week. To access comments in previous Sundays newspapers, you need to click on 'Archive' in the top right hand corner of the screen.

Fig 6.3 *Comments, tips and share recommendations in the Sunday newspapers.*

Financial News Digest

24.4.99 / Issue 43

Free Every Sunday from 6.45am. Read on screen or print!

Archive

HS Equities Direct | Company Web Sites | Nasdaq UK News | Book Shop |

The Sunday Telegraph

• INVESTMENT BOOK BARGAINS •

Bradford & Bingley forced to prepare £2.5bn float as members opt for £1,000 windfalls. p1

Mission Energy of US wins auction to buy **PowerGen's** coal fired generating stations at Ferrybridge Yorks and Fiddlers Ferry Merseyside for up to £1.4bn.p1

Carlton considers £170m offer for quoted outdoor advertising company **Maiden Group**.p1

Manufacturing industry should be out of recession by the end of the year and enjoying strong recovery over next 2 years says **Lloyds TSB** Economic Bulletin out tomorrow.p1

Littlewoods to split pools and betting.p1

Peter Rowbotham, chairman of **Co-operative Retail Services** quit yesterday after the movement voted to pull out of non-food retailing and back a new strategy. See FMoS below.p1

Rebel shareholders in **Premier Oil & Gas** want extraordinary general meeting to oust chief executive Charles Jamieson and three other board members.p2

Unfortunately, you cannot access full news stories directly from this site. Only a brief headline is displayed together with the page number and the newspaper in which the story appeared. Usually the brief headline will give you enough information to decide whether it is worth buying the newspaper to read the full story. Often the story will appear in a newspaper which you can access via the internet. The 'Rescarch Index' site described in Chapter 4 provides a comprehensive list of online newspapers, and provides direct access to each site.

Financial News Digest *(con't)*

http://www.pigeon.co.uk

There is a quick way to find out whether a particular share has been mentioned in any of the newspapers covered at this site. At the very top of your computer screen, you should see a heading of 'Edit'. If you click on this, a menu of options should appear as shown in Figure 6.31. Click on 'Find', and a box will appear on your screen in which you can type the name of a company.

Fig 6.31 *Use the 'Find' function on your computer to search for a particular company.*

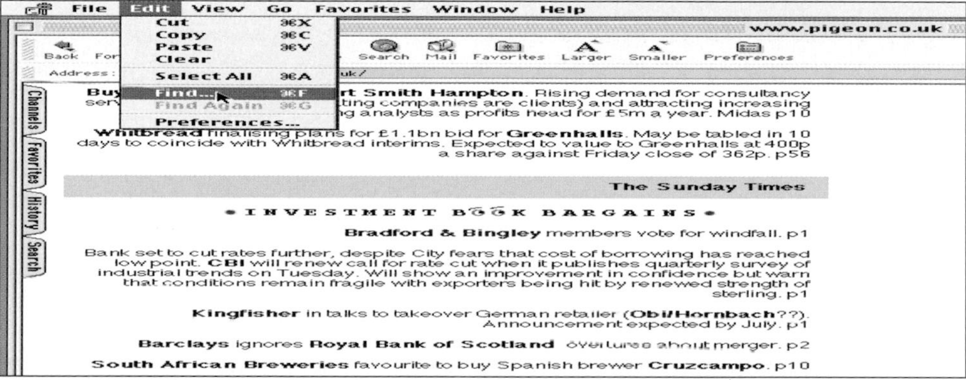

The 'Find' function is particularly useful for searching lengthy text documents for a particular word. In the example below, the name 'dixons' was typed into the 'Find' box. When you click on the 'Find' button, the screen automatically jumps to where the word you typed in is first mentioned. For your convenience, the word in the text is highlighted in blue as shown below.

Fig 6.32 *The computer will highlight any mention of that company in the text.*

AA, RAC, Burtons, Top Shop, Dorothy Perkins, Principles, House of Fraser and **Midland Bank** among household names charging customers over the odds to telephone them. RAC has received so many complaints it plans to offer freephone for all inquiries within 18 months. p3

US computer company **Gateway 2000** planning 10 fold expansion of UK High Street chain this year in challenge **Dixons**. p5

Robert Buckland & Jonathan Stubbs of **Saloman Smith Barney** say UK institutions will have to buy £59bn worth of **BP, Vodafone** and **Zeneca** after respective acquisitions of **Amoco, Arco, Airtouch** and **Astra** to maintain typical 60% institutional holding in the UK market. p9

Analysts reckon full bid for chemicals concern **Brent International** is only a matter of time following Friday sale of its inks and coatings business. Has £10m in cash. Could go for as much as 150p in an auction against Friday's 110p close. p9

Financial News Digest *(con't)*

http://www.pigeon.co.uk/pages/ftseweb.html

Fig 6.33 *You can also access FT-SE 100 web sites directly from this internet site.*

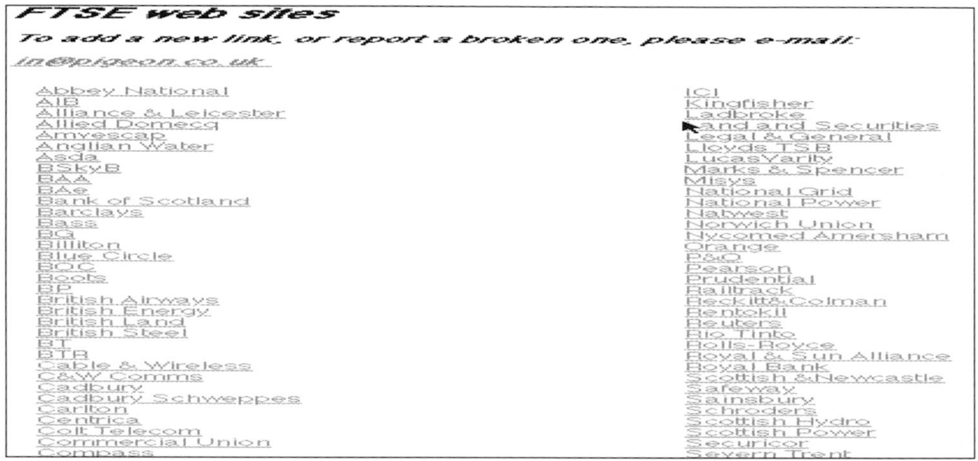

Fig 6.34 *Dixons Web Site can be accessed by clicking on 'Dixons' in the list above.*

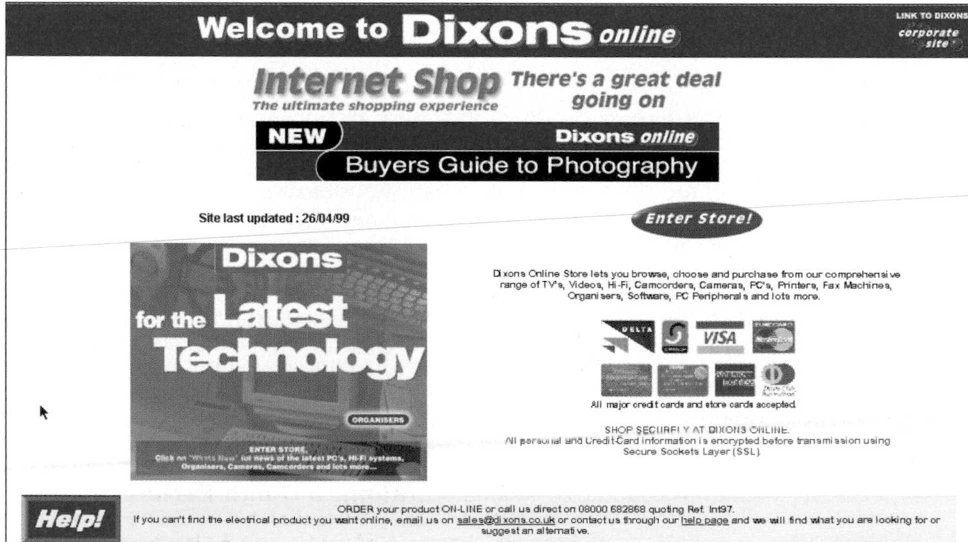

If you click on 'Company Web Sites' in Figure 6.3, an alphabetical list of FT-SE 100 companies which have a web site is displayed as shown in Figure 6.33. You can access a company web site directly by clicking on its name in the list. A company web site can often give you useful information about that company.

Hemscott

http://www.hemscott.com/EQUITIES/INDEX.HTM

Hemmington Scott are one of the major providers of financial data in the UK. Their internet site is an excellent place to access some of this information for free. You can view the 'Report & Accounts' for some companies 'online' at this site. To access this information, you start by clicking on 'Annual Reports' in the top left hand corner of the screen.

Fig 6.4 *The Hemscott site gives online access to some Company Report & Accounts.*

When you first click on 'Annual Reports', a list of headings appears in the left hand column. This site only provides access to a limited number of Company Statements and Reports. To display an alphabetical list of the companies which are covered, you need to click on one of the headings in the left hand column such as 'Chairman's Statement'.

Fig 6.41 *Click on 'Annual Reports' to find out which companies are covered at this site.*

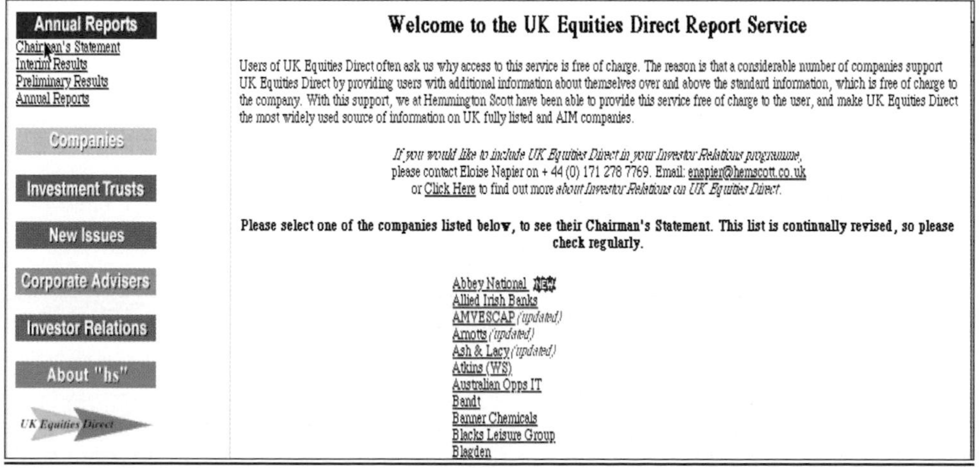

Hemscott *(con't)*

http://www.hemscott.com/EQUITIES/INDEX.HTM

Click on the name of a company in the alphabetical list and a list of all the data available on that company appears in the left hand column. Most of the data in this list is available for all UK listed companies at this site. In the example of Abbey National PLC, you can see that the list in the left hand column is headed by 'Chairman's Statement'. This additional data is only available for companies appearing in the list in Figure 6.41.

Fig 6.42 *Left hand column lists all the data which is available for Abbey National PLC.*

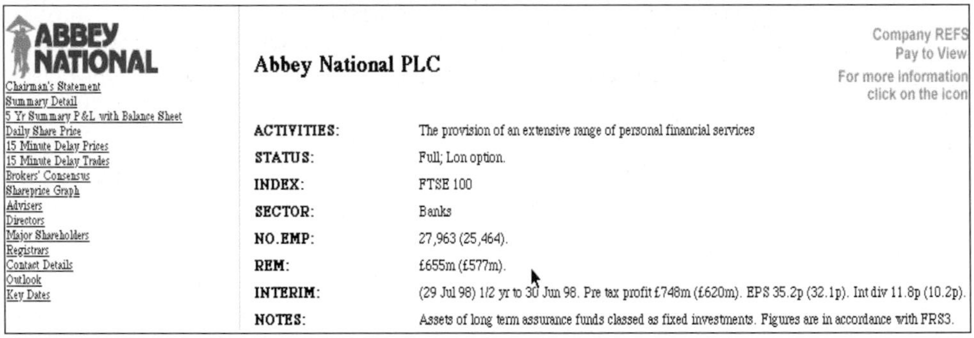

ABBEY NATIONAL

Chairman's Statement
Summary Detail
5 Yr Summary P&L with Balance Sheet
Daily Share Price
15 Minute Delay Prices
15 Minute Delay Trades
Brokers' Consensus
Shareprice Graph
Advisers
Directors
Major Shareholders
Registrars
Contact Details
Outlook
Key Dates

Abbey National PLC

Company REFS
Pay to View
For more information
click on the icon

ACTIVITIES:	The provision of an extensive range of personal financial services
STATUS:	Full; Lon option.
INDEX:	FTSE 100
SECTOR:	Banks
NO.EMP:	27,963 (25,464).
REM:	£655m (£577m).
INTERIM:	(29 Jul 98) 1/2 yr to 30 Jun 98. Pre tax profit £748m (£620m). EPS 35.2p (32.1p). Int div 11.8p (10.2p).
NOTES:	Assets of long term assurance funds classed as fixed investments. Figures are in accordance with FRS3.

Fig 6.43 *Clicking on 'Chairman's Statement' allows you to read the Statement online.*

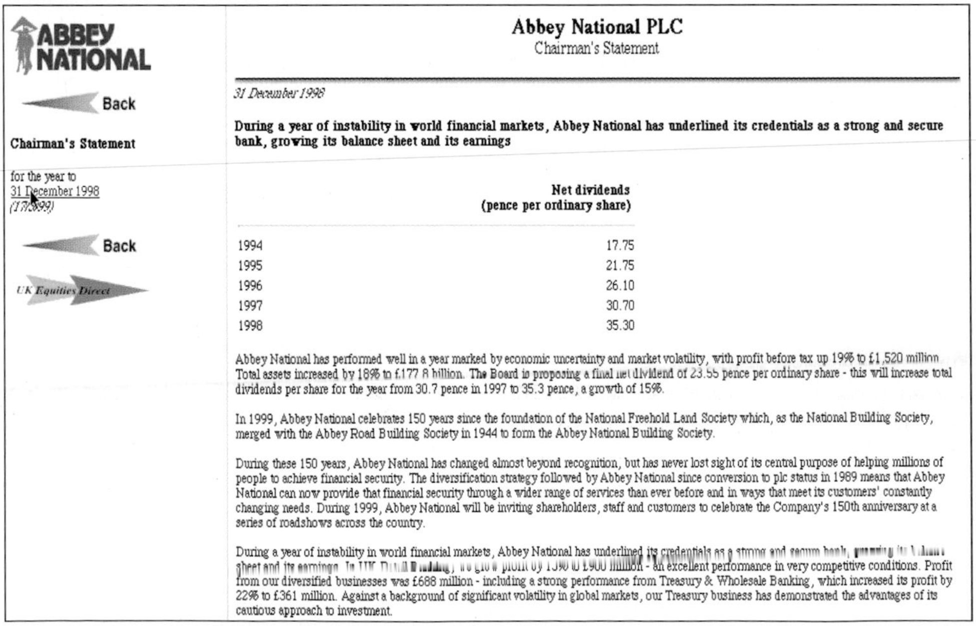

ABBEY NATIONAL

Back

Chairman's Statement

for the year to
31 December 1998
(17/3/99)

Back

UK Equities Direct

Abbey National PLC
Chairman's Statement

31 December 1998

During a year of instability in world financial markets, Abbey National has underlined its credentials as a strong and secure bank, growing its balance sheet and its earnings

	Net dividends (pence per ordinary share)
1994	17.75
1995	21.75
1996	26.10
1997	30.70
1998	35.30

Abbey National has performed well in a year marked by economic uncertainty and market volatility, with profit before tax up 19% to £1,520 million. Total assets increased by 18% to £177.8 billion. The Board is proposing a final net dividend of 23.55 pence per ordinary share - this will increase total dividends per share for the year from 30.7 pence in 1997 to 35.3 pence, a growth of 15%.

In 1999, Abbey National celebrates 150 years since the foundation of the National Freehold Land Society which, as the National Building Society, merged with the Abbey Road Building Society in 1944 to form the Abbey National Building Society.

During these 150 years, Abbey National has changed almost beyond recognition, but has never lost sight of its central purpose of helping millions of people to achieve financial security. The diversification strategy followed by Abbey National since conversion to plc status in 1989 means that Abbey National can now provide that financial security through a wider range of services than ever before and in ways that meet its customers' constantly changing needs. During 1999, Abbey National will be inviting shareholders, staff and customers to celebrate the Company's 150th anniversary at a series of roadshows across the country.

During a year of instability in world financial markets, Abbey National has underlined its credentials as a strong and secure bank, [illegible] sheet and its earnings. In UK [illegible] £900 million - an excellent performance in very competitive conditions. Profit from our diversified businesses was £688 million - including a strong performance from Treasury & Wholesale Banking, which increased its profit by 22% to £361 million. Against a background of significant volatility in global markets, our Treasury business has demonstrated the advantages of its cautious approach to investment.

Hemscott *(con't)*

http://www.hemscott.com/EQUITIES/INDEX.HTM

You can also search for information on a specific company at this site. When you first click on 'Annual Reports' in the left hand column, a 'Search' box appears in the centre of the screen. Type in the name of a company and click on 'Search'.

Fig 6.44 *You can search for financial data on specific companies at this site.*

A list of companies with the word 'dixons' in the title is displayed. To access the financial information for the company you are interested in, click on its name.

Fig 6.45 *The search finds all companies with the word 'dixons' in the title.*

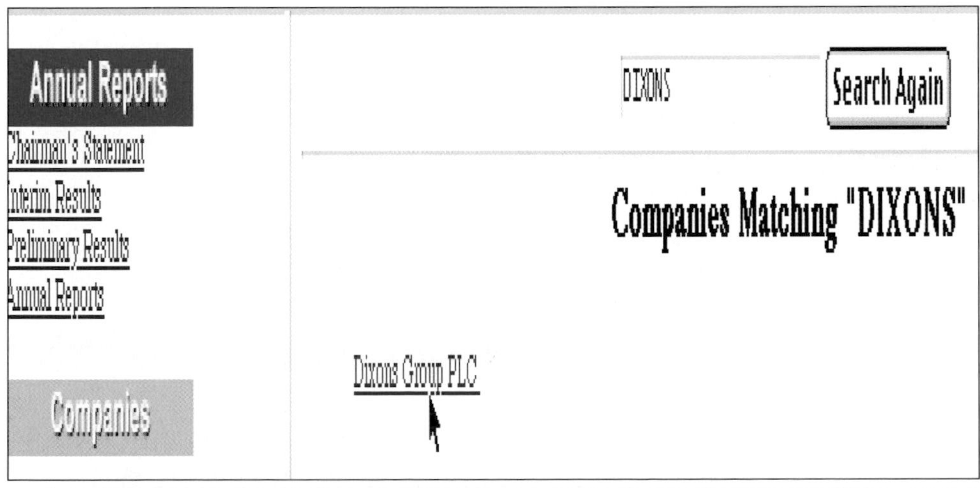

Hemscott *(con't)*

http://www.hemscott.com/EQUITIES/INDEX.HTM

Initially, a brief summary of 'Dixons Group PLC' appears in the center of the screen. The summary contains some useful financial ratios such as 'Gearing' and 'ROCE' (Return on Capital Employed). Gearing gives a measure of a company's borrowings and ROCE indicates how well the company is utilizing the capital at its disposal. The Glossary at the back of this book explains some of the more commonly used financial terms and expressions.

Fig 6.46 *Clicking on 'Dixons Group PLC' displays a brief company summary.*

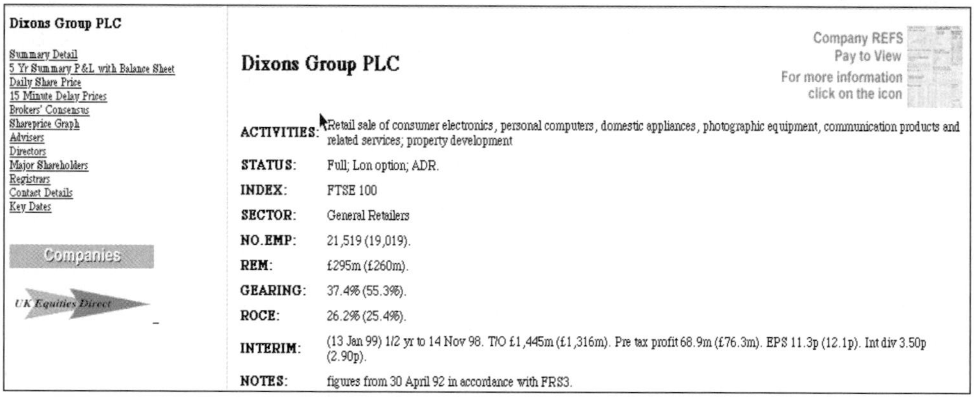

Dixons Group PLC

Summary Detail
5 Yr Summary P&L with Balance Sheet
Daily Share Price
15 Minute Delay Prices
Brokers' Consensus
Shareprice Graph
Advisers
Directors
Major Shareholders
Registrars
Contact Details
Key Dates

Companies

UK Equities Direct

Dixons Group PLC

Company REFS
Pay to View
For more information
click on the icon

ACTIVITIES: Retail sale of consumer electronics, personal computers, domestic appliances, photographic equipment, communication products and related services; property development

STATUS: Full; Lon option; ADR.

INDEX: FTSE 100

SECTOR: General Retailers

NO.EMP: 21,519 (19,019).

REM: £295m (£260m).

GEARING: 37.4% (55.3%).

ROCE: 26.2% (25.4%).

INTERIM: (13 Jan 99) 1/2 yr to 14 Nov 98. T/O £1,445m (£1,316m). Pre tax profit 68.9m (£76.3m). EPS 11.3p (12.1p). Int div 3.50p (2.90p).

NOTES: figures from 30 April 92 in accordance with FRS3.

On the left of the screen there are numerous headings which you can click on to display a variety of useful information about a company. The following pages use 'Dixons Group PLC' to show the screens which are displayed when you click on each heading in this list.

Fig 6.47 *A summary of the 5 year Profit & Loss Account for Dixons.*

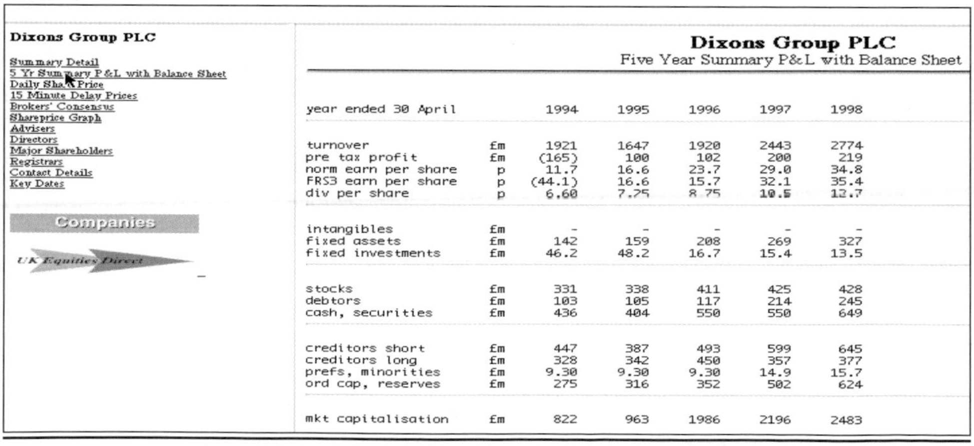

Dixons Group PLC

Summary Detail
5 Yr Summary P&L with Balance Sheet
Daily Share Price
15 Minute Delay Prices
Brokers' Consensus
Shareprice Graph
Advisers
Directors
Major Shareholders
Registrars
Contact Details
Key Dates

Companies

UK Equities Direct

Dixons Group PLC
Five Year Summary P&L with Balance Sheet

year ended 30 April		1994	1995	1996	1997	1998
turnover	£m	1921	1647	1920	2443	2774
pre tax profit	£m	(165)	100	102	200	219
norm earn per share	p	11.7	16.6	23.7	29.0	34.8
FRS3 earn per share	p	(44.1)	16.6	15.7	32.1	35.4
div per share	p	6.60	7.25	8.75	10.5	12.7
intangibles	£m	-	-	-	-	-
fixed assets	£m	142	159	208	269	327
fixed investments	£m	46.2	48.2	16.7	15.4	13.5
stocks	£m	331	338	411	425	428
debtors	£m	103	105	117	214	245
cash, securities	£m	436	404	550	550	649
creditors short	£m	447	387	493	599	645
creditors long	£m	328	342	450	357	377
prefs, minorities	£m	9.30	9.30	9.30	14.9	15.7
ord cap, reserves	£m	275	316	352	502	624
mkt capitalisation	£m	822	963	1986	2196	2483

Hemscott *(con't)*

http://www.hemscott.com/EQUITIES/INDEX.HTM

Fig 6.48 *Clicking on 'Daily Share Price' also gives no. of shares in issue and Mkt Cap.*

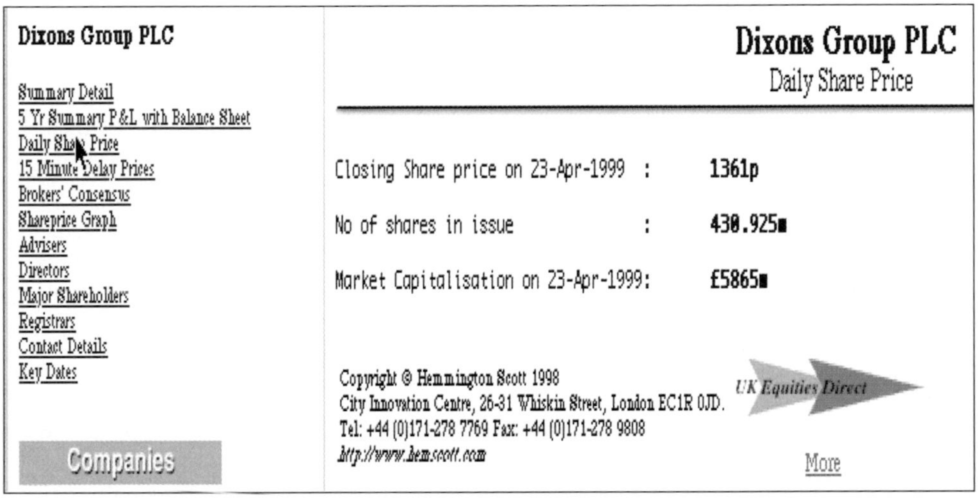

Dixons Group PLC

Summary Detail
5 Yr Summary P&L with Balance Sheet
Daily Share Price
15 Minute Delay Prices
Brokers' Consensus
Shareprice Graph
Advisers
Directors
Major Shareholders
Registrars
Contact Details
Key Dates

Companies

Dixons Group PLC
Daily Share Price

Closing Share price on 23-Apr-1999 : **1361p**

No of shares in issue : **430.925m**

Market Capitalisation on 23-Apr-1999: **£5865m**

UK Equities Direct

More

Fig 6.49 *Clicking on '15 Minute Delay Prices' shows 'intraday' share price movements.*

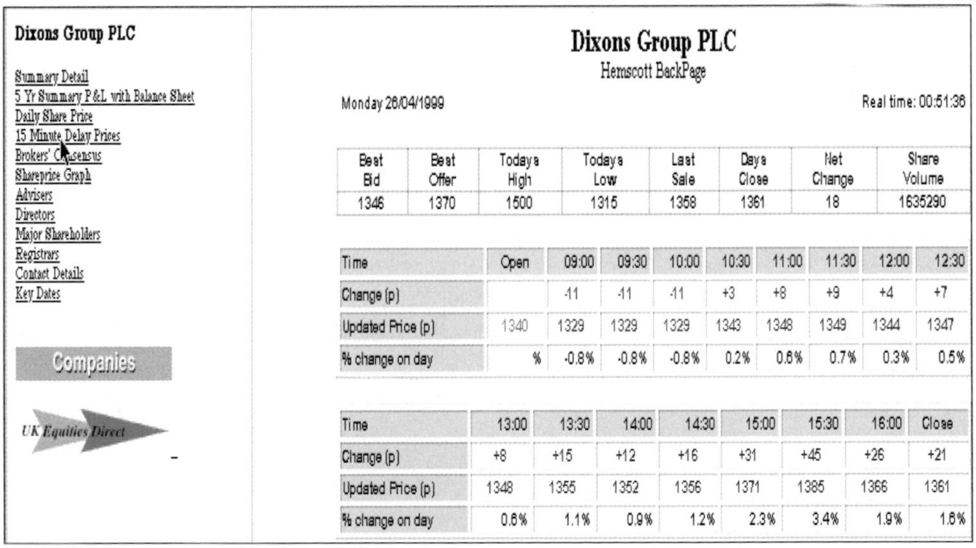

Dixons Group PLC

Summary Detail
5 Yr Summary P&L with Balance Sheet
Daily Share Price
15 Minute Delay Prices
Brokers' Consensus
Shareprice Graph
Advisers
Directors
Major Shareholders
Registrars
Contact Details
Key Dates

Companies

UK Equities Direct

Dixons Group PLC
Hemscott BackPage

Monday 26/04/1999 Real time: 00:51:36

Best Bid	Best Offer	Todays High	Todays Low	Last Sale	Days Close	Net Change	Share Volume
1346	1370	1500	1315	1358	1361	18	1635290

Time	Open	09:00	09:30	10:00	10:30	11:00	11:30	12:00	12:30
Change (p)		-11	-11	-11	+3	+8	+9	+4	+7
Updated Price (p)	1340	1329	1329	1329	1343	1348	1349	1344	1347
% change on day	%	-0.8%	-0.8%	-0.8%	0.2%	0.6%	0.7%	0.3%	0.5%

Time	13:00	13:30	14:00	14:30	15:00	15:30	16:00	Close
Change (p)	+8	+15	+12	+16	+31	+45	+26	+21
Updated Price (p)	1348	1355	1352	1356	1371	1385	1366	1361
% change on day	0.6%	1.1%	0.9%	1.2%	2.3%	3.4%	1.9%	1.6%

This site is one of the few places you can access the intraday share price movement for a share. Sometimes knowing how and when a share price has moved during the course of a day may draw your attention to an event you didn't know about such as a company announcement for example.

Hemscott *(con't)*

http://www.hemscott.com/EQUITIES/INDEX.HTM

A valuable piece of information to know about a company, is whether Brokers are upgrading or downgrading their earning per share (EPS) estimates. Share prices often go up on the back of Brokers upgrading EPS. In the case of Dixons, the consensus of 20 Brokers, is that EPS will increase from 38p in 1999 to 41.2p in the year 2000. This puts Dixons on a prospective price earnings ratio of 33.1 in the year 2000. 'Detailed Broker Forecasts' are only available if you sign up to the Hemscott.net service which is free if certain conditions are met.

Fig 6.4.10 *Brokers are forecasting that 'earnings per share' at Dixons will increase.*

Dixons Group PLC

Summary Detail
5 Yr Summary P&L with Balance Sheet
Daily Share Price
15 Minute Delay Prices
Brokers' Consensus
Detailed Broker Forecasts
Shareprice Graph
Advisers
Directors
Directors' Share Dealings
Major Shareholders
Registrars
Contact Details
Key Dates

Consensus (Base eps 39.8p)

Period		00	01
eps	p	41.9	47.0
3M change	p	+0.24	+1.04
brokers	n	19	16
std dev	p	1.70	2.27
growth	%	5.29	12.3
prosp p/e	x	24.7	22.0

Sometimes a knowledge of who the major shareholders of a company are, can give an indication of how likely it is that the company will be subject to a take over bid. For example, if a large number of shares were owned by a family trust there may be less chance of an aggressive take over bid than if you spot a potential aggressor holding a large number of shares.

Fig 6.4.11 *Sometimes it is useful to know who the major shareholders are.*

Dixons Group PLC

Summary Detail
5 Yr Summary P&L with Balance Sheet
Daily Share Price
15 Minute Delay Prices
Brokers' Consensus
Shareprice Graph
Advisers
Directors
Major Shareholders
Registrars
Contact Details
Key Dates

Dixons Group PLC
Major Shareholders

Major Shareholders:
(23 Apr 99) 430.93m 10p Ords - Mercury Asset Mgmt Ltd 11.14%, Capital Group Companies Inc 5.72%, Prudential Corp Grp of Co's 5.01%, Putman Advisery Co Inc (The) 4.87%, Standard Life Assurance Co 3.85%, Other Dirs 0.57%.

Copyright © Hemmington Scott 1998
City Innovation Centre, 26-31 Whiskin Street, London EC1R 0JD.
Tel: +44 (0)171 270 7700 Fax. +44 (0)171-278 9808
http://www.hemscott.com

UK Equities Direct

More

Hemscott *(con't)*

http://www.hemscott.com/EQUITIES/INDEX.HTM

Fig 6.4.12 *The company 'Registrars' can tell you details of share splits, dividends etc.*

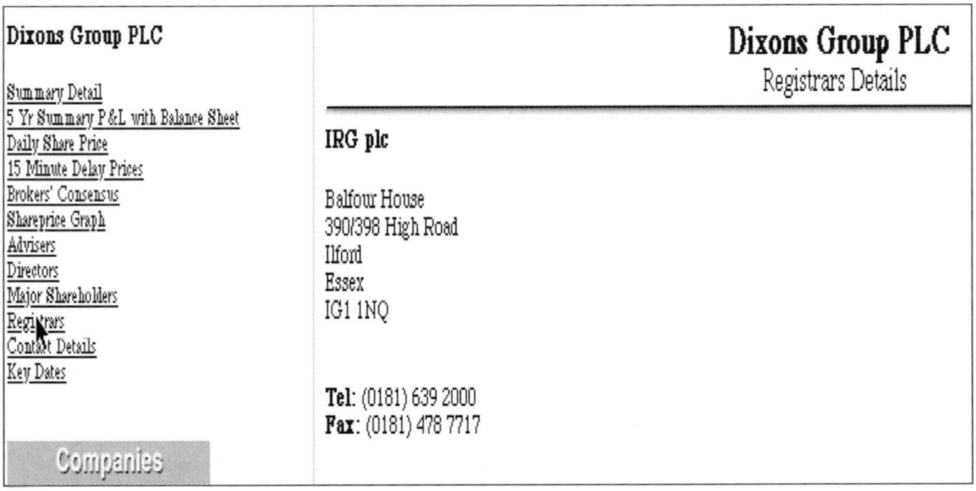

Dixons Group PLC

Summary Detail
5 Yr Summary P&L with Balance Sheet
Daily Share Price
15 Minute Delay Prices
Brokers' Consensus
Shareprice Graph
Advisers
Directors
Major Shareholders
Registrars
Contact Details
Key Dates

Companies

Dixons Group PLC
Registrars Details

IRG plc

Balfour House
390/398 High Road
Ilford
Essex
IG1 1NQ

Tel: (0181) 639 2000
Fax: (0181) 478 7717

Fig 6.4.13 *'Key Dates' covers the Report & Accounts and dividend dates.*

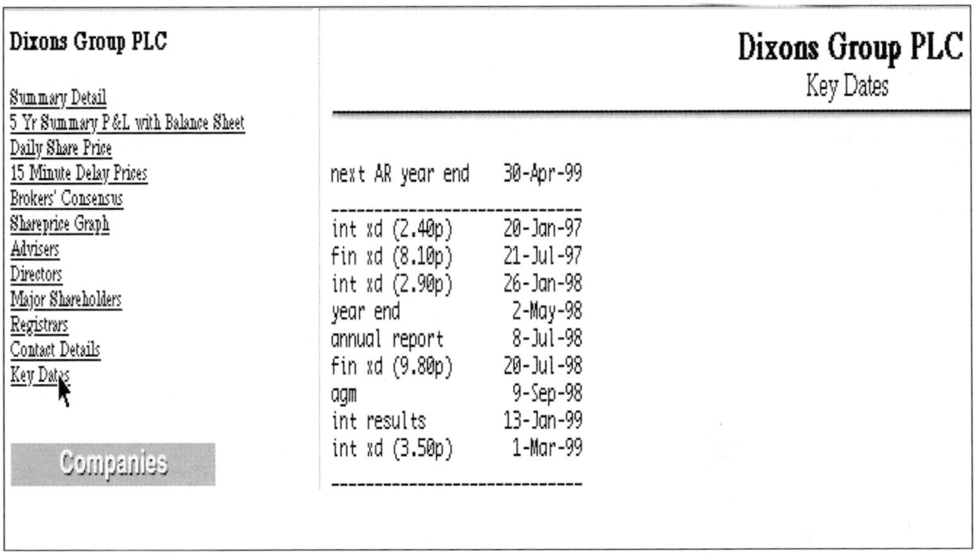

Dixons Group PLC

Summary Detail
5 Yr Summary P&L with Balance Sheet
Daily Share Price
15 Minute Delay Prices
Brokers' Consensus
Shareprice Graph
Advisers
Directors
Major Shareholders
Registrars
Contact Details
Key Dates

Companies

Dixons Group PLC
Key Dates

```
next AR year end   30-Apr-99
-----------------------------
int xd (2.40p)     20-Jan-97
fin xd (8.10p)     21-Jul-97
int xd (2.90p)     26-Jan-98
year end            2-May-98
annual report       8-Jul-98
fin xd (9.80p)     20-Jul-98
agm                 9-Sep-98
int results        13-Jan-99
int xd (3.50p)      1-Mar-99
-----------------------------
```

Ex-dividend dates will often be the reason for share prices movements, so it is as well to be aware when they are. Similarly, a share price can move significantly on the back of the Report & Accounts being published if they contain news or information which the stock market was not expecting.

Financial Times

http://www.globalarchive.ft.com/cb/cb_analysis.htm

The Financial Times internet site now includes a detailed summary of 'Analysts Estimates' for most UK companies. Normally, this information would be extremely costly to obtain and has until recently, only been available on a subscription basis. To display analysts estimates for a stock, you need to type in all or part of the name and click on search. The exact internet address for this page is scheduled to change so try http://www.ft.com if you experience any problems.

Fig 6.5 *The FT internet site gives investors free access to 'Analysts Estimates'.*

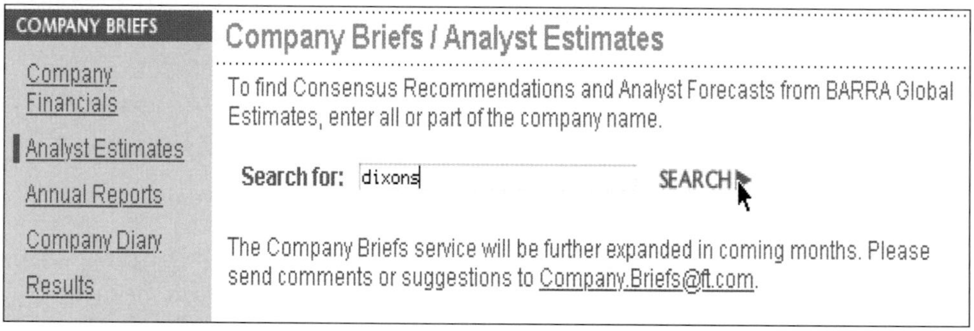

At present, it is not possible to search using the correct security code. If you type in part of the name of a company, the search returns a list of companies beginning with those letters. To display 'Analysts Estimates' for the company you are interested in, click on the company name as shown below.

Fig 6.51 *Click on the name of the company to display a list of 'Analysts Estimates'.*

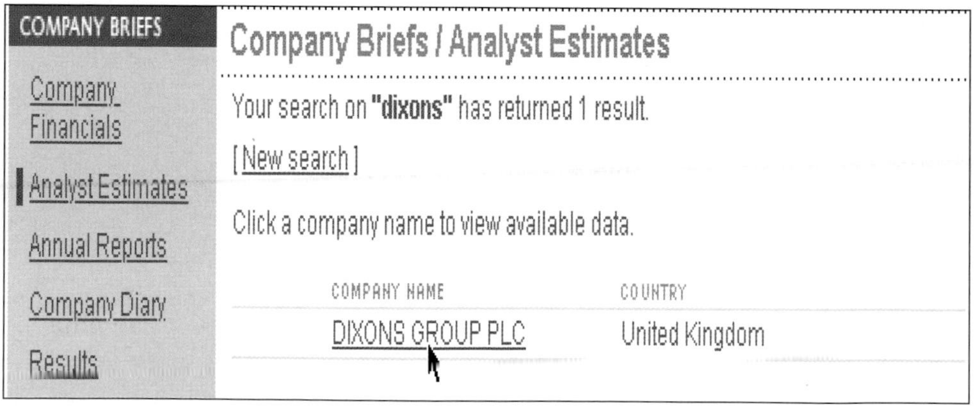

Financial Times *(con't)*

http://www.globalarchive.ft.com/cb/cb_analysis.htm

This internet site enables both private and professional investors to check whether leading stock market analysts feel positive or negative on a particular company. The display starts off with a 'Summary of broker recommendations'. This makes it easy to see at a glance whether brokers are on average recommending buying, holding or selling the shares. Below the Summary, is a 'Consensus' forecast for 'Net Profit', 'EPS' (earnings per share) and 'DPS' (dividends per share). The Consensus forecast can be important because share prices only tend to rise over time if profits, earnings and dividends are increasing. Once leading analysts start to predict a fall in earnings and profits, it can become difficult for a share price to make any significant progress.

Fig 6.52 *A detailed summary of 'Analysts Estimates' for Dixons PLC.*

Company Briefs / Analyst Estimates

DIXONS GROUP PLC

Summary of broker recommendations

38%	recommend a buy
33%	recommend a hold
22%	recommend a sale

[New Search]

Broker recommendations and estimates

	NET PROFIT GBP '000,000	EPS GBP	DPS GBP
Consensus Report Date: 9 Sep 1999			
3 May 2000	260.0	0.4	0.2
3 May 2001	290.0	0.5	0.2
ABN AMRO Equities - UK Forecast Date: 15 Jul 1999 Rec: HOLD			
3 May 2000	270.0	0.4	0.2
3 May 2001	295.0	0.5	0.2
Charles Stanley & Co Ltd Forecast Date: 28 May 1999 Rec: HOLD			
3 May 2000	265.0	0.4	0.2
3 May 2001	290.0	0.4	0.2
Charterhouse Securities Forecast Date: 31 Aug 1999 Rec: REDUCE			
3 May 2000	248.7	0.4	0.2
3 May 2001	279.0	0.5	0.2
Credit Lyonnais Securities Europe (UK) Forecast Date: 27 May 1999 Rec: REDUCE			
3 May 2000	265.0	0.4	0.2
3 May 2001	-	-	-
Credit Suisse First Boston Limited Forecast Date: 5 Aug 1999 Rec: BUY			
3 May 2000	-	0.4	0.2
3 May 2001	-	0.4	0.2

Automated City Analyst

http://www.homeusers.prestel.co.uk/tbird/disclaimer.html

This is an interesting site which highlights the 10 most and least attractive stocks using a complicated series of technical analysis tools. The method by which the predictions are arrived at is outlined at the site, and can be viewed by clicking on 'Return to ACA home page' at the bottom of the screen. Technical analysis tends to look at how share prices have moved in the past under certain conditions. This information is then used to predict future share price movements. To display the predictions, you need to click on either 'Top 10' or 'Bottom 10' in the right hand column of the screen.

Fig 6.6 *Using technical analysis to highlight stocks to potentially buy or sell.*

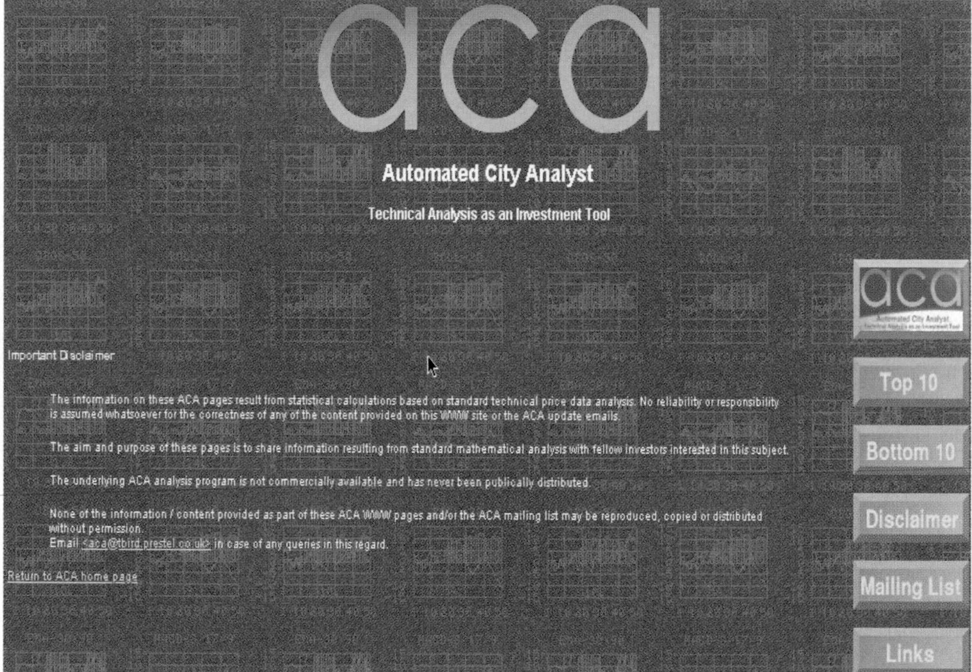

The site is independently maintained and it is difficult to ascertain how successful the predictions have been. Generally speaking, it is always safer to do your own fundamental research rather than relying on someone else's predictions. However, this site could draw your attention to stocks which are worth researching further. Conversely, you might be alerted to some potentially negative factors if a stock you hold or are interested in buying, crops up in the 'Bottom 10' list.

Automated City Analyst *(con't)*

http://www.homeusers.prestel.co.uk/tbird/top10.html

Fig 6.61 *Clicking on 'Top 10' displays the 10 most attractive stocks.*

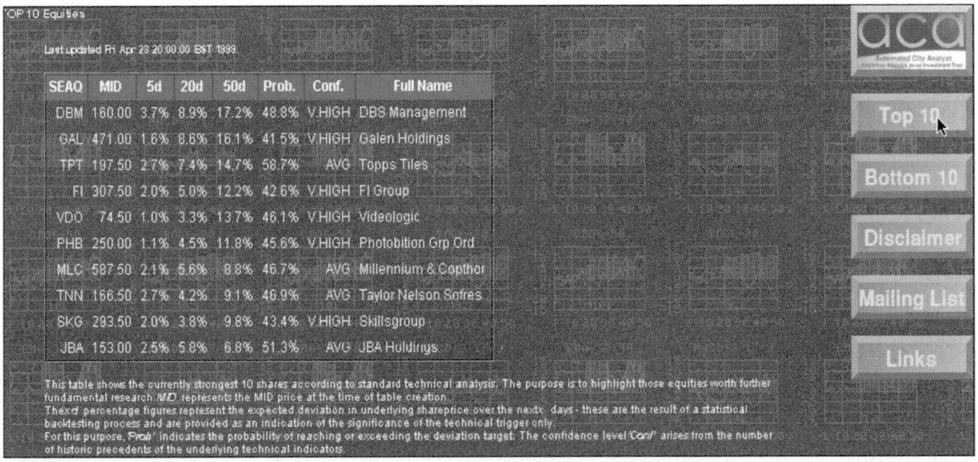

'OP 10 Equities

Last updated Fri Apr 23 20:00:00 BST 1999.

SEAQ	MID	5d	20d	50d	Prob.	Conf.	Full Name
DBM	160.00	3.7%	8.9%	17.2%	48.8%	V.HIGH	DBS Management
GAL	471.00	1.6%	8.6%	16.1%	41.5%	V.HIGH	Galen Holdings
TPT	197.50	2.7%	7.4%	14.7%	58.7%	AVG	Topps Tiles
FI	307.50	2.0%	5.0%	12.2%	42.6%	V.HIGH	FI Group
VDO	74.50	1.0%	3.3%	13.7%	46.1%	V.HIGH	Videologic
PHB	250.00	1.1%	4.5%	11.8%	45.6%	V.HIGH	Photobition Grp Ord
MLC	587.50	2.1%	5.6%	8.8%	46.7%	AVG	Millennium & Copthor
TNN	166.50	2.7%	4.2%	9.1%	46.9%	AVG	Taylor Nelson Sofres
SKG	293.50	2.0%	3.8%	9.8%	43.4%	V.HIGH	Skillsgroup
JBA	153.00	2.5%	5.8%	6.8%	51.3%	AVG	JBA Holdings

This table shows the currently strongest 10 shares according to standard technical analysis. The purpose is to highlight those equities worth further fundamental research. 'MID' represents the MID price at the time of table creation.
The xd percentage figures represent the expected deviation in underlying shareprice over the next x days - these are the result of a statistical backtesting process and are provided as an indication of the significance of the technical trigger only.
For this purpose, 'Prob' indicates the probability of reaching or exceeding the deviation target. The confidence level 'Conf' arises from the number of historic precedents of the underlying technical indicators.

Top 10

Bottom 10

Disclaimer

Mailing List

Links

Fig 6.62 *The 10 least attractive stocks.*

SEAQ	MID	5d	20d	50d	Prob.	Conf.	Full Name
CCC	483.00	-3.9%	-7.6%	-12.7%	47.6%	LOW	Computacenter
GIM	137.50	-1.1%	-5.3%	-14.9%	39.1%	AVG	Geo-Interactive Medi
SMDS	134.00	-1.9%	-4.8%	-6.0%	52.2%	V.HIGH	Smith (DS)
BRS	18.75	-0.8%	-3.8%	-7.2%	47.6%	HIGH	Burn Steward Dist
MFI	47.00	-1.7%	-3.6%	-6.0%	47.8%	V.HIGH	MFI Furniture Grp
JVP	85.00	-1.7%	-3.3%	-5.9%	48.7%	HIGH	Jarvis Porter
ELH	61.00	-2.6%	-6.1%	-2.1%	49.6%	HIGH	Eurodis Electron
WOC	67.50	-0.8%	-2.3%	-4.8%	46.6%	V.HIGH	Whittard of Chelsea
CSA	25.75	-0.7%	-3.7%	-3.0%	50.7%	AVG	Crestacare
LSB	123.00	-1.8%	-2.0%	-3.3%	46.1%	HIGH	Lon.Scot Bank

'MID' is the middle market price of the stock when the table was compiled. The figures under the headings of '5d, 20d and 50d' predict the percentage by which this price is expected to move over the next 5, 20 and 50 days respectively. 'Prob' indicates the probability of how likely this is to happen, and 'Conf' is a measure of how often the technical indicators have occurred in the past.

Money World

http://www.moneyworld.co.uk/rates/index.html

The Money Facts publication is an excellent source of information for the best rates on just about any type of savings vehicle from annuities to TESSA accounts. At the time of writing, Money Facts did not have a web site themselves. However, much of the information in the Money Facts publication can be accessed for free via the excellent 'Money World' internet site.

Fig 6.7 *The Money World site has information on most types of savings vehicles.*

ISAs
Latest Rates

Cheque Accounts
Latest rates

Children's Accounts
Latest rates or Savings Search

Fixed Rate Bonds
Latest rates

Guaranteed Income Bonds
Latest rates

Instant Access Accounts
Latest rates or Savings Search

Monthly Interest Accounts
Latest rates

National Savings
Latest rates

National Savings: Index Linked Certificates
Latest rates

Notice Accounts & Bonds
Latest rates or Savings Search

Offshore Accounts
Latest rates

Tessas
Latest rates

Regular Savings
Savings Search

Term Deposits
Savings Search

Annuities
Latest rates

Clicking on one of the categories will give you the best rates for that particular investment together with the telephone number of the provider.

Fig 6.71 *A quick and easy way to find out who is offering the best savings rates.*

Monthly Interest Accounts

The best rates available, last updated 5 November 1999.

Account Int Paid	Notice	£500 %	£1K %	£2.5K %	£5K %	£10K %	£25K %	£50K %	£100K %
Abbey National - 0800 174635									
Direct Saver	Instant	-	-	5.84	5.84	5.84	5.84	5.84	5.84
Monthly		Min bal £2K. Telephone A/c. Cash card available. Includes 1.00% bonus to 31.3.00.							
Alliance & Leicester - 0845 964 5660									
PhoneSave 75	75 Day	-	-	5.35	5.45	5.85	6.10	6.15	6.25
Monthly		Telephone A/c. Rate includes 0.50% bonus to 1.5.00. Transactions via nominated current A/c.							
Britannia BS - 0800 13[illegible]304									
Capital Trust 30	30 Day	-	3.90	3.90	4.65	4.85	5.10	5.35	6.05
Monthly		Postal A/c. 5.10% paid at £20K.							
Chelsea BS - 0800 132351									
POST-tel Gtee Bond	60 Day	-	-	-	5.84	5.84	5.84	5.84	5.84
Monthly		Postal A/c. Minimum withdrawal £250.							
Coventry BS - 0845 766 5522									
CallSave II	Instant	-	-	-	5.60	5.60	5.60	5.60	5.60
Monthly		Telephone A/c. Cash card available.							
Egg									
Internet [illegible]	[illegible]	[illegible]	5.84	5.84	5.84	5.84	5.84	5.84	5.84
Monthly		Internet A/c. Min bal £1. Includes 0.50% premium to 1.1.00.							

Bulletin Boards

http://www.freeyellow.com/members6/scottit/page7.html

Bulletin Boards are places on the internet where you can read comments from other private investors. Sometimes the answer as to why a particular share price has risen or fallen suddenly, can be found by reading comments on a Bulletin Board. Many investors who write comments on Bulletin Boards, have access to research or information that you may not be able to get hold of yourself. Good Bulletin Boards tend to act as an open forum where private clients can share their thoughts and ideas with other investors. In many cases, you can also post your own comments or ask questions relating to a particular investments.

Fig 6.8 *You can set up your own web page to access the best Bulletin Boards directly.*

HOT LINKS

- Market-Eye (with search engine)
- Hemmington Scott (with search engine)
- UK Shares (with a search engine).
- Interactive Investor

The bulletin boards covered in this Chapter all allow you to search for comments on particular companies. If you type in the internet address at the top of this page, the screen in Figure 6.8 will be displayed. You can click on any of the names under 'Hot Links' to access that Bulletin Board directly. This saves you having to type in the complete internet address for that Bulletin Board each time.

Market-Eye

http://www.market-eye.co.uk/scripts/forum/find.asp

The Market-Eye internet site has an excellent Bulletin Board called 'Investor Eye to Eye'. The thing that makes a Bulletin Board good, is the number and quality of investors who post comments. Those internet sites offering the best free financial information in the first place tend to attract the most investors. Market-Eye is mentioned frequently throughout this book because it undoubtedly has one of the best free investment based web sites on the internet. To display comments, type in the name of a share or topic in the white box under 'Keyword 1:' The company 'dixons' has been used in the example below. If you wanted to just display comments relating to 'dixons' and the 'internet' for example, you could type the word 'internet' in the 'Keyword 2:'. To display the results, click on 'Search' in the bottom left hand corner of the screen.

Fig 6.81 *The Market-Eye Bulletin Board allows you to search using two 'Keywords'.*

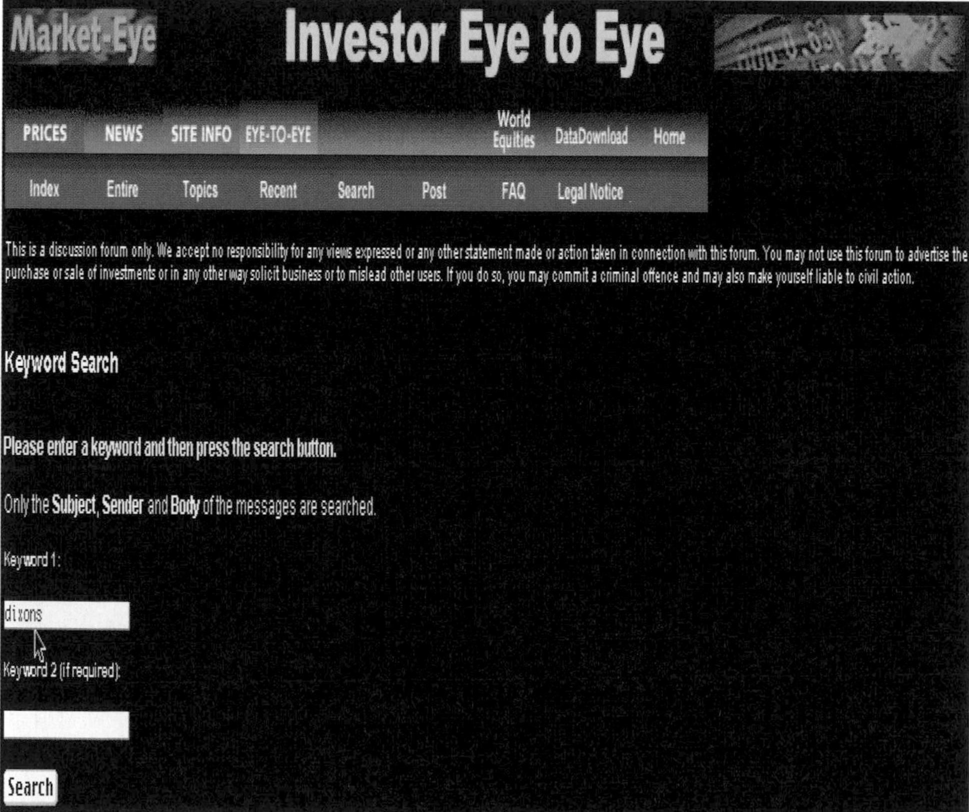

Market-Eye *(con't)*

http://www.market-eye.co.uk/scripts/forum/find.asp

The search displays a date ordered list of comments relating to the keyword you have typed in. The name of the writer, the date and the time, is posted alongside the headline. Over time, you will learn which people on the Bulletin Board post the most useful and informed comments. It is important not to believe everything you read on Bulletin Boards. Investors who post comments, often have a vested interest in promoting the shares they own.

Fig 6.82 *The search displays a date ordered list of comments relating to 'Dixons'.*

Search Results

Re: Dixons , niederhoffer, 29/04/99 17:27:15
Dixons , AFZ, 29/04/99 17:12:32
DIXONS , FAB, 29/04/99 13:22:39
Re: > Free internet access BT/WHS/Microsoft/Tempo , BornLoser, 27/04/99 18:38:19
Re: > Free internet access BT/WHS/Microsoft/Tempo , BornLoser, 27/04/99 18:37:24
Re: > Free internet access BT/WHS/Microsoft/Tempo , BornLoser, 27/04/99 18:16:00
Re: > KDC-Free internet access BT/WHS/Microsoft , Ducky, 27/04/99 17:05:55
Re: > KDC-Free internet access BT/WHS/Microsoft , Ducky, 27/04/99 17:04:56
Scotia Holdings & Dixons , FAB, 19/04/99 16:18:23
Dixons , FAB, 15/04/99 12:37:23

Someone may post a comment to which many people reply. In the example below, there were 6 replies to the question 'Am I missing something?' To reply to a comment or question, you need to click on 'Reply' in the bottom left hand corner of the screen. Before you can post comments yourself, you will need to register. The application form is usually very simple and a password is generally e-mailed to you almost immediately. Registration is covered in Chapter 7.

Fig 6.83 *Click on a headline to read the full comment.*

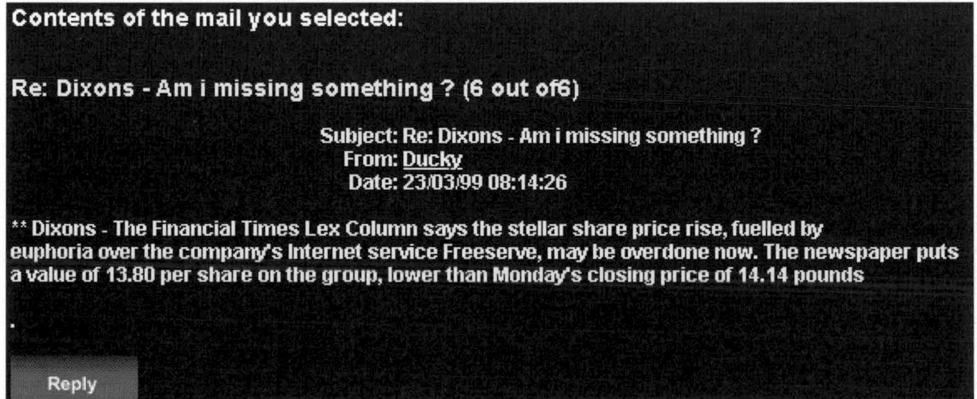

Contents of the mail you selected:
Re: Dixons - Am i missing something ? (6 out of6)
Subject: Re: Dixons - Am i missing something ?
From: Ducky
Date: 23/03/99 08:14:26
** Dixons - The Financial Times Lex Column says the stellar share price rise, fuelled by euphoria over the company's Internet service Freeserve, may be overdone now. The newspaper puts a value of 13.80 per share on the group, lower than Monday's closing price of 14.14 pounds
Reply

Hemscott

http://infoex.hemscott.com/search/query.htm

Hemmington Scott has one of the best internet sites in the UK and its Bulletin Board is particularly good. Type in the name of the company you are interested in and click on 'Search' to display the results.

Fig 6.84 *Search results can be displayed in either Descending or Ascending date order.*

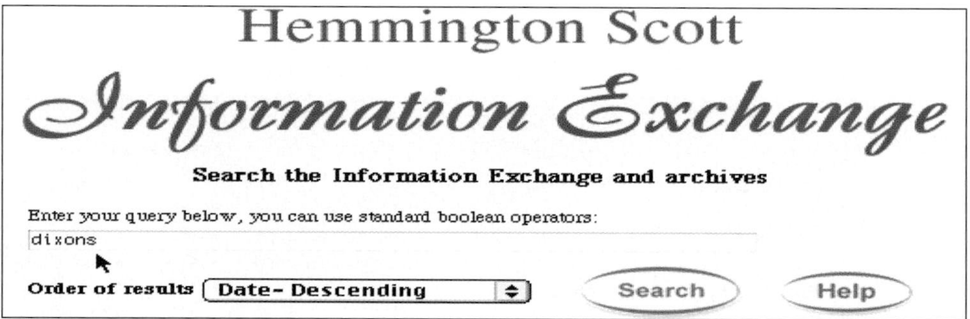

The search displays the first 10 headlines. Use the arrows at the top of the screen in Figure 6.85 to read more comments. To read the full comment, you need to click on the appropriate headline. You can post your own comments or questions once you have registered and received your password via e-mail.

Fig 6.85 *In this example, there are 641 comments posted mentioning the word 'dixons'.*

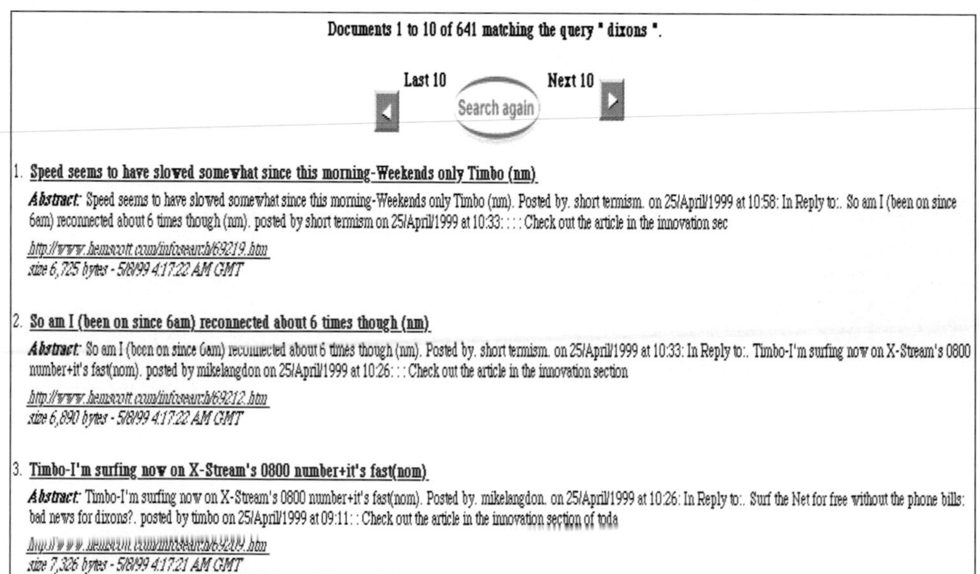

UK Shares

http://ukshares.com /cgi-bin/bb/Ultimate.cgi?action=intro&BypassCookie=true

This is an interesting internet site because it is privately run and maintained by an enthusiastic group of individuals. Indeed, some of the facilities at this site are far superior to those at sites run by well known investment companies. Although only the Bulletin Board is covered in this book, it is worth spending a moment or two to explore the other features of this site. The search engine is particularly good if not a little difficult to locate! If you look hard enough, you will find it in the top right hand corner of the screen in tiny writing.

Fig 6.86 *The UK Shares site has an excellent privately run Bulletin Board.*

UK Shares

UK Shares Bulletin Board

profile | register | prefs | faq | search

Perform a search by keyword, date, or name.

Today's Active Topics (all public forums)

Registered Members: **660**

Forum	Topics	Posts	Last Post	Moderator
UK Chatterbox				
UK Shares Info eXchange Our Main Forum **Remember that this is an advanced BB - amongst other nifty features you can edit YOUR OWN text at any time AFTER you let it go by using the notepad & pencil icon that's on each posting.**	957	4633	30 April 1999 20:11	richiec
Finance NOT! Anything (well almost) but finance. There is more to life than tracking share prices. So here's a Forum to talk about those *'best things in life'*.	31	88	29 April 1999 21:05	richiec
Computing & Software				
Ask Andy All your Computer Problems solved & more!	2	4	08 April 1999 22:37	Andy
Testing Testing 1-2-3 Testing Go on - have a play in this Playpen! Play with UBB Code, get the signature in your profile just right, experiment with activating links. No one is going to complain if you do it in here - we will clean up the mess after you! **YOU DON'T NEED TO REGISTER** to post here. Keep it clean and decent though!	9	16	04 April 1999 20:20	Andy
Let's Get Together				
Company Meetings Please post details of Company meetings here. AGMs, EGMs, locations, times, and possibly what colour of Carnation you will be wearing!	5	5	06 February 1999 14:28	Conkleschnott
Private Club Forums				

UK Shares *(con't)*

http://ukshares.com /cgi-bin/bb/Ultimate.cgi?action=intro&BypassCookie=true

To search for comments on a particular company, type in the name in the 'Search Words' box at the top of the screen, and click on 'Perform Search'.

Fig 6.87 *The Search Engine at this Bulletin Board gives you more options than most.*

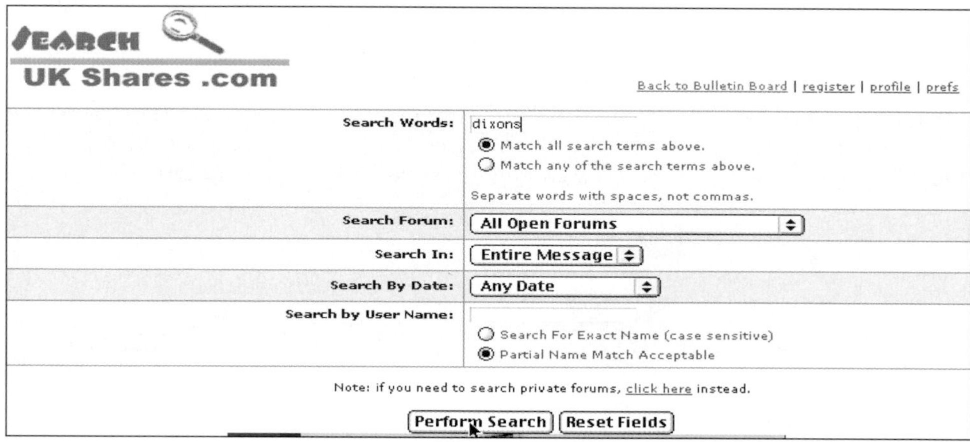

To read the the full comment, click on the relevant heading in the left hand column of the screen below. Once again, you can reply to recent questions or comments once you have registered.

Fig 6.88 *Search results are clearly displayed, but not in any particular order.*

SEARCH
UK Shares .com

Search Results:

Displaying Matches 1 - 10 (10 total)

New Search | Back to BB

Topic	Name	Date	Forum
JWE Telecom	Bobby Charlton	08-04-98	Archive - A READ ONLY Archive
Credit SuisseFB flags its "attractive stocks"	Earlybird	12-08-98	UK Shares Info eXchange
MFI - Sale starts today	KDC	12-20-98	UK Shares Info eXchange
Thursday's Business Headlines	Earlybird	01-14-99	UK Shares Info eXchange
Freepages - blasting off in pursuit of Zergo?	Stoker	01-19-99	UK Shares Info eXchange
Wednesday's Newspapers	Earlybird	01-20-99	UK Shares Info eXchange
Card Clear set to rise 50% - a chartist theory for you to test!!	Limpsfield Chartist	03-20-99	UK Shares Info eXchange
Tuesday's Newspapers	Earlybird	01-26-99	UK Shares Info eXchange
Dixons v Tesco	james	01-31-99	UK Shares Info eXchange
Tuesday's Newspapers	Earlybird	04-13-99	UK Shares Info eXchange

It is worth bearing in mind that not nearly as many people use this Bulletin Board as the Market-Eye or Hemmington Scott Bulletin Boards. This makes it less likely that you will find comments on smaller more obscure companies.

Interactive Investor

http://www.iii.co.uk/portfolio

The Interactive Investor internet site is one of the most popular financial sites in the UK. They are continually upgrading their site and a relatively new addition is the 'Discussion' board. You can access comments from other private investors directly from either the Quotes section or the Portfolio section. In the example below, an online portfolio has been set up to monitor internet related stocks. You can see that Affinity Internet Holdings are showing a gain of 13.95% on the day. In these situations, the best way to find out the reason for a sudden price move is often via a Bulletin (Discussion) board. Click on the 'Discussion' icon to display a list of comments from private investors regarding this stock.

Fig 6.89 *Click on 'Discussion' to show comments on a stock from other investors.*

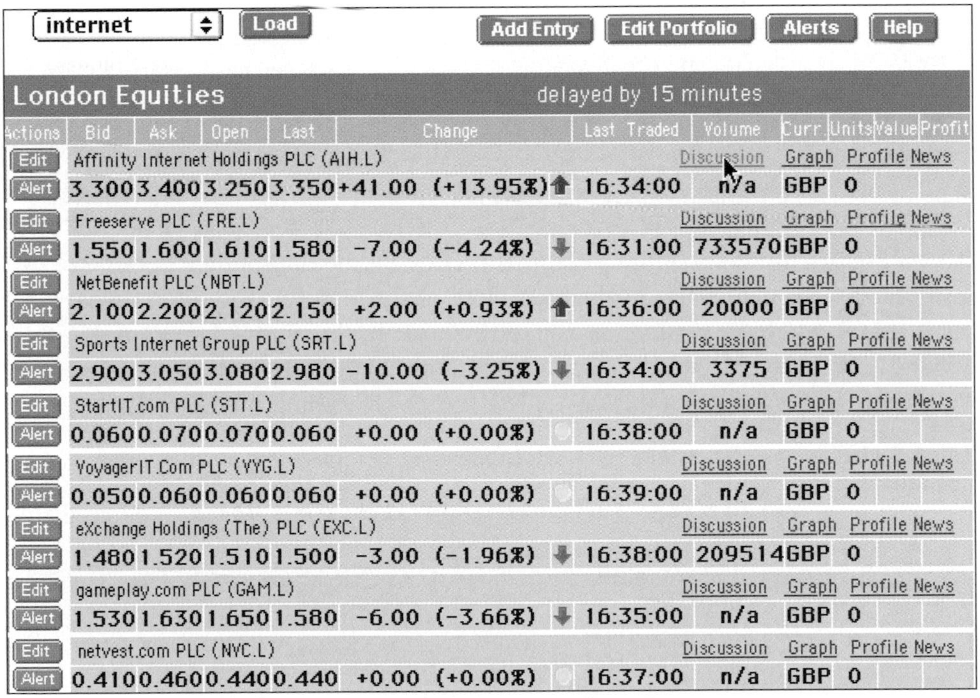

internet | Load | Add Entry | Edit Portfolio | Alerts | Help

London Equities — delayed by 15 minutes

Actions	Bid	Ask	Open	Last	Change	Last Traded	Volume	Curr	Units	Value	Profit
Edit	Affinity Internet Holdings PLC (AIH.L)					Discussion	Graph	Profile	News		
Alert	3.300	3.400	3.250	3.350	+41.00 (+13.95%) ↑	16:34:00	n/a	GBP	0		
Edit	Freeserve PLC (FRE.L)					Discussion	Graph	Profile	News		
Alert	1.550	1.600	1.610	1.580	-7.00 (-4.24%) ↓	16:31:00	733570	GBP	0		
Edit	NetBenefit PLC (NBT.L)					Discussion	Graph	Profile	News		
Alert	2.100	2.200	2.120	2.150	+2.00 (+0.93%) ↑	16:36:00	20000	GBP	0		
Edit	Sports Internet Group PLC (SRT.L)					Discussion	Graph	Profile	News		
Alert	2.900	3.050	3.080	2.980	-10.00 (-3.25%) ↓	16:34:00	3375	GBP	0		
Edit	StartIT.com PLC (STT.L)					Discussion	Graph	Profile	News		
Alert	0.060	0.070	0.070	0.060	+0.00 (+0.00%)	16:38:00	n/a	GBP	0		
Edit	VoyagerIT.Com PLC (VYG.L)					Discussion	Graph	Profile	News		
Alert	0.050	0.060	0.060	0.060	+0.00 (+0.00%)	16:39:00	n/a	GBP	0		
Edit	eXchange Holdings (The) PLC (EXC.L)					Discussion	Graph	Profile	News		
Alert	1.480	1.520	1.510	1.500	-3.00 (-1.96%) ↓	16:38:00	209514	GBP	0		
Edit	gameplay.com PLC (GAM.L)					Discussion	Graph	Profile	News		
Alert	1.530	1.630	1.650	1.580	-6.00 (-3.66%) ↓	16:35:00	n/a	GBP	0		
Edit	netvest.com PLC (NVC.L)					Discussion	Graph	Profile	News		
Alert	0.410	0.460	0.440	0.440	+0.00 (+0.00%)	16:37:00	n/a	GBP	0		

Although the 'Discussion' board on this site is a relatively new addition, it is none the less still extremely useful because of the wide popularity of this site. Bulletin boards become far more useful and valuable when there are lots of potential users. If you are trying to find out information on smaller companies or more obscure stocks, the popularity of a bulletin board is of paramount importance.

Interactive Investor *(con't)*

http://www.iii.co.uk/portfolio

Internet related stocks are particularly popular with the online investing community. The stock in this example (Affinity Holdings) is obviously widely followed by users of the Interactive Investor internet site as there are 181 messages pertaining to the stock as shown below. The third message in the list reveals why the shares have jumped up suddenly - a buy recommendation in the Times.

Fig 6.8.10 *Discussion board reveals that the shares have been tipped in the Times.*

181 Messages found, 1 to 20 shown.

Result Pages: 1 | 2 | 3 | 4 | 5 | 6 | 7 | 8 | 9 | 10

Date/Times	Comment	Author
today 10:43	[Comment] Re: Prestbury.	Net Solutions
1999/10/16 18:13	[News] More Money Making Deals	Andrew McAulay
1999/10/16 18:04	[Comment] The Times Says BUY AIH Shares	Andrew McAulay
1999/10/16 13:24	[Comment] Re: Share valuation	Nigel Hancock

To access the full text behind a comment, click on the appropriate comment. Bulletin boards can be an invaluable source of information and often reveal facts that it would be difficult to find elsewhere. In this particular example, it would have been extremely difficult to find out why these shares had risen so suddenly. To respond to a message, click on the 'Respond' button as shown.

Fig 6.8.11 *Click on 'Respond' if you have a further question or useful comment to make.*

Affinity Internet Holdings PLC

New Comment

Message Detail

Back | Next | Previous

Author:	Andrew McAulay
Date posted:	1999/10/16 18:04
Classification:	Comment
Subject:	The Times Says BUY AIH Shares
Message:	The Times 15.10.99 indicated that: 1. AIH customers are BETTER quality than Freeserve customers. 2. AIH customers are currently valued, according to the AIH share price, at £82 while Freeserve customers, even AFTER recent Freeserve share price falls, are still valued at £1100. The Times says 'buy if you can'.

Respond

7

Registration

The internet sites described in this book, all have free access to all or part of the financial information they provide. However, many of the best sites require you to fill out a simple online registration form. You should not be put off by this. There is no cost involved, and registration for each site generally only takes a few minutes. It is convenient to have the same login name and password for each site at which you register. With this in mind, choose a login name and password which both have at least 6 letters in them.

Hot Links

✍ Register for share price quotes, charts and news headlines with - *E*Trade*
✍ Register for real time price quotes and interactive charts with - *Stock Point*
✍ Register for real time price quotes and interactive charts with - *UK-iNvest*
✍ Register for charts, news & online portfolios with - *Interactive Investor*
✍ Register for share price charts and up to date news stories with - *Market-Eye*
✍ Register for detailed investment trust data with - *Trustnet*
✍ Register for online portfolios with - *Quicken*
✍ Register for news and real time quotes with - *Freequotes*
✍ Register with the - *Daily Telegrap*h
✍ Register for the bulletin board of - *UK Shares*
✍ Register for free e-mail with Hotmail - *Microsoft*

Some of the registration forms require you to have an e-mail address. Most people who use the internet will already have an e-mail address provided by their 'Internet Service Provider' (ISP). If you do not already have an e-mail address, you can contact your ISP to find out how to get one. Alternatively you can use one of the many free e-mail services available. Details of how to set up a free e-mail account with 'Hotmail' are given at the end of this Chapter.

Interactive Investor

http://www.freeyellow.com/members5/scott2b/page7.html

The simplest way to register for all the sites mentioned in this book is to visit the internet address given above. You will see a page almost identical to the first page of this Chapter. At the internet site, the 'Hot Links' become live so that you can click on them to go directly to the relevant registration page. Most registration pages are almost identical and require you to enter the same basic information about yourself. As an example, the Figure below shows what you would see if you clicked on the 'Interactive Investor' link at the internet address given above.

Fig 7.1 *The Registration page for the 'Interactive Investor' internet site.*

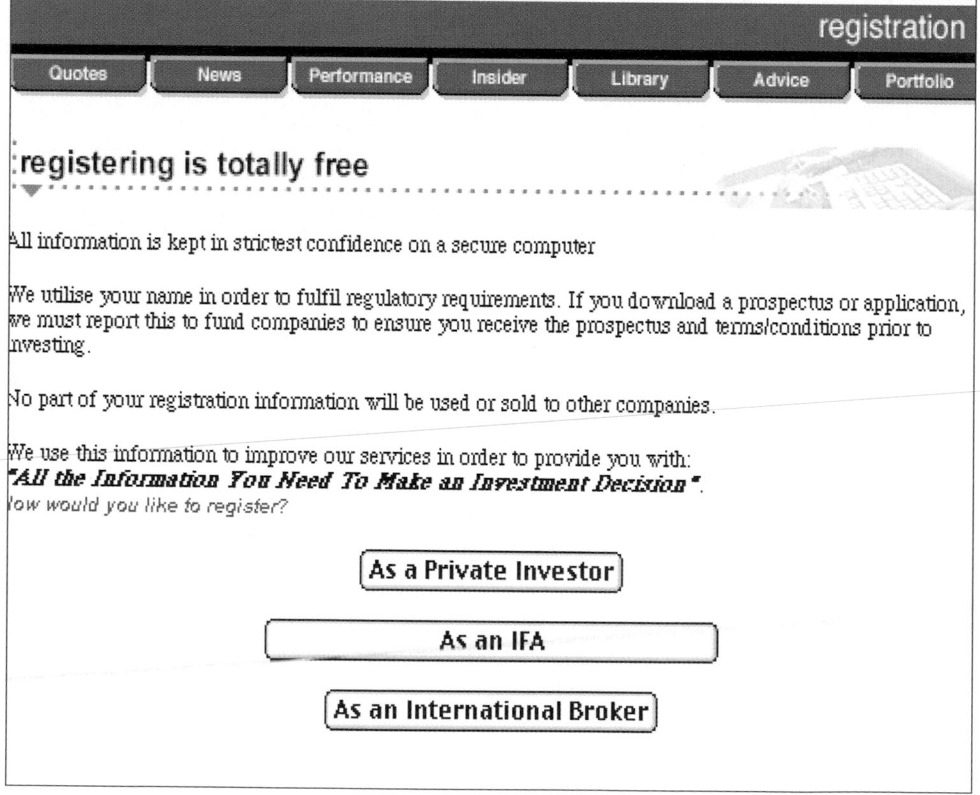

In this particular example, you have to specify on what basis you are registering. Most people would click on 'As a Private Investor'.

Interactive Investor *(con't)*

http://www.iii.co.uk/registration/

The 'Interactive Investor' internet site has a particularly simple application form as shown below. First, you must choose a 'User name'. At other internet sites, this is known as a 'login' name. Some sites will specify that your 'login' name must be at least 6 letters long, no spaces, symbols or numbers. With this in mind, choose a 'User name' with exactly 6 letters and type it in the box. Similarly, choose a 'Password' with exactly six letters. You will generally be asked to re-type the password to make sure you entered what you think you entered. Make sure you enter your full e-mail address which will look something like 'yourname@hotmail.com. Many registration forms have a small box somewhere on the screen which asks you if you wish to receive regular updates etc. via e-mail. If you do not wish to receive anything via e-mail, remember to click on the appropriate box (eg so that the small black tick disappears). At the end of each registration form you will have to click on the 'Submit' button.

Fig 7.11 *Interactive Investor has a particularly simple Registration Form.*

Register free for interactive investor

NOTE: If you wish to provide address and other information, please complete this form and then refer to 'Personal Profile' on the following page. **Note: The username and password fields are CASE SENSITIVE. All fields are required.**

Username	Password	Password (retype)
yourname	••••••	••••••

First Name: your
Surname: name
E-mail address: yourname@wherever,com
Country of residence: United Kingdom

☑ **iii Alerts**

Uncheck this box if you do not want to receive our regular investment newsletter detailing top performing funds, financial trends and new financial products.

Terms of Acceptance and Registration

Press register below to warrant the information you have supplied is accurate and you accept iii's Terms & Conditions and wish to use the services.

Register

Registration *(con't)*

http://www.hotmail.com

Setting up a free e-mail account with 'Hotmail' takes about 5 minutes and is relatively straightforward. The advantage of having an e-mail account with Hotmail, is that you can easily access your e-mail account anywhere in the world. Some people will find that the e-mail address they are currently using can only be accessed at the computer on which it was set up. This is not much good if you want to use e-mail when you on holiday abroad or using someone else's computer. Hotmail is owned by Microsoft who are one of the most powerful computer companies in the world. Microsoft have plenty of resources at their disposal to keep this service up and running and upgrade it with new technology etc. To open an account you need to type in the internet address given above. On many modern computers using the Explorer browser, it is sufficient to simply type in 'hotmail'. The screen shown below appears and you need to then click on 'Sign up now'. The screen shots illustrating this internet site have been reprinted by permission from Microsoft Corporation.

Fig 7.2 *The opening screen for the free e-mail service - 'Hotmail'.*

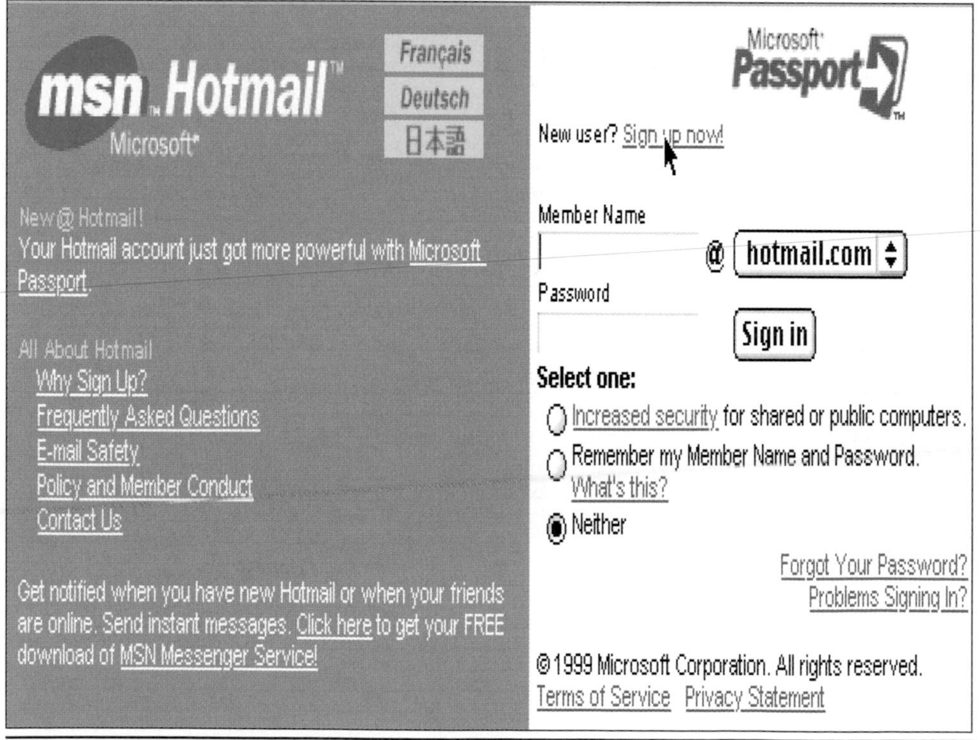

Registration *(con't)*

http://www.hotmail.com

Fig 7.21 *At the end of the terms and conditions click on 'I Accept'.*

Pursuant to Title 17, United States Code, Section 512(c)(2), notifications of claimed copyright infringement should be sent to Service Provider's Designated Agent. See Notice and Procedure for Making Claims of Copyright Infringement.

I Accept I Decline

Fig 7.22 *Fill out each part of the application form and click on 'Sign Up'.*

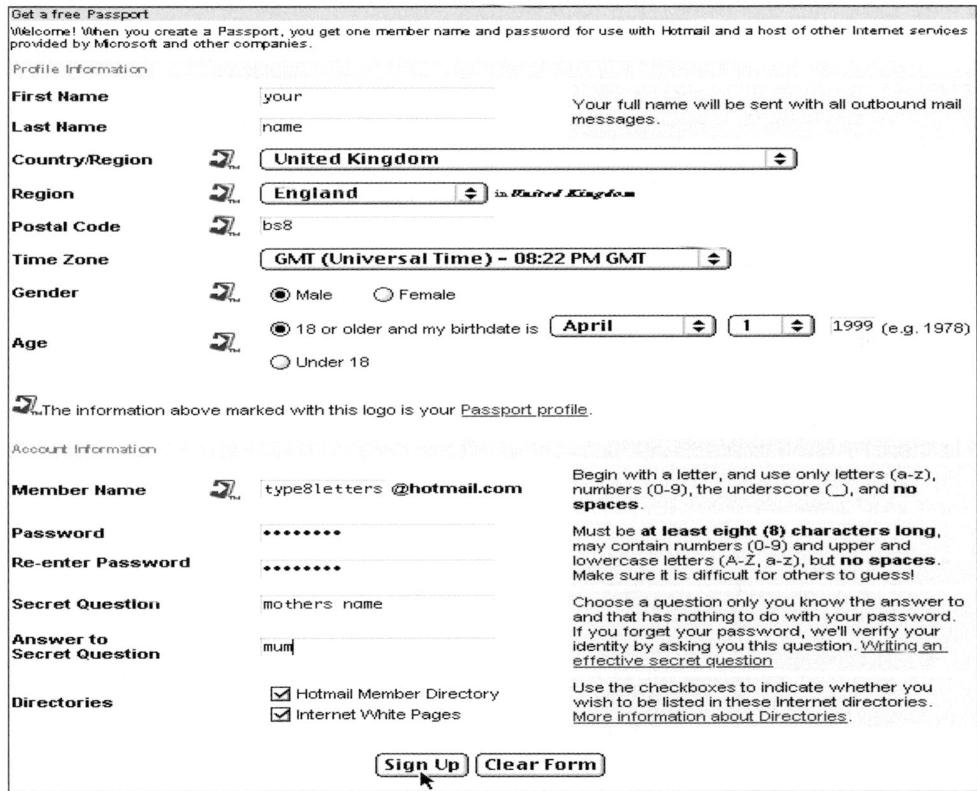

Get a free Passport

Welcome! When you create a Passport, you get one member name and password for use with Hotmail and a host of other Internet services provided by Microsoft and other companies.

Profile Information

First Name: your
Last Name: name
Your full name will be sent with all outbound mail messages.

Country/Region: United Kingdom
Region: England in United Kingdom
Postal Code: bs8
Time Zone: GMT (Universal Time) - 08:22 PM GMT
Gender: Male Female
Age: 18 or older and my birthdate is April 1 1999 (e.g. 1978)
Under 18

The information above marked with this logo is your Passport profile.

Account Information

Member Name: type8letters @hotmail.com
Begin with a letter, and use only letters (a-z), numbers (0-9), the underscore (_), and **no spaces**.

Password: ••••••••
Re-enter Password: ••••••••
Must be **at least eight (8) characters long**, may contain numbers (0-9) and upper and lowercase letters (A-Z, a-z), but **no spaces**. Make sure it is difficult for others to guess!

Secret Question: mothers name
Answer to Secret Question: mum
Choose a question only you know the answer to and that has nothing to do with your password. If you forget your password, we'll verify your identity by asking you this question. Writing an effective secret question

Directories: Hotmail Member Directory; Internet White Pages
Use the checkboxes to indicate whether you wish to be listed in these Internet directories. More information about Directories.

Sign Up Clear Form

Hotmail has recently become so popular that login names and passwords must now contain at least 8 letters. If you choose to have your name and location listed, it simply makes it easier for friend to look up your e-mail account which can be useful.

Registration *(con't)*

http://www.hotmail.com

In case you ever forget your password, you are asked to type in a hint question at the end of the form. For example, if your password was your mothers name, you could type in a 'Hint Question' like 'What is my mothers name?' The hint answer in that example would hopefully be fairly obvious to you!! As long as you don't leave these boxes completely empty, it doesn't really matter what you decide to type in. At the end of the form, you will be asked to type in the login name and password you have chosen just to make sure you remember them. When you have done this, click on 'Sign Up' at the bottom of the screen. If you have filled in the form correctly and chosen a login name that isn't already being used, the screen in Figure 7.23 will appear.

Fig 7.23 *If you have registered correctly the 'Sign Up Successful'! screen is displayed.*

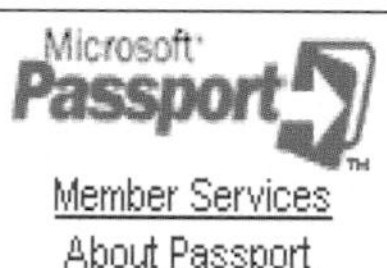

Member Services
About Passport

Sign Up Successful!

Congratulations. Your new Member Name is:

<type8letters@hotmail.com>

Important: For your Hotmail account to remain active, after today you must sign in at least once within the next ten (10) days. Also, after the initial 10 day period you must sign in at least once every 90 days to keep your account active.

Continue at Hotmail

Tips:

To Sign Out, click Passport sign out

To Sign In, click Passport sign in

You can use your Passport to access Hotmail as well as many other top internet sites. For a directory of Passport sites visit **http://www.passport.com/**.

 Terms of Service Privacy Statement

8

Buying and Selling

The procedure for setting up a dealing account which enables you to buy and sell investments over the internet is similar for all brokers. The Company's internet site will generally enable you to request an application form to be sent to you in the post. You will need to complete the application form and return it with a cheque for the amount you wish to invest. Your cheque will generally be deposited in an interest bearing client account and you will be able to deal as soon as it has cleared. Once you have set up an account, you can literally buy and sell shares at the touch of a button. There is no paper work involved and you can access your account to check valuations or view transactions etc.

Hot Links

✍ Market Master Account - *Charles Schwab*

✔ List of online brokers and dealing commissions - *Money World*

Competition is hotting up in the world of online broking and it is worth checking to see what special deals are being offered at the time. It can take up to 10 days to open an account with some online brokers and hence it is worth trying to pick a broker who is reliable and competitive on price. Think carefully before subscribing to any additional services with an online broker as this book tells you where to get most of the same financial information for free. This Chapter uses the Charles Schwab 'Market Master' A/C to illustrate some of the features of the UK's most popular Online dealing account.

Charles Schwab

http://www.schwab-worldwide.com/Worldwide/Europe/Sterling

Charles Schwab is an American company which some years ago took over the UK based 'Sharelink PLC'. This was the first internet dealing site to be established in the UK and is at present by far the largest. Although bigger is not always better, there is some comfort in knowing that this internet dealing site has been tried and tested by thousands of investors before you. Charles Schwab offers many different types of dealing account as shown below. The basic internet share dealing account is called 'Market Master'. To request an application form, click on 'Application Request' in the top left hand corner of the screen.

Fig 8.1 *To open an Online dealing account, you need to request an Application Form.*

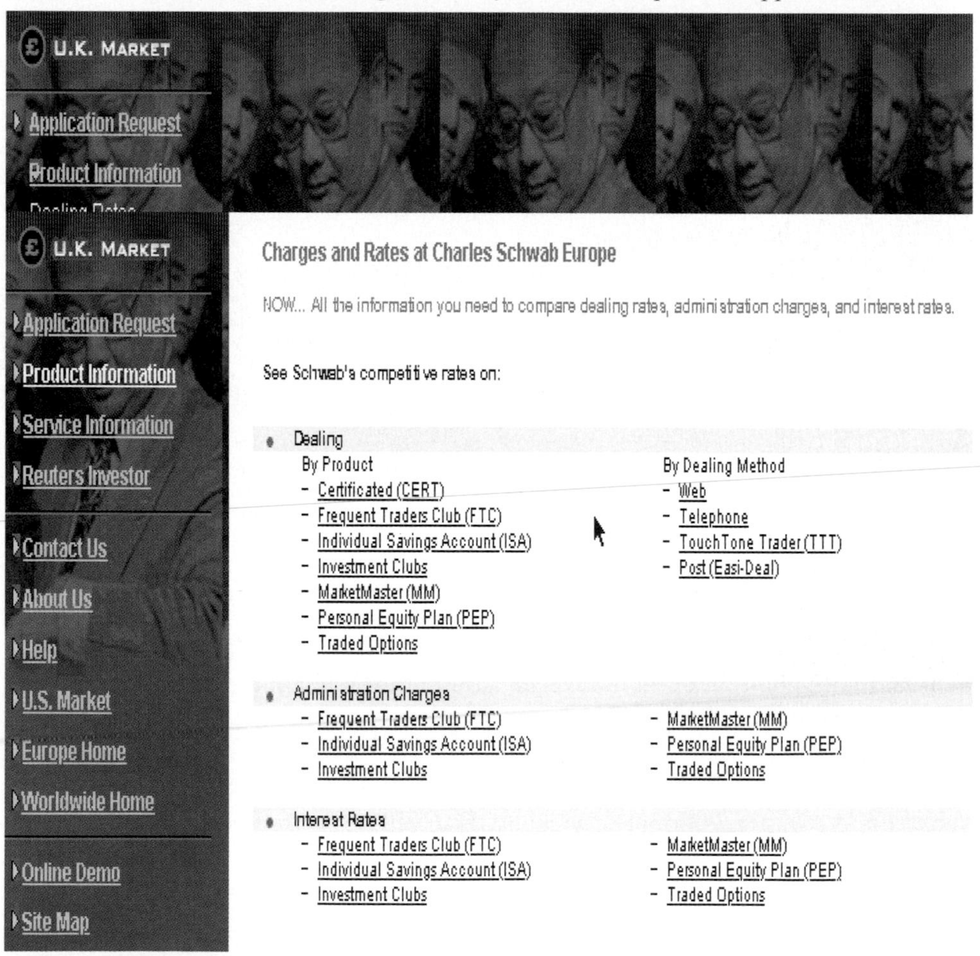

Charles Schwab *(con't)*

http://www.schwab-worldwide.com/Worldwide/Europe/Sterling

You can click on any of the headings in Figure 8.1 to get more details about the various dealing accounts offered by Charles Schwab. The figure below shows the dealing rates for buying and selling shares over the internet. To set up an internet account there is a one off charge of £25 known as the 'Connection Charge'. As competition increases, dealing rates are likely to fall and connection charges will become a thing of the past. For example, in America where there are over 90 Online Brokers, dealing rates are as low as $7 a trade - regardless of deal size. With dealing rates so low, internet trading in America has really taken off. On some days almost half the volume of trades on the American stock market are transacted over the internet.

Fig 8.11 *Charles Schwab offers relatively low commission rates for internet dealing.*

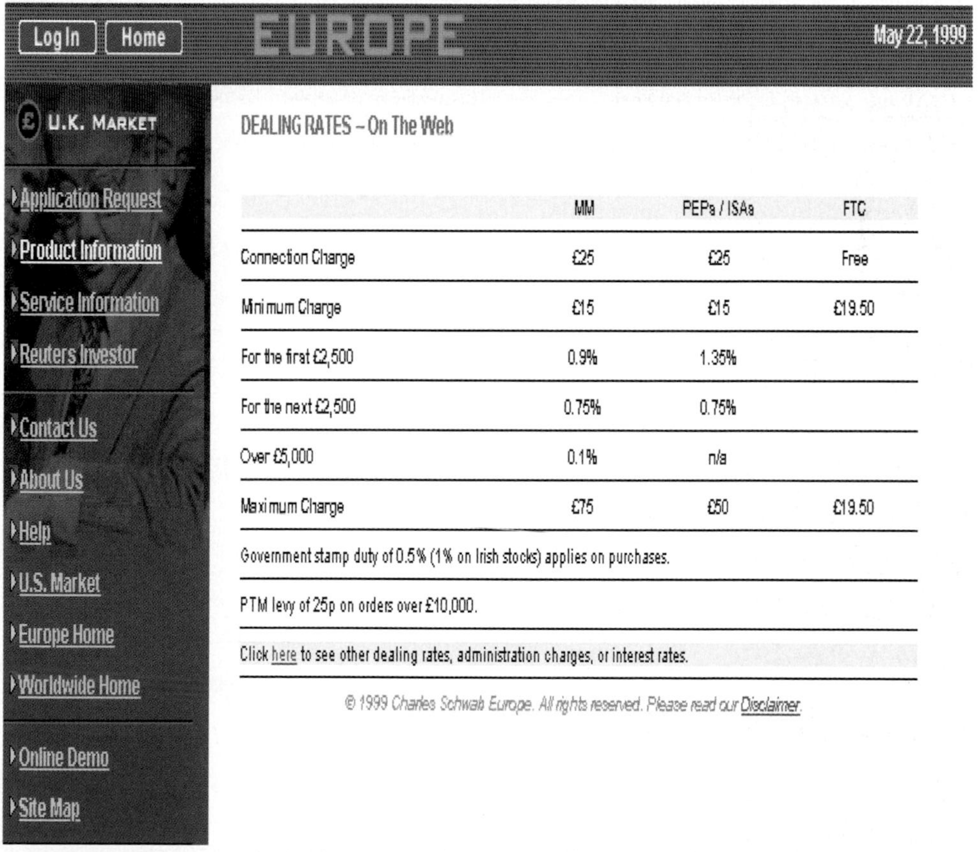

Log In | Home

EUROPE

May 22, 1999

U.K. MARKET

Application Request
Product Information
Service Information
Reuters Investor
Contact Us
About Us
Help
U.S. Market
Europe Home
Worldwide Home
Online Demo
Site Map

DEALING RATES – On The Web

	MM	PEPs / ISAs	FTC
Connection Charge	£25	£25	Free
Minimum Charge	£15	£15	£19.50
For the first £2,500	0.9%	1.35%	
For the next £2,500	0.75%	0.75%	
Over £5,000	0.1%	n/a	
Maximum Charge	£75	£50	£19.50

Government stamp duty of 0.5% (1% on Irish stocks) applies on purchases.

PTM levy of 25p on orders over £10,000.

Click here to see other dealing rates, administration charges, or interest rates.

Charles Schwab *(con't)*

http://www.schwab-worldwide.com/Worldwide/Europe/Sterling

Internet dealing accounts generally have interest bearing bank accounts associated with them. When you sell investments over the internet, the proceeds will automatically be paid into this bank account unless you request otherwise. Similarly, dividends from shares will also be paid into this bank account. One of the great benefits of an online share trading facility is that you can at any time look at a statement of your account by connecting to the internet.

Fig 8.12 *Internet dealing accounts pay reasonable rates of interest on your cash.*

INTEREST RATES – MarketMaster

Cash Balance	Gross Interest Paid
£20,000 plus	4.25%
£5,000 – £19,999	3%
£500 – £4,999	1%
£50 – £499	0.5%

Click here to see other dealing rates, administration charges, or interest rates.

Often internet dealing accounts will have administration charges associated with them. This is not unusual, but it is as well to be aware of how much you will be charged before you open an account.

Fig 8.13 *The Administration charges associated with the 'Market Master' account.*

Quarterly charge	£1 per stock Minimum £5 Maximum £30	Yes
Insurance	Free	
Quarterly Account Statements	Free	
Quarterly Portfolio Valuations	Free	
Consolidated Tax Certificate (Annual)	Free (Duplicate £6)	Yes
Annual Company Report & Accounts (on request)	Free	
Attendance at Shareholders Meetings (on request)	Free	
Rights and other special events	Free	
Transfer in of Shares	Free	
Transfer in of Shares from New Issues	Free	
Transfer out of Shares	£10 per stock. Minimum £30	Yes
Ad hoc Statement or Valuation	£6	Yes
Automatic Reinvestment of Dividends	1% (no minimum charge, but reinvestment attracts stamp duty at the standard rate)	
Ad hoc Funds Withdrawal	Free	
Application for New Issue shares from Funds available	£10	n/a
Funds Wire	£30	No

Charles Schwab *(con't)*

http://www.schwab-worldwide.com/Worldwide/Europe/Sterling

Once you have set up an account and logged on, you will be able to access your online trading account. One of the unique features of having an online trading account is that you can access 'Real Time' share price quotes. Share price quotes elsewhere on the internet will nearly always be delayed by at least 15 minutes. See Glossary for a definition of a Real Time price.

Fig 8.14 *Click on 'Real Time' prices and enter the name or symbol of a share.*

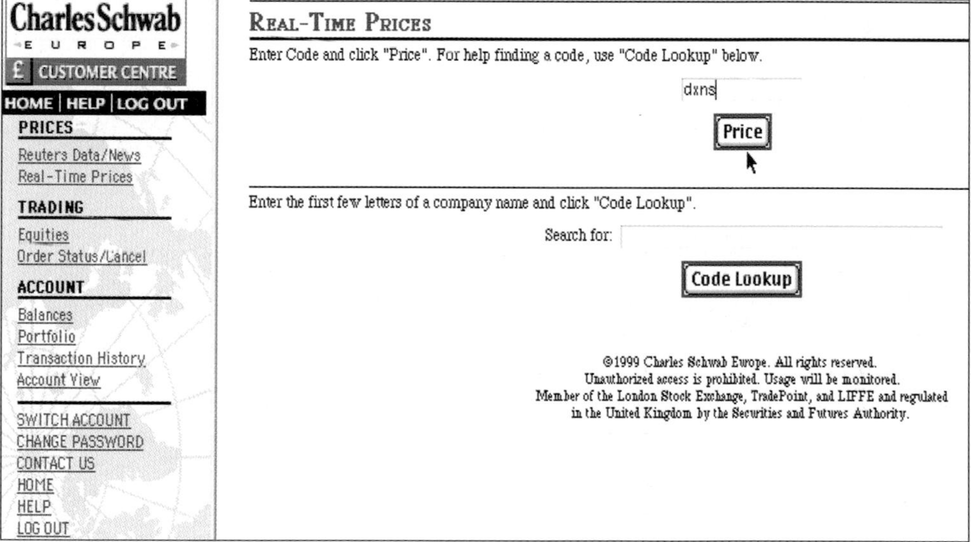

Fig 8.15 *A 'Real-Time' share price quote for Dixons Group PLC shares.*

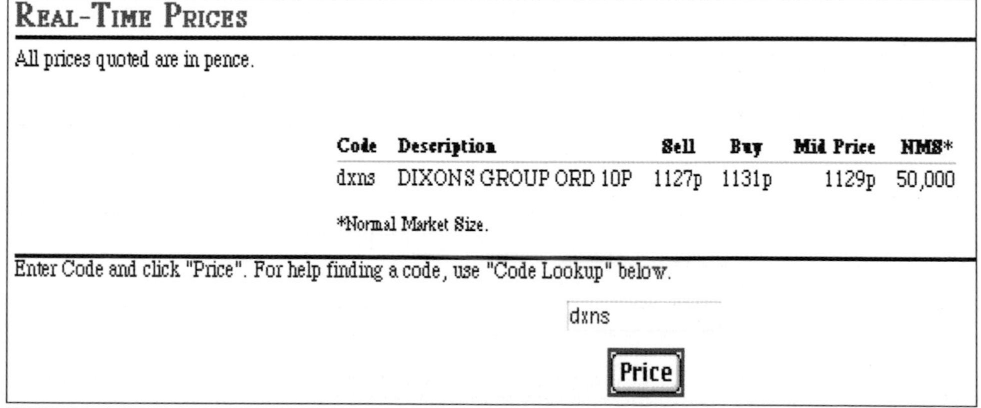

REAL-TIME PRICES
All prices quoted are in pence.
Code Description Sell Buy Mid Price NMS*
dxns DIXONS GROUP ORD 10P 1127p 1131p 1129p 50,000
*Normal Market Size.
Enter Code and click "Price". For help finding a code, use "Code Lookup" below.
dxns
Price

Charles Schwab *(con't)*

http://www.schwab-worldwide.com/Worldwide/Europe/Sterling

To buy or sell shares, you need to click on 'Equities'. This is located under the heading of TRADING in the left hand column of the screen shown in Figure 8.17. If you want to buy or sell shares at a specific price, then click in the 'Limit at' circle. Share prices can change rapidly and you may be disappointed or surprised to find out that you have bought or sold shares at a different price to the one you had looked at on the screen just moments earlier.

Fig 8.16 *Enter the dealing instructions on the screen below and click on 'Place Order'.*

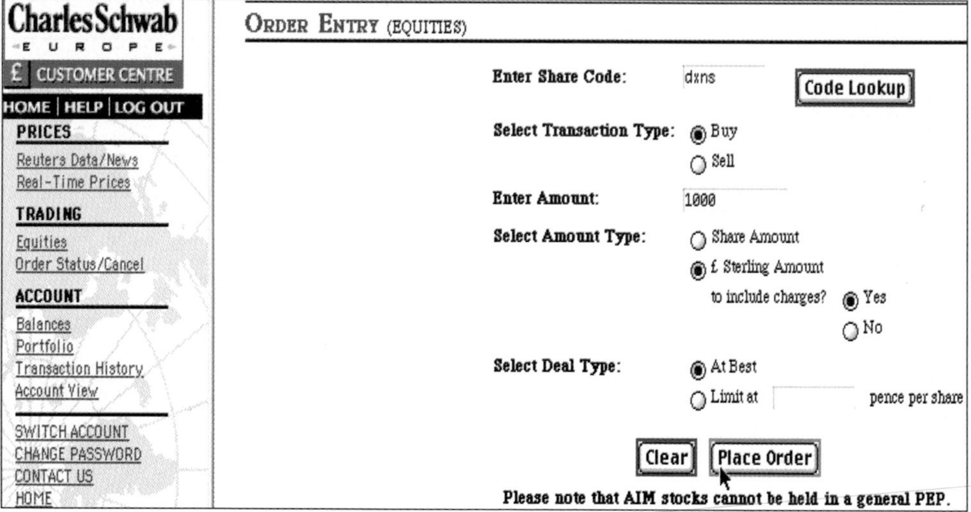

The screen which appears after clicking 'Place Order', displays the instructions you have entered, along with the current Real Time share price. If you are satisfied that you have entered your instructions correctly, click on 'Place Order' in Figure 8.17. It normally only takes a few minutes for a deal to be transacted. You can check whether your order has been dealt with, by clicking on 'Order Status/Cancel' in the left hand column of the screen shown in Figure 8.16.

Fig 8.17 *Last chance to double check that you have entered your deal details correctly.*

ORDER VERIFICATION (EQUITIES) Account

Please verify your order. To place this order and to receive an order number, click the "Place Order" button.

Action	No of Shares	Code	Description	Price per share
Sell	2000	SCFW	SCHRODER INCOME GROWTH FUND WTS TO SUBSCRIBE FOR ORD	At Best

Price Quoted	Estimated Commission	Stamp Duty	Levy Amount	Estimated Amount
42p	£15.0000	0.0000	0.0000	£825.0000

Do Not Place Order | Change | Place Order

Charles Schwab *(con't)*

http://www.schwab-worldwide.com/Worldwide/Europe/Sterling

The various headings under 'ACCOUNT' in the left hand column of the screen, enable you to check on various aspects of your account. If you click on 'Balances', a list of the cash balances in your various accounts is displayed together with the current stock value (at the mid price). These two figures are added together to give you the total value of your 'Market Master' account. Clicking on 'Portfolio', displays the investments currently held, the number of shares, mid price, book cost, market value and the percentage gain (or loss!!). Clicking on 'Account View' displays all of this information on one screen at the same time. An example of how this information is displayed is shown below.

Fig 8.18 *Clicking on 'Account View' displays your cash balance and current portfolio.*

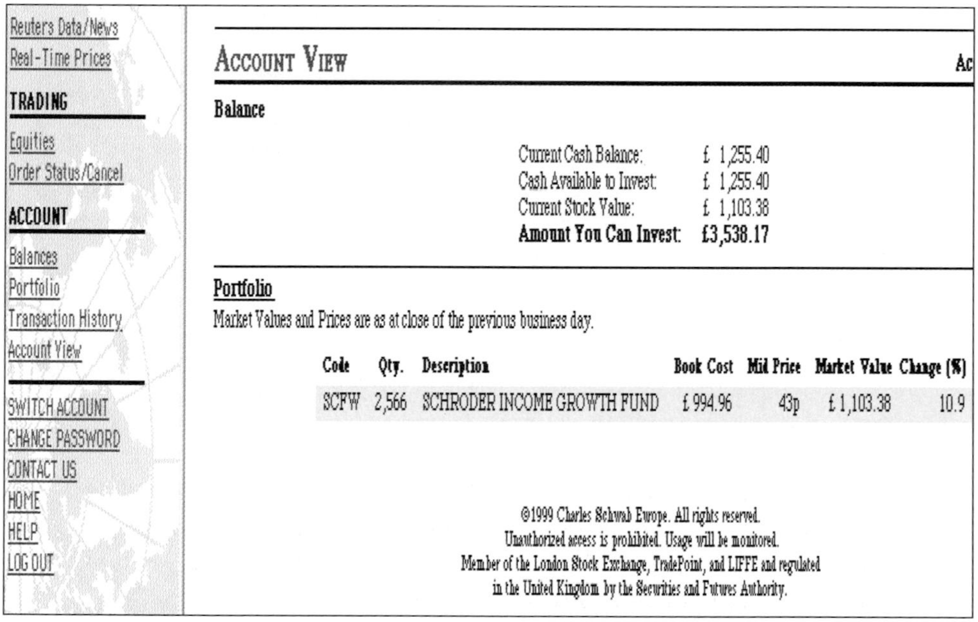

Reuters Data/News
Real-Time Prices
TRADING
Equities
Order Status/Cancel
ACCOUNT
Balances
Portfolio
Transaction History
Account View
SWITCH ACCOUNT
CHANGE PASSWORD
CONTACT US
HOME
HELP
LOG OUT

ACCOUNT VIEW — Ac

Balance

Current Cash Balance: £ 1,255.40
Cash Available to Invest: £ 1,255.40
Current Stock Value: £ 1,103.38
Amount You Can Invest: £3,538.17

Portfolio

Market Values and Prices are as at close of the previous business day.

Code	Qty.	Description	Book Cost	Mid Price	Market Value	Change (%)
SCFW	2,566	SCHRODER INCOME GROWTH FUND	£ 994.96	43p	£ 1,103.38	10.9

The heading 'Transaction History' is fully described on the following page. If you have more than one account with Charles Schwab (such as a PEP), you can click on 'Switch Account' to display similar details for that account. You can e-mail Charles Schwab by clicking on 'Contact Us' but bear in mind that you can not e-mail trading instructions. When you have finished using your online trading account, be sure to 'Log Out'. This ensures that no one can inadvertently (or purposely!!) trade on your account.

Charles Schwab *(con't)*

http://www.schwab-worldwide.com/Worldwide/Europe/Sterling

Clicking on 'Transaction History' enables you to check the price at which you have bought and sold investments in the past. At a glance you can also see what has been credited to your bank account (via BACS). Interest you have earned on cash held in your account, and dividends are also shown. Clicking on 'View Today' in the top right hand corner of the screen, displays that day's transactions.

Fig 8.19 *Clicking on 'Transaction History' displays a summary of your past deals.*

TRANSACTION HISTORY

Current View: Historical Transactions
Click dates that are underlined to see details.

View Today

Date	Action	Qty	Description	Debit	Credit	Balance
04-05-1999	Sold	2635	PROLIFIC INCOME		£ 1,243.21	£ 1,255.40
22-03-1999			Personal Cheque		£ 700.00	£ 12.19
21-03-1999			Interest Credited		£ 1.83	£ (687.81)
21-03-1999			VAT Charge	£(0.74)		£ (689.64)
21-03-1999			Admin Charge	£(4.26)		£ (688.90)
26-02-1999	Bought	2566	SCHRODER INC GWTH	£(994.96)		£ (684.64)
26-02-1999	Bought	2635	PROLIFIC INCOME	£(994.95)		£ 310.32
26-02-1999			Withdrawal BACS	£(700.00)		£ 1,305.27
24-02-1999			Withdrawal BACS	£(700.00)		£ 2,005.27
05-02-1999	Sold	237	DIXONS GROUP		£ 2,366.87	£ 2,705.27
11-01-1999	Sold	41	DIXONS GROUP		£ 333.91	£ 338.40
27-12-1998			Interest Credited		£ 2.47	£ 4.49
27-12-1998			VAT Charge	£(0.74)		£ 2.02
27-12-1998			Admin Charge	£(4.26)		£ 2.76
20-11-1998	Bought	278	DIXONS GROUP	£(1,992.98)		£ 7.02
04-11-1998			Personal Cheque		£ 2,000.00	£ 2,000.00

Fig 8.1.10 *Click on an individual entry in Figure 8.19 for details on that transaction.*

TRANSACTION HISTORY (DETAIL)

Click "Summary" to return to Transaction History Summary.

DIXONS GROUP

Transaction Date	05-02-1999	Bargain Reference Number	CY1237
Action	Sold	Contract Total Amount	£2366.87
Quantity	237	Settlement Date	12-02-1999

Summary

Charles Schwab *(con't)*

http://www.schwab-investor.rois.com

Most online trading accounts also give free access to certain financial data. In the case of Charles Schwab, you need a different logon name and password which is issued upon request. Clicking on 'Reuters Data/News' in the left hand column of the screen in Figure 8.14, displays the following screen.

Fig 8.1.11 *Click on 'Reuters Investor Site' to access the free information at this site.*

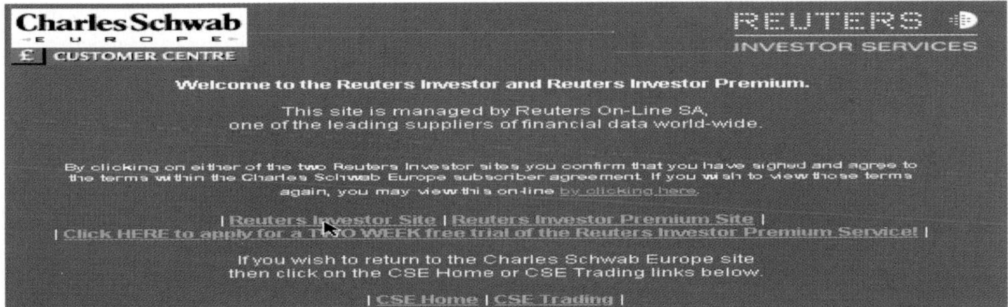

You can access the free data by clicking on the various headings in the left hand column of Figure 8.1.12. The opening screen is quite useful because it displays the mid prices and 'ticker symbols' of all the stocks which comprise the FT-SE 100 Index. You can click on any of these shares to get real time prices.

Fig 8.1.12 *Mid prices of shares in the FT-SE 100 Index shown on the same screen.*

Charles Schwab
EUROPE
£ CUSTOMER CENTRE

Quick Quote

REUTERS
INVESTOR SERVICES

News
FTSE 100
Search
Indices
Foreign Exchange
Premium Service
Help

FTSE 100 INDEX 6239.8 -82.3 H 6280.8 L 6184.8 at 16:13

Down 82 Unchanged 1 SEAQ VOL 920633430

ABF.L	461 2/8	BSCT.L	878 4/8	GUS.L	670	NXT.L	722 4/8	SDR.L	1272
ADZ.L	777	BSY.L	579	HAS.L	613	ORA.L	878 4/8	SEM.L	542
AL.L	907	BT.L	1065	HFX.L	790	PO.L	894 4/8	SGC.L	204 2/8
ALLD.L	574 4/8	CBRY.L	439 4/8	HG.L	263	PRU.L	831 4/8	SHEL.L	459 4/8
ANL.L	1296	CCM.L	549 4/8	HNS.L	544	PSON.L	1210	SLP.L	482
ASSD.L	178 6/8	CGU.L	931 4/8	HSBA.L	2040	PWG.L	699	SMIN.L	930
AVZ.L	602	CNA.L	123 4/8	ICI.L	677 4/8	RBOS.L	1358	SPW.L	531
AZN.L	2480	CPG.L	619	III.L	692	RCOL.L	715 4/8	SSE.L	591
BA.L	415	CTM.L	1358	IMT.L	666	REED.L	485	STAN.L	982
BAA.L	648	CW.L	790	ISYS.L	278 4/8	RIO.L	960	SVT.L	896
BARC.L	1878	DGE.L	663	KGF.L	800	RR.L	270	TSCO.L	172 2/8
BASS.L	915	DMGOa.L	3360	LAND.L	801	RSA.L	506	TW.L	936
BATS.L	560 4/8	DXNS.L	1125	LGEN.L	174 4/8	RTK.L	1359	TWT.L	277
BAY.L	467	EGS.L	1591	LLOY.L	857	RTO.L	245 6/8	ULVR.L	563 4/8
BG.L	350 6/8	EMA.L	1300	MKS.L	381	RTR.L	829	UNWS.L	648 4/8
BGY.L	576	EMI.L	448	MSY.L	539	SAB.L	503	UU.L	690
BLT.L	204 2/8	GAA.L	1245	NGG.L	426	SB.L	778	VOD.L	1252
BOC.L	1095 4/8	GEC.L	582	NPR.L	470 4/8	SBRY.L	378 2/8	WPP.L	517
BOOT.L	822	GKN.L	956 4/8	NU.L	434	SCR.L	574 4/8	WTB.L	1043
BPA.L	1131	GLXO.L	1725	NWB.L	1398	SCTN.L	731	WWH.L	405 4/8

Charles Schwab *(con't)*

http://www.schwab-investor.rois.com

If you click on the News icon, a menu of four choices appears. Clicking on 'UK Market Report' displays a list of news headlines relating to the UK stock market. The full story can be viewed by clicking on the appropriate headline. Unfortunately, there is no facility to search for specific news items which limits the usefulness of the news service at this site.

Fig 8.1.13 *'UK Market Report' tells you how the stock market is performing that day.*

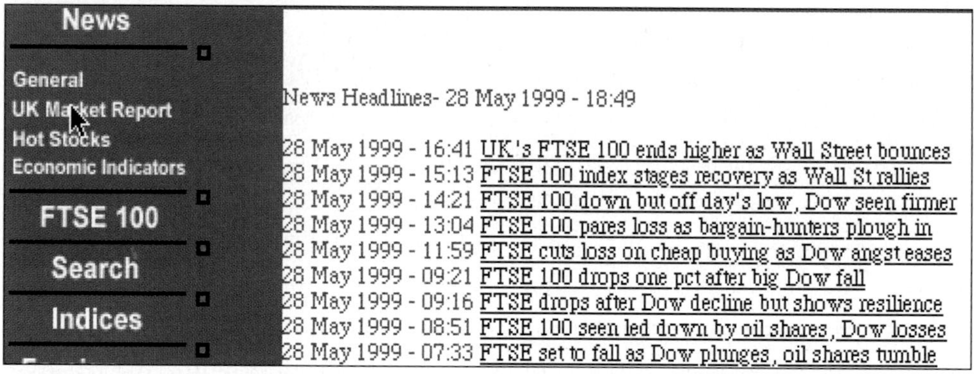

News
General
UK Market Report
Hot Stocks
Economic Indicators
FTSE 100
Search
Indices

News Headlines- 28 May 1999 - 18:49

28 May 1999 - 16:41 UK's FTSE 100 ends higher as Wall Street bounces
28 May 1999 - 15:13 FTSE 100 index stages recovery as Wall St rallies
28 May 1999 - 14:21 FTSE 100 down but off day's low, Dow seen firmer
28 May 1999 - 13:04 FTSE 100 pares loss as bargain-hunters plough in
28 May 1999 - 11:59 FTSE cuts loss on cheap buying as Dow angst eases
28 May 1999 - 09:21 FTSE 100 drops one pct after big Dow fall
28 May 1999 - 09:16 FTSE drops after Dow decline but shows resilience
28 May 1999 - 08:51 FTSE 100 seen led down by oil shares, Dow losses
28 May 1999 - 07:33 FTSE set to fall as Dow plunges, oil shares tumble

Clicking on 'Hot Stocks' displays a list of stocks which are featured in the news that day. Clicking on a headline displays the full story whereas clicking on the 'ticker symbol' gives the up to date share price of that stock. The 'Economic Indicators' heading produces a useful list of forthcoming economic figures such as inflation, producer prices etc.

Fig 8.1.14 *Clicking on 'Hot Stocks' displays a list of stocks in the news that day.*

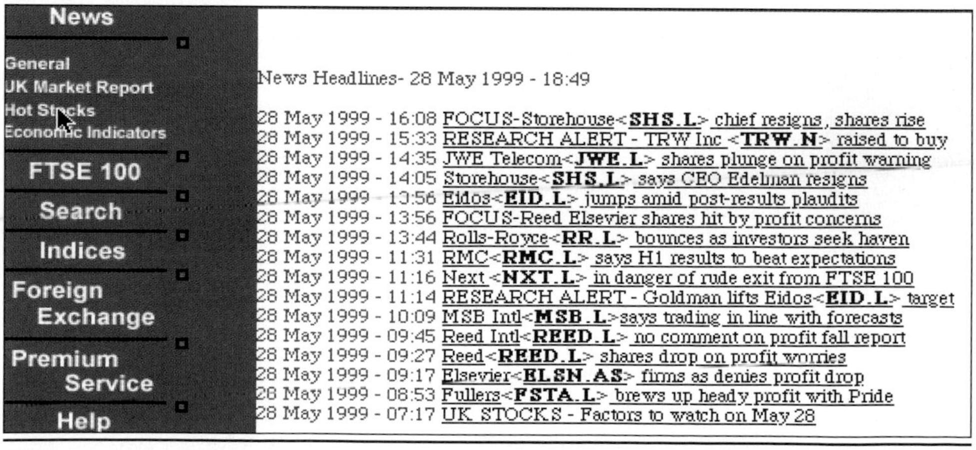

News
General
UK Market Report
Hot Stocks
Economic Indicators
FTSE 100
Search
Indices
Foreign Exchange
Premium Service
Help

News Headlines- 28 May 1999 - 18:49

28 May 1999 - 16:08 FOCUS-Storehouse<**SHS.L**> chief resigns, shares rise
28 May 1999 - 15:33 RESEARCH ALERT - TRW Inc <**TRW.N**> raised to buy
28 May 1999 - 14:35 JWE Telecom<**JWE.L**> shares plunge on profit warning
28 May 1999 - 14:05 Storehouse<**SHS.L**> says CEO Edelman resigns
28 May 1999 - 13:56 Eidos<**EID.L**> jumps amid post-results plaudits
28 May 1999 - 13:56 FOCUS-Reed Elsevier shares hit by profit concerns
28 May 1999 - 13:44 Rolls-Royce<**RR.L**> bounces as investors seek haven
28 May 1999 - 11:31 RMC<**RMC.L**> says H1 results to beat expectations
28 May 1999 - 11:16 Next <**NXT.L**> in danger of rude exit from FTSE 100
28 May 1999 - 11:14 RESEARCH ALERT - Goldman lifts Eidos<**EID.L**> target
28 May 1999 - 10:09 MSB Intl<**MSB.L**>says trading in line with forecasts
28 May 1999 - 09:45 Reed Intl<**REED.L**> no comment on profit fall report
28 May 1999 - 09:27 Reed<**REED.L**> shares drop on profit worries
28 May 1999 - 09:17 Elsevier<**ELSN.AS**> firms as denies profit drop
28 May 1999 - 08:53 Fullers<**FSTA.L**> brews up heady profit with Pride
28 May 1999 - 07:17 UK STOCKS - Factors to watch on May 28

Charles Schwab *(con't)*

http://www.schwab-investor.rois.com

Fig 8.1.15 *Clicking on 'Indices' shows the performance of major stock markets that*

Top Indices				
Name	Last	Net Chg	Pct Chg	Updated
FTSE 100 INDEX (.FTSE)	6235.8	-86.3	-1.37	16:14 25 MAY 1999
AMS EXCH INDEX (.AEX)	560.94	-6.23	-1.10	15:30 25 MAY 1999
ATX-INDEX OETOB (.ATX)	1187.99	-42.59	-3.46	14:01 25 MAY 1999
CAC 40 INDEX (.FCHI)	4373.78	-24.35	-0.55	16:24 25 MAY 1999
DJ INDU AVERAGE (.DJI)	10732.84	78.17	0.73	16:29 25 MAY 1999
DT. AKTIEN INDEX (.GDAX)	5143.10	-121.58	-2.31	16:05 25 MAY 1999
HANG SENG INDEX (.HSI)	12346.91	-89.95	-0.72	09:00 25 MAY 1999
MIB 30 IDX (.MIB30)	35549	-73	-0.20	16:30 25 MAY 1999
NIKKEI 225 INDEX (.N225)	16214.23	-176.26	-1.08	07:03 25 MAY 1999
S&P 500 INDEX (.SPC)	1315.94	9.29	0.71	16:30 25 MAY 1999
SPI GENERAL C (.SSHI)	4473.37	-98.67	-2.16	16:22 25 MAY 1999
STRAITS TIME IDX (.STI)	1896.21	-36.59	-1.89	10:01 25 MAY 1999
TSE 300 INDEX (.TSE)	6867.10	-98.87	-1.42	16:30 25 MAY 1999
CI-WORLD (.CIWL=USD)	1200.097	-11.905	-0.98	10:22 24 MAY 1999
CI-EU/AUS/FEAST (.CEAF=USD)	1423.584	-2.151	-0.15	10:22 24 MAY 1999

Fig 8.1.16 *Clicking on 'Foreign Exchange' displays bid/offer prices for currencies.*

Currency	Bid	Ask	Updated
GBP/USD	1.6013	1.6023	16:20 25 MAY 1999
GBP/JPY	196.69	196.81	16:29 25 MAY 1999
GBP/EUR	1.5110	1.5125	16:28 25 MAY 1999
USD/JPY	122.76	122.86	16:20 25 MAY 1999
EUR/USD	1.0598	1.0602	16:20 25 MAY 1999

Most of the free information offered as part of the 'Market Master' account is available elsewhere on the internet. Up until recently, the lack of competition has meant that online brokers have not really needed to offer their clients much in the way of free information. This is likely to change as ever more competitors enter the market.

Money World

http://www.moneyworld.co.uk/trading/onlinetrading.html

The Money World internet site has an excellent page which displays an up to date list of online brokers in the UK. The dealing commissions for various deal sizes are also listed which makes it very easy to check on who is offering the best dealing rates. With increasing numbers of new brokers entering the market all the time, it can be difficult to keep track of who is offering what at any given time. This site makes it particularly easy to monitor the best deals in the market.

Fig 8.2 *The Money World internet site helps you keep track of all the online brokers.*

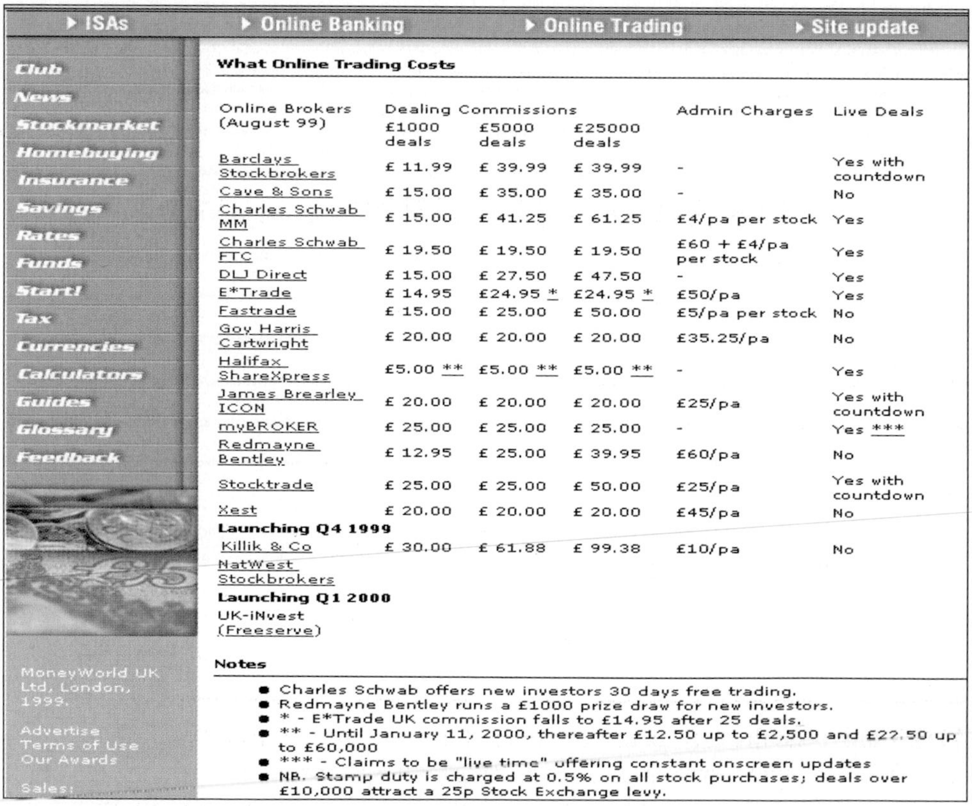

▸ ISAs ▸ Online Banking ▸ Online Trading ▸ Site update

Club
News
Stockmarket
Homebuying
Insurance
Savings
Rates
Funds
Start!
Tax
Currencies
Calculators
Guides
Glossary
Feedback

What Online Trading Costs

Online Brokers (August 99)	Dealing Commissions £1000 deals	£5000 deals	£25000 deals	Admin Charges	Live Deals
Barclays Stockbrokers	£ 11.99	£ 39.99	£ 39.99	-	Yes with countdown
Cave & Sons	£ 15.00	£ 35.00	£ 35.00	-	No
Charles Schwab MM	£ 15.00	£ 41.25	£ 61.25	£4/pa per stock	Yes
Charles Schwab FTC	£ 19.50	£ 19.50	£ 19.50	£60 + £4/pa per stock	Yes
DLJ Direct	£ 15.00	£ 27.50	£ 47.50	-	Yes
E*Trade	£ 14.95	£24.95 *	£24.95 *	£50/pa	Yes
Fastrade	£ 15.00	£ 25.00	£ 50.00	£5/pa per stock	No
Goy Harris Cartwright	£ 20.00	£ 20.00	£ 20.00	£35.25/pa	No
Halifax ShareXpress	£5.00 **	£5.00 **	£5.00 **	-	Yes
James Brearley ICON	£ 20.00	£ 20.00	£ 20.00	£25/pa	Yes with countdown
myBROKER	£ 25.00	£ 25.00	£ 25.00	-	Yes ***
Redmayne Bentley	£ 12.95	£ 25.00	£ 39.95	£60/pa	No
Stocktrade	£ 25.00	£ 25.00	£ 50.00	£25/pa	Yes with countdown
Xest	£ 20.00	£ 20.00	£ 20.00	£45/pa	No
Launching Q4 1999					
Killik & Co	£ 30.00	£ 61.88	£ 99.38	£10/pa	No
NatWest Stockbrokers					
Launching Q1 2000					
UK-iNvest (Freeserve)					

Notes

- Charles Schwab offers new investors 30 days free trading.
- Redmayne Bentley runs a £1000 prize draw for new investors.
- * - E*Trade UK commission falls to £14.95 after 25 deals.
- ** - Until January 11, 2000, thereafter £12.50 up to £2,500 and £22.50 up to £60,000
- *** - Claims to be "live time" offering constant onscreen updates
- NB. Stamp duty is charged at 0.5% on all stock purchases; deals over £10,000 attract a 25p Stock Exchange levy.

MoneyWorld UK Ltd, London, 1999.

Advertise
Terms of Use
Our Awards
Sales:

Not all brokers who are planning to offer online trading will necessarily be listed at this site. For example, at the time of writing, Hargreaves Lansdown were planning to become the first online broker to offer a standard minimum dealing commission of less than £10.00 (£9.95). Sometimes brokers who are planning a market beating deal, will not always be keen to alert the potential competition of their plans.

ADR's

Some British companies choose to have a portion of their shares listed on one of the American stock exchanges. This is achieved via an American Depository Receipt commonly known as an ADR. A company will deposit ordinary shares with a bank which is called the 'depository'. This bank then issues certificates in America which represent and are backed by the deposited ordinary shares. These certificates are freely traded and are commonly called American Depository Receipts or ADR's for short. The Bank of New York maintains a list of companies which have an ADR. The complete list can be found at: http://www.bankofny.com/adr

AMERICAN INTERNET SITES

- ✔ http://www.Bridge.com
- ✔ http://www.Quicken.com
- ✔ http://www.Datek.com
- ✔ http://www.Cnnfn.com
- ✔ http://www.Quotewatch.com

ADR's are basically US securities covered by US regulations although the underlying company may actually be British. One of the advantages of a stock with an ADR, is that you can access a whole host of free share information that would normally only be available for American companies. The price of an ADR will generally move in tandem with the price of the underlying security to which it is linked. For example, the ADR price chart for Dixons Group PLC will generally look almost identical to the UK share price chart. See Figure 2.123.

American Depository Receipts (ADR'S)

Company	Symbol
Abbey National PLC	ABYNY
Albert Fisher Group (The) PLC	AFHGY
Allied Domecq PLC	ALDCY
Allied Irish Banks PLC	AIB
AMVESCAP PLC	AVZ
Anglo Irish Bank PLC	AGIBY
Arcoplate Holdings PLC	ARHUY
Arjo Wiggins Appleton PLC	ARWGF
ARM Holdings PLC	ARMHY
Astra Zeneca PLC	AZN
Atlantic Caspian Resources PLC	ALCRY
Avis Europe PLC	AVRPP
BAA PLC	BAAPY
Barclays PLC	BCS
Bass PLC	BAS
Bespak PLC	BPAKY
BG PLC	BRG
Blue Circle Industries PLC	BCLEY
BOC Group PLC	BOX
Body Shop Intl PLC	BDSPY
Booker PLC	BKERY
Boots PLC	BOOOY
BP Amoco PLC	BPA
British Aerospace PLC	BTASY
British Airways PLC	BAB
British American Tobacco PLC	BTI
British Biotech PLC	BBIOY
British Energy PLC	BHEGF
British Sky Broadcasting Group PLC	BSY
British Steel PLC	BST
British Telecommunications PLC	BTY
BTR Siebe PLC	BTSBY
Bunzl PLC	BNL
Burmah Castrol PLC	BURMY
Cable and Wireless PLC	CWP
Cadbury Schweppes PLC	CSG

American Depository Receipts (ADR'S)

Cantab Pharmaceuticals PLC	CNTBY
Caradon PLC	CRDOY
Carlton Communications PLC	CCTVY
Centrica PLC	CNRKY
Chloride PLC	CDGPY
CML Microsystems PLC	CMLMY
Coats Viyella PLC	COAVY
Colt Telecom PLC	COLTY
Compass Group PLC	CMSGY
Cookson PLC	CKSNY
Cordiant Communications PLC	CDA
Cortecs PLC	DLVRY
CRH PLC	CRH
Danka Business Systems PLC	DANKY
Delphi PLC	DELEY
Denison Intl PLC	DENHY
Diageo PLC	DEO
Dialog Corporation PLC	DIAL
Dixons Group PLC	DXNGY
Ecsoft Group PLC	ECSGY
EIDOS PLC	EIDSY
ELAN PLC	ELN
EMI Group PLC	EMIPY
Energis PLC	ENGSY
Enterprise Oil PLC	ETP
Eurotunnel PLC	ETTFF
Frontline Ltd	FRONY
Futuremedia PLC	FMDAY
GKN PLC	GKNPY
Gallaher Group PLC	GLH
General Electric Co PLC	GNELY
Glaxo PLC	GLX
Glencar Mining PLC	GCM
Great Universal Stores PLC	GRUSY
Hanson PLC	HAN
Hartstone Group (The) PLC	HSTPY

American Depository Receipts (ADR'S)

Company	Symbol
Hibernia Foods PLC	HIBNY
Hillsdown Holdings PLC	HDYHY
Horace Small Apparel PLC	HSACY
HSBC PLC	HSBHY
Huntingdon Life Sciences Group PLC	HTD
Imperial Chemical Industries PLC	ICI
Imperial Tobacco Group PLC	ITY
Independent Energy Holdings PLC	INDYY
Insignia Solutions PLC	INSGY
Invensys PLC	INVSY
JD Wetherspoon PLC	JDWPY
Kingfisher PLC	KNGFY
Ladbroke Group PLC	LDBKY
LASMO PLC	LSO
Laura Ashley Hldgs PLC	LARAY
Legal & General Group PLC	LGGNY
London International Group PLC	LONDY
London Pacific Group Ltd	LPGL
Marks and Spencer PLC	MASPY
Medeva PLC	MDV
Merant PLC	MRNT
National Grid Group PLC	NGGPY
National Power PLC	NP
National Westminster Bank PLC	NW
NFC PLC	NFC
Nycomed Amersham PLC	NYE
Omnimedia PLC	OMMDY
Orange PLC	ORNGY
Pearson PLC	PRSNY
PowerGen PLC	PWG
Premier Farnell PLC	PFP
Premier Oil PLC	PMOIY
Professional Staff PLC	PSTF
Proteus International PLC	POTUY
Prudential Corporation PLC	PPLCY
Racal Electronics PLC	RCALY

American Depository Receipts (ADR'S)

Company	Symbol
Railtrack Group PLC	RTKHY
Ramco PLC	RCO
Rank Group (The) PLC	RANKY
Reed International PLC	RUK
Rentokil Group PLC	RTOKY
Rexam PLC	REXMY
Reuters PLC	RTRSY
Rio Tinto PLC	RTP
Skypharma PLC	SKYEY
Smallworldwide PLC	SWLDY
SmithKline Beecham PLC	SBH
South African Breweries PLC	SBWUY
Smurfit (Jefferson) Group PLC	JS
Sun Life and Provincial Holding PLC	SNLLP
T & N PLC	TNNSY
Tate & Lyle PLC	TATYY
Taylor Nelson Sofres PLC	TYNLY
Telewest Communications PLC	TWSTY
Tesco PLC	TSCDY
Thistle Hotels PLC	THTL
TI Group PLC	TIGUY
Tomkins PLC	TKS
Top Jobs PLC	TJOB
Townpages Net Com PLC	TPN
Transport Development Group PLC	TDVGY
Trinity Biotech PLC	TRIBY
Unigate PLC	UNGAY
Unilever PLC	UL
United Biscuits (Holdings) PLC	UTBCY
United News & Media Group PLC	UNEWY
United Utilities PLC	UU
Utility Cable PLC	UTCBY
Virgin Express Holdings	VIRGY
Vodaphone PLC	VOD
Wace Group PLC	WCGRY
Waterford Wedgewood PLC	WATFZ

American Depository Receipts (ADR'S)

Company	Symbol
Wellington Underwriting PLC	WLUNY
Wiggins Group PLC	WGGGY
Williams Hldgs PLC	WIHGY
WPP Group PLC	WPPGY
Xenova Group PLC	XNVAY
Yorkshire Food PLC	YKSHY

B

Home Pages

Most internet sites have a home page which tells you what information and services you can access at that site. Wherever possible this book has supplied the addresses of the actual internet pages being described. Having the precise internet page address usually saves time, although a potential problem can arise if a company decides to change the address of an internet page. Although individual internet page addresses may change, the home page address will almost always stay the same. Similarly, when you move house, your telephone number may change, but your name will always stay the same.

Hot Links

- http://www.freeyellow.com/members5/scott2b/page15.html

If you find that an internet address given in a Chapter no longer works, type in the home page address for that company. All the sites described in this book can be accessed via that company's home page. When the web page you are interested in is displayed on your computer screen, make a note of the new internet address if necessary. The address of the page displayed, usually appears in the 'location bar' at the top of the screen.

Home Page internet addresses

ACA *http://www.homeusers.prestel.co.uk/tbird/index2.html*
Bank of New York . . . .*http://www.bankofny.com*
Bloomberg . . . .*http://www.bloomberg.com*
CNN . . . .*http://www.cnn.com*
Charles Schwab . . . .*http://www.schwab-worldwide.com*
Daily Telegraph . . . .*http://www.telegraph.co.uk*
Datastream . . . .*http://www.datastream.com*
Datek . . . .*http://www.datek.com*
E*Trade . . . .*http://www.etrade.co.uk*
Financial News Digest/Pigeon . . . .*http://www.pigeon.co.uk*
Financial Times . . . .*http://www.ft.com*
Freequotes . . . .*http://www.freequotes.co.uk*
Free Yellow . . . .*http://www.freeyellow.com*
Hemmington Scott . . . .*http://www.hemscott.com*
Hotmail . . . .*http://www.hotmail.com*
Interactive Investor (*III*) . . . .*http://www.iii.co.uk*
Market-Eye . . . .*http://www.market-eye.co.uk*
Micropal . . . .*http://www.micropal.com*
Moneyworld . . . .*http://www.moneyworld.co.uk*
News Review . . . .*http://www.news-review.co.uk*
Quicken US . . . .*http://www.quicken.com*
Quicken UK . . . .*http://www.quicken.co.uk*
Quotewatch . . . .*http://www.quotewatch.com*
Research Index . . . .*http://www.thedataindex.co.uk*
Stock Point . . . .*http://www.stockpoint.com*
Trustnet . . . .*http://www.trustnet.co.uk*
UK-iNvest . . . .*http://www.ukinvest.co.uk*
UK Shares . . . .*http://www.ukshares.com*
Wright Research Center . . . .*http://www.wisi.com*
Yahoo . . . .*http://www.yahoo.co.uk*

Research Master

You can create your own 'Research Master' by copying the computer code and modifying it to suit your own needs. The official name for the computer code/language associated with the internet is HTML (Hyper Text Mark up Language). As a consequence, you will often see internet addresses ending with either 'html' or 'htm'. The method for copying HTML computer code and modifying it to suit your own needs is actually very easy. Modern computers have a simple command which displays the underlying computer code of any web page on your computer screen. The underlying computer code for a web page is known as the 'source' code.

Hot Links

- Research Master: *http://www.freeyellow.com/members5/scott2b/page6.html*

Once you have displayed the computer code on your screen, all you need to do is copy it onto your own web site and modify it to suit your own needs. The following pages show you how to display the 'source' code associated with a web page on your computer screen, and copy it into your own web site. Appendix D shows you how to create your own free web site.

Research Master

http://www.freeyellow.com/members5/scott2b/page6.html

Type in the internet address of the 'Research Master' which is given at the top of this page. When the page is displayed on your computer screen, click on the 'View' icon at the top of your screen. At the bottom of the window which appears, click on 'source' as shown in Figure 9.1.

Fig 9.1 *Use the 'Edit - View' function to display the HTML source code for a web page.*

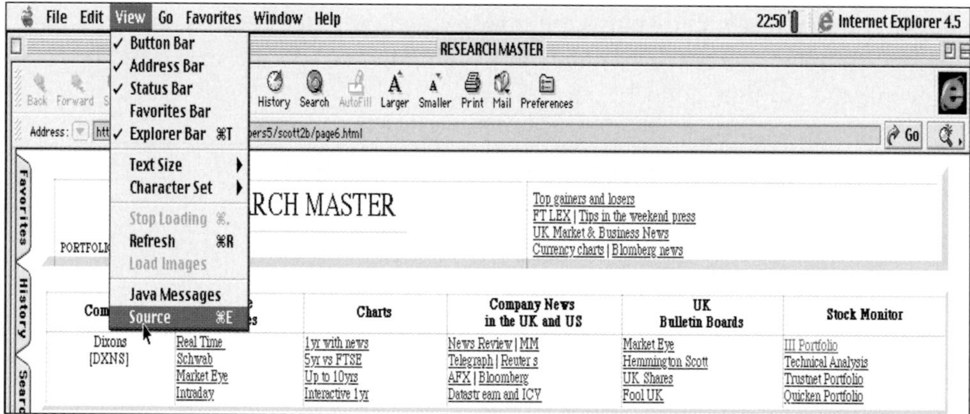

The underlying HTML source code used to create the 'Research Master' should be displayed on your screen. Click on the 'Edit' icon and then click on 'Select All' to highlight all of the computer code. When you have highlighted the code to be copied, click on 'Copy' as shown in Figure 9.2 below. The computer code has now been stored in your computer ready to 'Paste' into your Web Page.

Fig 9.11 *Use the 'Edit - Copy' function to copy the HTML source code for a web page.*

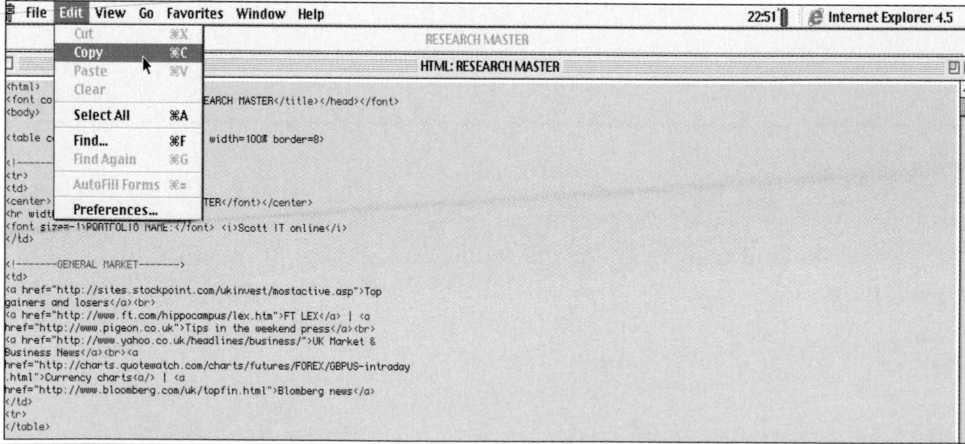

D

FreeYellow

There are many companies offering a free service which allows you to create your own web site. FreeYellow is one such company which is relatively simple to use and understand. In return for offering you free web space, the provider will generally advertise on your web page. Most companies which provide free web space also have computer software which allows you to build web pages very simply. Rather than you writing all the computer code, the computer software does it for you. This computer software is often referred to as a Web Wizard or Web Page Builder. When you use a Web Wizard, your web pages generally have a similar layout.

Hot Links

- *http://www.freeyellow.com*

To create a web page which looks like the 'Research Master', you need to write (or copy!!) your own computer code. The next few pages show you how to create a 'Research Master' using free web space provided by 'FreeYellow'. This Appendix should be read in conjunction with Appendix C.

FreeYellow

http://www.freeyellow.com

Before you can start creating your own web pages, you will need to register with FreeYellow. Click on 'Start Here' in Figure 10.1 and complete the online registration form. You will be asked to choose a 'User Name' and a 'Password'. If possible these should be the same as the ones used for registering at other internet sites described in this book.

Fig 10.1 *Once you have registered, enter your User Name and Password as shown.*

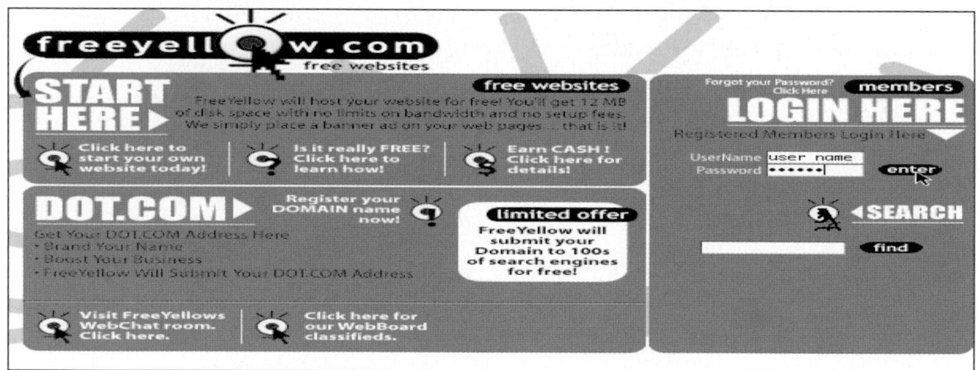

The first page you will see when you have logged on at this site is shown below in Figure 10.2. The 'Web Site Manager' icon is what you would click on to see a summary of all the web pages you have created. From there, you can edit existing pages, delete pages or display pages. Click on the 'Webpage builder' icon to build a web page.

Fig 10.11 *Click on 'Webpage Builder' to create a new web page.*

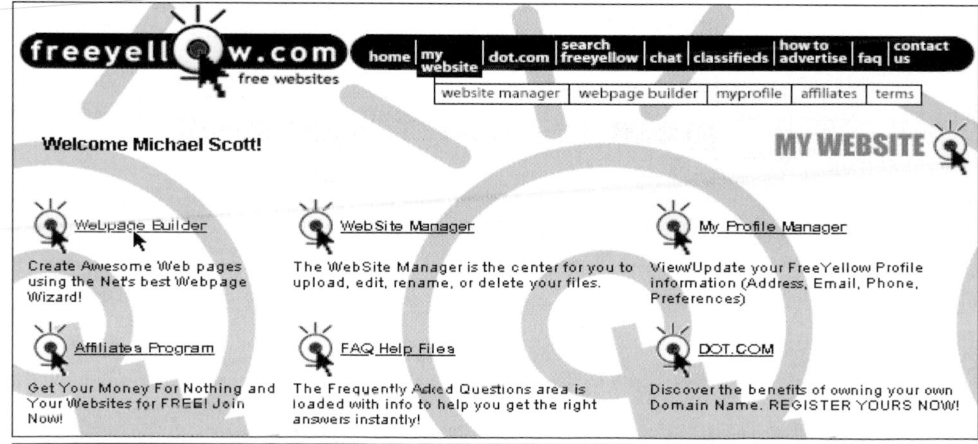

FreeYellow *(con't)*

http://www.freeyellow.com

When you are creating a new web page, you will always be asked whether you want to create a web page using the 'Web Page Builder', or using customised HTML code. The 'Research Master' was created using customised HTML computer code, so you need to click on the 'click here' icon at the top of the the right hand column as shown in Figure 10.3

Fig 10.12 *Click on the option which allows you to type in your own HTML code.*

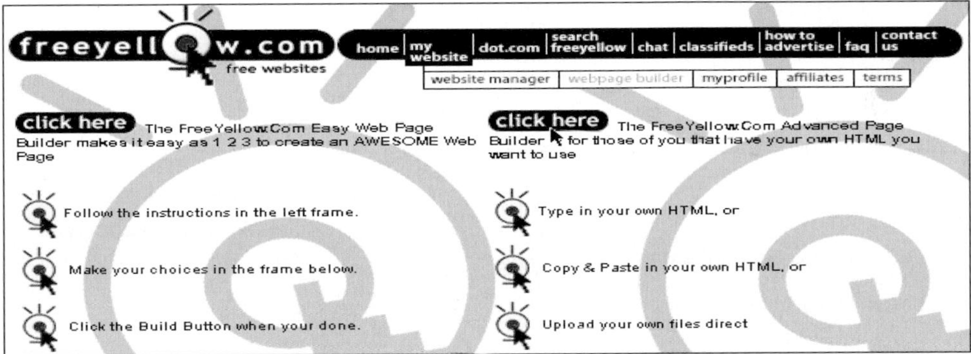

A large white empty box should appear on your screen. This is the place in which you type in, or in this case 'Paste' in your HTML computer code. First click in the empty box so that your computer knows where to 'Paste'. Next, click on the 'Edit' icon at the top of your computer screen. In the window that appears, click on 'Paste' as shown in Figure 10.4.

Fig 10.13 *Click on 'Edit- Paste' to reproduce the HTML code for the Research Master.*

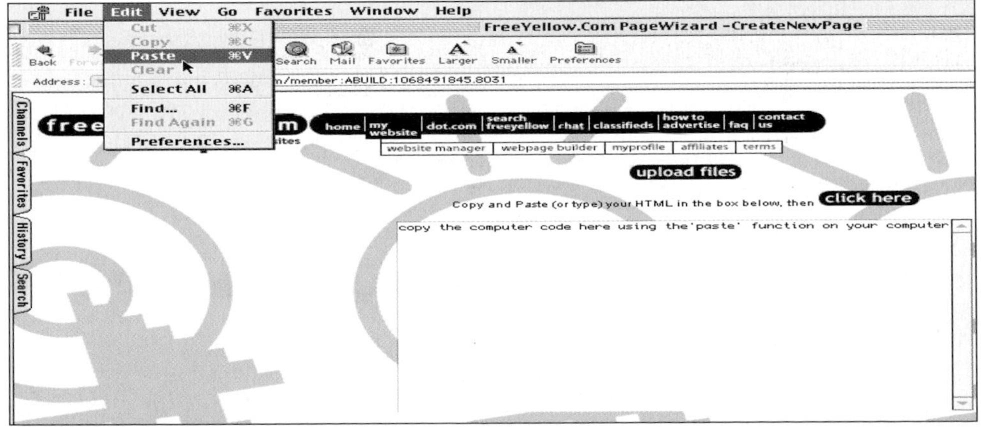

FreeYellow *(con't)*

http://www.freeyellow.com

To modify the 'Research Master' all you need to do is change parts of the code. For example if you wanted to change the name, simply delete 'Research Master' and re-type a new name. If you want to know more about HTML code then an excellent and simple to understand book to read is: *HTML for the World Wide Web - Elizabeth Castro.*

Fig 10.14 *You can delete and re-name headings or titles in the Research Master.*

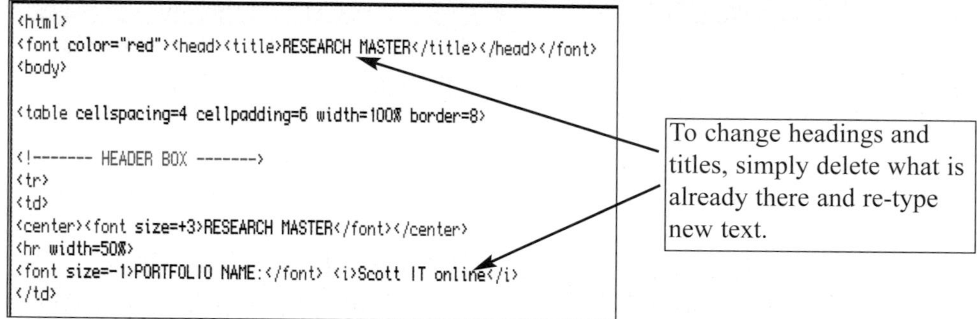

```
<html>
<font color="red"><head><title>RESEARCH MASTER</title></head></font>
<body>

<table cellspacing=4 cellpadding=6 width=100% border=8>

<!------- HEADER BOX ------->
<tr>
<td>
<center><font size=+3>RESEARCH MASTER</font></center>
<hr width=50%>
<font size=-1>PORTFOLIO NAME:</font> <i>Scott IT online</i>
</td>
```

To change headings and titles, simply delete what is already there and re-type new text.

To change any of the 'links' within the Research Master' look for computer code that begins with "http........". For example, at the time of writing, the Research Master was set up to go directly to a chart of Dixons Group PLC when you click on the '5yr vs FTSE' link. To change this to another stock, simply replace 'DXNS' in the computer code shown below, to another security code.

Fig 10.15 *To change links, simply change all or part of an existing internet address*

```
<a
href="http://www.market-eye.co.uk/scripts/indices.dll?HandleEquityLink
?symbol=dxns">1yr with news</a> <br>
<a
href="http://www.iii.co.uk/reg-tools/quotes/equity/detail?code=DXNS.L&
history=5+years&user_codes=&index=UKX.L&graphtype=Line">5yr vs
FTSE</a><br>
<a
href="http://www.hemscott.com/EQUITIES/ATOZ.HTM">Up to 10yrs</a><br>
<a
href="http://www.stockpoint.com/quote.asp?Mode=JAVACHART&Symbol=LS:dxn
s">Interactive 1yr</a>
</td>
```

To change a link, either change the whole internet address, or just substitute a new security code.

FreeYellow *(con't)*

http://www.freeyellow.com

There is quite a lot of computer code associated with the 'Research Master'. You can save time and effort by using the 'Edit - Find' function (see Figure 6.31) on your computer to quickly locate the computer code that you want to change. For example, you could ask you computer to find all the instances of 'DXNS' if you wanted to modify the Research Master for another stock. Another time saving function is the 'Edit Copy/Paste' described in Appendix C and D. Each time you look at a web page, the internet address of that page will appear in the location bar at the top of your screen. If you want to add a link to that web page in the Research Master, highlight the address and copy it using the 'Edit - Copy' function. When you are building your web page, paste in the internet address to save you having to manually type it in.

Fig 10.16 *Click on 'click here' in Figure 10.4 when you have finished making changes.*

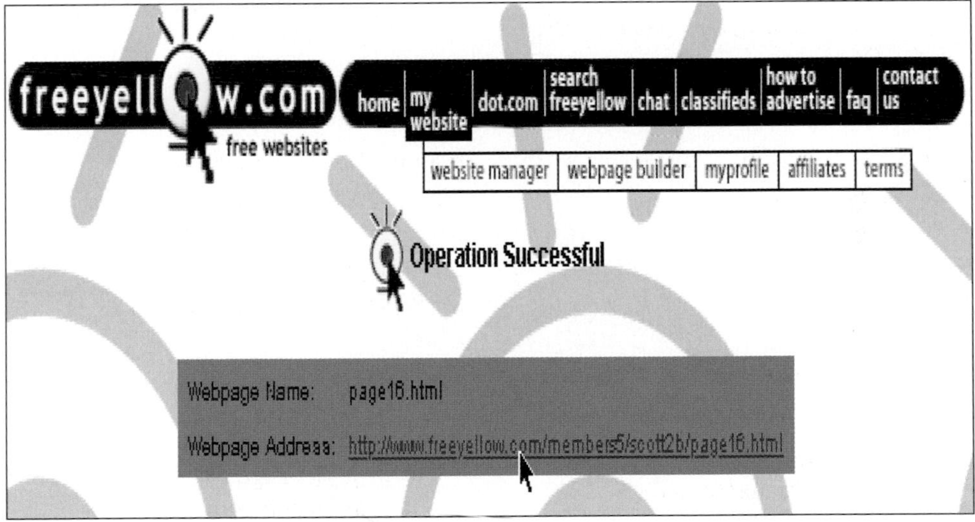

When you have made a change to the Research Master, you need to click on 'click here' in Figure 10.4 to save that change. The screen in Figure 10.7 should appear and you can click on 'Webpage Address' to display the web page you have created. Don't forget to click on 'Refresh' or 'Reload' at the top of your computer screen, otherwise any changes you have made will not initially be displayed. One final tip, is to 'bookmark' your web page address so you can easily access it in the future.

E

Stock Codes

Stock codes for shares which comprise the FT-SE 250 index are listed in this Appendix. Broadly speaking, these are the largest companies by market capitalisation in the UK. Most financial internet sites have search engines which enable you to look up a stock code if you do not know it. However, it saves time and money if you know the correct stock code before logging on to the internet. The E*Trade internet site has a comprehensive alphabetical list of most UK listed investments. If you are likely to use the internet frequently to look up financial information, it makes sense to print out a complete list of stock codes. There are blank pages at the end of this book to note individual stock codes.

Hot Links

✍ http://research.etrade.co.uk/free/esifinder/Find_share.cgi?page=quick_quote

Some internet sites have either a prefix or a suffix with the stock code. For example, the stock code 'dxns' (Dixons PLC) has the prefix 'ls:' at the Stock Point internet site. To obtain a price quote or chart for Dixons PLC at this site you must enter a stock code of 'ls:dxns'.

Stock Codes for FT-SE 250 Index

Shares in FTSE-250

EPIC	Stock Name	EPIC	Stock Name
ADC	ADMIRAL	AGS	AEGIS GRP.
AGG	AGGREGATE IND.	AGK	AGGREKO
AIR	AIRTOURS	ATST	ALLIANCE TRUST
AUN	ALLIANCE UNICHM	AMEC	AMEC
AW.	ANGLIAN WTR.	AG.	ARCADIA GRP.
AWA	ARJO WIGGINS	ARM	ARM HLDGS.
ARI	ARRIVA	AHT	ASHTEAD GRP.
ABP	ASS.BR.PORTS	ATK	ATKINS(WS)
AVE	AVIS EUROPE	BNKR	BANKERS INV.TST
BDEV	BARRATT DEVEL.	BBA	BBA GRP.
BZR	BEAZER	BWY	BELLWAY
BRFD	BERISFORD	BKL	BERKELEY GRP.
BICC	BICC	BOY	BODYCOTE
BVS	BOVIS HOMES	BWTH	BOWTHORPE
BPB	BPB	BPT	BPT
BSET	BR.ASSETS TRUST	BBOR	BR.BORNEO OIL
BLND	BR.LAND	BVIT	BR.VITA
BKB	BRAKE BROS	BRT	BRITANNIC
BTX	BRITAX INTL.	BXTN	BRIXTON EST.
BWNG	BROWN(N.) GRP.	BRYN	BRYANT GRP.
BTP	BTP	BNZL	BUNZL
BUO	BURFORD HLDGS.	BMAH	BURMAH CAST.
CLDN	CALEDONIA INV.	CWG	CANARY WHARF
CPI	CAPITA GROUP	CAP	CAPITAL RADIO
CRN	CARADON	CTT	CATTLES
CCH	CELLTECH CHIRO.	CET	CHARTER EURO.
CHTR	CHARTER	CLF	CHELSFIELD
TRCD	CITY LONDON IT	CBG	CLOSE BR.GRP.
CMG	CMG	COB	COBHAM
CCB	COCA-COLA BEV.	CCC	COMPUTACENTER
CKSN	COOKSON GRP.	CRI	CORDIANT COMMS.
CWA	COUNTRYWDE.ASRD	CRDA	CRODA INTL.
DVSG	DAVIS SERVICE	DLAR	DE LA RUE
DEB	DEBENHAMS	DIG	DUNEDIN INC.
EDIN	EDIN.INV.TST.	EUS	EDIN.US TRACKER
EID	EIDOS	EBQ	ELECT.BOUTIQUE
ELTA	ELECTRA INV.TST	ECM	ELECTROCOMPS.
ELM	ELEMENTIS	EMA	EMAP
ETI	ENTERPRISE INNS	ETP	ENTERPRISE OIL
ETL	EUROTUNNEL UTS	EXD	EXPRESS DAIRIES
FI.	F.I.GRP.	FAY	FAIREY GRP.
FTC	FILTRONIC	FCD	FIRST CHOICE
FSL	FIRST LEISURE	FGP	FIRSTGROUP
FKI	FKI	FAM	FLEM.AMER.I.T.
FUT	FLEM.CONTL.	FLMJ	FLEM.JAP.
FMN	FLEM.MERC.	FOV	FLEM.O'SEAS
FLXT	FLEXTECH	FCU	FOR.&COL.EURO.
FRCL	FOR.&COL.IV.TST	FNET	FUTURE NETWORK
GAL	GALEN HLDGS.	GLH	GALLAHER GRP.
GER	GERRARD GRP.	GLYN	GLYNWED INTL.
GOG	GO-AHEAD GROUP	GVS	GOVETT STRAT.IT
GPOR	GR.PORTLAND	GREW	GREENALLS GRP.
GNK	GREENE KING	GWG	GWR GROUP
HLMA	HALMA	HMSO	HAMMERSON
HSL	HEND.SMALL COS.	HPW	HEPWORTH
HEWS	HEWDEN-STUART	HLND	HIGHLAND DIST.
HYR	HYDER	ICE	ICELAND GROUP
IMI	IMI	INCH	INCHCAPE
IIG	INDEP.INSUR.	INF	INFORMA GRP.
ICAP	INVEST.CAP.GWTH	JLT	JARDINE LLOYD
JRVS	JARVIS	JJB	JJB SPORTS

Stock Codes for FT-SE 250 Index *(con't)*

JMAT	JOHNSON,MATTH.	JPR	JOHNSTON PRESS
KEL	KELDA GRP.	KCOM	KINGSTON COMM.
LARD	LAIRD GROUP	LPRT	LAPORTE
LSMR	LASMO ORD.	LEX	LEX SERVICE
LII	LIBERTY INTL.	LIM	LIMIT
LOG	LOGICA	LNB	LON.BRIDGE SOFT
LMI	LONMIN	EMG	MAN(ED&F)GROUP
MNU	MANCHESTER UTD.	MTN	MATALAN
MFW	MAYFLOWER	MKNE	MCKECHNIE
MDV	MEDEVA	MGGT	MEGGITT
MEPC	MEPC	MRN	MERANT
MRP	MERC.EURO.INV.	MRCH	MERCHANTS TST
MDK	MERSEY DOCKS	MYER	MEYER INTL.
MLC	MILLENNIUM &COP	MNKS	MONKS INV.TST.
MGCR	MORGAN CR.	MRW	MORRISON (WM)
MUT	MURRAY INC.TST.	MYI	MURRAY INTL.TST
NEX	NAT.EXPRESS	NSR	NESTOR HEALTH.
NEW	NEW LOOK GRP	NXT	NEXT
NFC	NFC	NFDS	NTHN.FOODS
NRK	NTHN.ROCK	NAM	NYCOMED AMER.
OGP	OCEAN GRP	PIC	PACE MICRO
PEEL	PEEL HLDGS.	PNN	PENNON GROUP
PND	PENTLAND GRP.	PER	PERPETUAL
PSN	PERSIMMON	PHTM	PHOTO-ME INTL.
PILK	PILKINGTON	PLL	PILLAR PROP.
PIZ	PIZZAEXPRESS	PJP	POWDERJECT PH.
PDUF	POWELL DUFFRYN	PFL	PREMIER FARNELL
PFG	PROVIDENT FIN.	PON	PSION
RCAL	RACAL ELECT.	RNK	RANK GRP.
RDW	REDROW GRP.	RSW	RENISHAW
REX	REXAM	RCP	RIT CAPITAL
RMC	RMC GRP.	RM.	RM
ROR	ROTORK	RBY	RUGBY GRP.
SSI	SAATCHI&SAATCHI	SFW	SAFEWAY
SCAM	SCOT.AMER.INV.	SCIN	SCOT.INV.TST.
SSM	SCOT.MEDIA GRP.	SMT	SCOT.MORTGAGE
SAT	SEC.ALLIANCE	STS	SECS.SCOTLAND
SLA	SELECT APPMNTS.	SLF	SELFRIDGES
SNR	SENIOR	SRP	SERCO GRP.
SKS	SHANKS GRP.	SHP	SHIRE PHARMCTCL
SIG	SIGNET GRP.	SLOU	SLOUGH ESTATES
SN.	SMITH&NEPHEW	SMDS	SMITH(DS)
SMWH	SMITH(WH)GRP.	SMIN	SMITHS INDS.
SOF	SOMERFIELD	SPX	SPIRAX-SARCO
SSL	SSL INTL.	SIV	ST.IVES
STJ	ST.JAMES'S PLAC	SGC	STAGECOACH
SHS	STOREHOUSE	SWW	SWALLOW GRP.
TARM	TARMAC	TATE	TATE & LYLE
TNN	TAYLOR NELSON	TWOD	TAYLOR WOODROW
TBI	TBI	TMPL	TEMPLE BAR
TEM	TEMPLETON EMRG.	THO	THISTLE HOTELS
TRV	THOMSON TRAVEL	TI.	TI GRP.
TOMK	TOMKINS	TRG	TR EUR.GROWTH
TFC	TRAFFICMASTER	TPK	TRAVIS PERKINS
TNI	TRINITY MIRROR	UTF	ULTRAFRAME
UNIG	UNIGATE	UAG	UNITED ASS.GRP.
UBIS	UTD.BISCUITS	VLL	VERSAILLES GRP.
VICK	VICKERS	VRD	VIRIDIAN GRP.
WSSL	WASSALL	WRC	WASTE RECYCLE.
WEIR	WEIR GRP.	JDW	WETHERSPOON(JD)
WLMS	WILLIAMS	WLB	WILSON BOWDEN
WSNC	WILSON(CONN)	WMPY	WIMPEY(GEO)
WTAN	WITAN INV.	WLY	WOLSELEY
WOLV	WOLVER.DUD.	YULC	YULE CATTO

Stock Codes for UK Government Gilts

CN2H	CONS.2H%	CN4	CONS.4%
CV02	CONV.10% 2002	CV99	CONV.10Q% 1999
CV3H	CONV.3H% LN	25JB	CONV.9 1/2%2001
CV9	CONV.9% 2000	CV11	CONV.9% 2011
84GO	CONV.9H% 2002	CV04	CONV.9H% 2004
CV05	CONV.9H% 2005	CV01	CONV.9T% 2001
CV03	CONV.9T% 2003	CV06	CONV.9T% 2006
EX05	EX.10H% 2005	EX12	EX.12% 2013/17
EX09	EX.9% 2002	FD04	FUNDNG.3H%99/04
T001	TR.10% STK 2001	T003	TR.10% STK 2003
TR04	TR.10% STK 2004	T11H	TR.11H%STK01/04
T11T	TR.11T% 03/07	T12H	TR.12H%STK03/05
TR13	TR.13% STK 2000	T13H	TR.13H%STK04/08
T03	TR.13T3%2000/03	TR2	TR.2% IL 2006
TR2H	TR.2H%I-L 2011	TR16	TR.2H%I-L 2016
T299	TR.2H%IL 1999	TR01	TR.2H%IL 2001
TR03	TR.2H%IL 2003	TR09	TR.2H%IL 2009
T13I	TR.2H%IL 2013	T2HI	TR.2H%IL 2020
T24I	TR.2H%IL 2024	T2H	TR.2H%
T3UD	TR.3%	T30I	TR.4E%IL 2030
T04A	TR.4TE%IL 2004	TR5	TR.5%STK2004
T12	TR.5H% LN 08/12	T009	TR.5T% STK 2009
T6H3	TR.6 1/2% 2003	TR28	TR.6% 2028
T6Q	TR.6Q% STK 2010	T6T	TR.6T% STK 04
T07	TR.7 1/4% 2007	TR7	TR.7% STK 2001
T702	TR.7% STK 2002	TR7H	TR.7H% 2006
TR6	TR.7T% STK 06	T15	TR.7T% STK12/15
TR21	TR.8% 2021	TR8	TR.8% STK 2000
T83	TR.8% STK 2003	TR08	TR.8% STK 2009
T813	TR.8% STK 2013	TY8	TR.8% STK 2015
T06	TR.8%LN 2002/06	T8H	TR.8H% LN 2000
TR8H	TR.8H% LN 2007	TR05	TR.8H% STK 2005
TR17	TR.8T% STK 17	T09	TR.9% LN 2008
TY12	TR.9% STK 2012	TR02	TR.9T%STK 2002
TS01	TR.FR STK 2001	WAR	WAR 3H% LN

G

Glossary

There are many technical terms associated with both the internet and investments. This Glossary should throw some light on the more commonly used terms that crop up in the text and pictures in this book. In some cases, the internet sites described in this book have their own 'Online Glossary' which can be useful.

Internet addresses for some Online Glossaries

- http://profiles.wisi.com/profiles/wisexnote.htm - *Wright Research Center*
- http://www.datastreaminsite.com/glossary.htm - *Datastream*
- http://www.moneyworld.co.uk/glossary/glmur.htm - *Money World*

Often, it is possible to obtain free guides relating to certain types of investment. In these cases, the Glossary gives the telephone number or internet address of the provider.

Glossary

ADR - The abbreviated name for an 'American Depository Receipt'. If a foreign company wants to have their shares listed on one of the American stock markets, they can do so via an ADR. The company deposits a number of shares with a bank which is known as the 'Depository'. The bank issues share certificates which can then be traded just like any other American share. ADR's are dollar denominated and pay dividends in dollars. A comprehensive list of UK companies with ADR's is given in Appendix A.

Address - Short for an internet address. Internet addresses usually start with *http://www.......* The 'http' stands for Hypertext Transfer Protocol, and the 'www' stands for World Wide Web.

BACS - Bank Automated Clearing System. The means by which money is transferred directly into you bank account.

Bid Price - This is the price at which an investment can be sold.

Bid Offer Spread - The difference between the buying and the selling price of an investment. The bid/offer spread is quoted either in pence, or as a percentage. If the buying price of a share was 11p and the selling price was 10p, then the bid/offer spread would be 1p or 10%.

Bookmark - A term used to describe the function on your computer which saves internet addresses.

Browser - A term used to describe the computer software that enables you to look at (eg browse) internet pages. The two most common 'Browsers' are 'Internet Explorer' and 'Netscape'. Browsers are constantly being updated and modified so there are many different versions of the same browser in existence. Often you need a recent version of a browser to view certain internet pages.

Bulletin Board - This is a term used to describe a place on an internet site where private investors post comments and ask questions. Other common names include 'Message Board' or 'Investors Forum'.

Glossary *(con't)*

Check - The word used to describe the process of clicking in a box or symbol on your computer screen. Usually a tick or a dot will appear in that box to indicate that that condition or command will be implemented.
DJ Industrial - Dow Jones is the name of the main stock market in America. It is comprised of just 30 shares.

Discount - A term often used with reference to Investment Trusts. If an estate agent tells you your house has a 'Net Asset Value £100,000 but a buyer is only prepared to offer you £90,000, then you would be selling it at a 'Discount to Net Asset Value' of 10%. Similarly, Investment Trust shares often trade at a 'Discount' to their underlying 'Net Asset Value'. For more information on Investment Trust shares, request a free guide from the Association of Investment Trust Companies (AITC) at *http://www.aitc.co.uk*.

Download - A term used to describe the transfer of information to your computer. If an internet page takes a long time to 'download' it means that it takes a long time for the information to appear on your computer screen.

Epic Code - see symbol.

Explorer -This is the shortened name for Microsoft's 'Internet Explorer' browser. Many new computers come with the 'Internet Explorer' software already installed to give you easy access to the internet.

FRS3 - An accounting standard used in the calculation of 'Earnings Per Share' (EPS).

Gearing - Another word for borrowing. A highly 'Geared' company is one which has borrowed a lot of money.

Hot Links - This is an expression given to text at an internet site which, when clicked on, will take you (eg link you) to another internet site. At some internet sites, the term is shortened to 'Links'. One of the unique

Glossary *(con't)*

features of the internet is that you can write computer code which will link you to another part of the internet. Often, 'Hot Links' will change colour once you have clicked on them once. A common setting for computers is for 'Links' to change colour from blue to red after they have been clicked on. When you move your mouse over a 'Hot Link', an internet address is usually displayed at the bottom of your computer screen. This is the internet address of the web page which will be displayed if you click on that 'Hot Link'.

Icon - A small picture or symbol used to describe something on your computer. Internet pages will often have 'icons' which when clicked on will take you to another internet page or site.

Location bar - A space at the top of your computer in which to type in internet addresses.

Mid Price - This is the average of the buying price (also known as offer price) and the selling price (also known as the bid price). To get the mid price, add the offer price and the bid price together and divide by two. Most newspapers print the 'mid price' for shares. When you are buying and selling shares, you will usually pay slightly more than the 'mid price'. Similarly, when selling shares you will generally, receive slightly less than the 'mid price'.

Mnemonic - Another term for 'Symbol' which is often used with reference to currencies.

Moving Average - A mathematical function often used to generate an additional line on a share price chart. The amount by which the share price chart deviates from the moving average chart can sometimes give an indication of whether a share pricc is likely to rise or fall.

NAV - Short for Net Asset Value - see below.

NMS - Normal Market Size. The number of shares you can buy at the quoted price. If you want to buy a greater number of shares than the

Glossary *(con't)*

'NMS', the price may be different from that quoted.

Net Asset Value -This term is generally used with reference to Investment Trust shares. Most Investment Trusts have a portfolio of shares which have a certain underlying value after all charges and debts have been accounted for. This is referred to as the Net Asset Value of that Investment trust. For more information on Investment Trust shares, request a free guide from the Association of Investment Trust Companies (AITC) at *http://www.aitc.co.uk.*

Netscape Navigator - This is the brand name of one of the most popular internet browsers.

Online - A term used to imply connection to the internet. For example an 'Online Portfolio' is a collection of investments (eg a portfolio) which can be viewed and modified over the internet.

Preference Shares - This is a type of share issued by a company which has preference over 'ordinary shares' when it comes to the payment of dividends. Preference shares generally pay a fixed dividend and are generally classed as 'fixed interest investments'. The dividend on 'ordinary shares' generally rises (or falls!) in line with the company's earnings.

RPI - Retail Price Index. This index measures inflation and is based on the price increase of a basket of UK goods.

Real Time Quote - This is a actual price of an investment at that moment in time. Most share prices which are displayed at an internet site are delayed by at least 15 minutes.

SEAQ - Stock Exchange Automated Quotes. The SEAQ Volume refers to the volume of trade in individual shares or for the market as a whole.

Search Engine - A term used to describe the computer software which enables your computer to search for the internet address you have entered.

Glossary *(con't)*

Sedol Number - This is a unique number code which defines an investment.

Site - This term refers to an internet site.

Spread - See 'Bid Offer Spread'.

Standard Deviation - A mathematical function sometimes used to generate share price charts. Put very simply, the 'Standard Deviation' is a measure of how far a share price deviates from its normal trading range.

Symbol - Each stock market investment has a unique identity code which is often referred to as the symbol. In many cases the code consists of a series of letters. For example the symbol for Dixons Group PLC is DXNS. Most internet sites will accept either capital letters such as DXNS of small letters such as dxns. The letters in a symbol will generally be the same for all internet sites. However, for some internet sites you have to add a suffix such as '.L' so that the symbol becomes DXNS.L The 'L' signifies that the stock is listed on the London stock market. Most financial internet sites enable you to look up share information either by their name, or by their symbol.

Technical Analysis - see online technical analysis glossary at:
http://www.e-analysis.com/glossary/glossar1.htm

Ticker Symbol - See 'Symbol'.

Warrants - These are a type of investment which give you the right to buy a particular investment at a fixed price in the future. Warrants are listed on the stock market just like shares and can be bought or sold at any time before their expiry date. For more details on warrants telephone Hargreaves Lansdown 0117 988 9880 and ask for a free copy of their 'Guide to Warrants'.

Web Page - The 'Web' is another word for the internet. The full

Glossary *(con't)*

expression is the 'World Wide Web' which is where the three W's which appear in at the beginning of many internet addresses come from. An internet site usually consists of many different pages which you can display on your computer screen. The internet addresses given at the top of most pages in this book, are the internet addresses of individual web pages at an internet site.

Web Site - This is another name for an internet site. A web site will generally consist of a number of web pages. If you think of a web site as representing a block of flats, then a web page represents an individual flat. The address of a flat, always includes the address of the block of flats. Similarly the address of a web page will generally start with the address of a web site. For example *http://www.iii.co.uk* is a web site address and *http://www.iii.co.uk/quotes/search* is a web page address.

I

Index

Index *(con't)*

Index *(con't)*

Index *(con't)*

Index *(con't)*

Index *(con't)*

O

P

Index *(con't)*

Index *(con't)*

Index *(con't)*

Name of share	Stock Code